A European Memory?

Studies in Contemporary European History

Editors:

Konrad Jarausch, Lurcy Professor of European Civilization, University of North Carolina, Chapel Hill, and a Director of the Zentrum für Zeithistorische Studien, Potsdam, Germany

Henry Rousso, Senior Fellow at the Institut d'histoire du temps présent (Centre national de la recherche scientifique, Paris) and co-founder of the EURHISTXX research network

A EUROPEAN MEMORY?

Contested Histories and Politics of Remembrance

Edited by

Małgorzata Pakier and Bo Stråth

Berghahn Books

NEW YORK • OXFORD

Published in 2010 by

Berghahn Books
www.berghahnbooks.com

© 2010, 2012 Małgorzata Pakier and Bo Stråth
First paperback edition published in 2012

Library of Congress Cataloging-in-Publication Data

A European memory? : contested histories and politics of remembrance /
edited by Małgorzata Pakier and Bo Stråth. — 1st ed.
p. cm. — (Studies in contemporary European history ; 6)
Includes bibliographical references and index.
ISBN 978-1-84545-621-4 (hbk.)—ISBN 978-0-85745-430-0 (pbk.)
1. Europe—History—Philosophy. 2. Collective memory—Europe.
I. Pakier, Małgorzata, 1979–. II. Stråth, Bo, 1943–.

D104.E887 2010
940.01--dc22

2009025366

British Library Cataloguing in Publication Data

A catalogue record for this book is available
from the British Library.

Printed in the United States on acid-free paper

ISBN 978-0-85745-430-0 (paperback)
ISBN 978-0-85745-605-2 (ebook)

CONTENTS

Section 4 Towards a Europeanisation of the Commemoration of the Holocaust

Section 5 Coming to Terms with Europe's Communist Past

Section 6 Coming to Terms with Europe's Colonial Past

ILLUSTRATIONS

❦

ACKNOWLEDGEMENTS

This book is the outcome of a series of seminars at the European University Institute in Florence in the spring semester of 2007, which was organised by the two editors. The contributions have been discussed and revised as a result of the discussions. The theme of the seminar series dealt with the question of a European collective memory, and the aim was to develop a critical distance to this question and to key concepts such as collective memory. An important topic was the connection between memory and history and why during recent years there seems to be a shift from history to memory. Another crucial question was how the entanglement of memory and history relates to the concept of Europe. Our normative point of departure was that the dark aspects of Europe's past must be integrated into European commemorations of that past. An additional goal was to incorporate perspectives of both the East and the West. We therefore organised the seminar series into four distinct clusters – the Holocaust, the Second World War, communism and colonialism – while a fifth cluster dealt with more theoretical issues in terms of the questions concerning Europe and memory/history.

We want to thank all of the contributors for their cooperation and for showing so much forbearance and goodwill. We are also grateful to the other participants in the seminars, who greatly enriched the discussions. Special thanks go to Sylvie Pascucci for her help in organising the meetings and for tireless secretarial assistance. Lucy Turner Voakes efficiently edited and fine-tuned a first version of the volume. We are very appreciative of her work and that of Shawn Kendrick, who edited the final version.

Finally, we wish to express our appreciation to the staff of Berghahn Books. Marion Berghahn showed an early faith in our project. We are further grateful to two anonymous reviewers, who gave valuable suggestions for revising and tightening the text.

– Małgorzata Pakier and Bo Stråth

Contributors

Péter Apor is working as a Research Fellow for Pasts, Inc. Center for Historical Studies at the Central European University. After finishing his PhD on communist representations of history in Hungary at the European University Institute in Florence in 2002, he spent a year in London at the School of Slavonic and Eastern European Studies as a teacher/fellow in Hungarian studies. His main research themes include the politics of history and memory, popular culture and historical memory, and the history of historiography. He has recently published, with co-editors Sorin Antohi and Balázs Trencsényi, *Narratives Unbound: Historical Studies in Post-communist Eastern Europe* (2007).

Cecilie Felicia Stokholm Banke, PhD, is a Senior Researcher and Head of the Research Unit at the Danish Institute for International Studies in Copenhagen. Her current research focuses on the normative impact of the Holocaust in post-war Europe and the way it has been dealt with politically, legally, socially and culturally. Her publications include *Demokratiets Skyggeside: Flygtninge og menneskerettigheder i Danmark efter Holocaust* (2005), which is forthcoming in English as *Welfare, Refugee and Rescue: Denmark and the Jewish Escape from Nazi Germany*.

Stefan Berger is Professor of Modern German and Comparative European History at the University of Manchester, where he is also Director of the Jean Monnet Centre. Between 2003 and 2008, he chaired the European Science Foundation programme, 'The Writing of National Histories in Nineteenth and Twentieth Century Europe'. He has published widely on comparative labour history, the history of historiography, national identity and nationalism, and British-German relations. His most recent books are *Friendly Enemies: Britain and the GDR, 1949–1990* (2010); *Kaliningrad in Europa: Nachbarschaftliche Perspektiven nach dem Ende des Kalten Krieges* (2009); and, co-edited with Chris Lorenz, *The Contested Nation: Ethnicity, Class, Religion and Gender in European National Histories* (2008).

Lars Elenius is an Associate Professor of History at Luleå University of Technology in Sweden. His fields of research include minority policy, ethno-political mobilisation and the creation of transnational identities in the context of globalisation. He is writing a history book and encyclopaedia of the Barents region and is conducting a research project about indigenous rights and nature conservation in the Nordic countries. His most recent book in English, co-edited with Christer Karlsson, is *Cross-Cultural Communication and Ethnic Identities* (2007).

Jan Jansen, MA, is a historian and lecturer at Konstanz University. He is finishing his PhD thesis on commemorative politics and public space in colonial Algeria. He has published articles on forms of public commemoration and archaeology in colonial North Africa and on contemporary life in Algeria. His research interests include modern North African and Middle Eastern history, colonialism, collective remembrance and historiography.

Konrad H. Jarausch is a Senior Fellow at the Zentrum für Zeithistorische Forschung in Potsdam and Lurcy Professor of European Civilization at the University of North Carolina at Chapel Hill. He has written or edited about three dozen books on modern German and European history. Recent titles include *After Hitler: Recivilizing Germans, 1945–1995* (2006); with co-editor Hans-Hermann Hertle, *Risse im Bruderbund: Die Gespräche Honecker-Breshnew 1974 bis 1982* (2006); and with co-editor Thomas Lindenberger, *Conflicted Memories: Europeanizing Contemporary Histories* (2007).

Heike Karge, PhD, is a historian and Assistant Professor in South-Eastern and Eastern European History at the University of Regensburg, Germany. She works primarily on the cultural history of Europe in the nineteenth and twentieth centuries, with a special focus on Eastern and South-Eastern Europe. Her current fields of interest include historical discourses of insanity, as well as practices of war remembrance. A forthcoming publication is titled *Steinerne Erinnerung – versteinerte Erinnerung? Kriegsgedenken im sozialistischen Jugoslawien.*

Klas-Göran Karlsson is Professor of History at Lund University, Sweden. He has written extensively about historical cultures and the uses of history, ethnic conflicts and genocide. His recent publications include, with Kristian Gerner, *History of Genocide: Perspectives on the Dark Side of Modern Society* (in Swedish, 2005) and, with co-editor Ulf Zander, *The Holocaust on Post-War Battlefields: Genocide as Historical Culture* (2006). Since 2001, he has been the leader of a research project titled 'The Holocaust and European Historical Culture'.

Wolfgang Kaschuba is Professor of European Ethnology at the Humboldt-Universität zu Berlin and Director of the Institute of European Ethnology.

His research interests lie in daily routines and civilisation in European modernity, national and ethnic identities, and urban and metropolitan research. Recent publications include, with co-editors Beate Binder and Peter Niedermüller, *Directing the National: History, Civilisation and Politics of Identities at the End of the 20th Century* (2001), and, with co-editor Kaspar Maase, *Trash and Beauty: Popular Culture around 1900* (2001).

James Kaye, PhD, is a historian, having recently completed a post-doctoral fellowship and work as a project coordinator at the European University Institute's Robert Shuman Centre for Advanced Studies. He also held the position of key researcher at the Ludwig Boltzmann Institute for European History and Public Spheres in Vienna. He is currently a Fondazione Rausing Research Fellow at the Swedish Institute in Rome and a lecturer in Intercultural and Global Studies at the Johannes Kepler University Linz/ Centre for Social and Intercultural Competence. His research and expertise are in historiography, photography and comparative discourses of modernity, community and conceptual history.

Clemens Maier, PhD, is a graduate of the Freie Universität Berlin, where his concentration was in contemporary history and the history of the Nazi era. In his PhD thesis, *Making Memories: The Politics of Remembrance in Post-war Norway and Denmark*, he analysed how certain dominant narratives about the Second World War and the German occupation developed in Scandinavia and the ways in which they were perpetuated and used by political agents throughout the whole post-war period. He is currently a Research Fellow at the Institute for the History of German Jews, where his project on transnational networks of Jewish emigration from Nazi Germany is being financed by the Deutsche Forschungsgemeinschaft.

Kevin Morgan is Professor of Politics and Contemporary History at the University of Manchester, where he works on comparative communist and labour movement history. His recent publications include a biography of Ramsay MacDonald (2006) and *Bolshevism and the British Left Part One: Labour Legends and Russian Gold* and *Bolshevism and the British Left Part Two: The Webbs and Soviet Communism* (both 2006), as well as the co-authored volume, with Gidon Cohen and Andrew Flinn, *Communists in British Society 1920–91* (2007). He is a founding editor of the journal *Twentieth Century Communism: A Journal of International History*, which was launched in 2009.

Jan-Werner Müller is an Associate Professor in the Politics Department, Princeton University, and directs the History of Political Thought Project, University Center for Human Values, Princeton University. He is the author of *Constitutional Patriotism* (2007), *A Dangerous Mind: Carl Schmitt* *in Post-War European Thought* (2003) and *Another Country: German Intellectuals, Unification and National Identity* (2000).

Senadin Musabegović is a professor at the School of Philosophy, University of Sarajevo, where he teaches courses in the sociology of culture and art theory. A former soldier and journalist, he began publishing poetry, essays and stories during the siege of Sarajevo. His second book of poetry, *The Maturing of Homeland* (1999), received two awards in Bosna and Herzegovina and was translated into French. He presented his doctorate thesis, 'War – Reconstruction of the Totalitarian Body', at the European University Institute in Florence in 2004. He has published theoretical papers in international magazines and books and has given lectures as a guest professor at European and American universities.

Ruth Nattermann, PhD, is a collaborator at the German Historical Institute in Rome and former Visiting Researcher at the European University Institute, Florence. Her research fields include German-Jewish history, Italian history, historiography, biography and diplomacy. She is the author of *Deutsch-jüdische Geschichtsschreibung nach der Shoah: Die Gründungs- und Frühgeschichte des Leo Baeck Institute* (2004) and the editor of *I diari e le agende di Luca Pietromarchi (1938–1940): Politica estera del fascismo e vita quotidiana di un diplomatico romano del '900* (2009).

Małgorzata Pakier has recently received a PhD title from the European University Institute in Florence. In her thesis, she analysed representations of the Holocaust in German and Polish cinema after 1989 in a comparative perspective and in the context of the question about the Europeanisation of the Holocaust memory. She was awarded with a Charles H. Revson Fellowship at the United States Holocaust Memorial Museum in Washington, DC. Her publications include book chapters and articles in English and Polish on discourses and images of the Holocaust in popular culture and film. Her research interests include film, collective memory and Holocaust studies.

Arfon Rees is Reader in Soviet and Russian History at the University of Birmingham. From 2000 to 2008, he was Professor of Eastern European History at the European University Institute, Florence, and he has taught at the University of Keele. A specialist on Russian history, he has published widely in this field. He is the author of *Political Thought from Machiavelli to Stalin: Revolutionary Machiavellism* (2004) and the editor of *Centre-Local Relations in the Stalinist State, 1928–1941* (2002) and *The Nature of Stalin's Dictatorship: The Politburo, 1924–1953* (2003).

Bo Stråth was Professor of Contemporary History from 1997 to 2007 at the European University Institute, Florence. Since October 2007 he has held the position of Academy of Finland Distinguished Professor of Nordic, European and World History at Helsinki University. His interests lie in questions of modernity and the use of history in a European and global perspective. Current research projects include 'Between Restoration and Revolution, National Constitutions and Global Law: An Alternative View on the European Century 1815–1914', co-directed with Martti Koskenniemi, and 'Conceptual History and Global Translations: The Euro-Asian and African Semantics of the Social and the Economic'.

Stefan Troebst is Professor of Eastern European Cultural Studies at the University of Leipzig, Germany. He holds a PhD in Russian and Eastern European History and Slavic Studies from the Free University of Berlin, where he also completed his habilitation. His recent publications include *Postkommunistische Erinnerungskulturen im oestlichen Europa* (2005), *Kulturstudien Ostmitteleuropas* (2006) and *Das makedonische Jahrhundert* (2007). He is the co-editor, with Farimah Daftary, of *Radical Ethnic Movements in Contemporary Europe* (2003).

Stanisław Tyszka, who graduated in law at Warsaw University, is a doctoral candidate in the Department of History at the European University Institute, Florence. He is preparing a dissertation about property restitution and collective memories in the Czech Republic and in Poland after 1989. His research interests include legal history, transitional justice and collective memory.

Heidemarie Uhl is a Senior Researcher at the Austrian Academy of Sciences in Vienna and is a lecturer at the University of Vienna and the University of Graz. Since 2001 she has been contributing to the research programme on the sites of memory run by the Institute for Culture Studies and History of Theatre at the Austrian Academy of Sciences. Her major interests are memory politics, the theory of cultural studies and modernity, and culture and identity in Central Europe.

Frederick Whitling is a doctoral candidate in history and civilisation at the European University Institute, Florence. His academic interests lie in the reception of antiquity and the classical tradition, in twentieth-century European history, and in memory and history studies. Recent publications include reflections on international scholarly collaboration in postwar Rome, as well as on memory and history studies in relation to the classical tradition.

A EUROPEAN MEMORY?

☙❡❧

Małgorzata Pakier and Bo Stråth

The French and Dutch rejection of the European Constitution in 2005 was, among other things, a rejection of the historical grounding for further integration as it was formulated in the proposal. The grand design of a United Europe with a common foreign policy and a common market, which was simultaneously to be sufficiently diverse so as to allow for cultural and social differences, was turned down.

The historical motivation for the constitution contained vague references to 'cultural, religious and humanistic traditions' and emphasised the necessity to overcome old divisions. The Enlightenment heritage and the tradition of a particularly social Europe were remarked upon, yet, in contrast, darker elements of Europe's past were absent. There was no mention of colonialism, ethnic cleansing, world wars, totalitarian regimes or genocide.[1]

It would be a mistake to try to repeat the role played by professional historians during the building of the nation states. Their teleological master narratives equated the 'reason of history' with the nation, the latter being depicted as the carrier of progress. While such narratives may have been popular during the nineteenth century, in the twenty-first century the long-term legitimacy of European unification requires a more critical historical understanding – one that acknowledges the conflicts, contentions, complexity and ambiguity of Europe's past and thereby recognises the fragility of its future.

The rejected constitutional proposal displayed a lack of understanding of the historical complexity of this past upon which visions of the future might be built. The case of the constitution demonstrates that there is an urgent need for a critical European history. This book aims to contribute to such a critical history, in which Europe is seen not as a harmonious whole but as the outcome of violent and bloody conflicts, both within the continent

---

Notes for this section are located on page 20.

and with its Others. Religious wars, class struggles and genocides such as the Srebrenica massacre are not exceptional cases. Rather, they are core dimensions of the landscape of the past, whose horrors and dark shadows must necessarily be integrated in a critical history worthy of the name. Transnational cultural transactions and peaceful commerce must be viewed in relation to violent conflicts between the European nation states. Moreover, memories about Europe are contested: there is not one history but many.

Having said this, we also want to emphasise that our goal is not to replace self-satisfaction with self-flagellation. We are arguing for a better balance between opposing sides in the outlines of the European past.

The Holocaust, the atrocities of the Second World War beyond the Holocaust, the Stalinist gulags, colonialism and imperialism are often forgotten or repressed when the key questions about the origin of Europe and its telos are posed. These dark shadows and bitter experiences are notably absent from the commemoration agenda, notwithstanding the Stockholm declaration on the Holocaust in 2000. The purpose of this volume is to thematise and reintroduce them to the historical imagination of Europe's past.

One crucial question is whether the remembrance of these catastrophes and atrocities is from a European viewpoint or from that of a specific nationality – German, Soviet, British, French, Dutch, Spanish, Polish, Czech, etc. This question relates among others to the locus of historical responsibility. It is easier to find a common European dimension when references are made to the positive sides of an argued European heritage, as in the case of the Enlightenment. Although in one sense the Enlightenment references a French core, which includes the *république des lettres*, Enlightenment philosophy and the French Revolution, figures such as Kant, Vico, Hume and Smith go beyond this core to develop a European dimension. Even with regard to the positive legacy, however, controversies may arise, as in the case of Polish protests against excluding from the Constitutional Treaty a reference to Christianity as an important constituent of European heritage. The perceived impossible co-existence of the Enlightenment and Christianity in the planned European Constitution exemplifies this conundrum.

However, must it not also be the case that the crisis of liberal and Enlightenment values – which began in the 1870s and was later manifested in the emergence of totalitarian regimes, aggressive imperialism and nationalism, and world wars, as well as atrocities such as the Holocaust and gulags – is also European to some degree? Although arguments for a European incorporation of these dark sides of Europe's past do exist on a normative level, the extent to which the production of history and the so-called memory boom actually outline a *European* dimension is quite a different question. Has not the genocide against Europe's Jewish population been reduced to a German problem and the gulag to a specifically Soviet problem?

In the period after the Second World War, the European self-understanding was from a Western European perspective in which black-and-white moral categories were easily produced through two demarcations, one temporal, the other spatial. The temporal divide depicted 1945 as a zero hour, a point of departure for a commitment expressed by the catchphrase 'Never again!' With the emergence of the Western European welfare states in the 1950s and 1960s, the 1930s and their attendant experiences and memories of mass unemployment became a supplementary zero hour. The spatial divide was between Western Europe and Eastern Europe, characterised respectively by social welfare capitalism and communism. The dark side of the temporal divide of 1945 was Nazi Germany and to a certain extent fascist Italy. The light side was the rest of Europe and, through reference to the heroic resistance movement against Nazism, also Italy and communism.

This world of yesterday, as we see it today, collapsed in 1989–91 with the end of the Cold War. The old points of orientation in time and space no longer functioned. In order to understand better the dramatic and turbulent movements around 1990, the search for new heuristic points of departure began. The year 1989 was constructed as a new zero hour, and the East-West divide was to be bridged through the project of a unified Europe, with the heroism of the resistance movement being critically questioned by some. In reflections on the Second World War, whereas the previous emphasis had been on resistance, there now emerged standpoints which emphasised collaboration. The shift in interpretation from heroism to collaboration often occurred as a consequence of political appeals for a new history and truth. As a result, history commissions were established in order to investigate and reconsider the past. With the straitjacket of the Cold War no longer a factor, there was obvious political interest in rethinking the past all over Europe.

There was certainly a critical confrontation with idealised and heroic national pasts, but translated into a European future this confrontation was naive. Drawing on Francis Fukuyama's fantasies about the end of history, a unified Europe that had overcome the historical East-West divide was proclaimed. The triumph of liberalism in 1989 – and the rhetoric of the globalisation narrative that followed in its wake – implied the ideological unification not only of Europe but of the whole world. Such illusions ended with the civil wars in Yugoslavia and the onset of a new religious war viewed as a 'clash of civilisations'.

The Distinction between History and Memory

During the past ten to fifteen years, references to the past have increasingly been made in terms of memory rather than history. There is a connection between history and memory, of course, but what is it, and why the shift? The term 'memory' has come to be understood in many different ways. An elastic concept, it has lost ever more precise meaning in proportion to its growing rhetorical power (Gillis 1994: 3). The most common reasons for developing a usable past are linked to individual and collective identity claims. A sense of sameness over time and space is sustained by remembering. There is little overall coherence in 'collective memory' studies, but probably the most important dividing line is that between individual and collective memory (Wertsch 2002: 34–5).

The conceptual slide from history to memory clearly relates to the construction of legitimacy. Who are the analysts of the past whose statements produce social cohesion and political legitimacy? During the nineteenth century, historians were key actors in the construction of foundation mythologies and the building of the nation state. What role do professional historians play in this process today, and what degree of exclusivity do they have? Less than their predecessors, one would argue.

In the wake of the more general acceptance of the perspective developed by Hayden White, François Lyotard, Paul Ricoeur, Jacques Derrida and Michel Foucault, the distinction between history, memory and myth has been blurred, and these categories are now seen as overlapping and supplementary (Stråth 2000a). However, against this backdrop of blurred distinctions there remains the question of why there has nevertheless been an obvious conceptual slide from history towards memory. In particular, the contributions by Frederick Whitling and James Kaye in this volume address this problem, and Klas-Göran Karlsson's discussion on the uses of history is also relevant.

What are the origins of the notable career of the word 'memory' in historiographical discourse? Is the use of this word necessary and irreplaceable in today's historiography? When collective memory emerged in the 1980s as a subject of scholarly interest, it was imagined as a counterconcept for history and as a critique of the totalising aspects of the latter. The focus on cultural practices replaced the earlier interest in socio-economic structures. However, since this linguistic turn, the understanding of history itself has also changed, and there is a growing awareness of the rhetorical and linguistic limits of history writing.

The dramatic events around 1990 provoked a search for the historical roots of the turbulent present. The Cold War no longer fulfilled its role as an interpretative framework. The revision of the past in order to understand better both present developments and future prospects has resulted in what can be described as a 'memory boom'. At the time of this memory boom, when the past not only has been recognised as a subject of scholarly research but also has been widely employed and represented in politics and mass media, it is more useful to speak of different discourses on the past rather than recalling again the distinction between history and memory. These different types of discourses – academic, political-institutional, popular or everyday, media, etc. – are not easily separable as they intermingle and influence each other.

The questions remain, however: Do professional historians possess an exclusive capacity in dealing with the past? And what is their role vis-à-vis the use of history as entertainment, as political legitimisation or as the subject of non-professional inquiry? The cultural turn in the 1980s and the emergence of constructivist methodologies have resulted in the view that historians do not stand above or beyond the processes that they analyse. Rather, they are considered to be part of them, and thus their positions as interpreters of the past have been relativised. In the wake of Foucault, it is not only history but also epistemological schemes in general that are deemed ideological and more or less political. The past is thus constantly present in the present and changes with the present.

These epistemological developments and the search for new theoretical structures after the end of the Cold War have made the role of professional historians less exclusive. Politicians and media representatives participate more actively in the remaking of the past, and this fact is a crucial dimension of the conceptual slide from history towards memory. This democratising dimension of the new conceptualisation, with less exclusivity (and authority) for professional historians, is counter-balanced by a populist dimension that runs the risk of manipulation and abuse – rather than use – of history. Another growing trend conflates history with a more or less nostalgic interest in the past that lacks theoretical framing.

The new conceptual and symbolic topography affecting concepts like identity and memory must be understood in the light of experiences of intellectual disorientation and of the erosion, since the 1970s, of earlier established frameworks of interpretation. A result of fundamental changes in epistemology, technology and the organisation of economies, work and labour markets, these shifts have produced new views, both of the past and of the preconditions for history – the science of the past. History as 'science' is a translation from the German *Wissenschaft*. Since the nineteenth century, the writing of the past has been seen in Germany as analogous to the description of nature, or *Naturwissenschaften*. In English-speaking cultures, history was never categorised as a science; instead, it was relegated to the arts. This distinction between the two linguistic cultures, ignored for a long time, has recently begun to take on meaning. The insight that the writing of history is less a matter of the unproblematic discovery of a past 'out there' by means of refined techniques of source criticism and is more something dependent upon the context of the present in which questions about the past emerge has come to be generally accepted.[2] The recognition of the role of narration poses new problems along the science-art axis (Stråth 2000a).

In the early 1980s, German historians seized upon the television series *Holocaust* and similar media representations in order to criticise a perceived moralistic representation of Nazism. In the unfolding 'historians' controversy' and in the debate about the historicisation of National Socialism, this 'moralistic' and 'black-and-white' dimension of the representation of the events – and thus the limits of their historicisation – was at stake (Friedländer 2000: 11–15; Rüsen 1997). The intertwining between the writing of the history of the Holocaust and the unavoidable use of implicit or explicit moral categories in its interpretation and narration remains a major challenge, according to Saul Friedländer. It is around these shared moral categories that history and memory encounter one of their central differences: the way in which the significance of Chełmno, Bełżec, Sobibór and Treblinka, sites whose sole function was immediate extermination, is defined.

Approximately two million victims were murdered at these sites within a year. How can the significance of each of these deaths be integrated in the interpretation of the epoch? Is the real impact of this history only in the memory that it has left? Historical writing about the Holocaust has increasingly attempted to circumvent such problems by focusing on the mechanisms that led to the 'Final Solution' within Nazism itself, or on the logistics, the technology and the bureaucratic processes of its implementation. Major issues of interpretation, historical roots and historical categories have also been addressed from the very beginnings of this historiography. The historian cannot – and should not, in Friedländer's view – be the guardian of memory. The historian's perspective is analytical, critical, attuned to complexity and wary about generalisations. In the face of simplified representations of the past, the historian's duty is, according to Friedländer, to reintroduce the complexity of discrete historical events, the ambiguity of human behaviour and the indetermination of wider social processes. However, if the historian opens up a critical distance to the events under scrutiny, it is only the integration of the individual fate within the historical narration that can at the end enable the historian to overcome the dichotomy between the unfathomable abstraction of the millions of dead and the tragedy of each individual life and death in the time of extermination. The challenge at stake is how to render a history of the Holocaust that includes not only the shared history of the victims, but also the narration of the events according to the victims' perceptions and descriptions of their individual fates. This is a history that tries to close the critical gap that it is opening up through analytical distance (Friedländer 2000: 11–14). History is thus both a critical ordering from a distance and a narrowing towards the documented memories.

In the search for a critical distance to the Holocaust and other totalitarian developments, it is necessary to distinguish between memory as an individual experience and as a collective construction. Individuals have memories but collectives do not. As collective phenomena, memories are discourses based on processes of social work and social bargaining.

Against the backdrop of the commemoration of the fiftieth and sixtieth anniversaries of the end of the Second World War, Reinhart Koselleck, who had experienced the war as a soldier, felt himself massively confronted with the memory problem. Trying to cope with it, he distinguished between memories that only individuals themselves can have and second-ary, mediated memories. He challenged the thesis about collective memo-ries, arguing that they are only discursive constructs. He swore to the right of the individual to his or her own inalienable memory as part of human dignity. Recollections of violence and deadly fear are stored not only in one's memory. 'They grasp the heart, kidneys, bile, gut, all muscles and all nerves, and this not only metaphorically speaking', Koselleck argued (Meier 2007). All unreasonable demands through collective instruction and tutelage he decisively rejected: 'Man has a right to his own memory. This I do not allow to be collectivised.' He talked about the 'veto right of personal experiences' and insisted on having been neither victimised nor liberated. On 8 May 1945, he had heard bells tolling the peace on his way to a Soviet prisoner of war camp in Auschwitz. Is this liberation? he had asked. With such experiences it was difficult to judge uniformly such seemingly clear-cut concepts as liberation and peace, and it was objectionable to dictate to individuals what they had to remember collectively (Meier 2007).

The imagination of a collective memory can only be a discourse, a social and cultural construct. As such, collective memories are not unequivocal but rather a product of social forces. Emerging in social contention and debate, such constructs reflect power relationships, which might take on more or less hegemonic proportions with a corresponding impact on the recollections. However, even when the collective memory seems hegem-onic, it remains a discourse without essence.

Maurice Halbwachs used the term 'collective memory' with reference to individuals locating themselves within a social context in which memory was seen as non-essential and constructed in and by social contexts (Halb-wachs [1925] 1994, 1950; see also Kaye, this volume). The rediscovery of Halbwachs in the framework of the memory boom often led to essentialist views that represented the term 'collective memory' as a shared property by a social group. It is important to treat such memories, however, as non-essential and constructed. Collective memory is nothing but a discourse about past events and how to order and interpret them.

The discourses about collective memories shift between being hegem-onic and being contentious. Such discourses – which deal not only with what to remember and how but also with what to forget – are usually politically instrumentalised. For instance, pacts of silence emerged in Germany after 1945 and to a certain extent in Spain after 1975, and it is difficult not to relate such pacts to the fact that many people had strong interests in public forgetting.

Collective memories are often seen as analogous to individual mem-ories and referred to in terms of trauma, repression and other similar psychological models. In these cases, silenced experiences are referred to as trauma, drawing on a definition that hails from psychology and psychoanalysis as something that one can neither forget nor talk about. A critical question we pose is whether individual psychological and psycho-analytical models can be translated to express collective experiences. For example, can the fact that the Holocaust was more or less silenced until the 1960s or the fact that Srebrenica was silenced after 1995 until the present day really be understood as a mass psychological question circumventing all enquiry about moral and political responsibility? Or are more immediate political interests and power structures in operation?

With respect to what to remember and what to forget collectively, the involvement of political interests and power cannot be ignored. Did the thematisation of the Holocaust from the early 1960s onwards depend on the sudden passing of a traumatic shock after fifteen years of repression? Or should it rather be understood with reference to the state formation of Israel and the generational confrontation of young Germans who began questioning the actions of their parents during the war?

During this German generational dramatic confrontation with the past, the term *Vergangenheitsbewältigung*, or 'coming to terms with the past', was used. This term quite obviously contains a certain social-psychological dimension: a society learns to master its past. However, as Jan-Werner Müller demonstrates in this volume, Jürgen Habermas and, indeed, the academic debate in Germany since the 1950s, upon which Habermas's discussion about coming to terms with the past is based, instead empha-sised a political dimension closely linked to a militant defence of the achieved democracy. The original connection with social-psychological models was diluted when the concept was linked to another Haberma-sian key term, *Verfassungspatriotismus*, or 'constitutional patriotism'. The focus shifted from social psychology to political communication and con-tention under democratic forms. However, the use of the term *Geschichts-aufarbeitung*, or 're-work on history', would be more effective in removing any remaining connotation of social psychology and in laying the foun-dation for an open-ended process of social work rather than a final mas-tery of the past.

In a perspective that emphasises memory construction as a process of social contention and bargaining, Srebrenica is not understood as a kind of traumatic experience, the discussion of which is precluded for psychologi-cal and psychoanalytical reasons, but as an atrocity silenced for political reasons. The massacre was and is certainly traumatic for the Muslim vic-tims and their families, but what about the victimisers and the onlookers? Had it been openly admitted, the Dutch and French part of the responsi-bility for the massacre would have hit the core of the European Union in moral terms. The condemnation of this, the second European genocide of the twentieth century, directed not at Europe's Jews but its Muslims, was circumscribed through the politically safe condemnation of the Holocaust in the Stockholm declaration in 2000, more than half a century after the genocide of the Jews. Solidarity becomes a zero game when the solidarity is with the victims of yesterday instead of the victims of today. By this point, the indemnity question had been solved in material terms. World leaders talked about the Holocaust, but they meant Srebrenica. Moving outside Europe but remaining within the Western hemisphere, the discussion might be extended to include Abu Ghraib.

The approach to memory in this volume is thus demarcating itself from stances that focus on the connection to memory in psychological or biological terms (e.g. Chalmers 1996, 1999; Penrose 1997). Our aim is to view collective memory as a social construct and to emphasise its link to history and to the writing of history. We approach memory historically, although our diachronic perspective is different from that of Jan Assmann ([1992] 2007) and Aleida Assmann (2008), with their emphasis on cultural memory in the sense of a society's deep cultural codes and myths. Whereas their focus is on continuous reiteration over millennia in commemoration practices, our view is much more contextual and time-bound, whereby memories are socially constructed in response to specific historical situations and conjunctures. We do not question the fact that the constructors of collective memory might draw on and consciously or unconsciously refer to well-established cultural and mythical discursive codes of long permanence. Those who do so successfully might profit from such references, if they touch the right chord. However, we have not explicitly explored the link between historically constructed memory and cultural memory in the sense of the Assmanns (although Uhl in this volume discusses their approach to cultural memory). That would have required another book.

The construction of collective memories has a dimension of political instrumentalisation in which the memory boom might be exploited as a nostalgic trip to the past in order to avoid discussion about the future. In this usage, 'memory politics' has a depoliticising impact corresponding to the depoliticisation of the globalisation rhetoric, which, like the memory boom, emerged in response to the end of the Cold War. Memory becomes an alternative to progress – that is, progress seen in man-made as opposed to natural terms – and substitutes critical questions about the present-day economic and social situation. The growing role of history as kitsch, disconnected from political, social and economic structures, is another example of this instrumentalised usage of the past. This approach to memory does not look for responsibility in the past, whereas memory treated as history does.

The development that began after the fall of the Berlin Wall with historians becoming consultants in local government commissions for renaming streets and other similar tasks has considerably changed the role of professional historians. The construction of collective memories and commemoration practices has in important respects left the historians behind; commemoration has become memory politics without their participation. Collective memory is now subject to legislation, with more and more countries having introduced laws dictating that their citizens remember certain historical events in a certain way, sometimes under threat of punishment for publicly stating something different. For instance, in Switzerland it is a crime to deny the Armenian genocide, while in Turkey it is a crime to recognise it. French politicians in particular have been active on this front, beginning with non-controversial legislation in 1990 to criminalise the denial of the extermination of Europe's Jews and other crimes against humanity as they had been defined by the Nuremberg tribunal in 1945. In 1995, historian Bernard Lewis was convicted by a French court of justice for having argued that available documents do not prove that what happened to the Armenians in 1915 can be described in terms of genocide, according to the definition of international law. Another French law, passed in 2001, regards slavery as a crime against humanity. With reference to that law, a group of French citizens living abroad brought a procedure against Olivier Pétré-Grenouilleau, the author of a study of the African slave trade, accusing him of denying the slave trade as a crime against humanity. At about the same time, the French National Assembly adopted another law prescribing schools to recognise in their teaching the positive impact of the French presence abroad, particularly in North Africa. This decision provoked an outcry among the historians, who, in a wave of indignation, created the movement Liberté pour l'Histoire with Pierre Nora as its leading figure. The movement led to the withdrawal of the case against Pétré-Grenouilleau and to the abolishment of the paragraph about France's positive role in North Africa. In the autumn of 2008, the French movement released an international manifesto.

Appel de Blois, an initiative of Liberté pour l'Histoire, is a call for unrestricted historical research and a protest against attempts of governmental authorities to criminalise the past through legislation:

> Concerned about the retrospective moralization of history and intellectual censure, we call for the mobilization of European historians and for the wisdom of politicians. History must not be a slave to contemporary politics nor can it be written on the command of competing memories. In a free state, no political authority has the right to define historical truth and to restrain the freedom of the historian with the threat of penal sanctions.
>
> We call on historians to marshal their forces within each of their countries and to create structures similar to our own, and, for the time being, to individually sign the present appeal, to put a stop to this movement toward laws aimed at controlling history memory.
>
> We ask government authorities to recognize that, while they are responsible for the maintenance of the collective memory, they must not establish, by law and for the past, an official truth whose legal application can carry serious consequences for the profession of history and for intellectual liberty in general.
>
> In a democracy, liberty for history is liberty for all.[3]

Yet memory as political instrumentalisation does not always have to be seen in terms of strong manipulation; it might very well emerge in processes of political contention. Jan Jansen demonstrates this in his contribution to this volume through his analysis of the French construction of a collective memory of the Algerian War (1954–62). The process was marked by contradictions and divisive views on past events and on exactly what to commemorate. The *classe politique* initiated and staged the debate and, after a while, became spectators when the debate developed its own dynamics. Instrumentalisation is too complex to be dominated by the manipulation of a single entity. One might here also refer to the impact of Willy Brandt's genuflection in Warsaw in December 1970, which provoked a heated political debate in Germany about how to approach the past.

A different kind of instrumentalisation is the creation and control of collective memory mounted by modern states through their education systems. Here collective memory comes close to official historiography. It constitutes a kind of reference point for the contentious public discourse on the past in which collective remembering is active. In other words, it is understood in terms of mediated action distributed between active agents, on the one hand, and the cultural tools, especially narrative texts, that they employ, on the other (Wertsch 2002: 172–3). Textual resources employed in collective remembering belong to and reflect a social context and history. Collective memory in this sense often makes claims of stability and constancy, but in fact one of the few durable attributes of collective memories is that they undergo change. Collective memories are in a flux and in a certain tension to official historiography.

The view of this volume is thus that there is a considerable amount of overlapping between history and memory. The distinction is that history has higher structuralising and ordering ambitions, argues in a more nuanced way, and considers the complexity of historical situations and developments better – that is, if and when history writing is optimal.

A European Memory?

The critical questions in the book deal with the issue of a Europeanisation of the memory boom. Can parallel processes of coming to terms with the past and contentious negotiation about what to remember and what to forget in various parts of Europe be understood as a European process in a more inclusive meaning of this concept? Such a dimension would imply, for example, an increasing recognition of a European responsibility for the Holocaust, rather than seeing it with an exclusive reference to Germany. Can the experiences of communism in Eastern as well as Western Europe be commemorated within a European frame, where questions about responsibility and intellectual and political collaboration extend beyond exclusive reference to the Soviet Union? Corresponding questions can be posed for the experiences of Nazism and the Second World War and for the experiences of colonialism and imperialism. The volume addresses these questions critically in the contributions by Stefan Berger, Heike Karge, Clemens Maier, Cecilie Felicia Stokholm Banke, Stanisław Tyszka, Małgorzata Pakier, Ruth Nattermann, Arfon Rees, Péter Apor, Senadin Musabegović, Kevin Morgan, Jan Jansen and Lars Elenius. Before the empirical analyses of the four fields of investigation (the Second World War, the Holocaust, communism and colonialism), Jan-Werner Müller, Klas-Göran Karlsson, Stefan Troebst, Wolfgang Kaschuba, Heidemarie Uhl, Frederick Whitling and James Kaye discuss these questions in more normative and theoretical terms.

Beginning in the 1990s, historians in bilateral investigations (Germany and the Czech Republic, and Germany and Poland) had no difficulty finding common ground on which to discuss painful past experiences. At this stage the discussions were not politicised; rather, the negotiation of history was an intellectual enterprise. On principle, these examples would be translatable to a broader European framework trying to come to terms with borders in time (1945) and space (East-West). However, the German-Polish-Czech analyses were soon politicised by the Bund der Vertriebenen, an association representing the interests of Germans who either fled parts of Central and Eastern Europe or were forcibly expelled after the Second World War, and in that vein nationalism has progressed in the 2000s in the midst of contentious debates about where to locate commemoration sites and museums. The initial work on history has shifted to memory politics with a strong degree of instrumentalisation and has been influenced by nationally segmented European memory cultures. The attempt in 2000 in Stockholm to make *ex post* the commemoration of the Holocaust a foundation myth of the European Union has remained an illusion. Efforts to establish transnational self-critical memory discourses on colonialism, racism and war collaboration in Europe have hardly gained momentum. The growing European interest in the Turkish genocide of the Armenian population during the First World War is not an exception but rather confirms this general trend, since the critique focuses on an Other. National history politics influences increasingly not only domestic but also foreign politics in the EU. The events on the sun deck of costly, large-scale European commemoration and jubilee projects occur in sharp contrast to the work in the engine room of European history politics (Troebst 2006b; 2007b: 53–4).

The prospects of a European memory policy are undermined not only by national approaches but also by institutional rivalry. A case in point is the power struggle between the Council of Europe and the European Commission about the project on a Museum of Europe initiated by the Spaak family.[4] What at the end came out of the brave plan for the Musée de l'Europe – at least for the time being – was a poster session in the lobby of the Commission.

In his contribution to this volume, Jan-Werner Müller reflects on the prospects of a softer variant of European commemoration – as opposed to stronger forms wherein Europeanisation stands for homogenisation – and examines the Europeanisation of moral-political attitudes and practices in dealing with profoundly different pasts. The goal would be a stronger understanding of diversity. Such an aim is not only normatively recommendable but also practically feasible. This is the conclusion of our volume: to work not towards a European collective memory in the singular, in a homogenising and essentialising sense, but towards the construction of European collective memories in the plural, which strive for a growing understanding of diversity. However, it is important to emphasise that memory politics does not occur in a vacuum cut off from other developments. If nationalism, populism and protectionism gain ground within the European Union, the prospects for a softer form of memory construction diminish.

A point of departure for our work has been Avishai Margalit's *The Ethics of Memory* (2002). Although we are aware that this is a philosophical work, in contrast to our own, which is an inter-disciplinary, historical, cultural and sociological study, the former has been relevant to our considerations. In particular, we aimed to contrast our idea of public remembrance with Margalit's concept of shared memory and to stress different features of what is defined with the general term 'collective memory'. In the politics of remembrance as presented in our volume, remembering in public is depicted in terms of bargaining between conflicted visions of the past that can be rarely integrated into one cohesive narrative. Nonetheless, Margalit's thoughts on 'communities of memory' and 'ethical communities' are relevant to our interest in whether there is an emerging European community of remembrance – although the answer is most often in the negative.

In the chapters of this volume, perspectives on public politics and practices of remembrance are presented as both top-down and bottom-up processes. Memory and history production is more than symbolic production from a European centre. While the prevailing self-understanding in Brussels seems to be one of Europe 'making citizens', historical legitimacy also requires a perspective of citizens 'making Europe'. This was illustrated by the French and Dutch rejection of the European Constitution in 2005. While this reaction was clearly attributable to social problems in the present, the political legitimacy needed to tackle these problems requires some kind of historical framing. This volume seeks to contribute to such a framing.

The Structure of the Book

The volume is divided into two main parts. In the first part, the authors provide normative and theoretical discussions of the relevant fundamental concepts: history and remembrance, politics of remembrance and European frames of remembrance. This discussion takes the form of asking questions about relations between these fields. The second part is empirical. Based on more general analysis and case studies, subsequent contributions continue to deal with the Europeanisation of public remembrance. Since the 1990s there has been a revision of memory politics across the continent. The chapters in this part are ordered thematically and investigate four European 'dark pasts': the Second World War, the Holocaust, communism and colonialism. In remembering the past, these four areas are of course entangled and overlapping. It is only for analytical purposes that they have been separated.

Part I

The first part of the volume opens with a section titled 'Normative Perspectives and Lines of Division of European Memory Constructions'. In the first chapter, Müller discusses normative perspectives of memory discourse and the possible formation of a European memory. The first and elementary observation is about the elite and artificial character of the 'European' discourse from which a sort of transnational remembrance may emerge. Müller detects the formation of a European memory in the self-critical processes adopted by nations in dealing with their dark pasts, a development that has been apparent all over Europe for at least two decades and with much greater impetus following the events of 1989. A critical self-understanding may result in an opening for mutually deliberative engagement over the past. Such a transformation, however, entails particular risks. Instead of painful confrontation, self-critical processes tend to yield to the temptation of consolation.

The following chapters by Karlsson, Troebst and Kaschuba deal with European histories and memories as potential lines of division and conflict. In the chapter by Karlsson, it is the national aspect that presents the major challenge for a more global, European historical consciousness. The end of the Cold War was concomitant with a general historicising of society; a return to history was equal to a return to Europe as a figure of reunification in the years immediately after the collapse of the Soviet empire. The framework for this was the search for new pasts to provide better orientation in the dramatically changing present. However, Karlsson argues that the Europeanisation of the past had little ambition for self-critical analysis. Europe would merely provide a new opportunity for the rethinking of national pasts. The chapter presents the case that Europeanisation went hand in hand with the nationalisation of history and emphasises that in parts of Europe extreme nationalistic historical interpretations have been a powerful weapon in ethno-territorial conflicts.

Referring to Oskar Halecki's model of divisions of European history from antiquity to the Cold War, Troebst observes that in terms of cultures of remembrance, post-1989 Europe resembles Halecki's historical meso-regions: Western, West-Central, East-Central and Eastern Europe. In particular, the celebrations of the sixtieth anniversary of the end of the Second World War showed that the year 1945 is far from a European *lieux de mémoire*, but rather stands for the limits and divisions of Europe's culture of remembrance. While in Western Europe victorious remembrance prevails and in Germany the year 1945 is remembered as the year of liberation, in East-Central Europe it is the Yalta Conference and the Molotov-Ribbentrop Pact that shape national memories. In the Russian Federation and some other parts of the Commonwealth of Independent States (former Soviet Republics), the year 1945 functions as a new alternative to the now defunct founding myth of 1917. In Troebst's view, there are currently two fundamental memory conflicts: the first concerns the Yalta Conference, which divides post-Soviet Russia and Poland and the Baltic states, and the second concerns the Holocaust as the negative foundational myth, which divides Western and East-Central Europe.

Kaschuba's contribution, which ends this section, differs from those previous. Here, it is Europe that constitutes a point of departure for exclusion. As Kaschuba explains, an inward politics of integration means outward politics of difference. In the globalised world, European culture has become the new *Heimat*. European topoi of remembrance are organised and constructed in a way that allows Europe to profile itself as a still clearer and more accessible horizon. Europe, Kaschuba states, 'constructs itself as offering the charm of the close by, of the local'. In the context of the global politics of remembrance, Europe tends to develop dominating 'grand narratives' and regimes of remembrance and imagery. However, rather than Europeanisation of memory constructions, the matter at stake is, according to Kaschuba's convincing argument, the globalisation of remembrance by European standards. He refers to an emerging global memory management that lacks a centre but is informed by European norms. The iconic-suggestive is displacing the textual-argumentative in new forms of global media representation. New mytho-motoric qualities emerge at a global level under catchphrases such as 'clash of civilisations' in an attempt to create a homogeneous Europe.

The second section, 'Towards a Fluid Conceptualisation of Memory Constructs', begins with chapters by Uhl and Whitling that bring theoretical perspectives to the nature of public remembrance and to public practices of evoking the past and discuss the implications of this for the formation of remembrances that could be called 'European'. Just as culture should be seen not as a homogeneous entity but as dynamic processes of the negotiation of meanings, 'memory' at the collective level should be referred to as a field of negotiations between different memory interests. The two authors thus share a theoretical perspective which recognises a shift from essentialising uses of the term 'collective memory' (and 'collective identity') towards more fluid conceptualisations at the discursive level, such as 'politics' and 'practices' of public remembrance. Uhl focuses on the conceptual relationships between memory as culture and memory as politics, while Whitling examines the distinction between memory and history. Uhl connects the growing public awareness of memory to the break-up of national postwar myths in which the European peoples as a whole were represented as victims of the Nazi occupation and whereby guilt was projected exclusively onto Germany. After the fall of the Berlin Wall in 1989, a more complex thematisation of collective memories was imposed on the political agendas. Whitling suggests that the rhetoric about a European identity or memory seems to be a kind of substitute for the vision of a political and social Europe. On this point one might recall that the connection was the opposite when the European nation states emerged: political unification and social integration resulted in identification with national space and time.

The second section closes with Kaye's reflections on the historical uses of the term 'memory'. Based upon a discussion of the naming of the newly invented practice of photography in the nineteenth century and its metaphoric as well as discursive association with memory, Kaye addresses two forms of more general metaphoric connection to memory. These span from Plato's wax tablet metaphor, as an attempt to illustrate the way in which memory functions, to the contemporary use of memory in the framework of a developed 'memory industry'. Within this context, the little understood concept of memory is metaphorically promulgated as an attribute of collectivities, which were described as being in possession of a memory. This occurred at a time in which the belief in objective history was subject to fundamental criticism by Hayden White and the French postmodernist philosophers, all of whom emphasised the discursive, narrative and constructed dimensions of history. The chapter by Kaye serves at the same time as a link to the second, empirical part of the volume: the author continues the discussion referring to the key images in Europe's coming to terms with the Holocaust, the Second World War, communism and colonialism.

Part II

The second part of the volume opens with a section titled 'Remembering the Second World War'. This section deals with remembrances of the Second World War in different parts of Europe, and its authors focus on three locales: Western Europe (Berger), Eastern Europe (Karge) and Scandinavian countries (Maier).

Berger distinguishes the following common phases in the process of Western Europe's coming to terms with the Second World War. The first of these is the post-war attempt to return to traditional national narratives and to downplay the significance of the Second World War as a major rupture.

The second phase took place in the late 1960s and involves a process of revising national master narratives, together with the increasing realisation of the importance of the Holocaust. The third phase took place in the 1980s and 1990s, a period Berger refers to as a 'return of the nation'. However, what returns is substantially different from the discursive practices of the 1950s. In conclusion, the author doubts whether there is any basis for a common European memory – indeed, whether historical consciousness should be moved from a national to a European plane at all.

Following this, Karge's contribution questions a perspective that focuses on Second World War remembrance with 1989 as a benchmark and that sharply divides historical time in a Cold War period and a post–Cold War period. In the Eastern bloc, the period 1945–89 is usually framed in terms of an official – as opposed to collective – memory. To ignore the decades in between would constitute a kind of *ex post* reinforcement of Europe's Cold War division, leaving little room for an understanding of practices of collective remembrance in a uniting Europe.

In his study of post-war Denmark and Norway, Maier analyses the ways in which a dominant version of Second World War history, a narrative of resistance, was established by means of rituals and anniversaries. Throughout the post-war period, governments and political movements 'nationalised and glorified the resistance', applying to the nation at large the merits of the relatively small percentage of the population that had actually been active in the resistance.

The next section of the volume, titled 'Towards a Europeanisation of the Commemoration of the Holocaust', consists of four chapters dealing with the question of whether it is justified to talk about a Europeanisation of Holocaust remembrance. The first chapter in this section, by Banke, is a general analysis of the processes of commemorating the Holocaust in Europe since 1945. The author sees a trend from the initial neglect after 1945, through confrontation, to the acknowledgement of the Holocaust as common dark legacy. The debate in Poland several years ago about crimes committed against Jews by their Polish neighbours in Jedwabne is an indication that this last stage has also taken place beyond the traditionally defined parameters of Western societies.

The contributions that follow are based on analyses of the memory of the Holocaust in particular countries. On the basis of comparative analysis, distinct from that of Banke, the chapters by Tyszka and Pakier suggest that it is not possible to speak of a Europeanised memory of the Holocaust. They argue instead that the politics of Holocaust remembrance is nationally framed. Tyszka discusses the discourses of the restitution of Jewish property in the Czech Republic and Poland after 1989. Despite two diametrically different patterns of coming to terms with the Jewish past in the two post-communist countries, neither seems to support the idea that the issue of Jewish restitution has, or can, become one of the most important means of Holocaust remembrance in Europe. In the following chapter, Pakier analyses the press reception of the Holocaust film *Europa, Europa* in Germany and in Poland. Common to the discussions triggered by the film in the press of both countries is an excessive identification with the story of the Jew, which Pakier interprets in terms of the politics of remembrance being used as an attempt to appropriate the status of victim for these nations and their citizens.

The chapter by Nattermann examines the processes of remembering victims of the Holocaust in post-war Italy. Discussing the emergence of a 'survivor-orientated narrative', with a positively shaped image of Italian humanity towards Jews during the war, she subsequently asks whether a Europeanised memory of the Holocaust can, especially in Italy, contribute to an increasingly critical examination of the subject in question, or if instead it results in a 'de-Italianisation' of the persecution and deportation of Jews by Italians.

In the following section, 'Coming to Terms with Europe's Communist Past', the contributors deal with communism as a European historical legacy and with the uses of this past in different national contexts, asking at the same time about the possibility of a common European remembrance. In the first chapter of this section, Rees discusses strands of continuity after 1991 in the former communist states in Eastern Europe, with a focus on Russia and Ukraine, in particular on the case of the famine of 1932–3. He discusses the new role for historians in Russia after the collapse of the Soviet system, offering several interesting examples of recent developments in the historical field in Russia, including the publication of lists of victims of the Stalin terror of 1937–8 by the organisation Memorial, an international historical and civil rights society.

Focusing on the Hungarian case, but with an eye to other Eastern European practices, Apor argues that commemorative projects such as museums of communism, the day of the victims of communism, etc., try to construct the image of communism as a terror of European history comparable to that of Nazism. Analysing contemporary politics of commemoration on communism, the author deals with the question of the historically and socio-politically generated conditions and criteria of credibility in historical representation.

In the following chapter, Musabegović investigates the political use of symbols in former Yugoslavia, where communist symbols drew inspiration from war motifs. The author shows how nationalist symbols, while participating in destroying the communist order, also fed on fantasies of war.

The last chapter in this section, by Morgan, provides a Western perspective on the European communist past. Morgan stresses the difference between the Western experience of communism and that of the East, where communism primarily represents a delimitable past and an interruption in national history. The failure to come to terms with the communist past in Western Europe is not a simple issue of memory or amnesia but rather of alternative historical memory.

The final section of the volume, 'Coming to Terms with Europe's Colonial Past', consists of two chapters on colonialism. The core of Jansen's contribution is to reveal the practices of remembrance in the form of politics of concealment and, since the 1990s, the processes of remembrance in the case of the French presence in Algeria. The discussion focuses on pressure groups of public memory and official politics of remembrance. Jansen questions whether common European denominators of processes of remembrance can indeed be said to exist at all.

The chapter by Elenius deals with a different version of colonialism. The author attempts to reinterpret the colonial narrative of native minorities in the Barents region in northern Scandinavia and to overcome the traditional interpretative framework of the nation state. In discussing micro groups and 'neo-tribes', Elenius analyses the ethnicity of the Kven people in relation to the Sámi people, and the claims to the status of indigenous population, as well as the possible transnational content of 'pan-Kven identity'. Claims to an indigenous 'primary' status embody the tension between history and memory and the question of precisely what constitutes the normative status of mixed cultures with 'hybrid identities'.

In the book's conclusion, Jarausch begins with a reflection on the memory boom of the past few decades, which has taken professional historians by surprise. He then discusses the European dimension of that boom. As a response to the pressures of globalisation, the creation of a European cultural space that is based on a shared collective memory and is capable of resisting popular Americanisation or radical Islamicisation might seem appropriate. But in the struggle over the preamble of the European Constitution, the search for common roots has had the opposite effect of raising tensions and fostering disagreement. The quest for a collective European memory should therefore be considered a normative discourse that, in combining two problematic projects, fosters some of their difficulties. The call to Europeanise memory aims not just at inspiring a more profound understanding of the European dimension of the past in its component regions, but at creating a transnational public memory that can be used to legitimate the transformation of the EU into a superstate – a goal that is opposed by many European citizens and resisted by some countries, including Britain and Denmark. Although the availability of funding from Brussels makes it tempting to join in the project of providing historical justification for a shared European memory, Jarausch's suggestion is that historians should instead demythologise it, deflate its rhetoric and deconstruct its subtext. We hope that this book delivers a substantial contribution to such demythologisation.

Notes

1. Cf. 'The Treaty Establishing a Constitution for Europe: Elements for an Evaluation', 3. See http://www.comece.org/upload/pdf/pub_const_treaty_050311_EN.pdf.
2. For a ground-breaking development in this debate, see Hayden White (1973), who has built on a long tradition of philosophical thought. An important source of inspiration for White was Giovanni Battista Vico (1668–1744), a Neapolitan philosopher of history and law.
3. See http://www.lph-asso.fr/actualites/42.html.
4. See http://www.museu.be.

Part I

EUROPE, MEMORY, POLITICS AND HISTORY

A Normative and Theoretical Framing

Section 1

Normative Perspectives and Lines of Division of European Memory Constructions

Chapter 1

On 'European Memory'

Some Conceptual and Normative Remarks

∝ℰⱯℰ⌐

Jan-Werner Müller

Democracy is a matter of having a good memory.
– Kurt Schumacher

The sole function of memory is to help us regret.
– Emile Cioran

Everyone complains of poor memory, no one of weak judgement.
– La Rochefoucauld

In recent years, a number of politicians and intellectuals have openly expressed the wish to see the formation of a kind of 'Europeanisation' of collective memory or even a clearly discernible 'supranational European memory'.[1] Jorge Semprún, for instance, has claimed that European enlargement can succeed culturally and existentially only 'when our memories have been shared and brought together as one' (Leggewie 2007). Yet this wish for oneness has been shadowed by the suspicion that a specifically German model of *Vergangenheitsbewältigung*, or coming to terms with the past, might be imposed on the rest of the continent, or that a pan-European focus on Nazism and the Holocaust might actually be an attempt to redistribute German guilt across the European Union. In other words, might not such a vision of a shared European memory conjure up the nightmare that Thomas Mann famously formulated as 'a German Europe' (rather than a 'European Germany'), although in an anti-nationalist rather than aggressive-nationalist versions? And is there not in any case, from a normative point of view, something deeply troubling about the vision of a European memory or even a Europeanisation of memories? Given what we know about the formation of collective memories in other contexts, is this a conceptually coherent aspiration, and is it empirically plausible at all? Do not collective memories

---

Notes for this chapter begin on page 36.

frequently conflict? Would not a 'oneness' of memory necessarily require the exercise of power in the suppression of memories – individual or collective – that just do not fit? In any event, what would oneness mean for ordinary European citizens? Is it not likely that discussions about European memory will only ever be undertaken by those paid to do so, that is, a relatively small group of European academics (Kansteiner 2006)?

I want to start answering these questions with some conceptual ground-work on how to think about memory and politics. I will then focus more specifically on the challenges and pitfalls of what might at first sight appear as a rather unattractive vision of elites constructing supranational memory. In the following section, I shall discuss some normative and empirical problems that, in my view, are inevitably associated with the notion of European memory. Overall, I want to endorse – with due caution – a process of mutual opening and civilised confrontation of collective memories under the guidance of something like a Rawlsian 'public reason' (Rawls 1999). However, this process should not unfold simply along national lines but should take account of Europe's *histoires* (*et mémoires*) *croisées*, that is, its entangled histories (and memories). The hope is that a critical self-understanding of collectives would be fostered by such a mutual opening and by shared, deliberative engagement over the past. To a degree, therefore, *Vergangenheitsbewältigungswille* (a political will to work critically through the past) becomes a barometer for the liberal-democratic quality of a political culture.

Needless to say, there are many aspects of this process that cannot be addressed in a short essay like this, including the role of historians, who should not turn into what Henry Rousso once called 'agitators of memory', the precise mechanisms for transnational engagements and, not least, an explanation as to why this normative vision is not simply a version of 'liberal nationalism' (thereby reinforcing the notion that only nations have certain ethical duties) but better fits the notion of constitutional patriotism (Müller 2007a). A final caveat is that the very discourse of memory tends towards large reifications, or at least abstractions. The fact is that we simply know far too little about how people actually remember, let alone how elite discourses might or might not affect individual memories. I am convinced that they do make an important difference, but everything that follows is, in a sense, one-sided: what is missing are the audiences, the 'consumers' of collective memory.

What Does 'European Memory' Mean? or, How to Think about Memory and Politics

A self-critical European memory would seem to require at least one of two possible processes. The first would be a commitment on the part of European countries to 'work through the past' as individual nations – in the name of shared universal principles and through 'Europeanised' practices – while clearly addressing different, nationally specific pasts. In other words, this would not be a Europeanisation – or, less politely put, homogenisation – of the contents of different collective memories, but rather a Europeanisation of moral-political attitudes and practices in dealing with profoundly different pasts. Such a process may or may not be happening already. The 1990s saw the rise – not just in Europe – of what has been called a 'politics of regret'. National leaders increasingly began to assume collective responsibility for past misdeeds and engage in public acts of atonement (Barkan 2000; Brooks 1999; Coughlin and Olick 2003; Lübbe 2001). Whether this public repudiation of the past constitutes a new and effective form of political legitimacy is still open to question, but that it has spread as a form of political claim-making is beyond doubt.

The second possible process would be a genuinely shared European memory, with similar contents and not just shared practices. This approach is likely more demanding and more problematic than a series of apparently national instantiations of the politics of regret. Either it would have to include 'new pasts' for each member – strange as it might sound, Europeans would have to acknowledge the collective memories of other countries – or it would mean that 'transnational memories' or 'supranational memories' would compose a single homogenised European memory. Initially, the first option seems awkward, perhaps even absurd: a national collective *can* take responsibility for its past, much in the way that Karl Jaspers and Jürgen Habermas once suggested in the context of post-war West Germany, and even argue about its past in continuous public communication (Müller 2000). Yet it is far from clear that nations could, let alone should, argue about *other* nations' pasts. Should Germans judge France's 'Vichy syndrome', that is, the coming to terms with the occupation and French collaboration with the Nazis, which for some is still an unresolved issue? Why should the French debate the British treatment of the Irish? Are the Spanish in a position to apologise for Portuguese colonialism? Clearly, one nation might acknowledge (and, in form, even emulate) the success of another in coming to terms with its past. But one cannot do this for another nation or instead of it.

Also, given the sheer passion with which nationals often argue about other country's present-day politics, simple prudence might suggest that judgements about the pasts of others might be even more fraught with emotion. Approaching today's politics via irresponsible references to the past would appear most problematic of all. For instance, in the early summer of 2003, a minor diplomatic scandal erupted when the newly inaugurated president of the Council of the European Union, Italy's Silvio Berlusconi, referred to a German member of the European Parliament as resembling a concentration camp guard. Concerns about Berlusconi's suitability for representing the EU became inextricably mixed with fragments from the Fascist and National Socialist pasts of Italy and Germany, respectively. Populations split over the issue very much along national lines.

And yet some European countries are actually moving forcefully in the direction of dealing with other nations' pasts. For instance, in January 2001, the French National Assembly passed a resolution that classified (and condemned) the treatment of Armenians during the First World War as genocide. The resolution was approved against the explicit wishes of the French government and the French president. Subsequent legislation in 2006 made denial of the Armenian genocide a crime punishable by a year's imprisonment and a fine of 45,000 euros. The point of the initial resolution was officially – and internationally – to recognise the character of the events as genocide. Defenders of such a resolution argued that the fact of genocide did not depend on recognition or acknowledgement by the national collective of the perpetrators. The fact that it was *French* politicians who had named what had to be named was irrelevant. Regardless of the potentially dubious political motivation behind such actions, shameful truths are not national property.

It seems morally preferable that recognition and acknowledgement become 'nationalised', that the actual 'intersubjective liabilities', to use Habermas's term, of particular collectives are questioned. Clearly, the aim in this case was to prompt an acknowledgement from the Turkish government itself, a more open debate in Turkish civil society and, perhaps finally, an official apology. Yet deliberation about consequences was secondary to the acknowledgement of atrocity as such: the fact that nationalists in Turkey might be helped, rather than hindered, by such outside pressure was one, but only one, consideration (Dabag 2001; Özdemir 2001).[2] There might be well-advised reasons for refraining from such historical acknowledgements; however, in my view, there exist no genuinely moral ones. Once the character of past events has been admitted, historical truth cannot remain national property. It is another matter to claim that apology – as opposed to recognition or acknowledgement – is a matter only for the collective of the perpetrators.

It is not impossible to merge historical memories to some extent or to draw on transnational memories and to forge a common political culture in the process of arguing about these pasts. At first sight, this prospect might seem on an equal footing with the well-known nationalist manipulation of memories, or it might even evoke Orwellian images of the manipulation of individual consciousness. Moreover, it appears to come up against the argument – most powerfully advanced by Avishai Margalit (2002) – that only 'thick' ethical communities such as families and nations have a duty to remember in the first place, while 'thin' moral relations (and humanity at large) are not and should not be concerned with memory.

A number of distinctions need to be made here, as it is not sufficient simply to transfer concepts from individual psychology to the collective.

First of all, a distinction must be drawn between collective or national memory, on the one hand, and individual mass memory, on the other.[3] The former refers to frames of remembrance, while only the latter designates the memories of participants in actual historical events. And it is collective memory, as a kind of narrative that nations or other groups tell about themselves, that is subject to moral claims and counter-claims – and also inevitably to instrumentalisation by more or less well-intentioned *entrepreneurs de mémoire*.

In other words, at issue are public, collective memories and public claims about these memories – not private, unarticulated or even involuntary memories. Memory claims of the former sort are always political in the sense that they demand collective recognition and are aimed at creating legitimacy. They are consciously shaped and reshaped both by 'producers' and 'consumers' of memory. They are not a matter of trauma and repression, as false analogies with individual psychology suggest, just as public acknowledgement cannot be assumed to lead to private or even collective 'healing' (see Kansteiner 2002). Collective memories and public claims about these memories can and should be subject to shared public reason, historical scrutiny and moral argument in a way that individual memories are not.[4]

Which European Memory (or Memories)?

An example of a recent half-transnational, half-supranational memory might be the collective failure (and shame) over Bosnia in the early to mid-1990s. An 'overlapping moral consensus' seems to have emerged that Europe betrayed its own liberal ideals in its reluctance to intervene, and that practical lessons can be drawn about institutional changes that are needed to make Europe act effectively in politics and war. Of course, it is difficult here to draw a line between European and international, but given how fervently representatives of the EU claimed at the beginning of the Yugoslav wars that this was 'Europe's hour', the responsibility for successive failures would have to be attributed to the EU at least as much as to the UN or individual countries.

Moreover, the artificiality of such a transnational perspective should not be exaggerated: after all, so much of national histories and memories are already inextricably bound up with each other. This interconnectedness is brilliantly symbolised in Emir Kusturica's 1995 film *Underground*, in which vast tunnels join not only European cities but also different historical periods. Underneath an allegedly 'new Europe', it seems, various pasts remain linked in a way that above ground appears to be covered by historical amnesia. In fact – to stay with the symbolism of *Underground* for a minute – these subterranean connections allow for short cuts in political argument through historical allusion and analogy. But by definition, genuinely entangled histories require shared and potentially conflicting efforts at historical (and moral) reconstruction. It is against this background that Jean-Marc Ferry (2000: 177) has suggested a self-critical 'opening' of European national memories, as well as an attempt to achieve a kind of 'overlapping consensus' through civilised conflict and confrontation. To be sure, such a mutual opening is risky and always in danger of being hijacked by populist politicians in particular. However, it might serve to decentre national memories and could contribute to the creation of an 'enlarged mentality', as far as thinking about Europe's pasts is concerned.

The EU itself has always been a peculiar kind of monument to the Second World War – not a monument that commemorates battles, but an institutional edifice whose foundations contain the very lessons learnt from the experience of totalitarian war, subjugation and European-wide genocide. It is not simply starry-eyed pro-European propaganda to say that the European Union was constructed as a result of the memory of the war, which animated the likes of Robert Schuman, Konrad Adenauer and Alcide de Gasperi. Nor is it empty rhetoric to point out that politicians such as Helmut Kohl pursued a fusion of European interests on the basis of memories of large-scale violence and atrocity.[5] The fact that these memories often remained hidden behind the language of technocracy and economic benefits does not detract from the actual motives of the founders (and subsequent re-founders) of the European Union.

In the post-war period, Europeans attempted to develop a language for history that was both monumental and critical. It was about drawing negative lessons from the past and consequently building 'critical monuments' – *prima facie* an oxymoron (and a fusion of two seemingly incompatible Nietzschean categories), but, in practice, a new potential form of legitimacy (Nietzsche 1980). It is therefore not surprising that some European intellectuals have gone so far as to claim that the impulse 'critically to work through the past' is the essence of 'European civilisation'. For instance, Alain Finkielkraut (1987: 143–4) has argued that while 'it is at the expense of his culture that the European individual has conquered, one by one, all his liberties, it is also, and more generally, the critique of tradition which constitutes the spiritual foundation of Europe'. However, such rhetoric perches precariously between European self-deprecation and Eurocentrism – and the one can all too easily turn into the other. There is no point in replacing self-congratulatory national histories with what paradoxically could be called self-congratulatory, self-critical supranational histories.

Some historical perspective and relativisation are in order here. The very idea of European unification itself has a deeply conflicted history – a history that needs to be remembered not least in order to counter simplistic narratives of European progress against the background of negative national pasts. It is worth recalling that the last great project of European unification before the formation in 1957 of the European Community was Hitler's plan for a new Europe. In fact, attempts at formulating and founding such a new Europe are one of the prime examples of a mixing of memories (and guilt) across national boundaries (see Bruneteau 2003; Joerges and Singh Ghaleigh 2003; Mazower 1998: 141–84). Many intellectuals and bureaucrats across the continent enthusiastically supported Hitler's project, and an entire ideology – not purely identical with Nazism – was built around ideas of peace and 'European values'. Due to the cluster of associations that included Hitler, Europe, conquest and colonialism, many left-wing intellectuals were at the time opposed to the European Community. According to the French sociologist Edgar Morin (1987: 140–7), it was only through the experience of decolonisation that his generation could see the idea of Europe itself as becoming 'purified'.

Some commentators have even detected intimations of what has been referred to as a Europeanisation of the Holocaust – although on closer inspection it becomes clear that, for rather obvious reasons, British, French and German views of the Holocaust remain deeply divided (Evans 2000; Levy and Sznaider: 2001). Nevertheless, a pattern seems to have emerged according to which individual European nations acknowledge their role in the Holocaust, while at the same time affirming its 'universal significance'. In France, Italy, Switzerland, Denmark, Sweden and Holland, the last decade of the twentieth century saw extensive debates about collaboration, slave labour and 'Nazi gold'. Moreover, after the collapse of communism, memories of the Second World War were 'unfrozen' on both sides of the former Iron Curtain. This is not to say that it suddenly became possible to recover some pristine, pre-representational memory, free of political instrumentalisation. But it did mean that collective memories – and, to some degree, even individual memories – were liberated from constraints imposed by the need for state legitimation and the kind of friend-enemy thinking associated with the Cold War.

One consequence appears to be that many myths of resistance and of the purity of the post-war period have been dissolved – which, obviously, is not to claim that guilt or responsibility can ever be distributed equally across the continent. Immediately after the war, nations quickly needed to assert themselves and to find and legitimise their role in the global confrontation between East and West. Arguably, European integration has helped Western European countries gain distance from their own pasts, which ceased to serve their particular post-war function as the moral foundations of individual nations. Integration lessened the need for national self-assertion and homogeneous narratives of national continuity – and therefore the need to present a morally pristine past. *La hantise du passé*, or being haunted by the past, is thus no longer a German peculiarity (Jeismann 2001: 57–8).

It might be too much to claim that the Nazi experience as a whole has been Europeanised, but certainly there is now a common language of guilt, political entanglements and fateful exclusions across the continent. This language does not in itself prevent – and might well encourage – a kind of 'competition of victimhood', particularly with regard to the atrocities of Nazism and Stalinism (Leggewie 2007). But the point holds that national collective memories have become more heterogeneous and discontinuous and less 'mythical'. In turn, free-floating particles of these memories might coalesce into a 'thin' transnational European memory.

A similar process of 'unfreezing' and fragmentation has recently taken place in Central and East-Central Europe. The painful Polish self-interrogation over the massacre at Jedwabne, the debates surrounding Budapest's 'House of Terror' and the German-Czech disputes over the Beneš decrees are only a few examples of intense historical controversies in which, often enough, Nazism, communism and collaboration were simultaneously at issue. In each case, history and national identity have been linked more or less directly, and in each case a European dimension was eventually added to the discussions. For some Central and East-Central European countries that are set to join the EU, establishing Holocaust memorial days seems to have become almost a litmus test of their liberal, democratic morality (Reed 2001).

Arguably, European integration has helped these processes of critical self-reflection. The prospect of inclusion has made Central and Eastern European politicians and intellectuals more willing to question national identities. The security of 'belonging to Europe' – if sometimes on rather unfavourable terms – has also consolidated the practice of self-questioning. This counters the frequent claim that accession countries which have only just regained national sovereignty will necessarily resent supranational integration, even if they might consent to it out of sheer economic necessity.

Finally, in the EU itself, reference to the Holocaust has been associated explicitly with an affirmation of tolerance and diversity in the present. For all their inclusiveness, these measures have clearly been part of an adversarial structure, except that this is diachronic and not synchronic, political or national. Present political communities reaffirm themselves against an image of absolute moral evil in the past, thereby inextricably linking memory and morality.

The choice of the Holocaust as a horizon of absolute evil is of course not accidental and says much about European political realities since 1989. After the end of the communist 'evil empire', the Third Reich was brought to the fore as a new standard of political evil. Moreover, in the presence of 'rogue states' and genocide, considered the worst political spectres of the post–Cold War period, the Third Reich appeared to be the most 'useful' past.

Memories of the Holocaust have served to legitimate both multi-cultural integration and humanitarian intervention. At least until September

11, it seemed that, after the end of the Cold War, integration and intervention were the two major political projects of Europe (and the West more generally). These projects are also connected, although often in complex ways. The wars of Yugoslav succession flooded the continent with refugees in a way not seen since the Second World War and its aftermath. Military intervention was partly designed to manage (and limit) the problems of integration at home, while the goals of intervention often included visions of an integrated multi-ethnic society. For both purposes, the Holocaust proved a useful past.[6]

Yet, as critics have long pointed out, the Holocaust is perhaps the last form of acceptable, albeit negative, Eurocentrism. Its uniqueness in the annals of genocide, at least in the eyes of some, derives precisely from the fact that it occurred in Europe and, in particular, in 'highly cultured' Germany. Since we are still far from what sociologists have called a globalisation (or even 'glocalisation') of the Holocaust, a European 'Holocaust identity' could thus result in its own novel forms of 'mnemonic exclusion'.

Perils and Pitfalls: Historical Analogising, Crowding Out Solidarity, Negative Nation Building

Frequently drawing on the history – or, more accurately, histories – of the Holocaust is bound to open a Pandora's box of problems unavoidably associated with historical analogies. James Bryce's judgement ([1888] 1995: 9) that 'the chief practical use of history is to deliver us from plausible historical analogies' will not deter politicians, intellectuals and citizens from rummaging through the past. Yet analogical reasoning is likely to have poor results due to causes rooted in cognitive psychology (Foong Khong 1992). If nothing else, such thinking serves to reduce complexity and short-circuit critical reflection for the sake of creating what appears as 'instant legitimacy'. Invoking the Holocaust will inevitably be subject to such problems.

In general, summoning the past appears to furnish the participants in political debates with a moral certainty that is otherwise unobtainable in pluralistic democratic societies. For example, drawing on memories for the justification of foreign and military policies, as happened frequently during the 1999 war in Kosovo, can lend these policies an almost self-evident moral character when they might or might not have achieved this kind of legitimacy had there been a proper debate about their meaning in the present. In short, appealing to the past can function as a way to avoid political argument. Such appeals can even end up 'de-moralising' political argument. One example might be that reference to the Holocaust could set the standard for military intervention far too high.

There is also an ethical question about the use of analogies which has been debated most extensively in connection with extracting 'lessons' from the Holocaust. Drawing such lessons, as laudable as it might be in the abstract, can be part of a strategy of consolation, of deriving a comforting meaning from the past, rather than a more painful strategy of confrontation with the past (Langer 1995: 5). It is in any case often indeterminate what these lessons would be. For instance, Giorgio Agamben and Norman Geras have claimed that the Shoah can be read as a conclusive refutation of well-meaning universalist morality as well as its affirmation (Geras 1998).[7] Yet Auschwitz was also *philosophically* (or *conceptually*) devastating and therefore resists any facile appropriation for the sake of reinforcing moral doctrines (Neiman 2002).

Finally, there is the concern that an emphasis on such a momentous (and, in a negative sense, monumental) event as the Holocaust might shackle the present to the past, so that remembrance comes at the cost of promoting universalist values in the present. It might be noted that solidarity is scarce in politics, and 'anamnestic' solidarity – empathy with victims in the past – is likely to crowd out present-day consensus: the sheer enormity of the Holocaust might make it more difficult to perceive injustice in the present. As has often been pointed out, the rise of a politics of regret has also been associated with a retreat from the idea of social self-transformation thorough collective action and the replacement of a politics of mass mobilisation with a 'politics of legal disputation' (Torpey 2001). Some critics have gone so far as to claim that – like neo-liberalism – the politics of regret and reparations is, above all, directed against the state, that it leads to a private cultivation (or even competition) of victimhood and a juridification of public life – all of which are said to be ultimately apolitical (ibid.).

These quasi-empirical predictions might or might not be accurate. There is no way of demonstrating that anamnestic solidarity will drive out other kinds of solidarity – or that it might, instead, make societies as a whole more sensitive to wrongs and instances of open or hidden violence in the present. Furthermore, none of the arguments discussed above suggests that there should be a moral-political *cordon sanitaire* around the Holocaust – as if that was even a possibility. But they should warn against facile analogies, against the complacency of merely directing political attention to familiar images and against misguided strategies of consolation. After all, even if one holds the view that universally valid insights can be derived from the Holocaust, it does not follow that every universalism needs recourse to the Holocaust to be effective or even fully comprehended (Friedländer 1992: 19–20). And there is no compelling reason why the experiment of the EU necessarily needs it, either. As Elisabeth Lévy (2002: 45) has remarked pointedly, it would be 'astonishing if Europe determined its future in response to some "negationists", who are fortunately marginal'.

But are there not other memories to be shared and contested across the continent? This might be the case for memories of colonialism. Almost all

Western European countries have histories that are intertwined through imperialism – histories and memories that still profoundly shape the present, as these countries face similar challenges of trying to make immigrants from former colonies 'feel at home'. The imperative to acknowledge French crimes during and after the Algerian War, for instance, is inseparable from the question of how to open the French Republic to its minorities (Barou 1993). It is at least debatable, however, whether here past experiences, including moral failure, can yield universal lessons in the way often claimed about the Holocaust. This challenge then also places a particular burden on public reasoning, that is, on trying to think things through together and on the merits of keeping the past alive by comparing history to memory and by continuing to argue about it.[8]

Stressing the colonial past is a useful check on Eurocentrism and Europe's universalist pretensions in the present. It also calls into question narratives of national superiority and 'civilising missions'. According to some observers, such colonial narratives make even more demands on moral reflection than memories of collaboration or even the Holocaust. In many colonial memories it appears that 'good' and 'evil' cannot easily be separated, which is one reason why such memories have remained especially particularised (Raben 2002).

Moreover, a focus on colonialism is double-edged as far as confrontations between former colonial powers and the formerly colonised are concerned. The latter might legitimately resist lessons about overcoming nationalism which are being administered by those who have – or believe that they have – reached a post-national stage. Clearly, if violations of human rights and democratic principles are at stake, intervention – rhetorical or even actual – might be justified. But this is different from admonishing others, particularly former colonial subjects, about how and when to question their traditions.

Conclusion

A conscious 'memorialisation' of European politics entails significant risks. Even if drawing on different, criss-crossing and partially conflicting memories is in principle possible, it has to be remembered that European memories are not just divided – they are also divisive. This differs from the criticism frequently directed at the 'memory industry', namely, that memories are necessarily of a 'liturgical' and non-negotiable character, so that memory becomes quasi-sacred – unquestioned and unquestionable (Maier 1993).

Thus, a European collective memory is a conceptually coherent notion and empirically not implausible. It is also *prima facie* desirable from a normative point of view. As I pointed out above, it is in principle possible to subject collective memories – as opposed individual mass memories – to public contestation and public reason. Such a process, a civilised mutual opening and confrontation, is desirable. In any case, nothing will bring back either quasi-sacralised national memories or the quasi-natural, lived collective memories, whose disappearance the French historian Pierre Nora began to observe in the 1980s. It is precisely because national 'memory-habits' are being lost that memory has had to be fixed – and frequently cast in stone (see Booth 2006). But that casting process has also become contentious, and out of such contestation and, ideally, mutual, deliberative engagement, new public self-understandings might emerge.

Nevertheless, a Europe that tries to narrate a story about itself *ex negativo*, with the Holocaust as a negative foundation myth, can easily turn into a monumental enterprise of sentimentalising the past and, perversely, deriving consolation from it, while remaining politically passive in the present. Put differently, a shared public reasoning on Europe's pasts and the 'admonitory meaning and moral purpose' this might serve is profoundly desirable, whereas Euro-nation building through negative memory building is not (Judt 2005: 831).

Notes

I thank Bo Stråth, Małgorzata Pakier and an anonymous referee for comments and suggestions. The essay was written while benefiting from a fellowship at the European University Institute, Florence, and revised while being supported by an Open Society Fellowship at Central European University, Budapest.

1. This essay draws selectively on previously published work (see Müller 2000, 2002a, 2007a, 2007b).
2. A Turkish opposition party proposed a law that condemned the French for genocide in the Algerian War, while the mayor of Ankara considered erecting a monument for the Algerians killed during decolonisation and changing all street names that referred to French nationals.
3. I adopt this distinction from Timothy Snyder (2002). Of course, the former (collective or national memories) in many ways frame the latter (individual mass memories), but they are not reducible to them – which is the mistaken view of those who see memory in purely instrumental terms.
4. I use the term 'public reason' here in the sense of John Rawls's political liberalism (1993).
5. The indirect approach of the founders of the European Union and the lag between foundation and finding a language capable of coming to terms with the past suggest the inherent complexity of this task. Time must pass before 'critical monuments' can be built and recognised as such. This also suggests that the particular German model of coming to terms with the past probably cannot be exported and applied immediately. For some of the general, structural difficulties with transitional justice, see Elster (1998).
6. For instance, Britain and Italy held Holocaust Memorial Days for the first time in 2001. In Britain, the event was partly organised by the Race Equality Unit, now the Race Equality Foundation (see 'Britain Excludes Armenians from Memorial Day', *The Independent*, 23

November 2000). During the 1990s, Austria, France and Switzerland made Holocaust denial a crime (see Shermer and Grobman 2000).

7. Giorgio Agamben explicitly sees Auschwitz as a refutation of Karl-Otto Apel's and Habermas's discourse ethics, but goes further to claim that 'almost none of the ethical principles our age believed it could recognise as valid have stood the decisive test, that of an *Ethica more Auschwitz demonstrata'* (see Heller-Roazen 1999: 13, 64–6).

8. It is often said that even if Europeans could find some kind of consensus about the Holocaust and the moral lessons from the Second World War, such a consensus would in fact exacerbate the problems of integration, as immigrants from former colonies and their descendants would neither respond to appeals somehow to 'feel guilty', nor necessarily share the historical interpretations offered by a majority population. But this is a far too static and, in a sense, sociologically naive picture. As Ian Buruma (2006) has shown in his important essay on the Netherlands, fragments of collective memories of collaboration continue to play an important role in public debates, and they are used (or misused) politically by the representatives of Muslims as much as by those who speak in the name of the *autochtoon*.

Chapter 2

THE USES OF HISTORY AND THE THIRD WAVE OF EUROPEANISATION

Klas-Göran Karlsson

Problems concerning the practices and politics of remembrance and the uses of history in Europe belong to a third wave of the European integration process. The first wave, well on the road to completion, is economic integration, while the second, notably less successful, is political unification. The third wave, cultural Europeanisation, includes complex and strongly disputed processes such as linguistic homogenisation and the inculcation of a 'European' amalgam of knowledge, attitudes and values. The aim is to bring Europeans closer to each other in terms of everyday associations and life experiences. In addition, there is an obvious parallel objective to provide 'new Europe' with a suitable cultural-symbolic foundation for political guidance and legitimacy. It can be assumed that enhanced communication between European countries makes political and intellectual elites, as well as populations more generally, increasingly aware of their cultural and linguistic differences, which in turn may reinforce the ambition to find common references. Yet the task of cultural Europeanisation is far from simple. The process of linguistic homogenisation, for example, is slow and irresolute, with new languages being officially recognised as working languages by the European Union.

The Historisation of Europe

While the European integration process has been in progress since the early post-war era, the cultural wave did not begin until the 1990s. It was at this point that Europeanisation broadened and intensified due to the breakdown of communism in Eastern Europe and the end of the Cold War.

Notes for this chapter begin on page 54.

A concomitant process was the general historisation of society. That the 'return to history' was interpreted as a 'return to Europe' or a 'reunification of Europe' in countries recently situated on the eastern side of the Iron Curtain was not surprising, given that many of them had been integral parts of the European space and discourse before the Second World War. Furthermore, Central European intellectuals had already prepared the way by drawing attention to the unnatural post-war position of Central Europe (Gerner 1999). It is, however, apparent that Europe was being attributed a new meaning even in countries that had continuously and indisputably been part of the European space and where ideas of a European identity are long-standing. A significant watershed in this sense were the years of economic crisis in the 1970s. The breakdown of the Bretton Woods system (the collapse of the dollar in 1971 and the oil price shock in 1973), combined with mass unemployment for the first time since the 1930s, shook the confidence of the European Community and weakened support for its movement towards economic and monetary union, as proposed in the Werner Plan. The negotiations for the implementation of the Werner Plan became stalled. Instead, the political energy was invested in a more distant and more utopian project that would circumvent the problems of the time. At its summit in Copenhagen in December 1973, the European Community published a declaration on European identity in order to define Europe's place in the world. The idea of a European identity triggered an academic and political obsession with the concept that has lasted for decades (Malmborg and Stråth 2002: 11).

In large parts of Europe, Europeanisation has gone hand in hand with a nationalisation of history. In the Balkan and Caucasian parts of Europe, history in extreme nationalist interpretations developed into a powerful weapon in ethno-territorial conflicts that accelerated the disintegration of the multi-national Soviet Union and Yugoslavia. In Eastern Europe, the continuing nationalisation of history can to a great extent be explained as a reaction against long-term submission to Soviet communist historical formulas and interpretations and against a corresponding forced disregard for nationalist or bourgeois national pasts in historical scholarship and teaching, as well as in the general historical culture. The larger European context for the nationalisation of history includes a need for answers to identity questions of who 'we' and 'they' are in a situation not only in which the bipolar peace and security of the old world have disappeared, but also in which multi-culturalism, regionalism and Europeanisation have added to insecurity. As usual, the other side of the coin is political: all over Europe, representatives of nationalist and populist parties have capitalised on nationalisations of history.

The outcome of cultural Europeanisation is therefore difficult to foresee. No doubt, linguistic and cultural 'turns' of this grand scale will be long processes with many setbacks and will depend only to a certain degree on the success of the two first waves. It is unlikely that a successful cultural integration would be prescribed and implemented from above by European institutions as a matter of instrumental politics. To avoid alienation, activities from below, such as public discourses, scholarly thinking, educational systems and mass media, should be implemented, accompanied by consideration of the heterogeneity and persistence of national and other identities. It is also necessary to take into account the tendency towards cultural inertia. The narrower mindsets and experiences of individuals are not always on a level with the seemingly limitless technical-economic and political range of the European integration project.

The problem is closely connected to the meaning of the concept of Europeanisation. Among political scientists, the notion is both fashionable and contested, as it relates to supranational problems of governance and change that have an impact on national politics. Scholars within the humanities are generally more interested in European identities and the ways in which factual historical circumstances, as well as culture, literary texts and historical thinking, are involved in the identity process. In the following, I will offer some comments on the possible ways that cultural Europeanisation – including extreme interpretations of it – could be brought about. For instance, the construction and dissemination of a European canon could be seen as a counterpoint to efforts made recently in several European countries – in political-cultural life as well as in schools – to identify the essence of the cultural assets and values that constitute a nation or a national heritage. Such a canon would appear to be problematic on the grounds that it aspires to transcend existing diversities and divisions in European history and culture. It is also highly inconsistent with the position taken above – that is, that cultural Europeanisation must resonate with societal initiatives that are broader than the interests of a political elite.

The Holocaust as a European Canon

To date, the best example of a canonisation of history in the name of the European dimension is the case of the Holocaust, or Shoah, not least in political institutions such as the Council of Europe and the European Parliament.[1] There is no other historical event or process to which European institutions have demonstrated such a deep commitment, so far culminating in the European Parliament resolution on remembrance of the Holocaust, anti-Semitism and racism of 27 January 2005, the date of the sixtieth anniversary of the Red Army liberation of Auschwitz.

Two recent statements demonstrate the basic idea behind the decision to give prominence to the Holocaust. The first of these, dated 31 October 2005, is from the EU presidency:

The significance of the Holocaust is universal. But it commands a place of special significance in European remembrance. It is in Europe that the Holocaust took place. And, like the United Nations, it is out of that dark episode that a new Europe was born.

European Union member states work together to promote peace and democracy within its borders and beyond. This is something which we could not have imagined 60 years ago. Yet some members of our societies still face intolerance and prejudice. The best tribute we can pay to the victims and survivors of the Holocaust is to speak out against such attitudes in our own communities.[2]

The second statement, made at an OSCE conference in June 2005, gives a similar explanation with respect to the importance of the Holocaust in European education. Introducing a session titled 'Education on the Holocaust and on Anti-Semitism', Beate Winkler, the former director of the European Monitoring Centre on Racism and Xenophobia, declared: 'The Shoah is the traumatic experience of Europe's recent history. It has driven the EU's founders to build a united and peaceful Europe and thus been at the very root of the European integration project.'[3]

These quotations show that the Nazi genocide of European Jewry serves as a combined founding history and basic value system for the European Union. According to such a view, it was the horrendous Holocaust experience – and not the Marshall Plan or the incipient Cold War antagonism towards the Soviet Union – that brought the Western victors of the war together and forced through the European integration project to create a peaceful and democratic Europe. Furthermore, the common remembrance of the Holocaust has been the motivation for keeping this work going for several decades and the justification for fighting those who do not adhere to European values by denying or minimising the significance of the Holocaust, or by committing other misdeeds in the spirit of the Nazi genocide. Thus, in a more general sense, the history of the war atrocities is politically invoked to call attention to 'the necessity of humanitarian intervention' (Bell 2006: 16). This context suggests that, rather than a slip of the tongue, the infamous declaration made on Victory Day 2005 in Theresienstadt by Swedish EU Commissioner and Vice-President of the European Commission Margot Wallström – namely, that the Second World War was caused by nationalistic greed and international power rivalry, that the EU was founded to replace such evils with European cooperation and that Euroscepticism risked a return to the Holocaust – was in fact a well-considered ideological statement.

It is similarly worth noting the ways in which the lessons of the European Holocaust are *not* applied in other circumstances. Drawing on fresh experiences from the 1990s, when genocides were perpetrated both in distant Rwanda and in European Srebrenica, a plausible response would have been that Holocaust perspectives help us understand what human beings are capable of pursuing in the outskirts of Europe even today, that is, the systematic, industrial murder of entire communities of fellow human beings. However, such argumentation has obviously not been considered compatible with the idea of the European Union as a guarantor against genocidal violence.

The Holocaust, situated at the centre of a victorious Western narrative that Norman Davies (1996: 39–45) has termed both an 'Allied scheme of history' and 'Eurohistory', has provided the European integration project with ideological underpinnings or, as Davies puts it (ibid.: 44), 'a dynamic vision of a European community that would be capable of creating its own mystique'. It has also proven useful in the European expansion process, when previously communist potential member states were called to account for their actions related to the Holocaust. The logic of Europeanisation has meant that the same agenda has been set up in those states that have been granted membership without being called upon to write themselves into a Holocaust context.[4] The aim, also clearly visible in the political statements of the Stockholm International Forum on the Holocaust, is to bring new European states into line with their EU partners by having them enter the moral – and, given that Holocaust denial is considered a crime, sometimes also legal – road towards recognition, penance and forgiveness (Judt 2005: 803ff.).[5] In several European states, the goal has not only been to acknowledge the sufferings of European Jews, but also to recognise the many misdeeds against Jews perpetrated by titular nationals who either cooperated with the Nazis or carried out genocidal acts on their own. The much-discussed Polish Jedwabne massacre is just one of several examples of anti-Semitic deeds perpetrated against Jews outside the realm of Nazi occupation rule. In the course of this recognition, the respective strengths of the Europeanisation and nationalisation processes in various Eastern and Central European countries, and in Europe in general, have clearly been put to the test.[6]

In particular, in European states and societies where nationalisation has been strong, the Soviet communist terror, represented by the gulag, has taken precedence over the European Auschwitz discourse. This is sometimes justified by the fact that communist rule was comparatively longer and that the number of individuals to fall victim to communist terror was much larger. However, a better explanation is probably that local populations are more unequivocally considered victims in the Soviet terror process. Charles Maier's distinction between a 'hot' and 'cold' memory is useful here. Maier (2002) points out how deep experiences of terror and genocide 'have remained engraved' in human minds. The gulag is a hot memory in the Eastern, post-communist parts of Europe, while Auschwitz is relatively cold. Yet in the West, the temperatures of these memories are reversed (ibid.). Official European discourse has demonstrated no comparable interest in integrating the gulag into a European canon. It does not appear to be considered worth the risk of initiating a new *Historikerstreit* (historians' dispute) in official European politics. Leftist groups continue to link Stalin to an essentially progressive ideology, and thus the gulag cannot be used as a means to challenge the supremacy of Hitler as Europe's absolute evil or to destabilise cooperation within the European Union. In this sense, Tony Judt (2005: 826) is correct in distinguishing between a united Europe and a still divided, deeply asymmetrical European memory, thereby tangibly illustrating some of the problems attached to the third wave of Europeanisation. The different treatments of Auschwitz and the gulag clearly illustrate the contrast between Europe imagined as a unified cultural entity and Europe conceived as a space of diversity and many interests, with numerous histories of atrocity.

Needless to say, basic aspects of the European Holocaust interpretation as a founding history have no connection to historical facts. During the first post-war decades, the mass killings of Jews were, for the most part, collectively forgotten, albeit for different reasons in different European countries. The concept of the Holocaust to denote the Judeocide (Petrie 2000) was not yet in general use, and indifference to the Jewish tragedy prevailed. In the West, a progressive narrative located Nazi genocide as the tragic finale of a dark narrative that ended with the war (Alexander 2004: 197–9). In the East, Jews were much more systematically omitted from a historical culture that otherwise dedicated itself to the heroism and suffering of the Second World War. Jews were not allowed to compete with Russians and communists in the hierarchy of victimhood in the Soviet grand narrative of the war (Merridale 2005: 247–58). The guilt question was unproblematic: Nazism and the extermination of the Jews were German phenomena, while Vichy rule in France and Fascist rule in Italy were aberrations in both national and European histories. Private memories were not allowed to disturb the dominant public impression of modernist progress and social harmony.

Furthermore, when the Holocaust gradually turned into an important historical-cultural symbol, neither the inspiration nor the initiative was European. Yad Vashem, a forty-five acre complex in Jerusalem that was instituted in 1953 by the Israeli Knesset as an official memorial to Jewish victims, became the prominent site of Holocaust remembrance and research. It was in the State of Israel that the first Holocaust Remembrance Day was established in 1951, and it was the Israeli trial of Adolf Eichmann in April 1961 that signalled the great change in the world's attitude towards the Holocaust. Another event that served to trigger historical-cultural interest in the Nazi genocide was the screening of the television series *Holocaust: The Story of the Family Weiss*, produced by US broadcaster NBC and aired all over the Western world in 1978–9. From its foundation in 1993, the United States Holocaust Memorial Museum in Washington, DC, has been an additional global centre of public, educational and scholarly activity related to the Holocaust.[7] In other words, the Holocaust as represented in present European public remembrance is not rooted in historical achievements of the post-war era but rather gains strength from contemporary needs and interests. Consequently, there is a demand for a broader, as well as a deeper, context of European public remembrance.

European Historical Consciousness

In a second, non-canonical interpretation, cultural Europeanisation is a dynamic and multi-faceted process in which not only official European representatives but also scholars, intellectuals, journalists, teachers and others participate. A European cache of cultural valuables becomes the – temporary – result of an open and continuous cultural negotiation, a process that serves as a metaphorical reminder of Ernest Renan's famous description ([1882] 1994: 17) of a nation as 'an everyday plebiscite'. In this interpretation, a canonical content is less useful than a collection of intellectual concepts and analytical tools to guide and frame an ongoing debate on the characteristics of European culture, identity and public remembrance.

The most basic and problematic of these concepts is historical consciousness. Is there such a thing as a European historical consciousness?[8] How do we make historical consciousness, as a cognitive foundation of all human life, operable for intellectual analysis? Historical consciousness is a mental process which helps human beings orientate themselves in time by ascribing meaning to the past. At its base is the assumption that all human beings exist in time. We have a past and are part of history, and at the same time we are orientated towards what will come, that is, we make history. Thus, memories and other experiences of the past converge with expectations for – or fears of – the future to guide individuals' and collectives' understanding of and readiness to take action in life and society. The debate on the idea of Europe is a good example of how interpretations of the past are mobilised both to sharpen the analysis of the contemporary situation and to endorse a desired Europe of the future in which the consciousness of Europeanness provides a common frame of reference. The following example may be illustrative: on the eve of the Swedish referendum on membership in the European Monetary Union, an opponent to entry, also a party leader and now a minister, supported a statement that the EMU is similar to Hitler's economic plans for Europe. The example also proves that emotive traits are as constitutive as cognitive ones when historical consciousness is involved.

As an individual faculty, it is easy to imagine that historical consciousness is at work when someone close to us is born or dies. To make sense of a dramatic change, we more or less consciously extend our time horizons by remembering our own childhood or by reflecting on the idea that, next time, it may be our turn to pass away. When analysing historical consciousness as a mental orientational mode that we share with others, there is much to be learned from Maurice Halbwachs's analyses of the social character of our recollections of the past. In particular, history has more often than not been set in a national framework, to which Halbwachs dedicated surprisingly little attention. Nonetheless, in European societies in which nationalisation has not been a prominent feature, history has also been an important instrument in a national project, a fact that has a restraining influence on efforts to encourage cultural Europeanisation.

As regards consciousness raising, it may be instructive to stick to the same basic bipolarities of life that serve to activate individual historical consciousness. These should include not only life and death, but also 'we' and 'they', right and wrong, power and powerlessness, true and false. Historical consciousness can be triggered by problems and concerns related to existence and identity, ethics and morality, politics and ideology. This indicates why genocides in general, and the Holocaust in particular, in their capacity as borderline events that concentrate several of these basic and contradictory dimensions, have a special place in historical consciousness. Furthermore, scholars have underlined that crises, defeats and traumas are hotbeds of this kind of time-transcending historical thinking (Rüsen 2001, 2004; Schivelbusch 2001). According to political scientist John Keane (1988: 208), 'crises are times during which the living do battle for the hearts, minds and souls of the dead'.

Based on mental *longues durées*, historical consciousness is probably a phenomenon characterised by a certain inertia. However, the dramatic years round 1990 involved more immediate and fundamental changes in our thinking about history. The studious and multi-faceted uses of history made all over Europe since then are the most convincing evidence of this development. Historical consciousness is impossible to see and analyse. It should rather be understood as a heuristic concept to remind us that history is a profound and elaborated mental dimension. A scholar interested in the development of historical consciousness must either be content with its concrete traces left in historical culture (books, films, monuments, museum exhibits, geographical sites, etc.) or take a keen interest in the functional activations of historical consciousness in life and society, that is, in the uses of history.

History is made use of when it is activated in a communicative process so that certain groups can satisfy certain needs or look after certain interests. The uses of history presented in the following, produced to reach a more general, comparative understanding of the role of history in life and society, correspond to the basic dimensions of human life connected to historical consciousness: an existential use of history applied to problems of existence and identity, a moral use to aspects of right and wrong, an ideological and political use to questions of legitimacy and power, and a scholarly-scientific use to the true-false dimension. These uses of history, which are presumed to possess differing degrees of strength and urgency in different European societies and historical periods, are not mutually exclusive but can and do function simultaneously.

A typology of this kind has two main advantages. It can help to avoid both an extreme top-down approach to historical culture, which is inherent in some analyses of 'the power of history and memory', and a bottom-up approach in which all expressions of a history, without discrimination and analytical cogency, are gathered in an all-embracing history-memory discourse. Concepts such as the uses of history can encourage a more multi-faceted anthropological interpretation of history's work in society.

The systematic presentation of the uses of history will be combined with a concrete analysis of interpretations and representations of history in a European context in which they transcend a traditional national history–cultural framework and touch upon problems that can be viewed as common to and shared by all or at least several European societies. The emphasis will be, on the one hand, on those historical aspects considered by the history users to be within a European human reach, that is, a space created by subjectively interpreted information and experiences, and, on the other hand, a European technical range, that is, a space determined by historical developments and structural conditions that can be externally analysed.[9]

The relevant historical material is practically infinite, since phenomena in modern history, such as the defeat of Germany in the world wars or the fall of the Soviet Union, have had an indisputable impact on the entire European space. However, the focus is primarily on how these and other historical events actually have been used. In this sense, it is the memory of the Second World War that remains at the heart of the twentieth century. Some commentators anticipated that the 'long Second World War' would come to an end in Europe with the international changes of 1989, but the reverse has rather been the case (cf. Bosworth [1993] 1994: 4). However, the aim here is not to provide the reader with a full account of contemporary European historical debate, but to illustrate the various uses of history with empirical examples and thereby suggest what a European historical consciousness might be.

The Uses of History in Europe

Existential Use of History

An existential use of history is triggered by the need to remember, or alternatively to forget, in order to uphold or intensify feelings of orientation and identity in a society characterised by insecurity, pressure or sudden change. Memory is a retrospective, present-minded mental process in which we confront or integrate reconstructions or representations of the past – normally, images of concrete figures, times and places – with situations in the present. Thus, memory can provide the individual with a comforting notion of a connection or a continuity in relationship to history, a kind of 'presence of the past', which itself may bring about an understanding of being part of something larger than a single, isolated human life.

The existential use of history is normally well developed in a society where the function of memory has been strengthened as a result of conflicts and turbulence, external pressures and/or intra-cultural homogenisation. Amnesia may also develop in such a situation; the need to forget and to devote energies to practical reconstruction work was deeply felt among many of those who lived through the horrors of the Second World War. However, the existential use of history may also operate in a post-industrial society which has passed beyond a certain level of material satiation and in which 'post-materialist values', related to belonging, self-expression and the quality of life, are more present (Inglehart 1990: 66–103). In another interpretation, it is rather our efforts to face what is perceived as the acceleration of time that provokes an existential use of history (Huyssen 1995: 7–8). The use is often of a private nature, removed from 'large', publicly mediated history and not always leaving its imprint in empirical documentation. It should, however, be emphasised that an engagement with the intimate past, as expressed, for example, in genealogical trees, diaries and photo albums, often leads to an interest in relating to and participating in 'larger' pasts situated outside the narrow world of family (Rosenzweig and Thelen 1998: 115ff.).

Since all collective memories, even the most private, are social constructs, marked by the cognitive and emotional framework of the social group to which we relate, they can easily be retrieved, manipulated and mobilised on a collective level by those individuals, often educated and communicative, who are able to give utterance to the values and ideals of the social group in question. In that case, history can still be existentially useful but also fulfils other, more politicised and antagonistic societal functions. For the same reason, the production and survival of private memories with no political and social sanction is often problematic in non-democratic societies and states.

Historians seldom look into photo albums, which is to be regretted if the purpose is to analyse an existential use of history. Studies of private history making are rare. However, since the existential use of history thrives on proximity and intimacy, it seems reasonable to conclude that a European context of significance is not a very salient feature. A few qualifications of this general conclusion are nevertheless needed. One is that Europe is clearly well represented in photo albums. The question is whether a Swede's photos taken on holidays in Greece and Italy fulfil a European meaning by demonstrating, for example, an interest in the sights of the antique roots of Europe, or whether the photos, more often than not with children in the foreground, reflect the need to remember a much more intimate sphere of life. The same general problem concerns all those Europeans with sad, often traumatic individual or cultural memories of war, including expulsion, ethnic cleansing and genocide. These memories are indeed of an existential nature, but it remains to be analysed whether they actually make sense in a European context, or whether their human reach is different. In all likelihood, the European reach will increase if – as in the case of the Holocaust – private memories are accompanied by public remembrances all over Europe. To a certain extent, this also applies to the Armenian genocide, perpetrated by the Young Turks and their allies under cover of the First World War. This event has received a new contemporary meaning in light of the fact that the persistent genocide denial of the Turkish state has been made an argument against its EU membership.

In some instances in which strong images of external threats are involved, however, Europe can be supposed to have a more unequivocal existential meaning of security and normalcy in memories and remembrance. In the Baltic states, where Europe often is positively contrasted with Russia, and where the idea of the Baltic republics as eastern outposts of Europe is frequently put forward in private as well as in public discourse, this is certainly the case (Karlsson 2002a). The idea is supported by more elaborate ideological constructs, such as Samuel Huntington's or Yurii Lotman's ideas of the world's division into various cultural spheres. Both depict the borderline between Russia and the Baltic states as much more than political; it signifies a deep cultural cleavage between two different world views and cosmologies, with the Balts unambiguously living in a European space except during the 'unnatural' or 'parenthetical' Soviet era (Huntington 1996; Lotman 1992).

Moral Use of History

The moral use of history is based on indignation at the scant attention given to certain aspects of history in a society and on the endeavour to acknowledge, restore or rehabilitate the same history. Generally, the moral use has dominated where a culturally insensitive government at the head of an authoritarian state has for some reason, such as political-cultural liberalisation and newly gained openness, been suddenly exposed to criticism when it is revealed that essential details of the past have been concealed from the population. Thus, the point of departure for the moral use of history is often a specific event, such as the introduction of a political reform. An example of this kind was the policy of *glasnost* introduced by the last Soviet leader, Mikhail Gorbachev, in the years 1986–7. The reforms, intended to modernise the Soviet Union within the framework of a communist society, had a revolutionary outcome, to a great extent due to the historical revelations that gradually undermined the legitimacy of the Communist Party and the

Soviet state. However, the moral use of history may also be triggered by the publication of an article, a book or another kind of artefact with historical exposures or revelations that meet with a broad social response and obtain paradigmatic significance. The television series *Holocaust* is a case in point. Often, there is a generational aspect involved in the moral use of history; a young generation with no personal memories of the history in question rises in anger against the silence of those in power and the older generations. Since around 1990, the moral use of history has also been engineered by a general shift away from a politics based on ideology to a politics in which questions of morality and conscience are important ingredients. Nowadays, politicians apologise, do penance and make amends in a way hardly conceivable during the Cold War era.

In a strictly analytical sense, the moral use of history in Europe has had two principal contexts of significance. In the first context, events and processes which compose the dark side of the modernisation process have caused an indignant debate in many European countries. This has especially been the case in European countries in which the progressive master narrative of increasing prosperity and national harmony has gone largely unchallenged. Inspired by Zygmund Bauman's work *Modernity and the Holocaust* (1989), which describes the bureaucratic, inhuman culture of modern society, but also motivated by perspectives of history from below and various identity quests, journalists and historians have demonstrated how – in the name of a modernisation project – state authorities have taken repressive measures against subjects whose ethnicity, political-ideological conviction, sexuality or psychic status have 'deviated from normality'. Despite the fact that even before the 1990s a great deal had been written in several European countries about forced sterilisations of allegedly psychologically retarded persons, up until this point there had been little public interest and no moral indignation. The context of significance of this critical, moral modernisation perspective is normally national. The main reason it could be applied to a European context – apart from the Soviet one, with its revolutionary consequences for the entire European space – is that it has a European range, although there have been obvious differences in the character of state power and mechanisms of repression in Western and Eastern Europe during the post-war decades.

The second principal context of significance related to a moral use of history is the Second World War and totalitarian rule. Again, the perspectives of current interest are not those that for decades have imbued the 'Allied scheme of history', in which resistance to Hitler was a common feature. In particular, national reactions of compliancy with, support for or outright collaboration with Nazi rule in wartime Europe have been indignantly debated, but more recently a bystander position has also been critically assessed. It stands to reason that direct support for the Nazi war effort and an involvement in the Holocaust have given rise to the strongest outcries, but moral discussions have certainly not stopped there. For example, recent debates with moral implications have asked the following questions: Was a prohibitive or at least ungenerous immigration policy towards Jews in the late inter-war era and the first war years tantamount to being an accessory state during the Holocaust? Does Finland's war against the Soviet Union on the German side in the years 1941–4 imply Finnish guilt for the destruction of the European Jews? Did those neutral states deeply implicated in the Nazi war effort profit from genocide? Despite being aware of what happened in Auschwitz at an early stage of the war, why did the Allies fail to counteract the mass killings? In comparison, debates about collaboration with the Soviet communist regime have not had the same moral impact outside the former satellite states. Even inside the old communist system, the appearance of history in court has been limited. Timothy Garton Ash (2002: 268) has argued that this is because several of the Eastern and Central European power shifts were 'negotiated revolutions', in which representatives of the old system were left in high places.

Ideological Use of History

The extension of a prevailing moral use of history may be a trial or a history commission, organised by a harassed state power or a radically new government, to find out what 'really' happened in history.[10] A morally based settlement with a dictatorial or functional state, leading to historical disclosures that eventually undermine its legitimacy and end in a change of political power, can, however, also be followed by an ideological use of history. Such was the case in the former Soviet Union, where an effective moral use of history was transformed into an ideological, nationalist use. This came about when representatives of popular fronts and other political organisations started constructing historical narratives from newly 'discovered' facts, such as, in the case of the Baltic republics, the secret protocol of the Molotov-Ribbentrop Pact, the political Sovietisation and the large-scale deportations of Baltic peoples. In these constructs, there were apparent similarities with the Soviet ideological use of history, although the change of 'colours' was total: what was considered positive and benevolent in the old Soviet interpretation was interpreted as negative and malevolent in the new nationalist narration, and vice versa (Karlsson 1999: 207–61).

In a general sense, such an ideological use of history is related to attempts made, mainly by groups of intellectuals and politicians in control of public representations, to arrange historical elements into a relevant context of significance. This arrangement is defined not by its relationship to empirical evidence and scholarly standards in general, but by its correspondence to external tasks – or rather, by its capacity to convince, influence, rationalise, mobilise and authorise with the aid of historical perspectives. Consequently, the focus of the ideological use of history is not on separate historical elements, as is often the case with the moral use of history, but on the entirety of the historical construct – on its consistency, pretentiousness and pedagogical clarity.

The ideological use of history is intimately connected with the success of those systems of ideas that employ history in order to build up legitimacy and to rationalise mistakes and errors in the past by referring to historical necessities and laws. In practice, the objective of legitimation is often reached by means of absolute chronological boundaries and clear-cut periodisations, black-and-white descriptions, strong lines of continuity and perspectives of unproblematic progress. History has proven especially useful for nationalists, whose main interest is to ascertain a symbiotic relation between their own nation and a specific territory on which historical claims are staked. Consequently, this kind of history has proven extremely useful in ethno-territorial wars in the peripheries of Europe (Kaplan 1993; Karlsson 1998; Kolstö 2005).

It has been argued that ideology has generally withdrawn in favour of the politics of morality and conscience in Europe since the collapse of the Soviet Union and the short-lived advance of the 'end of history' thesis. Grand, ideological master narratives are not in vogue, if we do not choose to call the European, Holocaust-based narrative an ideological, Europeanist history. Nevertheless, the uses of history already mentioned often have ideological underpinnings. Behind the existential use of history there sometimes rests a conservative wish to 'stop the flow of time' in a Europe bent towards rapid, global technological change, and the debate on the moral use of history often mediates between a nationalist-conservative conception of 'eternal' guilt and a civic-liberal idea that guilt should be attached only to living individuals. Resolutions concerning the Soviet 'communist terror' regimes have not been looked upon with approval by groups of socialists and communists in Western Europe, who feel themselves implicated in the misdeeds engineered by Lenin and Stalin, and who do not hesitate to argue in terms of deviations, 'objective necessity' and the essentially good nature of communism and even of the Soviet era. Eric Hobsbawm (1998: 333), referring to the imagined memories of the former Soviet citizens, affirms this position: '[F]or most of its inhabitants who can remember, the old Soviet era certainly looks far better than what the former Soviet peoples are going through now, and will go on doing so for a good long while.' However, a more frequent strategy of rationalisation, trivialisation and denial of a terror regime is silence and omission. This leads to a special case of the ideological use of history: the *non-use* of history.

The non-use of history is not simply a question of remembering or forgetting a historical date, or of unconsciously omitting it from a historical context. Rather, the non-use of history is rooted in the deliberate and ideological adoption by some intellectual and political groups of an attitude according to which history, or some part of it, should be ignored. Here, too, reasons connected with the legitimacy of the non-using society or state or conscious efforts to rationalise historical misdeeds are involved.

Generally speaking, the non-use of history is a successful strategy in societies and states where it is strongly felt that legitimacy should be built not on tradition or cultural heritage but on the contention that the society in question constitutes a particularly praiseworthy contemporary phenomenon, or on expectations of a rewarding future. One conviction of this kind was the modernist or economistic notion that history, as an object of the past, is worthless for the cultivation of a qualitatively new society – a perspective characteristic of early post-war Sweden. Another example was the predominant view of the early Soviet state, especially among the influential members of the Proletkult organisation, that the new, socialist society had thrown off the yoke of the past. A socialist society, on its way to reaching the highest level of an ideal communist society, had nothing to learn from the past, it was argued, but should develop through everyday interaction between individuals in a society characterised by socialist virtues such as justice, solidarity and love (Karlsson 1993: 212–17). Although it can be difficult to support empirically, it is probably appropriate to talk about a non-use of history in a context where an aspect of history that is traditionally presented as important or even fundamental is passed over. An example with an obvious ideological motivation is when the Holocaust is left out of a historical construct by revisionists or deniers of the Nazi genocide.

Political Use of History

The political use of history may be characterised as a deliberate comparative, metaphorical or symbolic use in which the transfer effect between 'then' and 'now' is rendered simple and unproblematic, while the traditional scholarly idea that history is anchored in the structures of the relevant period is toned down. All this is in consequence of the main purpose, which amounts to summoning history as an aid in attacking what are felt to be severe and concrete political problems in a later era. The idea is that there are lessons from the past to be learned and taught by posterity. There is reason to believe that a political use of history is particularly hard to reconcile with a scholarly one. Thus, it is more or less a commonplace among historians discussing the use and abuse of history to launch a diatribe against 'historians, or would-be historians, [who] all too often become politicians and generals shaping and reshaping the historical record to score points, clinch arguments, and advance their own solutions and nostrums' (Dallin 1988: 181).

To be sure, the political use of history is a traditional and often-used instrument in foreign policy; for instance, references to Chamberlain's compliancy towards Hitler in Munich in 1938 were used to support the idea that a 'Munich syndrome' continued to guide foreign policy decisions long after the advent of the Second World War (Rystad 1982). There are, however, indications that history has been used politically on a broader scale and more frequently in the last full decade, in which politicians seem to have become aware of the mobilising power of the historical dimension. Two examples from the political debate in Sweden during the last few years are illustrative: a feminist-leftist party leader stated that Swedish men are like Talibans, while a former Swedish minister, frustrated by setbacks in his negotiations with a Norwegian colleague, accused Norway of being the last Soviet state.

As expressions of absolute evil, Hitler, Nazism and the Holocaust appear to be especially attractive objects of comparison for internal or external spokespersons seeking to draw attention to the allegedly exposed positions of 'their' historical or present-day parties. Swedish politicians not only have used Hitler and the Holocaust to combat the EMU and support the undersigning of the EU constitution, but also have placed NATO's bombings of Belgrade in 1996 on an equal footing with the Holocaust. A Swedish business executive, frustrated by a German truck company's ambitions to take over the company of which he is in charge, has recently remarked upon Germany's habit of starting blitz wars; Germans have not always been successful in these war efforts, he added confidently. Equating the Israeli treatment of the Palestinians to the Holocaust is a particularly troublesome political use of history in the early twenty-first century. The ambition behind such a comparison is hardly to do full justice to historical specificities; rather, the goal is to stir up a moral-political debate. Those who make a historical comparison that includes Nazism and the Holocaust can be confident that they will appear on the front page of the newspapers the next day.

Scholarly-Scientific Use of History

The scholarly-scientific use of history, finally, is based on professional, discipline-specific rules and standards. The criteria of historical relevance are more often than not determined from an internal, scholarly value judgement, which means that the history selected for research or teaching is chosen due to its qualifications to illuminate an analytical or a theoretical position considered fruitful to develop, or to give further empirical evidence to a historical phenomenon or setting that already has been subject to scholarly analysis. To be able to carry out an intellectual operation of this kind, professional training is normally considered necessary. One aspect of this ideal self-understanding is sometimes the opinion that it is a scholarly virtue to dissociate oneself from the history interests, needs and requests of the surrounding society. Another aspect is the belief in the possibility of dissociating the present from the past, as expressed in the anti-political argumentation of Herbert Butterfield in his classic text, *The Whig Interpretation of History* (1931: 10f.): 'The chief aim of the historian is the elucidation of the unlikenesses between past and present.... It is not for him to stress and magnify the similarities between one age and another.... Rather it is to work to destroy those very analogies which we imagined to exist.'

Thus, a claim of exclusivity is a traditional part of the scholarly-scientific idea of history: the professional use of history is legitimate and good, while all non-scholarly uses of history are to be branded as misuse or abuse of history, or at least judged less favourably. In general, at the university and scholarly level, the concept of historical consciousness is seldom used. This intensifies the impression that many professional historians are indifferent to questions about the role of history in society, or that they even actively dissociate themselves and their scholarly products from society. This background certainly goes some way in explaining why historians are less prominent in many of the discourses referred to above. Another explanation might be that European professional historians still are, to a great extent, occupied with carrying out national projects, which means that they write about the history of their own countries in which the European dimension normally is absent. On the whole, this is regrettable. A professional historical perspective is a vital component of cultural Europeanisation. A historian is capable of providing a critical and analytical framework for the debate on how to Europeanise history in the intersection between human reach and political range. The professional historian's contribution should be presented not as a final empirical result or as a superior use of history in what Judt (2002: 182) has described as 'the no-man's-land of mythical and preferable pasts', but rather as one of several necessary voices in the 'everyday plebiscite' on what might constitute European historical consciousness.

Notes

1. There are many examples of efforts to develop a 'European' history course for teaching purposes that would focus not only on the history of the European Union but on broad aspects of modern history (e.g. Slater 1994). The hitherto most conspicuous and controversial example of a European 'master narrative' is Duroselle (1990), which was subsidised by the Commission of the European Union.
2. See the EU presidency statement on Holocaust remembrance at http://europa-eu-un.org/articles/en/article_5224_en.htm.
3. For Winkler's address, see http://www.osce.org/documents/cio/2005/06/16402_en.pdf, 99–103. A report titled 'Education on the Holocaust and on Anti-Semitism: An Overview and Analysis of Educational Approaches' is available at http://www.osce.org/publications/odihr/2006/04/18712_586_en.pdf. It was produced following the OSCE Conference on Anti-Semitism and Other Forms of Intolerance at Cordoba on 8–9 June 2005.

4. A particularly interesting example is Sweden, where an extensive information project on the Holocaust, entitled 'Living History', was initiated by the government and received great international attention and appreciation. In 2003, it was transformed into a civil authority in Sweden, which is responsible for general problems concerning tolerance, democracy and human rights, but still mainly focuses on the Holocaust (see Karlsson 2002b).

5. For the Declaration of the Stockholm International Forum on the Holocaust, see http://www.manskligarattigheter.gov.se/stockholmforum/2000/page1192.html.

6. Since 2001, a research project at Lund University has been investigating how the Holocaust has been represented and used in various European states and societies since the Second World War, with particular attention to the opposition between the processes of Europeanisation and the nationalisation of the Holocaust (see Karlsson and Zander 2003, 2004, 2006).

7. For aspects of the non-European public remembrance, see Levy and Sznaider (2006), Linenthal (1995), Novick (1999), Tossavainen (2003), Wyman (1996) and Zander (2003).

8. The concept of European historical consciousness is so far used in a very general sense to address historiographical problems connected to Europe, to European standards and practices of history teaching, and to analyses of the role of history in orientating individuals towards a European identity (cf. Macdonald 2000).

9. The distinction between these two spaces is inspired by Jönsson et al. (2000: 183–4).

10. It is a matter of theoretical reflection and empirical analysis whether there is a distinctive legal use of history, or whether historical trials or commission works are examples of what in this text are denoted as a scholarly-scientific use of history, focusing on traditional scholarly values such as empirical verification or falsification, source criticism and intentionalist analysis (cf. genocide trials).

Chapter 3

HALECKI REVISITED

Europe's Conflicting Cultures of Remembrance

☙❦❧

Stefan Troebst

Images of textiles are among the most popular metaphors for the profession of the historian. In his *Fin-de-siècle Vienna*, Carl Schorske (1981: xxii) describes the 'diachronic thread' as 'the warp, the synchronic thread, the woof in the fabric of cultural history' and the historian as 'the weaver'. According to Carlo Levi's famous definition, history is the pattern woven *ex post* into the chaos. Sometimes the patterns of rather remote historical subjects resemble each other to such a degree that the question arises as to whether sheer coincidence is at work or whether there is a more substantial connection. This recalls the title of Oskar Halecki's still popular book of 1950, *The Limits and Divisions of European History*, and the lines dividing the landscape of memory of contemporary – that is, post-1989 – Europe.

There is a pragmatic reason for these remarks. In 2004, I was asked to give a paper on the conflicting cultures of remembrance in post-communist Eastern Europe (Troebst 2005a). The result of grouping the various societies of the region into analytical categories was reminiscent of Halecki's division of European history into four historical meso-regions. Almost automatically, a question arose: was this coincidence or the result of logic? In order to answer this question, I will present Halecki's model and provide an overview of conflicts and dividing lines in Europe's current cultures of remembrance. Before doing either of these things, however, I should point out the striking fact that the two phenomena 'memory' and 'space' (or, alternatively, 'place') seem to be tightly connected in a way that is still largely underexplored. Pierre Nora's term *lieu de mémoire* (place of memory) brings the two closely together, as does Aleida Assmann's term *Erinnerungsraum* (space of remembrance) (A. Assmann 1999a; cf. also A. Assmann 2006b: 217–34).

Notes for this chapter are located on page 63.

Halecki's Theory

A Habsburg Pole of Croat background born in Vienna, Oskar Ritter von Halecki became the leading historian of inter-war Poland (Bömelburg 2007; Kłoczowski 2006; Morawiec 2006). In 1923, his paper presented at the International Congress of Historical Sciences in Brussels triggered an intense and long-lasting international debate among historians from Czechoslovakia, Poland and Germany about whether the history of Eastern Europe is different from that of Western Europe (see Halecki 1924; cf. Wandycz 1992). In *The Limits and Divisions of European History*, Halecki (1950) expanded his frames of analysis both spatially and temporally, looking at the whole of Europe from late antiquity to the Cold War. Based on cultural and, in particular, religious criteria, he divided the historical macro-region of Europe into three historical meso-regions: Western Europe, Central Europe and Eastern Europe. In Halecki's view, however, Central Europe consisted of two rather different parts. These were West-Central Europe, that is, Germany (and probably Austria), and East-Central Europe, that is, the lands between Germany and Russia. Not surprisingly, Halecki's East-Central Europe historically resembled the Polish-Lithuanian Commonwealth of the early modern period, as well as the group of states which fell under Soviet hegemony in 1945 according to the decisions at Yalta (Troebst 2003).

Halecki's book became and remains influential among historians. This not so much due to its sophistication but rather to the fact that for decades after its publication historians dared not introduce an intermediary, transnational level between the various national histories of Europe and European history. Only in the second half of the 1970s did this change. The German historian Klaus Zernack took Halecki's divisions as a starting point. Firstly, Zernack combined Halecki's Eastern Europe and East-Central Europe into one historical region, again named Eastern Europe. Secondly, he subdivided this extended Eastern Europe into four parts: first, South-Eastern Europe, that is, the Balkan-Danube region; second, a narrower East-Central Europe, comprising Hungary, Poland and the Bohemian Lands; third, North-Eastern Europe, with the historical Baltic lands as its core; and, fourth, the Eastern Slavic lands, with the various Russian state formations from the Kievan Rus via Muscovy to Russia and the Soviet Union (Zernack 1977: 20–30, 88–92).

Furthermore, when the Hungarian historian Jenő Szűcs published a socio-economic model in 'The Three Historical Regions of Europe' (1983), it turned out to fit Halecki's model perfectly. The only difference was that Szűcs made no distinction between Western and West-Central Europe. Instead, he spoke, in a somewhat terminologically inconsistent manner, of Western, East-Central and Eastern Europe. Thus, Halecki's three main dividing lines – between Germany and Western Europe, between

East-Central Europe and Russia, and between Germany and East-Central Europe – were basically confirmed by later research (Troebst 2007a).

Memory Conflicts in Contemporary Europe

The following section moves from this historiographical context to a glance at memory conflicts in contemporary Europe. In my attempt of 2004 to describe the various post-communist cultures of remembrance from Tirana to Moscow and from Prague to Kiev, it was useful to form groups of the many cases, and I ultimately identified four categories (Troebst 2005a; cf. also Troebst 2005b, 2005c, 2005d). The first category was comprised of societies with a strong anti-communist consensus concerning recent history, for example, the Baltic states. The second category was of societies where such a consensus did not exist; instead, there was fierce public debate on how history should be remembered. One such example was Hungary, with its antagonistic camps of anti-communist liberals and post-communist socialists, while others included Poland and Ukraine. The third category was of societies where not only ambivalence but also apathy was dominant. In countries such as Bulgaria, Romania, Serbia and Albania, the urge to come to terms with the past was relatively weak. The fourth category was of societies where communism had not suffered a loss of legitimacy and where, accordingly, the communist past was hardly discussed. This was the case in Belarus, Moldova and, above all, the Russian Federation, where communism is perceived as part of the imperial legacy.

While aware of the fact that the natural frame of any given culture of remembrance – and thus also the adequate unit of analysis – is national, the transnational similarities within these four categories struck me as being historically connoted, if not charged. From 1918 on, the three Baltic states, Lithuania, Latvia and Estonia (category 1), had a similar political fate; Poland and Hungary (category 2) shared the same noble and imperial background; and the Balkan states (category 3) had a common Byzantine and Ottoman heritage. In other words, both Halecki's dividing line between Eastern and East-Central Europe and Zernack's distinctions between North-Eastern, East-Central and South-Eastern Europe were present.

The Commemoration of V-E Day

A fitting occasion to test this hypothesis on historically shaped meso-regional divisions of European cultures of remembrance was the sixtieth anniversary of the end of the Second World War in 2005. The year 1945, the European *lieu de mémoire*, functions as a litmus test for the hypothesis. Indeed, on 8 May 2005, the various transnational categories of national cultures of remembrance appeared on the radar screen of European politics. The Russian invitation to the former Soviet satellites and republics to participate in the Moscow celebrations of what was termed 'the victory over fascism' and 'the liberation of Europe' met fierce and unanimous disapproval – or disinterest. In the Baltic perspective, 1945 did not result in liberation; rather, it merely signified a change in occupation forces from one alien, dictatorial and genocidal regime to another. In Poland, the invitation triggered a heated debate; while some thought *raison d'état* required the presence of Poland as an ally in the wartime alliance against Hitler, others strongly resented the post-Soviet interpretation of history. In the eyes of the majority of the Poles, the crucial *lieu de mémoire* was not 8 or 9 May 1945, but the Yalta Conference, which had taken place three months earlier. Finally, in South-Eastern Europe the Russian invitation evoked little emotion. Hungary, Romania and Bulgaria had lost the Second World War on the side of Germany and had little interest in celebrating anything, while most of the post-Yugoslav states looked upon post-Soviet Russia through the prism of the Tito-Stalin split.

Interestingly enough, the Russian invitation was finally accepted by the post-communist Polish president, Aleksander Kwaśniewski. Yet in parallel and independently from Kwaśniewski, General Wojciech Jaruzelski (who had proclaimed martial law in communist Poland in 1981) travelled to Moscow on a personal invitation from the Russian president, Vladimir Putin. On 9 May 2005, Red Square therefore played host to two historical Polands: the democratic republic and the Soviet vassal. Similar emotions were caused by the decision of the Latvian president, Vaira Vike-Freiberga, to accept Putin's invitation, in sharp contrast to her Estonian and Lithuanian colleagues who declined. Vike-Freiberga explained her decision by stating that she was going to Moscow to confront the post-Soviet interpretation of twentieth-century history with the alternative Latvian and Baltic interpretation (Onken 2007; cf. also Veser 2005; Von Lucius 2005a, 2005b). Typically enough, in Lithuania and Estonia, but also in parts of the Latvian republic, Vike-Freiberga's move was attributed to the fact that she had spent most of her life not in Latvia but in Canada.

Indeed, that the transatlantic connection with Washington, DC, was an excellent one was proven by US President Bush's stopover in Riga on his way to Moscow on 7 May 2005. Bush's speech thoroughly subscribed to the Baltic interpretation of twentieth-century history: 'For much of Eastern and Central Europe, victory brought the iron rule of another empire. V-E Day marked the end of fascism, but it did not end oppression.... The captivity of millions in Central and Eastern Europe will be remembered as one of the greatest wrongs of history.'[1] In the eyes of Latvians, Balts and East-Central Europeans in general, Bush thus managed to combine the stress on democracy with the memory of the wartime alliance. Since there was no German gesture of this kind, no such signals issued from West-Central to East-Central Europeans. On the contrary, soon after the celebrations for 9 May, Putin invited German Chancellor Gerhard Schröder and French President Jacques Chirac to celebrate the 750th anniversary of the founding of the former Prussian city of Königsberg on the Baltic coast (now the Russian enclave of Kaliningrad). Neither Schröder nor Chirac protested about the fact that the heads of neighbouring Lithuania and Poland were deliberately not invited.

The terms of transnational cultures of remembrance of the sixtieth anniversary of the end of the Second World War, therefore, grouped the national societies of Europe into four camps: first, the Soviet-nostalgic host Russia; second, the anti-Soviet camp in East-Central Europe; third, a disoriented Germany, which after decades of being excluded from Allied celebrations viewed its participation in the Moscow ceremonies as something like an international rehabilitation; and, fourth, Western European societies clinging in this instance to a culture of remembrance less continental than Atlantic. Seen through the prism of 1945, today's dividing lines coincide perfectly with Halecki's division.

Holocaust versus Gulag

Yet Halecki's divisions do not fit all levels of European cultures of remembrance. For example, in March 2004, a few weeks before the European Union's major eastward enlargement, a controversy arose in Germany as well as in some other parts of Europe about the relationship between a Western Holocaust memory and an Eastern Gulag remembrance. In this case, the dividing line between East and West ran parallel to the Iron Curtain of the Cold War and not to the EU's new eastern border, which again retraces Halecki's line between East-Central and Eastern Europe. In a public speech entitled 'Old Europe, New Europe',[2] the former Latvian minister of foreign affairs and Latvian EU commissioner-to-be, Sandra Kalniete, stated in Leipzig in Eastern Germany that 'the two totalitarian regimes – Nazism and communism – were equally criminal'. Accordingly, Kalniete (2004) demanded that the victims of both regimes should be remembered equally. In Germany, this caused a vehement debate in which Kalniete initially was accused of 'illegitimate comparison', of 'downgrading the Holocaust' and ultimately, of 'anti-Semitism' (Troebst 2006a, 2006b).

In 2005, a certain rapprochement between Kalniete and her opponents took place, but in February 2006 the debate flared up again. In another speech in Germany, this time in Hamburg, Kalniete elaborated on her view that National Socialism and Stalinism were 'equally criminal'. Here, she came up with death figures for both regimes – 94.5 million for the Soviet version of totalitarianism versus 56 million for the German one (Kalniete 2006a; see also M. Bauer 2006; Jeismann 2006; Kalniete 2005, 2006b) – thus implying that communism was the greater evil. Despite the strong reaction from parts of the German public, Kalniete has managed to put the Gulag on the agenda of the politics of remembrance, at least in Germany. Thus, the exclusive focus on the Holocaust as a negative 'EU founding myth', propagated by the 2000 Stockholm International Forum on the Holocaust (Jeismann 2000; Kroh 2005; Levy and Sznaider 2001; Probst 2002), is giving way to multi-perspectivity. At the same time, Kalniete's views illustrate a political tendency in Germany to move from the self-perception of a nation of perpetrators to that of a nation of victims. The Allied bombing of Germany, the expulsion of Germans from East-Central Europe and other 'revisionist' topics figure prominently in media and politics. However, something like a 'Kalniete effect' can also be observed in other European societies and publics. This is the case in France, where in 1997 the publication of *Le Livre noir du communisme* was of crucial importance.[3] So it seems as if the divide running through EU's cultures of remembrance along the Gulag-Holocaust line is becoming even shallower.

The Central European Culture of Remembrance

My last example again affirms Halecki's perception of one Central Europe being subdivided into West-Central and East-Central Europe. For a number of years, Germany and to a lesser degree Austria, on the one side, and the Visegrád Group of states (Poland, the Czech Republic, Slovakia and Hungary), on the other, have periodically engaged in heated national as well as transnational debates on ethnic cleansing and processes of forced migration during the twentieth century in Central and Eastern Europe. In particular, these debates have focused on the mass expulsions of Germans from East-Central and South-Eastern Europe to Germany and of Poles from the former eastern part of inter-war Poland and what since 1944 became Soviet territories to the new People's Republic of Poland. Notwithstanding the militant overtones of larger segments of German and Polish society and media, in 2005 the political elites of the two countries came up with one of the rare instances of an institutionalised joint venture in the field of a common European culture of remembrance focusing on forced migration and ethnic cleansing. The European Network for Remembrance and Solidarity was initiated by Warsaw and Berlin and is supported by Budapest and Bratislava, probably also by Vienna, but not yet by Prague (Troebst 2007b; see also Quack 2007).[4] A similar initiative, again with Germany and Poland as the driving forces, was started in 2004 in the Parliamentary Assembly of the Council of Europe. The latter project is intended to establish a European remembrance centre for victims of forced population movements and ethnic cleansing (Troebst 2006b). Clearly, in terms of the politics of history and the culture of remembrance,

Germany and her neighbours to the east can indeed be grouped into a common Central Europe, such as that identified by Halecki.

The Connection between Halecki's Theory and Post-1989 European Cultures of Remembrance

At this point, I wish to return to the initial question of whether the resemblance between the patterns of Halecki's division of European history and those of post-1989 European cultures of remembrance is mere coincidence, or whether there is a logical, even causal connection between the two phenomena. Of course, one could argue that what Halecki has analysed from late antiquity to the mid-twentieth century – that is, the emergence of four historical meso-regions in Europe – remains valid for the twenty-first century. Such an argument, however, would be first of all something like a truism. It would furthermore imply that Halecki's *longue durée* interpretation is correct. The explanation for the resemblance of the two patterns may be much more simple and direct: Halecki's division of European history into four distinct meso-regions is very much a product of the Cold War. This conclusion can be reached because, upon closer inspection, his four-fold regional model turns out to be binary. Culturally, Halecki makes a distinction between two parts of Europe: the West, consisting of Western, West-Central and East-Central Europe, and the East, consisting of Eastern Europe, that is, Russia (aka the Soviet Union). Thus, Halecki sees East-Central Europe being under Soviet hegemony since Yalta as an ahistorical, deplorable, yet temporary political reality to be corrected in order to 'fit' history. This is the core thesis of Halecki's other book published in the 1950s, the somewhat dramatically entitled *Borderlands of Western Civilization: A History of East Central Europe* (1952). Despite his elaborate historical argumentation, Halecki's meso-regionalising model is essentially a child of its time. The missing links to today's actors in the politics of history in East-Central Europe and to the discussion in the 1980s on *Mitteleuropa* can be identified. Milan Kundera's view (1983) of East-Central Europe as an *occident kidnappé* – that is, a part of the West hijacked by Stalin – is in fact an unconscious reiteration of Halecki's time-bound world view of thirty years earlier.

Towards a Transatlantic Culture of Remembrance

This brings me to the final question: what should we make out of all this? To what degree are European national cultures of remembrance historically shaped, even historically programmed? And what is their average historical 'depth of focus'? Sixty years? A hundred years? Or, taking the

Serbian case, could this extend to five hundred years? Or even four thousand years – the point to which historical entrepreneurs in contemporary Greece trace back the latest flare-up of the Macedonian controversy in the early 1990s? Again, I believe that each national case is different. Yet national cases tend to form clusters and categories that can be identified, and Halecki has helped us to understand this. Halecki even offers us a hint as to whether the conflicting national cultures of remembrance of Europe will one day merge into a European, transcontinental or even global culture of remembrance. The last sentence of *Borderlands of Western Civilization* envisages 'a new era … for all those who today suffer in East-Central Europe, or at least for their descendants, because for the first time in history they would belong to the same great community, not only with Western Europe, but also with America' (Halecki 1952: 516–17). Thus, Halecki turns around Pierre Nora's dictum that history unites, while memory divides. In his North American Cold War exile, the East-Central European historian came to the opposite conclusion: that history divides, while it is memory that unites. Seen from this point of view, the emergence of a transatlantic culture of remembrance – out of the many national memories – indeed seems possible.

Notes

1. 'President Discusses Freedom and Democracy in Latvia', Riga, Latvia, 7 May 2005, http://georgewbush-whitehouse.archives.gov/news/releases/2005/05/20050507-8.html.
2. The title of Kalniete's speech is a somewhat provocative reference to the 2003 comments of US Secretary of Defense Donald Rumsfeld, in which he referred to countries that did not support the US invasion of Iraq as 'old Europe'.
3. The volume *Le Livre noir du communisme*, originally published in France in 1997, was edited by Stéphane Courtois. The English title, *The Black Book of Communism*, was published by Harvard Press in 1999.
4. The European Network for Remembrance and Solidarity, located in Warsaw, is a foundation under Polish law.

Chapter 4

ICONIC REMEMBERING AND RELIGIOUS ICONS
Fundamentalist Strategies in European Memory Politics?

෴

Wolfgang Kaschuba

This chapter offers some preliminary thoughts on the issue of European remembrance. These thoughts are especially concerned with two developments: firstly, national and European forms of collective remembrance after 1989, which could be described as having conventional formats; and, secondly, newer tendencies of globalisation and fundamentalisation in memory politics. In the past few years, these latter tendencies have also come from within Europe, where they have become visible in new cultural formats, often religious ones. My impression and my hypothesis is as follows: we are dealing with a new and fundamental 'iconic turn' in visual politics, or the politics of imagery. In terms of mnemotechnics, such a turn creates new situations. This relates in part to the advance of Islamist, as well as Christian, visual politics in Europe.

The Entangled National and European
Memory Construction

Against the background of European history, we have so far researched collective memory and collective politics of remembrance primarily in a national perspective. This is quite reasonable, since in Europe 'national remembrance' has embodied the prototype of all those enterprises of identity politics, which, from the late eighteenth century up until the present, have sketched collective images of selfhood (cf. Nora 1984–92). These images of national and ethnic communities had to seem historically plausible and culturally attractive, while at the same time they were supposed to perform a dual function: fostering an inward politics of integration and promoting an outward politics of difference.

Documentation for this chapter is located in the reference section.

The reason for this is that national identity politics was an attempt at an inner collectivisation, which essentially depended on its 'relation', on the existence of external concepts of the enemy and scenarios of threat. Furthermore, national identity politics necessitated a clear-cut opposition of self and other. Normally, this differentiation was produced along cultural lines, which were then essentialised: lineage, language, religion, mentality. National and ethnic collectivisation in a Weberian sense was thus accomplished primarily via culturalist strategies and formats, which could always be modified and newly adjusted. Here the ability to draw boundaries, both within society against the culturally foreign and at the national borders against foreign societies and power, was of vital importance. As Georg Simmel (1983) has shown, for Europe in particular this boundary paradigm – and with it the moral legitimation and cultural conceptualisation of 'difference' – has been a momentous idea. Even now we have difficulty thinking about specific concepts of the social and of social order in a border-less way. Border mentalities seem to disappear much more slowly than border guards.

These national memories of the late nineteenth and early twentieth centuries have always been layered with the columns and arches of a European culture of remembrance. The latter invariably referred to traditions of high culture: from philosophy to literature, from fine art to music – and from antiquity to the present. European elites proved themselves consistently committed to this project of 'Christian-Occidental civilisation', since it helped them to shape both the social orders and the historical imagery of Europe. Time and again, these elites engineered Europe's identity through their political, scientific and artistic practices. They did so by changing narratives and imagery in identity constructions, by means of which they could legitimate anew their own relevance and secure their own positions of power. Yet despite their commitment to the Christian-Occidental project, the elites remained primarily national actors. They thus provided for the existence of steady national orders, as well as firm ethnic and religious social structures. In this way, the nation became a community of lineage as well as one of maintenance, a community of defence as well as one of values.

Because of this, European identities could never compete with national ones in the sense of material or idealistic attractiveness. Without economic power, without being able to offer social welfare and without the potential for militaristic-imperial capacity, Europe remained a weak vision for the social majorities, in a political as well as an emotional sense. Along with this visionary weakness, there was a commemorative weakness: far into the post-war period, it was the national power of remembrance that dominated and structured the respective horizons of European landscapes of remembrance.

At this point, the post-war period appears to have lost its validity as a mnemotechnical arrangement. In addition, the political balance of power seems to have slowly shifted from the national level to the European level over the past few years. The Europeanisation of Europe by the European Union plays a central role in this context. It is especially the concentration of material resources and political competences with authorities in Brussels that has effectively changed the strategic framework (Shore 2000). We now appear to be able to think in new ways about national identity politics in terms of European structural policy.

For that purpose, some fundamental symbolic reinterpretations are required, especially in the realm of social perception and historical remembrance. In this sense, it is the European topoi of remembrance – dates, names, places, regions, works of art and values, usually assigned with specific cultural associations and meanings – that now gain importance. European memory is thus being organised and constructed in a 'culturalistic' way (A. Assmann 1999a). A more detailed analysis of European cultural awards, exhibitions and contests, as well as recent events in the visual and performing arts, would easily support this proposition.

This cultural Europeanisation profits from the fact that Europe can profile itself in the context of globalisation as a clearer and more accessible horizon. Europe presents itself as offering the charm of the close by, of the local, while at the same time providing security against the 'big world'. European culture has thus become 'home' (*Heimat*). Despite this Europeanisation, there is still an insistent stance on the national idea – on 'Germanness', 'Britishness' or 'Italianess' – and this approach is not without finesse. National actors denounce Europeanisation as a form of globalisation. In their narratives, the notion of the national then appears as that of the local, as the culturally 'real' and authentic, which itself requires protection and appreciation. Such protection is effectively against Europe by Europe, and is paid for by Brussels.

Western European member states have exercised this strategy over the past few decades, while Eastern European accession countries have followed their example in recent years as a result of intense 'mnemopolitical labour'. In the latter states, pre-socialist traditions and symbols, including history narratives, kings' crowns, rulers' bones and hymns, are again being pushed to the fore and rearranged as national myths. However, these life worlds (*Lebenswelten*) are being saturated with new national and ethnic symbolism. In Hungary, for example, land property is being described as a sanctuary, while in Poland this tendency is encountered in discussions on energy. In the Czech Republic and in Slovakia, the strategy is apparent in respective mutual dissociation in all public realms, from politics to sports.

These messages, put forward as necessary re-nationalisations, prove to be extremely powerful. It is through their motives and imagery that social bonds are being strengthened and political loyalties are being activated anew (see Binder et al. 2001). A crucial contribution to this development is a new aestheticisation of the national. From film to video clip, from pop music to cultural events, from cell phone to Internet communication, there is a constant evolution of new media and performative patterns of the construction of 'collective memory' that are designed to appeal in particular to younger people. They thereby assume a national fervour, whose purpose is twofold: to create a new form of patriotism, on the one hand, and to cease to appear as 'second-class Europeans', on the other. The goal is thus to become the 'new Europe'.

In Western Europe, however, a slightly different development has occurred. There has appeared a politics of remembrance with stronger reflexive tendencies that questions precisely this national devotion of *lieux de mémoire* and of cultures of remembrance. On 24 November 2006, the *Frankfurter Allgemeine Zeitung* commented, without irony, upon British politics of remembrance as follows:

> Gestures of penitence with regards to British mischief have cumulated. Tony Blair has apologised for the failure of the British during the Irish famine; his government is currently debating about a 'declaration of regret' on the occasion of the second-hundredth anniversary of the abolition of slavery next spring. The Queen has apologised to the Maori for the deprivation of land in the nineteenth century, as well as to the Indians for the 1919 Amritsar massacre. Now she has, together with Prince Philip, attended the unveiling of a memorial for Chief Mahomet of the Mohegan tribe, who protested against British deprivation of land in London in 1735, but who never actually appealed to King George II because he soon died from pox.

Yet at the same time, the German debates on remembrance demonstrate a heightened potential for reflexivity. Examples include the controversy over the design of the various Holocaust memorials in Berlin and the painful corrections to the German self-perception evoked by the much-attended exhibition on the German Wehrmacht and its role during the Second World War. The contemporary Europeanisation of the *lieux de mémoire* concept also clearly points to this direction.

New Trends: Global Politics of Remembrance with European Standards

These few remarks were intended to help outline the horizon of the hitherto existing politics of remembrance. On this basis, I would now like to advance a few thoughts about new developments in cultures of remembrance and memory politics. It seems that new formats, which diverge from the tradition of national or European remembrance and try to utilise new strategic options, are increasingly playing a role. Their goal appears to be a globalisation of the politics of remembrance in order to gain new powers of definition and to achieve new forms of political mobilisation.

Often primarily motivated by civilising and religious impulses, these new configurations promote a memory politics with transnational images in supranational formats. Clearly, they are attempts to instal new regimes of remembrance and imagery, which in their strategic intent aim at a new 'global politics of remembrance' in the aftermath of grand narratives and the unsuccessful 'end of history'.

Although these are preliminary thoughts, I want to try to outline two levels of such a global politics of remembrance that seem to differ mainly with respect to the role that 'the European' plays in each of them. The first level includes the terms 'world cultural heritage' and 'genocide' and seems to relate to a *European* regime in the globalisation of the politics of remembrance. The second level is a discussion of the Crusades and the Turkish wars. Here I want to follow up the idea of a new religious imagery, as this becomes visible in the periphery of Islamism, which seems to stand for a *global* regime of the politics of remembrance.

I will begin with the Europeanisation of a global politics of remembrance. This tendency is illustrated by UNESCO's World Heritage programme, which began in 1972. A highly successful and effective instrument of cultural politics, this programme was and remains intended to implement global standards in memorial politics and the politics of remembrance. Disputes associated with the programme, ranging from Afghanistan (the destruction of two ancient statues by the Taliban) to Dresden (the idea of a new bridge crossing the river Elbe and the romantic site of Dresden), have caused even more sensation than the large number of successful projects, thereby increasing the programme's significance.

Nevertheless, it is not difficult to reconstruct how many of the programme's underlying concepts are geared to European cultural formats. From the materiality of the 'Cultural Heritage concept (stone and brick)' (Strasser 2005: 66) and its artificial orientation and aesthetic code to its conceptions of masterpieces of global culture, it is European standards that predominate. Newer ideas, such as that of a textual inventory, a so-called Memory of the World Register, or of a media archive, Digital Heritage, also reveal this conceptual origin. Only a few marginal programmes, which put a stronger focus on oral traditions or cultural protection, indicate a non-European imprint.

At the same time, most formats clearly revert to repertoires of the European heritage of the eighteenth and nineteenth centuries. Such is the case with the idea of the monument as a symbol of national remembrance, or the museum as a site for the construction of identity. This applies as well to the idea of the individual art genius, or of the landscape as an open-air archive of European 'nature-culture' aesthetics. Such historical models are of course being updated correspondingly. However, within the World

Heritage programme they are, above all, generalised and universalised. Once again, therefore, it is monument and memory, artwork and landscape – themselves the basic themes of a European iconography – which are supposed to attribute meaning to this securing and conserving of global culture.

Presenting European culture and aesthetics as the universal mode of thinking and practice results in a European power of definition over global culture politics. Despite the cosmopolitan intention, this means that non-European ideas of culture are conversely being shut out or decontextualised. Thus, this version of a global politics of remembrance can be seen as a form of European cultural fundamentalism.

The second example that illustrates this European dominance is the discourse and politics of remembrance that surround the Turkish genocide against the Armenian minority in 1914–15. The Armenian approach to the politics of remembrance is demonstrated regularly each year on 24 April at the dedication ceremonies of the genocide memorial in Yerewan, which was erected in 1967 during the Soviet era and is now a veritable pilgrimage site. The related campaign around the ceremony and the memorial has been the subject of a research project which investigates the way in which Armenia took advantage of the specific moment. This was done in two steps. For several years Armenia has been intensively involved in European cultural programmes and has therefore aligned its politics of remembrance with European cultural politics. At the same time, it has come to identify the opportunities resulting from Turkey's present efforts for EU accession negotiations and the fact that a candid discussion about historical remembrance and guilt is regarded as a crucial criterion for accession capability.

By means of preparative books and films, academic conferences and the monumental inauguration of a memorial, attended by almost a million people, Armenia has pursued a European concept of remembrance politics (Darieva and Kaschuba 2008) – one that is based on the premise of public discourse, a clear-cut correlation of victim and perpetrator, an ethos of acknowledgement of guilt, and, finally, the memorial as a territorial principle of remembrance. The Armenian memorial is thus intended to position itself as a constant *lieu de mémoire* in the map of global sites of memorials. It is a map, formed in Europe, that initially denoted only the sites of the Holocaust.

Due to its dislike of this Europeanisation of memory politics, Turkey's reaction towards this effort has been negative. In the run-up to the accession negotiations, Turkey already regards itself as being subjected to various other European impositions, and these additional conditions would be hard to present domestically. Furthermore, to accept Armenia's version of the politics of remembrance would threaten to tip Turkey's own, nationalistically conceived version out of balance. Nor is it insignificant that besides remembrance, such a balance requires forgetting. The stakes are apparently too high for Turkey to accept the ethnic genocide against the Armenians as an accusation of guilt. Such a confession would signal the beginning of a more general ethnic opening of the national question, and this would result in official fragmentation of what has been constructed as the nation's collective memory.

Although this is only a rough outline of the situation, the Armenian strategy is understandable, and there may be little sympathy for the Turkish position. However, the description of the scenarios reveals some of the difficulties which follow the intervention of 'external' regimes of interpretation in processes of remembrance that remain open and not yet fully negotiated. The politics of remembrance is being 'culturalised' still further.

'War of Civilisations': The Iconic-Suggestive Displacing the Textual-Argumentative

The second level of the global politics of remembrance, which in my view is even more important, is the dramatic rise of 'civilisational-religious' imagery in the global discourse on remembrance. What counts for 'world heritage' apparently counts for 'the religious' in an exceptional way. Grand narratives are consciously being put into position, much like the ideological concept of the 'clash of civilisations'. Currently, this is happening most noticeably in the discord between Christian-Occidental and Islamist-Oriental adherents, which seems to be heading towards open confrontation.

This present development is related to a new Christian agenda in Europe and the US and to contemporary reversions into allegedly helpful value systems of the Christian-Occidental tradition. Another factor is that Christianity is being strengthened by its popular acceptance in post-socialist societies, for example, in Poland and Hungary, and by the growing influence of the Christian Right in the US and its respective movements in Asian and African societies. Above all, however, this 'religious turn' is being driven by the new and aggressive appearance of Islamist ideology and movements, in Europe as well as the Middle East.

Both Islamic and Christian cultural and religious fundamentalists aim at regenerating old figures of remembrance (Meyer 2005): the Muslim avenger against countries of the Crusader coalition, on one side, and the Christian defender of Vienna in the seventeenth and eighteenth centuries against the Turks and Islam, on the other. Fundamentalist positions being staked out in both the Muslim and Christian camps consciously construct an identity based on differences. By sharply defining these differences, each side endeavours to reinforce its sense of cultural authenticity and legitimacy. In both cases there is a reciprocal reference: the overreaching rejection and the overreaching idealisation of the European. Islamists in Europe also experience the further aggravating aspect of their faith being condemned and depreciated as a 'European' and hence 'infected' version of Islam.

Thus, both fronts are formed *by means of* a visual politics as well as *in* a visual politics. Symbols and icons are being substituted for texts and arguments in a radical way: the 'iconic-suggestive' is displacing the 'textual-argumentative' – at least, what remains of the latter. With the rising speed of scheme and counter-scheme, a dangerous spiral effect develops. Actors are forced to take sides and to show commitment, leading to a pure iconisation and aestheticisation of collective memory and thus to a remembrance that is regulated solely by the repertoire of imagery and by its iconography. The remembrance then ceases to be accessible to discursive arguments and reflexive considerations.

Last but not least, the situation is being dramatically aggravated because this 'mnemopolitical war of religion' is also unfolding in the field of European (as well as global) politics of migration. Since September 11, migration has been seen as the dominant event in Europe and, at the same time, as a central threat. This attitude is not restricted to security policy; rather, a decided cultural reassessment of migration is taking place. In politics and the media, migration is being targeted more fiercely than ever before as the cause of a growing cultural foreignness and a new disruption of European societies and cities. In particular, Arab, African and Turkish immigration is believed to threaten a cultural overloading of European national societies, since it is often accompanied by a 'foreign' religion.

These arguments seem to be effective, despite the fact that immigration has actually decreased considerably in most European countries in recent years. In addition, the majority of people who are marked as migrants were born in Europe and have European citizenship. Although they are European by geographical origin, they are consciously being attributed a non-European identity of a 'foreign' ethnic origin and of 'foreign' cultural belonging. In civil society as well as mnemopolitically, this is a non-identity. It excludes and relegates migrants to a geographical-cultural no man's land – to migration itself as a social space of transit.

Thus, within European societies a new external border is being constructed, politically as well as symbolically. It is an imaginary borderline around enclaves of 'foreign' culture, around apparently parallel societies of migrants. This boundary is being fixed in a mnemopolitical way, first, by means of the open or tacit reference to 'own' history, remembrance and ethnicity, and, second, through an insurmountable opposition to the other.

This ethnic coding of belongingness, which aims at origin and lineage, reveals a clearly racist concept that appears to be more and more dominant in the present discourse on migration. It is, in fact, a form of racism that has already reached the centre of numerous societies, including Germany, Britain, Scandinavia and Russia. Everywhere migration is the current focus for those memories and feelings of insecurity that have resulted from the economic crises and social disruption of past years. And the European media eagerly contribute to the production of the imagery of 'foreign' migrants.

Since the New York City terror attacks, and perhaps even earlier, a useful and narrowly constructed chain of association has been propagated that puts migration and terrorism into a causal relationship, with old images of the treacherous Oriental being mobilised. Such thinking refuses to accept that the self-proclaimed 'holy warriors' are usually not immigrants affiliated with al-Qaeda but rather 'home-grown terrorists'. In particular, this misinterpretation ignores the fact that the latter's motives originate to a large extent from domestic social conflicts in Europe, and that their strategic concept and media structure have been developed in the shadow of mosques in London or Hamburg. The suras of the Qur'an and the slogans of the jihad thereby serve only as styles of reasoning – as symbolic practice and ideological justification.

In the past years, therefore, several developments have taken place, including strategies of a systematic 'collectivisation' via religion, which, in turn, has had dramatic effects. To young men who have been excluded as 'foreign migrants', Islamist groups offer an identity as a respected member of a community that defines its own values. This allows a means of distancing from the hostile social majority. In these instances, the Islamist concept of a religious memory provides striking images as examples and role models. References to the Muslim trauma of the Christian Crusades and to the iconic figure of the Muslim 'holy warrior' are numerous. To some young men, the only truly achievable models appear to be the committed Muslim or the historical avenger. Such models also function as a kind of symbolic 'self-Orientalisation' against 'the European'. Other models from the realm of civil society – or even that of consumer society – often seem to be impossible for them to strive for on their own, due to lack of education.

This increased Islamist activity leads to a concurrent Christian-Occidental effort to build up its own cultural defences, thus adding to the argument of the incompatibility of cultural and religious precepts and heightening the sense of the imminent loss of one's own tradition, culture and authenticity. One outcome is the formation of angry citizens' action committees in almost all European cities in which new representative mosques are being built. Such groups regard the future minarets as army flags of a foreign cultural infiltration, and thus they seek to defend 'the Occident' in their neighbourhood. That which remains entirely unnoticed in this controversy is the fact that the construction of such mosques actually brings Muslim communities closer to Christian communities and, in turn, serves to make their religious spaces and rituals more transparent.

What is clear is the speed with which the Christian Crusades to Jerusalem and the defence of Vienna in the so-called Turkish wars have become subjects of popular interest. A sudden multiplicity of publications contrast 'holy warriors' and Crusaders, the Turkish Janissaries and the defenders of Vienna. Both sides deploy opposing yet interchangeable attributes: on one side, hero and believer; on the other side, child murderer and rapist. These figures are iconographically present and passed on, with the image of the Turkish knifer as a current version of the sabering Janissary. But these images have been only weakly outlined in collective memory, especially in the case of their present carriers. The process of 'remembering' has therefore required a great deal of pulling out of context and, indeed, making anew.

It is in this way that a 'community of remembrance' emerges. This invention of remembrance becomes a carrier of knowledge and an alleged absolute truth, which thereby becomes a social movement. Religious iconography seems to be very well suited for a medium of group identity because, in relation to national and social remembrance, 'religiously' impregnated memories are much less subject to reflection. Integrated in religious practices and rituals, their imagery is hard to question and to discuss. More significantly, they allow for emotionalisation and mobilisation – even, to a degree, in the case of the secularised Christian churches in Germany. This applies all the more when the localistic and communitarian culture is tied up in the politics of difference between true believers who consider themselves answerable only to their own faith – a circumstance that can be found in the backyard mosques of Berlin as well as the Christian parishes at the base of the Rocky Mountains (Kaschuba 2007).

The media setting of this religious politics of remembrance stands in explicit contrast to its messages of archaic origin. 'Religious' video clips and films, 'info-tainment' and Internet databases, chat rooms and games are 'normal'. For example, Islamist 'history videos' in which 'holy warriors' are fighting Crusaders – and to which fantasy motifs and pop music have been added – have long been in circulation. In terms of their rhetorical content, these forms of media resemble the national memorial inaugurations of the German Empire. However, in their impact and imagery, they function as postmodern communication and aesthetics. This has a great deal to say about the media agents as well as their audience. Culturally speaking, many 'believers' are equally late-modern 'users' and 'players'; some Muslims ask IslamOnline, not the mullah, for advice about how to pray and how to kiss. Viewing Islam as a 'stone-age religion' often precludes this important realisation.

Transformed into 'toys' long ago, the icons of remembrance also have become effective counters in this clash of cultures. Spread via the Internet and through oral communication, they are easily accessible and particularly attractive to children and teenagers. As a result, even those forms of Muslim and Christian religious fundamentalism that consider themselves 'pure' doctrine have in reality been 'hybrid' cultures for a long time. A possible outcome of this hybrid mixture of iconic images, of cultural fundamentalism, of religious memory politics and of the World Wide Web has been demonstrated by the 2005 case of the *Jyllands-Posten* Mohammed caricatures. In this instance, the Danish cultural fundamentalists evidently underestimated the Islamist religious fundamentalists.

Global Memory Management without a Centre

In summary, these phenomena allow us to observe a new 'memory management', which is operated globally by new regimes and with new media and formats. This management has existed for some time, and it is no longer controlled exclusively by the regulative triangle of Western Europe, Israel and the US. Rather, Arab, African and Asian agents also are involved at a key level; examples of this are media such as Al-Jazeera, political religious activist groups and NGOs, and even political parties and national governments. The screenplays of historical memories are being rewritten more and more quickly in order to change and sharpen roles, often in an aggressive way. Hence, we see anti-Semitism among French teenagers with Arab migratory backgrounds, a deepening fundamentalism of European and American Christians, the hatred expressed by European Islamists towards Europe, nationalistic tendencies of Eastern European post-socialist countries and racism in Western European middle-class milieux.

In the meantime, the message of memory politics is now only partly directed towards national societies or local minorities. Increasingly, it aims at groups that are held together by common beliefs and world views but that are scattered globally. Regardless of whether they refer to linguistic, ethnic or religious mutuality, it is iconic images and aesthetic formats that control these feelings of belonging. It is for this reason that memory management has ceased to occupy an actual centre, as in the classic model of social organisations or elites that dominate and control. Organised more like a network or campaign, it intensively integrates the possibilities of global communication such as the Internet, visual media and info-tainment. Memory is simultaneously being carried over into new culturalistic frameworks that, in turn, enable new political and ideological implementations.

Five points seem to be crucial. Firstly, memory is being decontextualised. Detached from previous interpretative contexts of remembrance in order to achieve new effects, it is simultaneously and directly being combined with patterns of practice and is thus orientated towards instantaneous usage. Secondly, memory is being despatialised. Removed from its stable place in the memory landscape of the *lieux de mémoire*, it is being carried over to new spaces of remembrance (often supplied by the media). Thirdly, remembering is being moralised in a new form. As in the case of religion, memory is being charged with moral-ethical meanings that emotionalise and mobilise. This constitutes a new mytho-motoric quality by means of which the circle of the 'community of remembrance' is enlarged and strengthened. Fourthly, and as a result of this, a globalisation of figures of remembrance is taking place. While previously this had occurred only in the case of the Holocaust, new representatives of a global memory politics are emerging. Lastly, these figures are thereby successfully and increasingly being 'fundamentalised'. 'Remembrance' is being forged as 'icon'. In the process of what I refer to as 'iconic remembering', memory is being detextualised and isolated, symbolically dramatised as images, and made absolute in its validity.

– Translated by Friedrich von Bose

Section 2

Towards a Fluid Conceptualisation
of Memory Constructs

Chapter 5

CULTURE, POLITICS, PALIMPSEST
Theses on Memory and Society

⚜

Heidemarie Uhl

In 1971, the Reichstag in Berlin was the site of an exhibition entitled 'Fragen an die deutsche Geschichte' (Questions about German History). The project was representative of a critical-historical self-enquiry, while the reconstruction of the building at that time, in purposely omitting the original cupola that had been destroyed in 1945, served as a memorial for the destruction of parliamentary democracy by National Socialism. The location of the building, immediately next to the Berlin Wall with a view of the Brandenburg Gate in the 'capital of the GDR', also recalled the continuing influence of the past on the Federal Republic's present withdrawal from any kind of 'normalisation'.

Today, the German Parliament is hosting a different exhibition, 'Wege, Irrwege, Umwege – die Entwicklung der parlamentarischen Demokratie in Deutschland' (Paths, Meanders, Detours – the Path to Parliamentary Democracy in Germany)', in the German Cathedral, formerly located in the Eastern section of the city. The Wall has disappeared, and the Reichstag building – now with its reconstructed cupola – is the seat of the German Bundestag and represents a new landmark of the German capital. The Brandenburg Gate, on the other hand, has turned into a normal, almost banal component of the everyday urban landscape, arousing only the faintest déjà vu about the threat of the Cold War. Instead, it is the Memorial to the Murdered Jews of Europe, commissioned in May 2005 after years of ongoing debate, which confronts the political centre of reunited Germany with a memento of those events that are antithetical not only to the fundamental values of the Federal Republic of Germany but also to the universal global community orientated towards humanity and human rights (Levy and Sznaider 2001).

Notes for this chapter are located on page 86.

The transformation of Berlin's memorial landscape serves as the point of departure for some considerations on memory and society. This correlation arises from two related aspects. The first is the genesis and rise of memory as the 'leading term' of the cultural turn in the humanities (A. Assmann 2002), which is closely related to processes of social transformation at the close of the twentieth century. The second consists of the differing conceptions of society inscribed in the theoretical bases of the paradigm of memory. These conceptions and the thesis discussed in this chapter constitute specifically designated forms of practice within the arena of memory which can be described with the terms 'culture' and 'politics'. However, memory does not arise from intentional generative acts themselves respectively derived from intentional acts of alteration. Rather, it is influenced by the logic and processes of a quasi-social *mémoire involontaire*, for which I propose the term 'palimpsest' (A. Assmann 1991: 19f.).

Memory – Social Frame Requirements for the Rise of a Term

It is no coincidence that scientific and social interest in forms of social memory gained visible contours in the mid-1980s, a period of increased discussion about the end of the modern age and the exhaustion of its 'utopian energies' (Habermas 1985). This period was also characterised by fading certainty about the future and the belief in progress, as notions of 'advancement' and 'development' began to decline. Not least, the 'grand narrative' (Lyotard 1986) was delegitimised by the failure of the real socialist experiment inscribed with the vague remains of a utopian potential. While debates concerning the replacement of the modern age with its *posthistoire* might seem less relevant to contemporary historical debate, they do indicate the erosion of the epistemological fundaments of modern societies and, in particular, the notion of a teleological process of modernisation.

Together with the loss of teleological visions of the future, the horizon of orientation for the system of social norms and values increasingly shifted towards the past. Jan Assmann (1988: 16) substantiates this moral-ethical dimension to the social relevance of memory as follows: 'A society becomes visible in its cultural tradition: to itself and to others. The past it allows to become visible within and which is allowed to emerge in the value perspective of its identificatory appropriation says something about what it represents and about where it wants to go.' Assmann's concept of a theory of cultural memory is regarded as the founding text of a cultural-scientific memory paradigm. However, by interpreting memory as a normative instance of a collective, it also locates the crucial *surplus* of this approach to Maurice Halbwachs's theory of collective memory, explicitly referred to by Assmann. It is not only Assmann's adoption of Halbwachs's constructivist credo that can be interpreted as an anticipation of cultural-scientific positions. What remains of the past is solely 'what society in each epoch is able to reconstruct with its present frame of reference' (Halbwachs 1985: 390). Assmann ([1992] 2007) defines this closing sentence of Halbwachs's script as the basis of his own memory theory, which naturally assumes that the past exists 'only as a social construction'.

However, Assmann's concept of cultural memory goes beyond the intertwinement of the terms 'memory' and 'identity' to arrive at a definition of memory as a symbolic form of expression of the self-conception of society. In this way, the socio-political potential of a collective memory is uncovered. This also explains the controversy over the representations of cultural memory, which are not at all neutral. Rather, they are charged with identity politics and accordingly contested, as Assmann (1988: 13) asserts: 'The objects of cultural memory are characterised by a kind of identificatory endowment in a positive sense ("this is us") or in a negative sense ("this is our opposite").' The link with the concept of identity alone has provided the foundation for the longevity of the memory term.[1]

This connection can be taken as an indication of additional basic social and epistemological conditions that are meaningful for the genealogy and resonance of cultural-scientific memory theory. Since the middle of the 1980s, these processes have undergone what Tony Judt (1993) has described as 'renegotiations' of the view on history with regard to the place of National Socialism within national historical narratives.

In a speech delivered on 8 May 1985, forty years after the end of the war, Richard von Weizsäcker suggested that the day of German capitulation should be commemorated as a 'day of liberation ... from the inhuman system of National Socialist tyranny'.[2] Among other factors, the explosiveness of this statement resides in the fact that the question of whether 1945 is to be assessed as liberation or occupation continues to generate politically controversial disputes up to the present day. In 1986, in the Federal Republic of Germany and in Austria, respectively, the historians' dispute and the conflict regarding Kurt Waldheim's wartime past provoked social principle debates about the 'undealt with' past that are now generally recognised as the signature of European political culture at the end of the twentieth century (Judt 1993: 101f.).

Hence, the scientific interest in memory and remembrance emerged parallel to the process of the break-up of European post-war myths in which the people were represented as victims of the brutal suppression of the National Socialist occupation and the question of guilt was projected onto Germany and hence externalised (Judt 1993: 91f.). A new generation that was personally uninvolved in the National Socialist experience posed new questions about history. Of particular importance was the question concerning individual and collective involvement in crimes of the National

Socialist ruling apparatus, of which Dan Diner's *Auschwitz: The Breach of Civilization* (1988) was increasingly conceived as the centre.

The shift in perspective onto the Holocaust as a leitmotif of the history of the twentieth century (Bartov 2004) breaks with the tradition of national creations of identity, which, as a rule, aim to evoke feelings of pride in one's 'own' history. In addition, the new culture of remembrance conceives of itself as a space of moral-ethical reflection – as a critical corrective of prior national traditions of remembrance, their strategies of suppression and their blind spots. Concerning this, Volkhard Knigge (2002), the director of the Buchenwald Memorial in Weimar, coined the term 'negative commemoration' – the memory of what 'we' did to others rather than what others did to 'us', the latter being characteristic of national memory politics. This is a memory of guilt which orientates itself according to the 'guilt of nations' (Barkan 2000).

Memory as Culture – Memory as Politics

Regardless of the central role of terms such as 'society', 'collective', 'group', etc., in cultural-scientific memory theory, their conception in society itself remains vague and undefined. Essentially, a differentiation can be drawn between an understanding of memory as culture and an understanding of memory as politics. While both concepts often overlap, these two approaches are based upon different ideas about the arena of memory and the connected forms of action.

The conceptualisation of memory as *culture*, developed through the works of Aleida Assmann and Jan Assmann, questions how societies hand down the 'fixtures' of a collectively shared 'knowledge' about the past (J. Assmann 1988: 9). The answer lies within the cultural mould of the ritualisation and institutionalisation of social memory. The perpetuation of this 'collectively shared knowledge' and its 'inheritability' within the culturally institutionalised heritage of a society necessitates continuous care. Religiously defined 'islands of time', relating to incidents which often go back thousands of years, are a paradigmatic example of this process (ibid.: 12–14).

The idea of a *longue durée*, a stable (if unalterable) canon of historical points of reference of social memory, forms the basis of Pierre Nora's concept (1984–92) of 'places of remembrance'. However, Nora's definition intertwines 'memory' and 'nation' (an outcome that Jan Assmann manages to avoid by speaking of 'groups' and 'society'). Accordingly, places of remembrance are 'places' in every meaning of the word, wherein 'the memory of the nation of France has condensed, embodied itself or crystallised imminently' (Nora 1990: 7). Nora's intention directs itself towards the ascertainment of the French nation's inventory of symbols – an 'inventory of the house of France' – by means of which the country sees itself as engaging in a 'return to national historiography'. However, this historiography, no longer in the traditional form of national writings, is now viewed 'in terms of the analysis of all that constitutes the idiosyncrasies of a country' (ibid.: 9).

The functionalisation of memory for the purpose of establishing national identity has evoked numerous critiques. Moritz Csáky has paid particular attention to the background of experiences affecting the ethnically, linguistically, culturally and religiously paradigmatic and heterogeneous region of Central Europe. Csáky (2002) has highlighted the fundamental ambiguity and complexity of places of remembrance, referring to the danger of the retrospective construction of national identifiers. Furthermore, the task of the historian is to contribute not to the construction of a national memory but to the *de*-construction of the connected repertoire of myths.

The success of the phenomenon of *lieux de mémoire* is comparable to that of national historiographies at the close of the nineteenth century. For the most part, contributions to the former attempt to distance themselves from the paradigm of national historiography. For example, the introduction to *Deutsche Erinnerungsorte* states that 'this project does not serve to support the state or to endow it with meaning' (François and Schulze 2001: 23). Equally, the editors of *Memoria Austriae* refuse to be defined as nationally orientated (Brix et al. 2004–5). However, the format of these compendiums is performative, and their focus includes the 'crystallisation points of collective memory and identity, outlasting generations' (François and Schulze 2001: 18). Thus, these audits of national places of remembrance also serve to frame a national foundation of identity with the connected mechanisms of inclusion and exclusion from the feeling of togetherness, to which critical theories of national identity call attention (Wodak et al. 1998).

The conceptualisation of memory as *politics*, on the other hand, is primarily concerned with negotiations around the collective understanding of history. At the same time, historical points of reference are precarious and temporary, the result of a continuous 'staging of the past'[3] in the arena of public communication in which prior traditions can be reproduced and fixed, but also changed. This suggests an ongoing contestation regarding the perpetuation and alteration of the canon of identity-generating conceptions of history that may sporadically become attached to memory. This perception of memory as politics recalls the interest of the field of cultural studies in the construction of collective identities within the frame of social power structures.

In order to 'translate' the theoretical and socio-critical potential of cultural studies on the category of memory, Oliver Marchart (2005) formulated a hegemonic-theoretical theory of memory which stipulates that a 'collectively shared knowledge' about the past cannot provide a neutral account. Rather, such knowledge is always 'situated' (ibid.; see also Haraway 1995).

Discourses on the past correspond not to the perceptions of an imagined collective, but to those of social groups. Different social groups, in turn, enjoy varying powers of definition and seek to promote their own perspectives. Consequently, negotiations about memory relate to struggles over the space of the universal, the imagined 'we-community' (Marchart 2005). According to this view, objects of cultural memory provide information about social power structures and indicate the success of certain groups in rooting their particular conception of history as a universal, binding memory of a collective.

Within the conception of memory as politics, therefore, there is less emphasis on the themes of public debate and the transmission of knowledge. Instead, the focus is on how defined modes of interpreting the past are implemented in a space characterised by diverse power resources. In this way, social action is conceptualised using terms such as 'struggle for memory', 'competition for the power of definition', 'strategies and calculations in the field of history' and 'memory politics'.

Memory as Palimpsest

However, memory does not merge entirely with either the forms of action of a culture of perpetuation or the politics of implementation. Rather, epistemological changes or shifts of interest in the past that cannot be traced back to the specific actions and strategies of actors serve to counteract the notion of memory as an intentionally, and therefore rationally, substantiated project. Transformations of social remembrance also occur as a result of the fading of places of remembrance and the lessening of the social energy previously directed at them. Such places lose their controversial value and potential to provoke conflict.

Metaphors of fading can be contrasted with processes of transcription and interference through new perspectives on the past. The radically new 'questions about history' are not the result of a strategic calculation; reactions to planned interventions in the views of history can be anticipated only to a limited extent. Accordingly, the creators of the popular and controversial exhibition 'Vernichtungskrieg: Verbrechen der Wehrmacht 1941 bis 1944' (War of Annihilation: Crimes of the Wehrmacht 1941 to 1944) did not anticipate the extent of public response. Shown exclusively at the Hamburg Institute for Social Research, it generated more interest than the institute's major exhibit, '200 Tage und 1 Jahrhundert' (200 Days and 1 Century), which dealt with the history of violence in the twentieth century (Manoschek 2002). However, fading and transcription are not necessarily synonymous with the temporal distance of an incident to the present moment of its reconstruction. Rather, the aim is to determine which obsessions, passions and emotional energies can be evoked through historical points of reference.

Collectively shared knowledge about the past is not to be regarded as an available inventory of rational information about a historical event. Such knowledge requires an emotional-affective dimension in order to be able to invoke the repertoire of feelings connected to memory.

It has been argued that the renegotiations of the Austrian past towards the end of the 1980s illustrate the concept of memory as a social palimpsest. The aforementioned debate surrounding Kurt Waldheim's wartime past served to shatter Austria's particular variation of European post-war myths and confronted Austrians with their 'suppressed' National Socialist past. However, at the same time the debate is a convincing illustration of the fact that transformations of memory do not depend exclusively on strategic interventions. The negative reactions of many Austrians, especially the younger generation, to Waldheim's justification that he did nothing other than 'carry out [his] duty', were astounding. Just ten years before, the chairman of the Austrian Freedom Party (FPÖ) and a former SS member, Friedrich Peter, successfully vindicated himself from allegations of involvement in war crimes using exactly the same argument (Uhl 2004, 2006).

The 1986 Waldheim debate in fact marks an epistemological turning point in Austrian contemporary history research itself. Ernst Hanisch (1994) identifies the debate as the stimulus for the obsession of an entire generation of contemporary historians with National Socialism and its long shadow over the Second Republic. These themes now eclipse all other aspects of Austrian history, especially the period after 1945. However, this observation should be qualified by the fact that it was the generation of historians of 1968 who were confronted in 1986 with the fact that their questions about history suddenly faced the charge of irrelevance. The interest and passion of this previous generation for the debate on the responsibility of the various political factions for the downfall of the First Republic and the evaluation of the authoritarian *Ständestaat* or Austrofascism were no longer shared by a young generation of historians. Like the conflict around the Austrian nation and its historical substantiation which dominated the 1950s and 1960s, this controversy now belongs to the archives of socio-political debates on principles of Austrian memory politics (Uhl 2003).

Apparently, the logics of the field of memory are not defined exclusively by intentional forms of cultural processes and political calculation. Their dimensions are also emotionally affective. Recognising this can enhance the analysis of the dynamics of social memory between tendencies towards perpetuation and those towards change. In addition, it promises to shed light on the question of why certain historical points of reference are present within the functional memory of a society, while others remain inside the storage vault of history – or simply disappear.

– Translated by Adrian Ortner

Notes

1. Aleida Assmann also referred to this during a lecture titled 'Generationsspezifische Vorurteile in der Neuen Erinnerungsliteratur', Wiener Vorlesungen, Universität Wien, 27 April 2005.
2. See http://www.grasse-kucht.de/pdf/weizsaecker.pdf.
3. The phrase is borrowed from Bucur (2002). See also Breuss et al. (1995).

Chapter 6

DAMNATIO MEMORIAE AND THE POWER OF REMEMBRANCE

Reflections on Memory and History

☙❧

Frederick Whitling

To live, you have to forget.

– Andrzej Wajda's 1970 film, *Landscape after the Battle*

Memory is too tied to the idea of immortality to expect that anonymous humanity can serve as a community of commemoration when it fails miserably as a community of communication.

– Avishai Margalit, *The Ethics of Memory*

Ours is a time characterised by the redefinition of academic boundaries as well as the role of historians in society. The following comments and reflections have sprung from discontent with the terminological confusion and lack of conceptual definition in the ongoing debate on collective memory. The capacity of memory is closely linked with consciousness and is indeed a prerequisite for the idea of thinking historically. In the words of Jan-Werner Müller (2002a), 'memory matters'.[1] Without the human faculty of memory, history could not be imagined. This chapter discusses history in relation to conceptualisations of memory and identity, focusing on the use of the term 'memory' and the notion of the 'politics of remembrance' in historical writing.[2]

It is important for the development of historical enquiry to attempt to overcome the Hegelian dialectic of the dichotomy between the two extremes of memory and history. The divide between these extremes remains too conspicuous, and this piece will highlight some ways of potentially bridging that gap and of overcoming differences and *différance* (after Derrida) in making memory – or memories – an accessible source

---

Notes for this chapter begin on page 96.

material category for historical investigation.[3] The insecurity in distinguishing between memory and history has to a large extent been shaped in the wake of the Cold War legacy of negotiating a fair view of the past, a product of post-1989 Europe that Tony Judt (2002: 180) refers to as an 'interregnum' between new myths.[4]

In debating the concepts of memory and identity in relation to history, certain key counter-aspects emerge, such as forgetting, indifference, and regional and transregional levels of study. The quest for a collective, value-based European identity as an end in itself is discussed here; 'official' public or collective *memory* is juxtaposed with 'unofficial' private *memories* (deliberately in the plural). In addition, the ancient Roman practice of *damnatio memoriae* will be employed as a contrasting example of forgetting.

In imperial ancient Rome, *damnatio memoriae* signified the opposite of deification of the deceased emperors. Rather, this practice functioned as senate decrees of 'damnation of memory'. If this choice was opted for, the former emperor was to be symbolically removed from remembrance in retrospective dishonour: all symbols of the emperor were to be eradicated, all statues destroyed, all depictions and inscriptions annihilated. In short, every trace of the person in question was to be removed. Ironically, this often had the opposite effect. One poignant case is that of Domitian (emperor 81–96 AD), the 'memory' of whom lives to this day.

I choose to revive the concept as a way of emphasising the force of forgetting as a backdrop to public remembrance, and because of its association with the political sphere. It also has an emancipatory element that may appeal to modern sensibilities. Most importantly, it highlights an active agency, here associated with public remembrance.[5] In this way, *damnatio memoriae* might be perceived as a conceptual cultural tool for discussing censorship, forgetting and indifference.

This chapter is divided into three parts. The first discusses aspects of the methodological instrumentarium of the memory and history debate. The second examines specific examples in the field of enquiry, highlighting memory and history in practice. The third offers concluding remarks and suggestions for possible ways in which to proceed with investigating memory in relation to history.

Theoretical Perspectives

> Apart from the power of memory to influence the present, there is also the power of the present to influence memory (Müller 2002a: 34).

The discourse on memory and history has been ongoing for over twenty years, the initial spark having been provided by Jan Assmann's notion of 'cultural memory'. The idea of a collective memory can be traced back to, for example, the 'super-individual memory' of Hugo von Hoffmansthal in 1902, and to the work on *mentalités* and 'social memory' (*soziales Gedächtnis*) of Aby Warburg, as well as that of Maurice Halbwachs (see Confino 1997: 1392). The term 'collective memory' was introduced to the social sciences by Halbwachs in 1925 (see A. Assmann 2006a: 222). Jan Assmann (1988, 1995) triggered the revival of the notion in his discussions of cultural identity.

At present, terms such as 'politics of remembrance', 'processes of remembrance', 'memory theatre' and 'commemoration' permeate academic discourse. Alon Confino (1997: 1394–5) observes that 'if social history reduced the cultural to the social, cultural history reduces the cultural to the political'. The use of the term 'politics of remembrance' is aimed at acquiring control of historical narratives.

Discussing Memory Terminology and Definitions

The concepts of remembrance and forgetting in memory terminology, or memory semantics, presuppose the existence of certain memories. Collective memory remains an abstraction unless deconstructed in order to detect nuances and deviances in memory trajectories.

Heidemarie Uhl, in this volume, discusses different complexes of memory: memory as culture, memory as politics and memory as shared knowledge. To these might be added another: memory as private narrative. This can be compared with Edward S. Casey's 'four major forms of human memory' (in Phillips 2004: 20–32): individual, social, collective and public. Aleida Assmann offers a similar categorisation of four 'formats of memory': individual, social, political and cultural. Stressing the importance of collective participation, Assmann (2006a: 211–21) argues that '*history* turns into *memory* when it is transformed into forms of shared knowledge'. In his employment of the notions of 'vernacular and official memory', John Bodnar (1992) provides another example of dichotomies in memory terminology (see also Confino 1997: 1401).

Spatial Manifestations of Memory

Transformation or (ex)change of knowledge can reasonably be analysed on three levels: a local or regional level, a national level, and a transnational, European or global level, which is orientated towards the future rather than aiming to reclaim the past. The national level has long enjoyed an elevated status, with the nation state as the traditional framework of reference. Yet in many ways this focus is unfortunate. Regional levels may provide us with the necessary tools for discussion concerning possible 'transregional memories', divergences and commonalities regarding concrete specificities, tropes and themes of memory.

Memory effectively seems to replace utopia and visions of the future with nostalgia, which becomes strikingly apparent in Pierre Nora's 'melancholic' conceptions of *lieux de mémoire,* focusing on national identity.[6] Memory studies require the analysis and deconstruction of memories, not only their reification. Tadhg O'Keeffe's take on Nora (in Moore and Whelan 2007: 8) is clarifying: 'Nora laments what he sees as a decline of a national, collective, identity-forming memory in the age of globalisation ... [the] *Lieux de mémoire* [project] will thus become a *lieu de mémoire* in its own right.'

Memories have time sequences, and if memory is allowed to replace history, this results in a tendency to 'freeze' certain experiences or interpretations into a solid and unchallengeable whole. In stressing memory as the uniting factor, Oskar Halecki (1950) in a sense reversed Nora's dogma that history unites and memory divides. One might rather speak of *milieux de mémoire* or, even better, spheres of private and public memory. Jan Jansen, in this volume, refers to *lobbies de mémoire* – what might be termed a politics of concealment – in the case of post-colonial remembrance of French Algeria.

Part of the challenge of debating memory studies lies in distinguishing and identifying scales of analysis and their relation to time. The role of imagination in the (re)constitution of remembered events also requires further attention. Paul Ricoeur's discussion (2004: 504) of the three 'figures' of forgetting identified by Marc Augé highlights the difficulties of traversing the past, present and future simultaneously on a conceptual level. It is important to distinguish between active and passive forgetting – hence the parallel here with the ancient concept of *damnatio memoriae.*[7]

Individual and Collective Memories

Wittgenstein (2001: 5.6, 68) stated that 'the limits of my language mean the limits of my world', which can serve as an illustration of the importance of the communication of an event (or an 'event-story') in relation to the individual and private level of memories.[8] Collective memory is a retrospective phenomenon; it must be discussed as a thing of the past.

What is being legitimised and justified in generalisable patterns of memory, if not present and future political actions? One might argue that the European *demos* is constructed on a particular notion of sovereignty, or (more importantly) that common identity is essential to the upkeep of 'transconstitutional continuity'. Jürgen Straub (in Friese 2002: 71) brushes off the term 'collective identity' as 'scientifically untenable'. The same applies to collective memory. Tadhg O'Keeffe prefers the term 'collected memory'.[9] This has also been picked up by Jeffrey Olick, who distinguishes between 'aggregated individual memories – or "collected memory" ... and collective memory understood as the "frame" or "profile" of national memory' (in Müller 2002a: 26; see also Olick 1999).

Collective memory (and collective identity) cannot be pinned down to an exact moment in time precisely because its constituent body is constantly in flux. Constructing collective memory – 'transposing' individual experiences onto collectives – makes the potentially concrete unmistakably abstract. Identity narratives offer new interpretations of the world in order to modify it, while collective memory can be interpreted as an evoked past framing the present. I propose conceptualising a third level in between remembering and forgetting: a 'neutral', *indifferent* memory (cf. the notion of 'benign collective neglect' in Judt 2002: 166, 182).

Intermediary levels of possible shared memories might be found in many strata of society, for example, clubs and associations. Konrad Jarausch (2007) discusses the possible essential and unifying features of 'group memories', striving towards an awareness of the multiplicity of groupings or 'clusters' of individual memories as pre- and post-collective levels of memory. The absence of visible actors in relation to constructed collective memory is conspicuous: they are too often anonymous. Collective memory and collective identities thus have no official authors, which undermines the stability of both concepts.[10]

National, Transnational and Regional European Memories

Memories, as histories, fall in and out of fashion; the swing of the pendulum dictates whether a synchronic or diachronic shift of commemoration is currently in vogue. Historical analogies tend to spring from a tight, short circuit that relies on the shaky premise that we are prepared to learn from history (paraphrasing Hegel's comment that the one thing we do learn from history is that we do not learn from history). Multiple and diverging uses of memory can be applied simultaneously in the name of legitimisation and alleged rationalisation.

National and Nationalist Memories

In the interplay between different interest groups, the European Union indirectly puts pressure on potential new member states to discuss and 'come to terms' with their respective national pasts. The EU arguments advocating a 'return to the past' and a critical revision of ideas entangled with the notion of 'paradise lost', a 'golden age' or the unfulfilled promise of the past are indicative of a desire to construct new forms of collectivity or commonality.[11]

There is an inherent ambiguity in downplaying the darker side of memory in public manifestations, for example, in commemorations in the context of public (national) holidays.[12] 'Memory culture' cannot afford to be solely affirmative and celebratory: its negative aspects need to be visible and present. Conflicting memories are to a large extent the result of the nationalisation of contemporary history. Ethnic nationalism can be juxtaposed with civic nationalism (as 'required' for entry in the European Union) with regard to the use of memory. The notion of collective memory is fuel for nationalist fires: in this context, memory is easily confused with nostalgia. The crucial question is how to overcome and transcend nostalgia and the double traps of political passivity and nationalist political activism in a European framework of belief in pragmatic progress.

Transnational and Transregional Memories: European Spheres of Remembrance?

Transnational perspectives present a multitude of problems and challenges, which are also found internally in individual nation states, as in Italy, for example, with its strong focus on regional identities. The communication and use of history are crucial to this discussion. The transnational or transregional aspect of this field remains largely unexplored territory.[13]

The politics of remembrance can operate according to diverging multiple narratives. For instance, the Holocaust is interpreted and perceived in clearly different ways in Germany and Poland to the extent that they appear to be 'two different Holocausts'.[14] The desire to create a common European identity, or the idea that it remains a goal unquestionably worth striving for, is often left unchallenged. Collective memory and collective identity cannot be taken for granted, and the same applies to ideas concerning European permanence and stability. A multi-cultural conception of Europe has to rely on the acceptance of mutual recognition, with diversity as the word of the day and tolerance as the master value. This implies a range of tacit, common normative values – or the acceptance of implicit double standards – as well as a redistribution of guilt and 'negative nationalism' across Europe with an extended dimension of responsibility.

Multi-culturalism is a fact, not a norm, which would thus disqualify any commitment from individual countries to engage with 'collective national pasts'. The focus on collective memory in this context remains unconvincing. The word 'memory' in the singular is prone to manipulation. Cultural practices of memory represent a fragmentation of coherent and cohesive constructed master narratives.

The European Union aims at creating, strengthening and maintaining solidarities and ties between European peoples. Stefan Berger's plea (2005) for focusing on a specific political project rather than on enforcing collective memory narratives would fit well with that idea. Constructed collective memory would not. Article 1 of the 'Convention for the Protection of the Archaeological Heritage of Europe' (the Valletta Convention) boldly refers to 'the archaeological heritage as a source of the European collective memory'.[15] This memory is thus seemingly taken for granted, which in effect imposes a *fait accompli* 'identity product' on Europeans.

Concluding Remarks

Memory functions as a process – as a transitional structure between history and myth in resurrecting the past. In taking common values, memory and identity for granted, we make an illogical move, confusing the construction of memory with its reception and contestation. If the nation is simply to be replaced by a larger unit (such as Europe), we fall into a similar methodological trap. The fundamental or 'normal' logic of identity is binary, with an identification of the self in relation to the 'Other'. In a multi-cultural European reality, this logic is undermined, which should be regarded as a positive development.

Centralised directives and constructed political taboos are sitting ducks for potential exploitation by xenophobes and extreme political groups prone to making infringements on national identities. Memory culture is then characterised by ongoing instrumentalisations of itself in reconciliation and by constant reminders of violations and atrocities in the past – all judged from a modern perspective and frame of reference – as a way of proceeding and dealing with a 'common' present and, above all, with a shared future.

Memory is narrative, and from this perspective we may safely say that a common European memory culture does not exist. One telling sign of this is that 'monuments honour national heroes rather than significant Europeans' (Jarausch, this volume). Jarausch (2007) emphasises that there are good reasons why a common European memory culture does not exist: the problems associated with definitions are seemingly endless; the idea is infected with essentialism and implications of the Judaeo-Christian heritage; Europe has not truly worked through its relationship with the Anglo-American sphere of the world; and the 'cultural othering' of post-colonial discourse continues to take its toll. One particular problem is that the notion of a European *demos* through a European identity (the European Community's 1973 Copenhagen Declaration) or a European collective memory seems to have emerged as a substitute for the visualisation of a social Europe that failed with the collapse of the Werner Plan in the 1970s (cf. Karlsson in this volume). During the historical development of the European nation states, the situation was the opposite: political unification and social integration resulted in identification with national space and time and the spread of identity and memory/history discourses.

The myriad of individual memory narratives might be organised in groups according to themes or clusters of individual memories. However, the problem then arises of distinguishing and identifying certain essential, unifying features. For example, which stories are European and which are local or regional? Reference points would be required with a clear *terminus ad quem* – with points of departure and of arrival.

The potential scope and character of European memory culture cannot be celebratory and affirmative. This 'dark continent' (Mazower 1998), with a history of tremendous barbarity and seemingly endless conflicts and wars, often emerges in historical writing as a West suffering from amnesia. The writing of European history remains incomplete in this regard, implying a free-trade aspect of memory culture that encourages a survival-of-the-fittest approach to the construction of the straw man of collective memory.

The heart of the matter of the problematic aspects of a Europeanisation of collective memory is the lack of a long-term perspective. Attempting to create one common European memory culture, therefore, seems a fruitless endeavour in a field immersed in a myriad of methodological problems as well as issues concerning translations; for example, is English to be considered *the* European language *par excellence*? If countries were to engage with the pasts of other countries, the transfer or exchange of individual memories would enhance mutual understanding and increase the possibility that forgiveness and catharsis might, in the long term, come to replace a politics of regret and apologies.

A one-dimensional *herrschaftsfrei* (or objective) 'Eurohistorical' identity narrative is ultimately censorial, as there are some stories that we simply do not want to hear. (Hi)stories are in general locally contained within national frames, which would advocate a regional approach to integrating memories as historical source material. The notion of a 'Eurohistory' with unconnected and hostile multiplicities is not constructive; linked or entangled multiplicities should offer a more productive way ahead.

Paraphrasing Beverley Southgate's recent publication *What is History For?* (2005), we might well ask what *memory* is for. Following Southgate (ibid.: 54–5), a general answer would be to identify some sort of 'therapeutic function' as a more general 'duty to memory' (see also Todorov 2003). If collective memory is regarded as 'official' discourse, we may therefore speak of 'counter-memory' on an individual and private scale. This implies a strong generational character to memory discourse.

Collective memory therefore becomes a public abstraction that takes over an individual concept and immerses it in vague psychoanalytical terminology, which historians might not always be most suited to employ. History and memory are ultimately mutually dependent, entangled categories, which is why 'memory versus history is something of a false dichotomy … what we are interested in is precisely memory *in* history' (Müller 2002a: 24).

Memory can successfully come into play in historical writing only through specific uses of sources that integrate private memories in historical narratives. The concepts of public memory and collective memory should more accurately be referred to as rituals of remembrance, public acts of commemoration or official acknowledgements. This would illuminate and clarify the driving political forces behind the phenomena and help recognise the agenda involved, carried out by actors for a specific purpose.

Ceremonies of public remembrance assume a cathartic function in taking on and acknowledging the *peccata mundi*, or 'sins of the world'. Historical writing needs actively to accommodate myths, memories and testimonies of a private dimension, integrating perspectives that take both remembrance and forgetting into account. History and memory are perfectly capable of peaceful academic co-existence.

Notions of collective identity stem from a multitude of diverging individual memories. Hence, rapid moves from individual to collective memory are not legitimate, in agreement with Marita Sturken's observation (1997: 5) that 'there is so much traffic across the borders of cultural memory and history that in many cases it may be futile to maintain a distinction between them'. The dichotomy between memory and history is therefore no longer tenable.

Joining forces with Confino's appeal (1997: 1391) for a historicity of memory in fighting the trend of 'studies of memory in symbolic isolation', it should be stressed that discussions regarding collective memory and collective identity tend to focus on symbols, which in turn leads to an emphasis on reception in debating the employment of memories as a source category in historical investigation.[16] The parallel drawn earlier with the ancient practice of *damnatio memoriae* might thus be interpreted here in a contemporary context as an annihilation of the symbolic value of the individual in manifestations of remembrance as a constructed collective category.

Considering the agency associated with public remembrance as well as its opposite (*damnatio memoriae*), it should prove more fruitful to conceptualise common themes of individual memories, focusing on their intermediaries and interrelationships on regional levels rather than on collective memory on a national scale. *Damnatio memoriae* provides another way of expressing forced forgetting, censorship, indifference and 'selective memories' (after Ilaria Poggiolini, in Müller 2002b: 225–7). The use of individual memories as a valid source in historical writing would assist in gradually overcoming the fear of erratic dissonance in a multiplicity of memories, with the historian providing the integrative gesture in approaching sources.

History should take memory seriously, if for no other reason than the opportunity it presents for transcending master narratives and national frameworks. History needs memory – or, rather, memories – as a serious and methodologically sound source material category, transcending the limitations of its confinement to the sub-discipline of oral history. However, this also means that historians need to define, clarify and contextualise each specific employment of the concept of memory in order to secure and justify its place in historical writing.

Notes

1. Müller (2002a: 19) emphasises the numerous 'pitfalls' in the study of memory in relation to power, most notably 'the dangers of reification, reductionism and "collectivisation"'.
2. Memory and identity studies have become increasingly fashionable paradigms of late, and the number of publications in the field is immense and continually increasing. The selection of references here is therefore exactly that: a selection. For the concept of memory, see, for example, Ashplant et al. (2004); A. Assmann (1996, 1999a, 1999b, 2001, 2006a, 2006b, 2006c, 2006d); J. Assmann ([1992] 2007); Confino (1997); Connerton (1989); Crane (1997); Giesen (2004); Gillis (1994); Glassberg (1996); Goebel (2001, 2007); Halbwachs ([1925] 1994, 1992); Hölscher (1989); Kansteiner (2002); N. Klein (1997); Le Goff (1988); Mangos (2007); Margalit (2002); Müller (2002a, 2002b); Ricoeur (2004); Samuel (1994); Sauter (2002); Stråth (2000a); Sturken (1997, 1998); Todorov (2003); Wägenbaur (1998); Weinrich (1997); Whitling (2009); Winter (2000, 2006); Winter and Sivan (1999); as well as a range of publications in the journal *History and Memory*, from 1989 to the present. For memory in relation to identity, see, for example, Friese (2002); Giesen (1991); Judt and Lacorne (2004); Müller (2000); Niethammer (2000); Sassatelli (2002); and Thomas (1996). For specifically *European* perspectives on identity, see Ichijo and Spohn (2005); Stråth (2000b, 2002); and Wintle (2006). For a general historical survey of memory in relation to history, see Le Goff (1988: 105–77).
3. Müller (2002a: 13–16) offers the following explanations for the 'memory boom' paradigm shift in the humanities: (1) the development of 'recollection associated with the electronic media'; (2) the transformation from living, first-hand oral memory with the 'generation of experience' to 'cultural memory' with historians as 'the guardians of collective memory'; (3) the fin-de-siècle account of the 'short twentieth century'; (4) the final disappearance of the 'undifferentiated societies' of *Alteuropa*; and (5) the 'rise of multiculturalism'.
4. To some extent, Müller (2002a: 11) balances the issue: 'Unlike "hot wars", the Cold War does not lend itself to memorialisation.' Aleida Assmann (2001: 6827) points out that it is significant that the journal *History and Memory* was founded in 1989, signalling a 'shift in historical interest ..., ethically committed to the participatory perspective of the victims', with 'history becoming a form of memory and vice versa'.
5. For *damnatio memoriae*, see, for example, Born and Stemmer (1996) and Varner (2004). For forgetting, see Hölscher (1989: 4), who emphasises that 'forgetting' for Sigmund Freud and his contemporaries should be interpreted in the tradition of the Platonic concepts of 'amnesis' and 'anamnesis'. In his analysis of the *Dasein*, Heidegger viewed remembrance and forgetting as implications of being itself. Forgetting as discussed by Hölscher (1989: 9–10) relates more to existential issues (in a Kantian, Gadamerian and Heideggerian tradition) than to collective remembrance. In Hölscher's opinion, collective forgetting is 'a matter of conceptual definition' (ibid.: 11–12).
6. See, for example, Nora (1989, 1996). For the *Lieux de mémoire* project, see Ricoeur (2004: 401–11). For Nora's 'nostalgic' view of memory and its relation to history, see Rodell (2005: 106–7).
7. For active forgetting, see Hölscher (1989: 3).
8. See also Wittgenstein (2001: 5.61, 5.62). On language and memory, see Halbwachs ([1925] 1994, esp. 40–82; 1992: 43–5). For the 'event-story' concept, see Margalit (2002: 60).
9. Opposing the concept of an essentialist 'intuitive collective memory', O'Keeffe (in Moore and Whelan 2007) argues that collected memory is a 'product of external programming', while emphasising the problematic aspect of penetrating the 'strong scent of nostalgia' in dealing with individual recollections.
10. One case of highlighting individual memories retrospectively is that of the Russian Memorial project, which was responsible for the publication of lists of victims of the Stalin terror of 1937–8, as well as hitherto non-official and neglected archival documents

(Arfon Rees, from the seminar 'Coming to Terms with Europe's Communist Past: A Europeanisation of Practices and Politics of Remembrance?' at the European University Institute in Florence, 5 February 2007). See also Passerini (2005: xiv); and A. Assmann (2006b: 274).

11. For constructed identities based on commonality, see, for example, Jürgen Straub (in Friese 2002: 71). An example of the *a priori* status of memory in relation to history can be found in the case of the Casa della Memoria e della Storia (House of Memory and History) in Rome, which focuses on individual testimonies from the events surrounding the Fosse Ardeatine massacre in Rome on 24 March 1944. The Casa della Memoria e della Storia was inaugurated on 24 March 2006. For the Fosse Ardeatine massacre, see, above all, Portelli (2001, 2003). The very name of the Casa implies a common hierarchical arrangement: memory precedes history.

12. Aleida Assmann (2001: 6824) makes the important point that celebrations of long-term anniversaries 'do not recur within the lifetime of individuals. Therefore, it is rather a mode of spotlighting historical dates than a form of creating a continuous, communal memory'.

13. One recent development in this field is the online Internet project entitled 'What Story Should Europe Tell?', initiated by Timothy Garton Ash (http://www.europeanstory.net). Ash argues that grand narratives and 'Euromyth' are no longer sufficient: 'Europe has lost the plot.' Ash thus proposes a 'new story' founded on six strands: 'freedom, peace, law, prosperity, diversity and solidarity' (http://www.prospectmagazine.co.uk/2007/02/europestruestories/). Judt (2002) argues that the years 1945–8 were crucial in moulding Europe's post-war memory. He also highlights that at a time 'when Euro-chat has turned to the happy topic of disappearing customs barriers and single currencies, the frontiers of memory remain solidly in place' (ibid.: 182).

14. Małgorzata Pakier, from the seminar 'Remembering the Holocaust: A Europeanisation of Practices and Politics of Remembrance?' at the European University Institute, in Florence, 5 February 2007. If the Holocaust is to be interpreted as *the* central event of a collective or common European memory, this creates a memory culture based on guilt as part of a public negotiation of the past. Confession then becomes a prerequisite for purification (cf. Southgate 2005: 158–63). Stressing the importance of transnational connectedness, Konrad Jarausch offers Jewish minorities as a key link in historical transnational ties (from the seminar 'A Europeanisation of Practices and Politics of Remembrance?' at the European University Institute, in Florence, 12 February 2007).

15. Council of Europe, 'Convention for the Protection of the Archaeological Heritage of Europe' (revised), Valletta, 1992. The text is available at http://www.coe.int/t/dg4/cultureheritage/Conventions/Heritage/valletta_en.asp. The classical tradition provides an interesting case concerning the difficulties in overcoming or summarising preconceptions regarding shared values in relation to cultural diversities (Whitling 2009).

16. Confino (1997: 1395) underlines the importance of reception to memory studies: 'The study of reception is not an issue that simply adds to our knowledge. Rather, it is a necessary one to avoid an arbitrary choice and interpretation of evidence.'

Chapter 7

SEEING DARK AND WRITING LIGHT
Photography Approaching Dark
and Obscure Histories

❧

James Kaye

Photography, Mirrors and
the Mass Marketing of Memories

The daguerreotype process, named after Luis Jacques Mandé Daguerre, was the first commercially viable, practical and reliable chemical process by which images could be fixed on a surface. Human vision recognised the resulting images as identifiable objects, the subjects of which were perceived to be both accurate and of scientific value. Stable visions of the past could now be preserved during an ever-shifting present created by visual interpretations and changing discourses. The longevity of Daguerre's name was secured with the naming of the daguerreotype, yet his discovery was not patented, nor was it kept private or used for the maximisation of personal or corporate profit. In 1839 it was acquired by the Académie des Sciences and made available to the public as a gift *à tout le monde* (Eastlake 1857). In line with this spirit and perception of progress, another pioneer of the practice, William Henry Fox Talbot (1980: 23), referred to this new procedure as the 'process by which natural objects may be made to delineate themselves without the aid of the artist's pencil'.

Two decades after the announcement of the daguerreotype and further technological advances, photography was metaphorically associated with memory. In an article in the June 1859 edition of the *Atlantic Monthly*, the polymath Oliver Wendell Holmes extolled the invention as more important than contemporary advances in rail travel, telegraphic communication and even chloroform anaesthesia. Holmes (1980: 54) lyrically dubbed photography the 'mirror with a memory'.[1]

Notes for this chapter begin on page 113.

In addition to raising the expressive potential of photography, memory sold. Explaining Eastman Kodak's marketing strategy, its founder, George Eastman, declared that Kodak 'does not sell film.... It sells memories'. Eastman employed memory to make millions selling film. Kodak film was promoted as a medium whose manufacture of memories was superior to any other, thus raising the value of the product from the mundane to the transcendental. Following the introduction of the Kodak camera in 1888, millions of people began to use photographs to identify and remember, spurring the use of photography as a mnemonic aid. Figures 7.1 and 7.2 are advertisements for Kodak film and cameras in *Punch or the London Charivari*, the popular British weekly. The images, which depict the Kodak Girl in her characteristic striped dress, attempt to sell film and cameras by selling memories. The Kodak Girl made her debut in 1892 (West 2000). Photographs were used extensively on graves and 'in memoriam' cards since the 1860s. With the advent of amateur photography in the 1880s, those practising photography as a leisure activity took photographs in the quest to preserve personal memories of places, people, times and events. An advertisement of 1919 drew on the notion of selective memory to market film, entreating the photographer to 'let your Kodak retain the memory of the scenes that please you' (*Punch*, 23 July 1919, in Taylor 1994: 36).

These developments took place in a climate in which the perception of progress had begun to give way to alienation and a world characterised by the acceleration of time, with the gulf between experience and expectation widening at an alarming rate. Photography contributed to this transformation by changing the way that the world was seen. Susan Sontag (2001: 3) wrote that since the invention of photography, '[j]ust about everything has been photographed. This very insatiability of the photographing eye changes the terms of confinement in the cave, our world. In teaching us a new visual code, photographs alter and enlarge our notions of what is worth looking at and what we have a right to observe. They are a grammar and, even more importantly, an ethics of seeing'.

In addition to being party to this transformation, photography eased its effects because it was perceived to preserve with verisimilitude things that had existed and had occurred. As it had the appearance of preserving the past, photography could be seen as analogous to individual memory. However, photographs are not the past; rather, they are a seemingly real description of and imaginary transportation to the past. As such, photography has become fused with and part of – as well as an aid to – memory. Visual sensations produced by looking at a photograph merge with other images seen through human eyes and remembered. Images of the past emblazoned on minds include both episodes from private lives and photographs seen repeatedly in private collections and the mass media. The power of photographic verisimilitude has long been used as a tool in the construction of personal memories and discourses of groups. In fact, many

FIGURE 7.1 'Save your happy memories with a Kodak'.
Source: *Punch, or the London Charivari*, 31 May 1922.

of the imaginary scenes we recall are not scenes of direct experiences but recollections constructed through repeated viewings of photographs. As a new element, photographs had a profound effect upon social structure and discourse, contributing to the construction of what Norbert Elias (1995) called habitus. They are tools in world making and thus influence 'the vision of the world and the practical operations by which groups are produced and reproduced … [they have a] [s]ymbolic power, whose form par excellence

FIGURE 7.2 'The only holiday that lasts forever is the holiday with a Kodak'.
Source: *Punch, or the London Charivari*, 7 July 1920.

is the power to make groups (groups that are already established and have to be consecrated or groups that have yet to be constituted ...)' (Bourdieu 1989: 23). This is true in Bourdieuian terms as photographs impose upon minds visions and values that are perceived to be founded in reality due to their verisimilitude.

Through images repeatedly viewed in mass media, photography has had an important impact on collective social psychology and has become an important element in collective discourses. From this perspective, photography has transformed the structures of the social world. It has altered habitus fundamentally for those who have seen often reproduced (and similar private) photographs spanning time, social classes and national affinities. In doing so, photography has become a mnemonic device.

Ten years after Holmes used photography as a metaphor for memory and long before it became a dominant discourse in the social and human sciences, the concept of photography was metaphorically associated with memory in the field of psychology. In 1868, the psychologist Henry Maudsley referred to the capability of a man to read a text he had just seen backwards as a type of visual memory 'in which the person seems to read a photographic copy of former impressions with his mind's eye' (cited in Draaisma 2000: 130). This psychological concept of 'photographic memory' was developed in Vienna at the beginning of the twentieth century (Hehlmann 1965). The renowned cognitive scientist Marvin Minsky (1988) has classified the notion as little more than 'unfounded myth'. The phenomenon referred to as photographic memory is actually the result of trained mnemonic techniques that can be employed in specific circumstances.

Due to its relative ease of use and the fact that it could quickly provide a 'recognizably accurate description of the shape of objects reproduced in one point perspective, [photography] displaced painting and the other visual arts as the prime representational medium almost as soon as it was invented' (Mirzoeff 1999: 44). The volume *Egypte, Nubie, Palestine et Syrie*, a travel documentary by Maxime Du Camp (1852), is among the first publications to be illustrated with photographs. Du Camp, who was not expressly a photographer, noted: 'I had realised upon my previous travels that I wasted much valuable time trying to draw buildings and scenery I did not care to forget. I drew slowly and not very correctly.... I felt that I needed an instrument of precision to record my impressions and reproduce them accurately' (cited in Newhall 1986: 50). The subtext here is the acceleration of time and the expansion of requirements for which photography was a solution, a tool that was believed to preserve and reproduce detail and be effective against unwanted forgetting.

This chapter will continue to discuss two forms of general metaphoric association with memory. The first, 'metaphors for memory', is an attempt to illustrate the way in which memory functions. The second, 'memory as a metaphor', pertains to the way that memory has been metaphorically promulgated as an attribute of collectivities at a time when history was subjected to fundamental criticism in the wake of the linguistic turn. The chapter argues that memory is a poor substitute for history – that it devalues history instead of emphasising the ironic, critical value of the problematics of contemporary historiography – and proposes photography as an alternative to memory to expand the historical discourse. The chapter concludes with the presentation of four key photographs that reveal important aspects of Europe's recent dark pasts.

Memory Metaphors and History

Photographs have been connected with memory both factually and rhetorically, the former through individual practice and the latter metaphorically, as in Holmes's 'mirror with a memory'. The use of memory in connection with metaphors long precedes the invention of photography. One of the earliest recorded and longest-lived metaphors for memory is that of writing. Photography, in name, is also related to writing – the term literally means 'light writing' or 'drawing' in Greek.

Plato used a 'wax tablet' metaphor for memory in *Theaetetus*. In this dialogue, Socrates declares that wax tablets of different sizes and capacities in different individuals are a gift of Mnemosyne,[2] the personification of memory and the mother of all Muses (Plato 1987: 99f.). The wax tablet as a technical device can be referred to as the medium. Writing became widely recognised as a superior practice or surrogate for memory, and the metaphoric association of writing and memory continues to this day. The superiority of writing to memory became commonly accepted during the nineteenth century when historiography began to privilege written sources produced in temporal proximity to events above all other source material.

The first form of the concept of memory, metaphors for memory, presents the workings of individual memory as in Plato's wax tablet. If this metaphor helps us understand memory, it is positive; if it leads to erroneous understandings of how the mind works, it is negative. The second form of the concept of memory, memory as a metaphor, does not aspire to explain memory. It uses memory to explain or even construct other phenomena, as in Holmes's 'mirror with a memory'. This approach might also be assessed according to utility. Holmes's analogy emphasises his conviction about the importance of photography.

The use of metaphors for memory aspires to give meaning to individual memory, yet memory continues to be one of the most complex and least understood of human faculties. Cognitive neuroscientists themselves claim only a fragmentary understanding of the workings of memory (Kandel and Schwartz 2000). Perhaps due to such uncertainty, this most complex human capacity has been, and continues to be, associated with simpler objects in order to make it comprehensible. In addition to the wax tablet, phosphorous, labyrinths, archives, phonographs, photographs, notepads, computers, holograms and looms have all been used as metaphors for memory (Draaisma 2000).

The Memory Boom and the Obscurity of History

Historians and social scientists are seldom concerned with explaining how memory functions and how metaphors for memory have been created.

Nevertheless, numerous scholars use memory as a metaphor, and this points to a crisis in the disciplines. History and the past have progressively lost importance in politics, art and public discourses, even among historians themselves. Memory has come to occupy much of the intellectual space vacated by history. Within the context of what has become known as the 'memory boom', historians and academics in cultural studies have widely exploited memory as a metaphor, with politicians and artists having made significant contributions. Within this contemporary context, the memory boom is propagated as an attribute of collectivities. This phenomenon is commonly traced to pioneering studies undertaken in the inter-war years by Maurice Halbwachs, who coined the phrase *la mémoire collective* (collective memory). To an extent, Halbwachs's reference (1992) was singular in so far as it referred to what an individual does within a social context or social settings: '[A] person remembers only by situating himself with the viewpoint of one or several groups and one or several currents of collective thought' (ibid.: 33). This conception of collective memory explained individual thought as non-essential and as constructed in and by social contexts.

Although Halbwachs was the first academic to collectivise memory, memory had an earlier and intriguing metaphoric use as the essential possession of a group. In 1902, the intellectual Hugo von Hofmannsthal referred to the 'collected force of the secret line of ancestors within us, the towering layers one upon another of accumulated super-individual memory' (Heumann 2001: 76).[3] The phrase was cited by Theodor Schieder (1978) in a discussion about historical consciousness. Schieder discounted Hofmannsthal's use of the memory metaphor, declaring that Hofmannsthal was probably referring to history in the sense of 'events that influence later generations, leave wounds ... and represent real or imagined climaxes', that is, popularly believed narratives as opposed to academic narratives, which Schieder termed 'knowledge of the past ... filtered through the process of artistic recreation and ... the scientific method' (ibid.: 2).

But this calls into question Hofmannsthal's use of the word *geheimnisvoll* (secretive or mysterious), with reference to the ancestors, and the unmistakably essential character of his language. Events that influence later generations are no more mysterious or secret than the work of historians. Even if partly a rhetorical flourish, Hofmannsthal's choice of the term *geheimnisvoll* and his use of emotive essentialist language may be a reference to memory's capacity to devalue the mundane practice of history (K. Klein 2000).

A former member of the Nazi Party, Schieder authored the infamous *Polendenkschrift*. This text demanded the elimination of Jews from Polish cities and provided the basis for the *Generalplan Ost*, the notorious National Socialist plan to create a new order in Central and Eastern Europe (Ebbinghaus and Roth 1992). In 1971, Schieder was awarded the high order Pour le Mérite für Wissenschaften und Künste. Prior to this period, the Holocaust had not been a crucial issue in European historiography or politics; nevertheless, in the era subsequent to the linguistic turn, it became central to the reassessment of history as the bitter past. Parallel to the beginning of the memory boom in the 1980s, the Holocaust became the 'test case of critiques of the historical discourse' (K. Klein 2000).

It has often been said that the Holocaust poses a challenge as 'the limit case of historiographical theory' (Dintenfass 2000). In much of the West, the Holocaust has become sacrosanct to the point that – despite the proclaimed sanctity of Enlightenment concepts such as freedom of expression – Holocaust denial has been made illegal. This process began with the Austrian *Verbotsgesetz 1947* (Prohibition Act 1945). Following an interlude, additional measures have been enacted since the mid-1980s, including the ban of Holocaust denial in Germany (cf. J.-W. Müller in this volume).[4] Despite the legitimacy afforded by legal recognition, it has been asserted that the Holocaust is somehow unrepresentable and thus presents a special challenge to traditional forms of historical narration (Friedländer 1992).

Yet the Holocaust is neither more nor less representable than any other event. The Holocaust does not problematise history; what it does is illustrate just how problematic all history is. In addition to the Holocaust, significant recent tests for European historiography include the wider Second World War, repressive communist pasts and ignominious colonial pasts. No one past event is easier to represent than another. All but the last of these categories have achieved a quasi-sacred and concomitant debated status following the fundamental transformation of the continent since 1989. The last category, colonial pasts, remains almost entirely in oblivion in European narratives. This is the case although colonialism endured for centuries and reverberates through the present. It may be that these pasts have indeed become the 'detail of history in general' that Jean-Marie Le Pen believed gas chambers were to the particular history of the Second World War.

Those who deny the Holocaust ironically profess the very same aspiration to 'reconstruct past reality' (Evans 1997: 249) as do the defenders of history, such as Richard Evans, Gertrude Himmelfarb, Lynn Hunt and Omer Bartov. The explosion of the memory industry was an ironic repudiation of the efforts of these figures, confirming the central importance of the linguistic turn for historiography. The vigorous rise of memory, nevertheless, offered an alternative to disempowered and divided history. While debates focusing on history have thrived, memory as it pertains to the masses has been, and continues to be, applied in an all-encompassing, plurally possessed discourse. The latter assumes the essentially sacred characteristics of history prior to its contextualisation within the framework of the linguistic turn and the reassessment of historiography as a genre (H. White 1973). The memory industry does not simply imply a step forward in historiography; it also results in a step backward.

Having undergone exponential expansion in this context, collective memory is often admittedly diffuse and imprecise. It lacks both the academic standards of history and the openness to criticism and self-criticism that history came to embody. Starting in the 1980s, memory as a collective possession has been associated with objects, street names, ceremonies, legends, myths, laws, rules, standardised procedures and records. It is 'even [found] in historical works' (Winter 2000; see also Schudson 1992). The use of memory as a metaphor has since been combined with numerous concepts, including trauma, narration, identity, culture, society, communication and the public. It is even possible to identify discourses of 'post-memory' (Hirsch 1997). Certain scholars do consider these applications of memory, but their arguments are weak (K. Klein 2000), and discourse on the topic tends to take place in an arbitrary manner. Doyens of the field such as Aleida Assmann and Jay Winter have pressed for a specification of the meaning of memory in order to develop further research (Winter 2000). To borrow the phrase of Kerwin Lee Klein (2000), the result of these processes has been the growth of a 'memory industry', which might be said to rival that of Kodak a century earlier. Klein's fundamental criticism of the use of memory as a metaphor is that it represents little more than a veiled, mystic/religious attack upon the discipline of history. Interestingly, Marianne Hirsch (1997) comes close to this religious interpretation in her description of post-memory as an illusive object of desire, sought after by a generation that attempts to capture, as in transubstantiation, the often-unenviable experiences of a previous generation in their entirety.

Although memory as a metaphor (to interpret collective phenomena) and photography as a metaphor (to explain individual mnemonic capacity) are spurious concepts, photographs may prove to be useful tools in the practice of historiography. Following its invention, photography was perceived to contribute significantly to processes that widened the gulf between experience and expectation. In addition, its apparent capacity to transgress time meant that it could be a means to bridge this same gulf. It became one of the most significant techniques of precise representation and scientific documentation of the nineteenth and twentieth centuries.

The Holocaust

Of the more than two million photographs that, it is estimated, document the Holocaust, one in particular stands out. A single child portrayed in this image has become the 'poster boy' of the Holocaust (see Hirsch 2002). This photograph was found in the photographic appendix of the 75-page *Stroopbericht* (Stroop Report), a daily account written by Jürgen Stroop, the commander of the German forces responsible for the liquidation of the Warsaw Ghetto. After systematically burning it down, literally smoking the Jews from their bunkers, he documented this act in a report to his commander, Heinrich Himmler. The report was triumphantly entitled *Es gibt keinen jüdischen Wohnbezirk in Warschau mehr!* (The Jewish living area in Warsaw is no more!). The appendix is a 48-page *Bildbericht* (photographic report) containing 52 photographs. On its thirteenth page appears an image (Figure 7.3) entitled 'Mit Gewalt aus Bunkern herausgeholt' (Forcefully hauled from the bunkers), which was taken between 19 April and 16 May 1943 (Stroop 1943). According to the documentation of the US Holocaust Memorial Museum, the girl on the far left is identified as Hanka Lamet, and the woman next to her as her mother, Matylda Lamet Goldfinger. The boy with a sack on his shoulder has been identified as Leo Kartuzinsky, and the woman in the foreground as Chana Zeilinwarger. The 'poster boy' in shorts has alternatively and inconclusively been identified as Arthur Domb Semiontek, Israel Rondel, Tsvi Nussbaum and Levi Zeilinwarger. The soldier holding the submachine gun is SS-Unterscharführer Josef Blösche.

This photograph has become an iconic image of the Holocaust. It is used repeatedly on the covers of popular and scholarly books and has appeared in fictional and documentary films, novels, works of poetry, CD-ROMs,

FIGURE 7.3 'Mit Gewalt aus Bunkern herausgeholt'. Source: *Bildbericht* of the Stroop Report (Stroop 1943).

brochures, paintings, etc. (Hirsch 2002). Although it is not often acknowledged, the photograph is from a National Socialist document that celebrates criminal acts as heroic accomplishments. In this image, the sense of evil is enhanced by the evident pride of the armed, elite soldiers as they herd civilians – mostly women and children – from a bunker to their death. Although the photograph was taken from the perpetrators' gaze, the humanity of their victims is amplified, whereas the stern and disgusted faces of Blösche and the Germans are dehumanised. Looking at their victims as vermin, the soldiers become vermin. While this image is not important solely on the grounds of its ubiquity, its ubiquity may well be due to the importance of its visual message.

The Second World War

A second image of holocaust is an allegorical depiction of *Güte* (Goodness) on the tower of the City Hall of Dresden. In a photograph taken by Richard Peter in 1945, the statue, an early twentieth-century sandstone sculpture by August Schreitmüller, looks and gestures over the skeleton of the city. In the night between 13 and 14 February 1945, 1,500 British and US bombers dropped around half a million bombs on Dresden. A firestorm ensued in which temperatures rose to 1,500° C, and people were literally sucked into the fire. The number killed is a question of intense and often polemic debate. The photograph (see Figure 7.4 opposite), which appears in Peter's *Dresden: Eine Kamera klagt an* (1950), reveals a devastated cityscape, burnt and devoid of life, juxtaposed with an angelic representation of goodness unconscious of the holocausts that were imminent. The city is petrified. The image challenges Gerhart Hauptmann's claim (1974: 1205f.) that '[t]hose who had forgotten how to cry relearned it as Dresden disintegrated, this joyous morning star of youth illuminated the world until that point'.[5] Dresden was not a new occurrence, nor did it endure as a warning or an example. This photograph perhaps symbolizes a final conclusion and suggests the terrible and surreal banality that led to the crimes Europe committed against itself.

Communist Repression

As a result of economic and social crises within Czechoslovakia in the early 1960s, CSSR Central Committee member Ota Šik led a technocratic opposition that proposed the social market economy as an alternative to the planned economy. Calls for economic reform were accompanied by political and artistic liberalisation. Examples include the rehabilitation of Franz Kafka and the fundamental debates on the possibility of Marxist alienation of the workers within a socialist society. A major forum for discussion was

FIGURE 7.4 August Schreitmüller's sandstone sculpture *Güte*. Photographed in 1945 by Richard Peter (1950).

the literature review *Literární Noviny* (circulation 140,000). Following the brutal suppression of student strikes, leadership was transferred to Alexander Dubček, who began a course of widespread reform and liberalisation in a movement that he described as 'socialism with a human face' and for which he received popular support. The 'Prague Spring' was born.

Criticism emerged from the Soviet Union and other communist states, and orthodox Czechoslovak communists demanded intervention to quell the 'counter-revolution', culminating in an invasion by Warsaw Pact armies during the night of 20 August 1968. Figure 7.5 shows a man, Emil Gallo, baring his chest while facing a tank in Bratislava on the first day of the invasion of Czechoslovakia. Captured by the sports photographer Ladislav Bielik, who remained anonymous until 1989 due to fear of reprisal, the image was smuggled out of the CSSR. The photograph received worldwide attention. This photograph tells a story of Europe in which an exceptional individual refuses to bow to power. Wielding neither cobblestones nor a Molotov cocktail, Gallo protests by offering himself to injury, thus presenting his oppressors with his own act of resistance.

FIGURE 7.5 'The Bare-Chested Man in Front of an Occupying Tank', Bratislava, 21 August 1968 © Ladislav Bielik.

The Colonial Crime

The themes of the Holocaust, the Second World War and the era of communist suppression have become transcendent, sense-giving and at times essential components of a pan-European historical consciousness. These events have assumed importance across Europe and beyond. Their influence is not limited to spaces connected directly with the specific events of which they are constituted: for example, there are Holocaust museums and institutes in Sweden, and a segment of the Berlin Wall is in Brussels. In contrast, Europe's colonial pasts have often been reduced to near oblivion in former colonising states and remain absent in European states that were not directly involved in colonialism as part of the European narrative. This is true even in works that emphasise Europe's most ignominious pasts. In essence, colonialism is a void in European historiography. The last of the images of Europe's dark pasts to be presented here is a photograph that is representative of the colonial pasts (Figure 7.6).

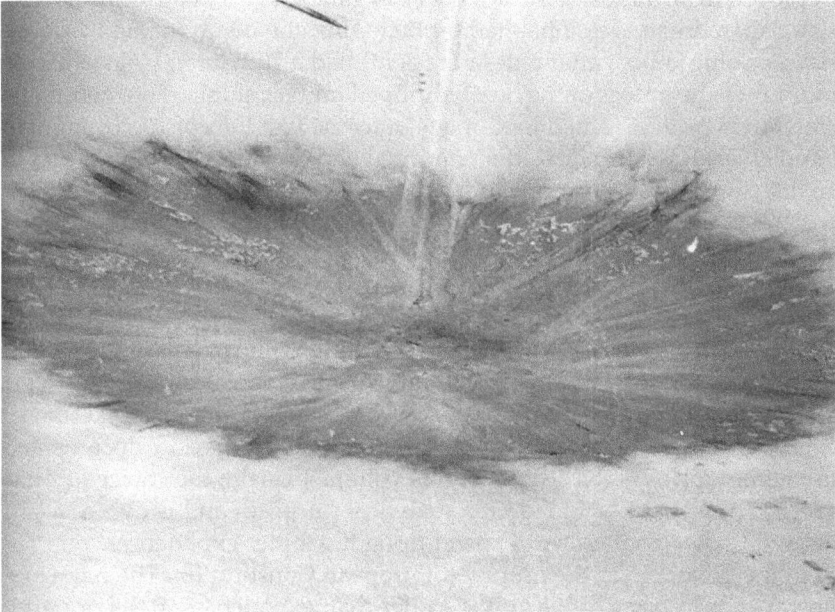

FIGURE 7.6 *Gerboise bleue.* Source: Anonymous.

The notion of a 'civilising mission', deemed absurd by Joseph Roth 70 years ago, is alive and well in France. This is evidenced by a bill of 23 February 2005 (see Jansen in this volume). This bill stipulated that '[s]chool courses should recognise in particular the positive role of the French presence overseas, notably in North Africa'.[6] In this volume Kevin Morgan provides a telling example of the absence of narratives of colonialism in France in the sphere of academia. Morgan notes that even in so seemingly comprehensive an exploration of the national memory as Pierre Nora's *Les Lieux de mémoire* (1984–92), Algeria and Indochina are barely mentioned. The absence of Algeria is surprising in a work edited by Nora, as his first monograph (Nora 1961), entitled *Les français d'Algérie*, was published the year before Algerian independence was declared in 1962. To cite Perry Anderson's memorable comment, what prevails is in fact *union sucrée* (see Morgan in this volume). This itself is an argument for critical history over memory. Similarly, despite citing Roth's question, 'Why then do the European states claim for themselves the right to spread civilization and manners to other continents, why not to Europe itself?' in the preface to his volume *Dark Continent*, Mark Mazower (1998) makes little mention of Europe's dark colonial pasts.

Upon his return to the French presidency in 1958, Charles de Gaulle accelerated the already substantial French weapons programme, and on 13 February 1960 France detonated its first atom bomb in *Algérie française*.[7] Deployed in an atmospheric test near Reggane, a town in the central Algerian Sahara in an area inhabited by Bedouins, the bomb (named *Gerboise bleue*, or blue jerboa, after a desert rodent) had a 70-kiloton yield, roughly four times the power of the bomb dropped on Hiroshima. The man-made crater in Figure 7.6 is an image of one outcome that Europe has brought to its colonies. It is a legacy seldom narrated and of which there continues to be little awareness in Europe today.

Conclusions

The Holocaust – interlaced with the wider context and events of the Second World War – and the repressive communist and colonial histories form the three or four of Europe's dark pasts confronted in this volume.[8] Like almost everything since the invention of the daguerreotype, they are documented in photographs. As the editors of this volume explain, the choice of these specific cases has been made for analytical purposes and is by no means essential. They contain and expand upon the 'bitter experiences' referred to in the preamble of the proposed European Constitution. The reference, however, is to pasts or narratives rather than experiences. Pasts or narratives of continents, polities or proto-polities are clearly defined entities as opposed to indeterminate experiences. The selection of photographs that tell stories of these pasts is in itself revealing. The first three events (the Holocaust, the Second World War and communist pasts) have produced numerous photographs that have been accorded iconographic value and have been republished widely. Photographs that critically document colonial pasts have not been vested with comparable iconic value.

Photographic images from the past have contributed to the production of myth and history, although they are often complex and may hold the plural meanings ascribed to Hofmannsthal's towering accumulated layers of memory. Photographs are not always as logical, rational and unified as science would demand. Instead, they are sensual like the events they document, themselves representing climaxes and contributing to narratives. As such, they are partial and incomplete. Taken from a specific viewpoint, they impart a selective vision. In addition, photographs are characterised by a verisimilitude with which they have been accorded, and in specific contexts they have been given iconic status.

Nevertheless, photographs are specifically abstractions and simplifications within the limits and boundaries of time and space – the time and duration of their production, and the primarily two-dimensional space that they occupy. They can also be perceived to be bridges of time and space. In these images, a number of time-space units are united. Three primary dimensions may exist: the present, in which a photograph is observed; the time of duration and the space of its production; and possibly, as with an architectural object, the times and spaces of its reproduction, restoration or disintegration. Photographs are thus the past(s), the present and the past(s) *in* the present. They connect on a sensual level, and this connection causes the viewer to analogise, equate and reflect. Some images, including those analysed above, may be said to do this for Europe's dark pasts and European historiography in opposition to memory. The images might be termed mirrors from the past, and as projections they contribute to Europe's self-constructions. These images do not exist intrinsically but emerge non-essentialised during processes of self-reflection. Like Europe itself, they exist in tension and none are equivocal. They are also icons, beacons, symbols or points of reference in the discursive construction of individual memories in collectivities.

Notes

I thank the editors for including my essay in this volume and for the stimulating discussions during its production. I also owe my gratitude to K. N. Chaudhuri for his comments and suggestions. This chapter was completed within the framework of the FP6 research project EMEDIATE: Media and Ethics of the European Public Sphere from the Treaty of Rome to the 'War on Terror' (CIT2-CT-2004-506027) supported by the European Commission, as well as with research supported by the Ludwig Boltzmann Institute for European History and Public Spheres in Vienna.

1. The substrate of the daguerreotype was in fact an exquisitely polished and mirroring silver-plated sheet of copper.
2. It is no accident that 'Mnemosyne Atlas' was the title chosen by Aby Warburg for his unfinished project supporting the idea of the continued existence of antiquity in European culture. History would not promote such clear links between modernity and antiquity; at the very least, it should problematise them.
3. 'Aufgesammelten Kraft der geheimnisvollen Ahnenreihe in uns, die übereinander gethürmten Schichten der aufgestapelten überindividuellen Erinnerung.' The English translation is by the author of this chapter.
4. Countries with laws or penalties against Holocaust and genocide denial today include Austria (1945/1992), Belgium (1995/1999), Czech Republic (2001), France (1990), Germany (1985), Israel (1986), Italy (2007), Lichtenstein (1987), Luxembourg (1997), Poland

(1998), Romania (2002), and Switzerland (1993). During the German presidency of the European Union in 2007, a law prohibiting Holocaust denial was proposed on a pan–European Union scale. Following protests fearing the curtailment of civil rights, a compromise solution was reached in the form of the European Union Directive for Combating Racism and Xenophobia (2007).

5. 'Wer das Weinen verlernt hat, der lernt es wieder beim Nachgelassene Werke; Fragmente Dresdens. Dieser heitere Morgenstern der Jugend hat bisher der Welt geleuchtet.'

6. Loi française n° 2005-158 du 23 février 2005 portant reconnaissance de la Nation et contribution nationale en faveur des Français rapatriés. The law was submitted by right-leaning MPs, led by Christian Vanneste.

7. Jan Jansen notes in this volume that since the 1990s, French Algeria (*Algérie française*) has become the subject of increasingly fervid academic and public debates, conflicting politics of remembrance and hurried commemoration activities sponsored by state and non-state actors alike.

8. The phrasing 'three or four pasts', instead of 'four pasts', is used here to highlight the political and moral problematic involved in distinguishing the Holocaust from the Second World War. There are convincing arguments that the Holocaust cannot – and should not – be separated from the European war. Others claim rightly that the Second World War cannot be reduced to the Holocaust. See Heer et al. (2003).

Part II

REMEMBERING EUROPE'S DARK PASTS

Four Fields of Commemoration

Section 3

Remembering the Second World War

Chapter 8

REMEMBERING THE SECOND WORLD WAR IN WESTERN EUROPE, 1945–2005

Stefan Berger

In his speech in 2005 commemorating the sixtieth anniversary of the end of the Second World War, German Chancellor Gerhard Schröder made explicit the link between German responsibility for the war and Germany's willingness to work with its European partners for a better future. Schröder proudly recalled his invitation from French President Jacques Chirac to attend the D-Day commemorations in Normandy on 6 June 2004, as well as further invitations from the Polish president, Aleksander Kwaśniewski, to participate in the commemoration of 60 years of the Warsaw Uprising on 1 August 2004 and from Russia's Vladimir Putin to take part in the sixtieth anniversary celebrations of the end of the Second World War in Moscow on 9 May 2005. Schröder described these invitations as testimony to Germany's desire to build European structures to prevent Europe from being dominated again by war and tyranny. Similar attempts to link the Second World War to the task of building a common European home were made by many leading politicians across Europe in 2005. But the question remains, is the Second World War, beyond all political rhetoric, really a common European *lieu de mémoire* shared by the nations of Europe, or are there national differences in how the conflict is remembered? What do different memories of the war tell us about who is perceived as victim, perpetrator, hero and villain? Since the war divided the nations of Europe into allies and enemies, is not the memory of the war therefore necessarily divisive, pointing to a lack of unity and common purpose? Are there attempts to overcome such divisiveness and commemorate the war in ways which emphasise common ambitions and goals for the present?

Collective memories of the Second World War have been expressed in a variety of genres, including literature (both fiction and non-fiction), cinema,

---

Notes for this chapter are located on page 136.

television, monuments, music and popular culture. The discussion below uses examples from different genres to analyse the memory politics of the war in different European nation states. While Heike Karge's chapter in this volume focuses on Eastern Europe and Clemens Meier's contribution deals with Scandinavia, the following pages will concentrate on the Western European story. Here Western Europe includes everything from Ireland to West Germany in the north and Italy in the south, including Britain, the Netherlands, Belgium, Luxembourg, France, Switzerland, Austria and Spain.[1] The national experiences of each of these countries differed substantially, but we can still discuss them in three groups. The first group we will examine is that of the perpetrator countries: Germany, Austria (itself part of Germany between 1938 and 1945) and Italy. These countries bore responsibility for the outbreak of war and were allied to one another. Secondly, we will discuss the countries attacked and occupied by the Axis powers: France, Belgium, the Netherlands and Luxembourg. Britain will also be discussed here, although it was never occupied. Finally, we will reflect on collective memories of the war in the countries that were neutral in the conflict: Ireland, Spain and Switzerland.[2]

Returning to National Normality

The Second World War turned Europe upside down. It was an event of such earth-shattering significance and unprecedented violence that it affected even those countries that managed to stay neutral in the conflict. During and immediately after the end of the Second World War, Italian and German narratives radically questioned the national developments of their respective countries, which had culminated in fascism and war. Many of these critical voices belonged to Italians such as Piero Gobetti and Guido Dorso and Germans such as Helmuth Plessner and Alexander Abusch who had been exiled by their fascist governments. Some also belonged to those who had remained, such as Germany's Friedrich Meinecke and Italy's Emilio Lussu.[3] The most radical rethink of the dominant national narrative occurred in Austria. Under the conditions of Soviet occupation, leading post-war politicians and opinion-formers developed the idea of Austria as the first victim of Hitler's Nazi Germany.

This was a daring construction, given the overwhelming support of Austrians for the Anschluss of 12 March 1938, when Austria became annexed to the Third Reich, but the unanimity with which the idea was put forward meant that it worked. German-speaking Austrians began to develop a sense of national belonging that was separate from that of other German speakers. The state and its leading representatives did everything to develop independent national narratives. In 1946, the government published the *Red-White-Red-Book: Justice for Austria!* which included a host of documents allegedly demonstrating beyond reasonable doubt that Austria was the first victim of Nazism. In the late 1940s, during the Allied occupation, the government lavishly financed a movie, *1. April 2000*. Released in 1952, the film was a review of Austrian history with a positive gloss, emphasising Austria as a nation with a cosmopolitan culture, *Gemütlichkeit* (cosiness or homeliness) and, above all, a peaceful past (Gigerl 2006).

Yet the radical questioning of the national past in Austria had a clear apologetic function, namely, to distance Austria from any responsibility for the Second World War and its atrocities, in particular the Holocaust. In contrast, in Germany and Italy, the questioning of the national past was meant to foreground alternative conceptions of national history. But these critical voices were soon silenced by others who stressed that fascism and Nazism were not the logical conclusion of the national past but rather aberrations from a positively accentuated national history. The resistance against fascism was used to highlight the continued existence of a 'good' national tradition. In Germany, the memory of those responsible for the attempt on Hitler's life on 20 July 1944 was used to draw a distinction between evil Nazis and good Germans. The good Germans continued in the vein of the founder of the Reich, Bismarck. The Borussian reading of German history was still the most popular one in West Germany in the 1950s.

In Italy, the resistance was presented as carrying on the struggle of the nineteenth-century Risorgimento, the political and social movement for national unification. It was described as the 'second Risorgimento' in contrast to Italian Fascism, which was depicted as anti-Risorgimento. The resistance thus became the crucial building block on which a renewed Italian state could be rebuilt after 1945. Of course, the communist memory of the resistance was different from the memory of the Democrazia Cristiana (DC, Christian Democratic Party), with the former emphasising the continuities between fascism and the post-war Italian state. Such a communist reading of the resistance could also be found in the German Democratic Republic, but in the Federal Republic of Germany (FRG) and Austria it was almost entirely sidelined.

Not only were the traditional national narratives about the past salvaged in Germany and Italy, but the perpetrator nations remembered, above all, their own suffering and their own victims. In Germany and Austria, the memorialisation of the war followed very similar trajectories: the Wehrmacht soldiers, who had allegedly fought a heroic battle and were misled by devilish Nazi leaders, stood in the foreground of commemorations of war in the 1950s. In many post-war publications and films, but also on stamps, posters and other objects of 'banal nationalism' (Billig 1995), we encounter pictures of tired, wounded and disillusioned soldiers, of bombed-out cities, of treks of German refugees ethnically cleansed from East-Central and Eastern Europe, and stylised images of POWs behind barbed wire (Moeller 1996, 2000). The moral superiority of heroic German soldiers and POWs over their Soviet tormentors was portrayed in well-received novels published in the late 1950s, including Fritz Wöss's *Hunde, wollt ihr ewig leben?* and Heinz G. Konsalik's *Der Arzt von Stalingrad*, which were made into films. The courage and daring of the German U-boat crew and commander in Lothar-Gunther Bucheim's *Das Boot*, first published as a best-selling novel in 1973, helped to turn the 1981 movie version into an international success.

Even if anti-fascism had been an important ingredient in the German and Austrian memory of the Second World War immediately after 1945, the onset of the Cold War pushed anti-fascist memories into the background during the 1950s and especially marginalised the communist resistance to fascism. Ordinary Austrians and Germans and their suffering were now remembered – regardless of whether they had been supporters or opponents of Nazism. The burning Stephansdom in Vienna became a potent symbol of the status of Austria as a victim of the war. The official Austrian response to the Jewish Claims Conference in 1953 was that Austria had been an occupied country and that sole responsibility for the Holocaust lay with Germany. Although, under pressure from international public opinion, Austria was to make payments later on, unlike the FRG it never accepted any responsibility for the Holocaust (Lillteicher 2006).

In Italy, official memory policy also concentrated on Italian victims, above all the victims of German-occupied Italy after 1943, thereby highlighting the national struggle against a foreign enemy. The history of Italian fascism was presented as a struggle of the Italian people first against fascism and then against foreign occupants. The civil war which raged in Italy between fascists and anti-fascists was thus marginalised by assuming an anti-fascist consensus of the people against the fascist leadership and the puppet regime of Germany in the north after 1943. Roberto Rossellini's 1945 film *Roma, città aperta* captures perfectly this image of a people united against Nazi fascism. Unlike in Germany and Austria, therefore, anti-fascism remained a central ingredient of the Italian memory of the war, as it was constructed as uniting and not dividing the nation.

Remembering the nation's own victims went alongside widespread silence about those victims perceived as not belonging to the nation. This is particularly true for the victims of the Holocaust. The greatest crime of the National Socialist regime and its collaborators all over Europe was also arguably the least discussed in post-war memories of the war. Forgetting and sidelining the most problematic and criminal aspects of the Second World War led to policies which were often advantageous to the perpetrators of war crimes across Europe (Frei 2006).

In those countries attacked and occupied by the Axis powers, we find a combination of victim narratives and heroic resistance narratives, which together pushed stories of collaboration out of public memory and into private remembrance. In some cases, this continued well into the 1970s and 1980s. The prevalence of post-war patriotic narratives in France, Belgium and the Netherlands often marginalised more critical assessments of the wartime experience (Lagrou 2000). Following a brief initial phase during which those deemed to be collaborators were tried before national courts, shamed and in some cases executed (Henke and Woller 1991), attention shifted to forms of memorialisation which were less nationally divisive. In France, in the autumn of 1944, approximately 20,000 women were shorn and paraded through the streets of their hometowns and villages for having had sexual relations with German soldiers (Virgili 2003). About 140,000 persons were tried before ad hoc law courts in 1944 and early 1945, and around 1,500 of the accused collaborators were sentenced to death and executed (Rousso 2001). Gaullist and communist resistance narratives alike shared the perception of Vichy as a historical aberration. The photographs of the 'liberation' emphasised national unity and ex-territorialised the (German) enemy.

In Belgium, the considerable sympathies of the Flemish movement for German National Socialism were rarely discussed. Instead, the memory of the Second World War was widely connected to the memory of the First World War and presented in terms of the collective resistance of the entire Belgian people against a barbarous and brutal foreign enemy. Fort Breendonk, which was situated between Brussels and Antwerp and had been used as an SS internment camp for political prisoners and Jews, became a powerful symbol of the suffering of the Belgian nation. In similar ways, the destruction of Rotterdam by German planes became the most potent symbol of the suffering of innocent Dutch victims during the Second World War. As Benoit Majerus (n.d.) argues, the notion of collective suffering was vitally important for Luxembourg's post-war self-legitimation: from 1945 to the present day, the Second World War has been its crucial foundational myth (ibid.).[4] The official national master narrative has firmly established the idea that the smallest European country made the biggest sacrifices during the war. It managed to sideline almost completely the importance of the Middle Ages for Luxembourg's national identity, despite the fact that the Middle Ages had still been the vital anchor point for national historical consciousness during the inter-war period. Luxembourg as a nation of martyrs, victims and resistance fighters has been memorialised on stamps, in street names, in publications such as Paul Weber's 1948 volume *Geschichte Luxemburgs im Zweiten Weltkrieg* and in specific monuments, such as the Musée Nationale de la Résistance (1956) in Esch/Alzette or the Monument National de la Solidarité (1971) in Luxembourg City (ibid.).

Britain was the only country in Europe which fought the war from beginning to end and was never occupied. Its own resistance and collaboration stories come from the Channel Islands, the only part of the British Isles occupied by the Germans, yet this was such a small part of the overall story that it had no significance with regard to memories of the

Second World War (Bunting 2004; Sanders 2005). The dominant storyline was that of Britain's 'finest hour' – the moment when the nation pulled together to 'stand alone' against what seemed to be an 'almighty' enemy. Britain, of course, never stood alone. Even between 1940 and 1941, many Commonwealth states fought alongside the small island on the western periphery of Europe. Proud memories of the war – the spirit of Dunkirk, the Battle of Britain, Churchill's rousing wartime speeches – served to create support for a post-war reconstruction of Britain that emphasised social justice, and this mood swept the Labour Party into office in 1945. However, one outcome of Britain's unique experience was to set British memories apart from those of continental Europeans, creating a strong mental barrier against a common European memory of the war.[5]

In neutral countries, the collective memory did not have to suppress direct collaboration with occupying armies and military authorities. Nonetheless, there were problematic aspects of the wartime record which became deeply buried in distant corners of the official national memory culture. As Jerrold Packard (1992) states in his comparative study of the European neutrals in the Second World War, no country had remained totally neutral: all had to make complex compromises, most of which threatened their neutrality. The Swiss memory discourse after 1945 was totally dominated by the image of a small country willing and able to defend itself against external enemies. One of the most popular national leaders was the head of the Swiss army, General Henri Guisan, and the war years were widely portrayed as a period of intense Swiss patriotism and solidarity. Such views were accompanied by the idea of a charitable Switzerland, home of the Red Cross, which gave asylum to the victims of Nazi Germany. Until the mid-1970s, the Swiss state was extraordinarily active in preventing a different memory of the Swiss war years from emerging. It restricted access to archives and documents, sponsored official publications and even intervened to prevent and sabotage research plans which might contradict the official memory of the Second World War. Switzerland as a nation had a long tradition of neutrality, and its memory discourse on the Second World War therefore fitted neatly with its construction of national tradition and identity (Marchal 2006).

This was not the case for Spain, Portugal and Ireland, the three other Western European nations that remained neutral in the conflict in Western Europe. The Spanish dictator Francisco Franco had emerged victorious from the Spanish Civil War with the help of Nazi Germany and Fascist Italy. During the war, at least up until 1943, the regime emphasised its closeness to the Axis powers; indeed, Franco's willingness to join the Axis powers early in 1940 was prevented only by Hitler's unwillingness to forge such an alliance (Bernecker 1989: 153ff.; Leitz 2000). In 1941, Spain sent an army of volunteers, the Blue Division, to fight alongside the German Wehrmacht against the Soviet Union. After 1945, this was a deeply problematic memory that needed to be suppressed. Instead, the Franco regime put considerable resources into proving to the Western world that Spain had been a strictly neutral country throughout the entire war. The opening of the borders for between 20,000 to 35,000 Jewish refugees was played up as a Spanish attempt to protect European Jews (Rother 2001). Under the conditions of the Cold War, this sanitised official picture of Spain and its actions during the Second World War was successful, and the US provided massive economic help and military protection in a treaty of 1953. The memory of the Blue Division could be used officially to legitimate the ongoing struggle of Spain as part of the Western world against the evil empire of the Soviet Union. The martyrdom of ordinary Spanish soldiers in the war and in Soviet POW camps became a theme of many books and films.

If Spain had been clearly biased in the direction of the Axis powers, Ireland was biased towards the Allies, in particular Britain. The Irish case, though, is complicated by the fact that the British had been the 'official' enemies of the Irish Free State, and the wartime cooperation over intelligence and defence matters was long kept secret, contrasting with a more popular perception in Ireland (and Britain) that Irish policies were sympathetic to the Axis powers (Girvin and Roberts 1999; Ó Drisceoil 2006). Neutrality was justified by all Irish politicians due to the young nation's sovereignty and the strength of anti-British feeling. Open support for Britain, it was argued, might well lead to civil war. Historiographical writing on Ireland and its role in the Second World War did not begin until the 1970s. Research over the next 30 years has revealed the full extent of Irish-British wartime collaboration, but work on the specific theme of the memorialisation of the Second World War remains rare. This is striking, given that up to 200,000 Irishmen from the Republic of Ireland volunteered to contribute to the Allied war effort.

The 1960s and After: Revising National Master Narratives

The various attempts in Europe to prevent the war from compromising the diverse national storylines were successful, but only in the short term. As Richard Bosworth ([1993] 1994) has rightly pointed out, the memory of the Second World War possessed such an overwhelming ethical force that it led to traumatisation, which in turn favoured silences and myths. However, in the 1960s and 1970s, many of these myths were questioned, and there were calls to end the silences surrounding particular themes of the Second World War, above all the Holocaust and the issue of collaboration (ibid.). In Germany, the repercussions of the Eichmann trial in Jerusalem in 1961–2, the Frankfurt Auschwitz trials between 1963 and 1965, the Fischer controversy in the early 1960s over Germany's responsibility for the First World War, the premiere of Rolf Hochhuth's drama *Der Stellvertreter* in

1963 and the screening of films such as Bernhard Wicki's *Die Brücke* in 1959 all contributed to a climate in which traditional national narratives were questioned. The student revolt of the late 1960s, which made the Nazi past a major topic, called for a new FRG that would rely on different constructions of the national past from what had emerged in the Adenauer years (Gilcher-Holtey 2001: 56ff.).

In Austria, the 1960s saw at least a partial revision of the victim theory. The 1961 drama *Der Herr Karl* by Helmut Qualtinger and Carl Merz portrayed the average Austrian's cynical functionalisation of the Nazi past. When protests about the anti-Semitic and neo-Nazi remarks of a Viennese professor of history, Taras Borodajkewycz, led to the death of Ernst Kirchwegger, a communist resistance fighter, a wave of anti-Nazi demonstrations took place in Austria in 1965. However, in the early 1970s several trials against concentration camp guards in Austria ended in acquittals, provoking storms of international protest. In 1974, the popular *Neue Kronenzeitung* published a 42-part series, 'The Jews in Austria', that was full of anti-Semitic stereotypes. The letters to the editor that followed were still more anti-Semitic (Pollak 2003).

Above all, it was the Waldheim debate of 1986 that confronted a wider Austrian public with the issue of Austria as a perpetrator nation. The controversy demonstrated the depth of the divide between those who continued to defend Austria's wartime record and those who were willing to come to a more self-critical interpretation of the war (Gruber 1991). In a cathartic process that continued throughout the 1980s, mainstream public opinion increasingly internalised the idea of Austrian responsibility for the war and the Holocaust. During the 1990s, a series of Holocaust memorials was erected in Vienna, symbolising this significant turn in Austrian memory culture (Uhl 2008).

In Italy as well, a far more critical reading of the national past had come to the fore during the 1960s. Some historians now interpreted Italian Fascism as an outcome of the Risorgimento, rather than its antithesis.[6] Hence, the traditional Italian national narrative was being severely questioned. At the same time, the unity of the resistance narrative was shattered by the increasing insistence of communist narratives that the struggle against the Italian state had to continue. The memorial discourse of the Partito Comunista Italiano (PCI, Italian Communist Party) emphasised the continuities between fascism and the post-war Italian state. Thus, a PCI poster for the twentieth anniversary of the end of the Second World War famously read 'La Resistenza continua!' (The Resistance continues). A class interpretation was thereby juxtaposed with a national interpretation of the resistance. The Italian Republic was faced with a serious crisis of legitimacy, as its foundational myths were increasingly challenged. It could no longer present itself as the outcome of a unified anti-fascist struggle that perpetuated the positive traditions of the Risorgimento and had the support of all social classes. The political attempts to come to some form of 'historical compromise' between the DC and PCI had their origins in this crisis of the 1970s. In all of the perpetrator nations, the radical questioning of the reconstituted traditional national narratives led to significant breaks with the dominant national storylines during the late 1950s and 1960s. The changing memory of the Second World War has therefore been responsible for a delayed break with traditional national narratives.[7]

During the 1960s and 1970s, the countries that had been occupied by German troops during the Second World War also underwent major debates focusing largely on the extent and character of collaboration with Nazi Germany. The older heroic resistance stories were now increasingly criticised as the extent of collaborationist activities became clear through new research and greater media attention. In France, starting in the early 1970s, the public discourse clearly shifted to a recognition of the widespread support within occupied France for the Vichy government. Historians at the Institut d'Histoire du Temps Présent (IHTP) were influential in re-examining the years of occupation (Flood and Frey 2000: 63). It was no longer only the Germans and the SS who were the bad guys in the narrative. The infamous massacre of civilians in the village of Oradoursur-Glane was now remembered increasingly as an atrocity committed by SS members who had been recruited from the Alsace. Fellow Frenchmen, not Germans, had committed the crime against their own countrymen, highlighting the divisions within wartime France.[8]

In Belgium, the memory of the Second World War increasingly became a weapon in the struggle between the Flemish and the Walloon parts of the country. In Wallonia, the resistance against the German occupation was glorified, and examples of Flemish collaboration with the Nazis were cited as evidence of the treacherous character of the Flemish. In Flanders, the persecution of collaborators was widely portrayed as a witch-hunt, and collaboration was often justified as a means to protect the nation from the excesses of German occupation policies (Beyen 2002: 99ff.). It was only in the early 1980s that a television series, *The New Order*, portrayed a more complex picture of Belgian resistance and collaboration, sparking a further round of self-critical investigations about the place of the Second World War in Belgium's national history.

In the Netherlands, Lou de Jong's popular 1960s television series, *De Bezetting* (The Occupation), screened in 21 episodes, portrayed the overwhelming majority of the Dutch people as courageous resisters. It was only in the 1970s and 1980s that more critical voices highlighted the extent of Dutch collaboration with the Nazi occupiers. Among them was the historian Johan C. H. Blom, who thoroughly researched the prevalence of various forms of accommodation made to comply with the German occupiers. Furthermore, the active cooperation of the population in rounding up Dutch Jews was now documented. Few Western European countries saw such a major decimation of its Jewish population as the Netherlands, where 75 per cent of Jews perished in death camps (compared to 25 per cent in France and 40 per cent in Belgium). These figures stand in marked contrast to the images of resistance to the Holocaust in the Dutch collective memory. After all, Anne Frank and the icon of the dockworker, symbolising the spontaneous strike movement in February 1944 against the deportation of Dutch Jews, indicate the importance of the image of the 'good' Dutch people to the memory of the war. It is thus understandable that revisionist accounts of the Netherlands' wartime experience caused considerable pain and anguish in Dutch society (de Haan 1997).

During the 1960s and 1970s, Luxembourg saw no real break with the self-legitimating narratives of the immediate post-war years, but even here some cracks appeared in the facade of national unity. The divisions between resistance fighters and those recruited to the German Wehrmacht provoked memory clashes, which led to a scandal in the 1970s when the representatives of those who had been *enrôlés de force* used the term 'died for the fatherland' on a central memorial dedicated to the memory of both the resistance and Wehrmacht soldiers. Since then, the competing memories of both groups have at times badly divided society in Luxembourg (Majerus n.d.).

It was more generally during the 1970s and 1980s that the memory of the Holocaust came increasingly to the fore in Western Europe. Prior to this time, the Jewish experience had tended to be overshadowed by national narratives. Only a few institutions had recorded the specific wartime experiences of Jews, notably the Wiener Library in London and the Centre de Documentation Juive Contemporaine in Paris. Members of the surviving Jewish communities were often crucial in developing a memorial culture. In Belgium, for example, the first 'monument for the Jewish martyrs' was erected in 1962 by the Belgian Association for Deported Jews. In many countries, the Jewish experience was nationalised, that is, Jewish suffering and victimhood were represented as national suffering and victimhood. In France, for example, many of the memorials to the deported, such as the Mémorial National de la Déportation (Struthof camp near Strasbourg, 1960) or the Mémorial des Martyrs de la Déportation (Paris, 1962), do not differentiate between those deported for political reasons or due to racial background. Hence, the deportation of the French Jews is thematised only in the context of the deportation of French men and women. A specifically Jewish memory of the Holocaust and the war has often been downplayed (Stone 2004).

In West Germany, as Wulf Kansteiner has pointed out, it was not only the screening of the American television series *Holocaust* in 1979 which brought the topic to mass public attention. A host of generational and political factors came together in the late 1970s to produce widespread interest in the darkest chapter of the German past (Kansteiner 2006: 115). British memorial culture around the Holocaust developed very late, a further indication of the view that the Second World War was fought on the continent by continentals. A central Holocaust museum opened as a permanent exhibition in the Imperial War Museum in London only in 2000, although other Holocaust centres, such as the one in Nottinghamshire, have existed since the 1990s.[9] In Luxembourg, Jewish experiences of the war and the Holocaust also played a comparatively minor role in the memory discourses of the war, arguably because of the centrality of the war for national identity. Up to this very day, heads of Luxembourg's government and state do not participate in commemorations of the Holocaust, in contrast to all other Western European countries. Luxembourg was also the last country in Western Europe to establish a commission to investigate what happened to confiscated Jewish property. The report was only published in the summer of 2009 (Majerus n.d.).

In Switzerland, a more self-critical memory discourse emerged in the 1960s. Alfred A. Häsler published a book in 1967 on Switzerland's wartime refugee policy in which he criticised the country for closing its borders and preventing a more substantial influx of refugees, especially Jewish refugees. Further critical introspection over the next 30 years culminated in 1996 with the establishment of the Independent Commission of Experts Switzerland – Second World War. The Commission's mandate was, among other things, to investigate the involvement of Swiss banks in dealing with gold and other assets stolen from European Jews. Its report documented the delivery of Swiss arms to Nazi Germany, the deportation of Jewish refugees back to Germany and the dismissal of Jews from Swiss companies. These findings contributed to the perception of Switzerland's wartime neutrality as being of dubious quality (Kreis 1985, 2000, 2002a, 2002b).

The move from Francoism to democracy in Spain in the mid-1970s was gradual and involved many compromises with the old order. Because of this, the past was deeply problematical and memory discourses were sidelined. Only during the 1990s and at the beginning of the twenty-first century have voices from within Spanish society begun to demand a more thorough de-Francoisation of Spanish society and a rehabilitation of the many victims of the dictatorship (Rey 2003). Attempts to remember the Republican victims of the civil war were accompanied by a renewed interest in the fate of Republican Spaniards in the Second World War. Thousands of Spanish Republicans were captured by the German Wehrmacht in occupied France and interned in concentration camps. The largest number, about 7,000, were imprisoned in Mauthausen near Linz. Reports about their fate, such as that produced by writer Jorge Semprún (captured as a member of the French resistance in 1943 and imprisoned in Buchenwald), could not be published in Spain until the late 1970s well after the change in government. Because of the general silence of memory politics for the next two decades, it is arguably only in the last decade that debates on public memory have begun to reach a wider audience.

The 1980s and 1990s: A Return of the Nation?

By the end of the 1970s, memories of the Second World War had been radically transformed across much of Western Europe. They had moved from the apologias of traditional national narratives to more self-critical storylines, which nonetheless remained overwhelmingly national. We hardly ever encounter transnational perspectives on the war.

The only democratic countries to experience no significant changes to the memory culture of the Second World War during the 1960s and 1970s were Luxembourg and Britain. In both countries, heroic and positive memories of the war and remembrances of solidarity in suffering continue to dominate memory discourses up to the present day. In Britain, wartime films about the country's 'finest hour' have been part and parcel of Saturday afternoon programming on all television channels. *Dad's Army*, one of the most popular television series ever, depicting the adventures of the Home Guard during the Second World War, was first shown on British television between 1968 and 1977. It confirmed the idea of a plucky, if somewhat chaotic, British nation facing a continental enemy. Memorialising a 'good war' also meant that war did not have the same negative connotations that it had acquired on the continent by the late 1970s. This in turn facilitated the enthusiastic public support for the Falklands War in 1982. The outburst of war mania in Britain was greeted with considerable levels of disbelief and shock among the British left and in many continental European countries. But Margaret Thatcher's rhetorical fireworks, concentrating on a potent combination of nationalism and liberty, directly linked the maintenance of freedom and liberty for the people of the Falkland Islands to Britain's stance for freedom and liberty in the Second World War. In 1995, on the occasion of the fiftieth anniversary of V-E Day, the British media once again bombarded the British public with singularly positive images and memories of the war. In the 1990s, 10 per cent of all history titles published in Britain were on the Second World War (Mandler 2002: 102). At the beginning of the twenty-first century, a Kentish Ale called Spitfire is still being sold, and the topic of the 'home front' during the Second World War remains firmly embedded in the primary school national curriculum.

However, if Britain, among the major countries of Europe, had a uniquely unbroken and positive collective memory of the Second World War, in the 1980s and 1990s other nations in continental Western Europe once again developed a more positively accentuated national memory of the war. During this period in France, Henry Rousso and Eric Conan called for an end to the allegedly obsessive concern with the Vichy regime (Conan and Rousso 1998). They did so against the background of important juridical attempts to come to terms with collaborationism. The much publicised trials of Paul Touvier and Maurice Papon and the murder of René Bousquet in

1993 drew renewed attention to the degree of French collaboration during the Second World War. French participation in the Holocaust was publicly acknowledged for the first time in a 1995 speech by President Chirac in which he emphasised the active support of the French state for the murderous policies of the occupiers and described it memorably as a 'dette imprescriptible'. Yet at the same time, as the interest in Vichy reached a highpoint in French society, a positively accentuated national history celebrated a major comeback.[10] In Luxembourg, the narratives of the Second World War had already been thoroughly nationalised, and it was arguably only the development of a more critical historiography in the 1990s that produced self-critical accounts of the war. These appeared in publications on the topic and in exhibitions such as '... et wor alles net sou einfach' (2002) and 'Le grand pillage' (2005), both of which were held in the Luxembourg City History Museum. The foundation in 2003 of the University of Luxembourg and the setting up of the Centre de Documentation et de Recherche sur la Résistance might further such self-critical perspectives on the myths of the war years (Majerus n.d.).

Even in the perpetrator countries, revisionist accounts of the war tended to emphasise aspects which appeared to present the nation in a more positive light. In Italy, historian Renzo De Felice emphasised the differences between Italian Fascism and German Nazism, in particular stressing the former's opposition to the Holocaust. In relation to the Holocaust, Italian revisionists could also build on the narratives established after 1945, according to which anti-Semitism and racism were German phenomena. The laws for the defence of the Italian race from 1938 were conveniently forgotten, as was the genocidal war in Ethiopia in 1936, in which the use of poison gas had been widespread.[11] In Germany, the *Historikerstreit* (historians' dispute) raged over the possibility of comparing the Holocaust with other wartime atrocities, including the ethnic cleansing of Germans from East-Central and Eastern Europe. Following the reunification of Germany in 1990, a new 'normalisation' patriotism has led to a variety of attempts to revive German national sentiment. The latest signs of this include the 2006 football championship tournament, when the media reported very widely and very positively on Germany's new-found patriotism.[12]

Ironically, at a time when revisionist accounts attempted to revise the more critical national perspectives on the war from the 1960s and 1970s, in Britain there was a significant attempt by military historian Corelli Barnett (1986, 1995) to portray the 'good war' as being simultaneously a 'foolish war', during and after which Britain had to pay dearly for its defence of Europe's liberty and freedom. Exhausted by the war, Britain lost its position as an imperial power and was put on a trajectory of economic decline. While this argument caused debate among historians and intellectuals, it remains doubtful whether it changed the wider public perception of the war as Britain's 'finest hour'.

What returned in the 1980s and 1990s, however, was rarely identical to the national apologias and narratives of the 1950s. Rather, the more self-critical discourses of the 1960s and 1970s opened the door to forms of memorialisation which attempted to accommodate greater complexity in the discourses about victims and perpetrators. More recent accounts of the war find it less necessary to think in terms of black and white, perpetrators and victims. There is greater exploration of the many shades of grey. Perhaps the best example of a major literary attempt to put all the different memories of war next to each other – thus allowing the reader to experience the very different faces of the war – is Walter Kempowski's multi-volume epic *Echolot* (Echo Sounder), a collection of documents recording life during the Second World War, which was published in German between 1987 and 2005 (Fritzsche 2002).[13] After reunification, Germany not only went through normalisation nationalism in the 1990s but also witnessed debates about the crimes of the German Wehrmacht (Heer and Naumann 1995) and the Goldhagen debate (Rosenfeld 1999). As Bill Niven (2002) points out, Germany has had considerable successes in facing its National Socialist past. On the basis of such success, he suggests that a national discourse which also pays homage to national achievements cannot be roundly condemned.[14]

Towards the Europeanisation of Memories of the Second World War

As this brief survey of the memorialisation of the Second World War in Western Europe demonstrates, the memory of the war between 1945 and the present has remained to a very large extent in the realm of national memory. In comparing the national narratives that have been analysed here, a number of common themes emerge. First, in the post-war years, we encounter a strong desire to return to national normality after the upheavals of the war. To achieve this, the war had to be portrayed as a period of aberration and confusion, after which the nation returned to its 'normal' self. The emphasis on the nation's own suffering during the war, which needed to be overcome and 'healed', reinforced the sense of exceptionality. Secondly, for perpetrator and victim countries alike, stories of heroic resistance to indigenous and foreign fascisms were crucial so that national memory could return to national normality. Thirdly, the 1960s and 1970s were decades in which those traditional national narratives were in many cases severely questioned on the basis of a radical reinterpretation of the Second World War. The following elements were instrumental in allowing more critical memories of the war to emerge at that time: the recognition of the Holocaust as a major aspect of the war, the highlighting of the collaborationist strategies of governments in occupied Europe and the acknowledgement of the overwhelming support of the people of the per-petrator countries for their fascist governments. Fourthly, these more criti-cal narratives were in turn revised from the 1980s onwards in an attempt to re-establish more positive national narratives, although what returned in the 1980s and 1990s was significantly different from what had been overcome in the 1960s and 1970s. Hardly anywhere was there a simple return to national apologias. Instead, the most recent developments can be described in terms of a thorough historicisation, which aims at allow-ing for less dichotomous and more complex memories of the war years to emerge. The boom in memory history and memory studies has undoubt-edly contributed to these developments in no small measure.[15]

The way that the war has been memorialised with striking similarity in Western European nations raises the question of a common European mem-ory of the Second World War. As early as the 1950s, popular support for the project of a united Europe could build on memories of the war. French and German students removing border posts between their two coun-tries acted in the idealistic belief that a common European future would end the national conflicts of the past, the most devastating of which had been the Second World War. The European wars, and arguably none more than the one between 1939 and 1945, have often been used as the negative foil against which politicians have tried to build a united Europe (Duch-hardt and Kunz 1997). From Winston Churchill's Zurich speech of 1946 to the address given by the president of the European Commission, Jacques Delors, in Brugge in October 1989, numerous speeches on the theme of a 'united states of Europe' have referred back to the Second World War as the hour of truth, after which Europe had realised the need to come together as a federation or as a 'Europe of fatherlands', in de Gaulle's famous words. It is not by chance that the beginnings of the European Union can be located in the discussions of those exiled by fascism and war. Their immediate experience of the Second World War served as a catalyst for the idea of a united Europe. Unity was seen as the motor for securing peace on the continent, for allowing democracies to prosper in stable economic circum-stances and for providing a minimum amount of social welfare for all of its citizens. Such a Europe was also widely perceived as a 'third way' between the United States and the Soviet Union (Stephan 2002).[16]

However, the way in which a united Europe initially took shape was through an economic alliance. The European Economic Community (EEC) was meant to overcome the serious financial problems of reconstruction. The aim was to re-establish European nation states, not to overcome them (Milward 2000). Even when the economic project of the EEC gave way to the political project of the European Union (EU) in the 1970s and 1980s, the goal was to overcome practical difficulties faced by all European nation states. At that time, little attention was given to creating a common public sphere and a common culture with collective memories. It was arguably only during the 1980s and 1990s that the perception of Europe as a cultural project was set in motion by policy makers in Brussels and Strasbourg (Shore 2000).

Thus, there arose the idea that a united Europe needed a common sense of culture and history, or at least a minimum consensus about what constituted European culture and history. The Second World War and the Holocaust became crucial elements in a strategy to construct a sense of Europeanness. Included was the long-established use of the Second World War in bilateral national relations to further processes of reconciliation, most prominently between France and Germany starting in the 1950s and between Poland and Germany from the 1970s onwards. Individual countries, such as Italy, have actively linked the memory of the liberation at the end of the Second World War with the building of Europe. On the occasion of the fifty-seventh anniversary of Italian liberation in 2002, the official poster connected the (self-)liberation of Italy through the resistance to the formation of the post-war Italian Republic and the construction of the European Union by depicting not only the Italian national flag but also the flag of the European Union. Speaking in 2005 at the UN General Assembly in New York on behalf of the EU and a range of European countries, Sir Emyr Jones Parry, at the time the Permanent Representative of Britain to the UN, stressed the importance of an annual Holocaust remembrance day and highlighted the special place of such memorialisation for the cause of a united Europe: 'The significance of the Holocaust is universal. But it commands a place of special significance in European remembrance. It was in Europe that the Holocaust took place. And, like the United Nations, it is out of that dark episode that a new Europe was born.'[17] The military intervention in Yugoslavia in 1999 was justified by EU politicians such as Joschka Fischer with explicit reference to the historic lessons provided by the Holocaust.[18]

Quite apart from the functionalisation of European history by politicians, several organisations are trying to promote the Europeanisation of history writing and history teaching. Prominent examples include Euroclio, the Georg Eckert Institute for International Textbook Research and Eustory. Euroclio (the European Association of History Educators) was first conceived of at a pan-European meeting in Bruges on the learning and teaching of history in Europe that had been organised by the Council of Europe in 1991. Its foundational event took place a year later in Strasbourg in November 1992, and by 2001 it had 76 full and associated members from 43 countries (van der Leeuw-Roord 2001). The Georg Eckert Institute is the leading research institution studying the development of European textbooks.[19] Eustory is an international network coordinated by the Körber Foundation in Hamburg, whose members carry out history competitions for young people in their respective countries.[20] History scholars have come together to form European consortia such as EurhistXX or to participate in

European-wide programmes such as those financed by the European Science Foundation (ESF).[21] There are now European history MAs and PhDs, and the profession is discussing few themes with more vigour than how best to write European history.[22] In all of these discussions and organisations, the Second World War and the Holocaust are important themes. There seems to be widespread agreement that the events connected with both phenomena have a truly European dimension.

Comparative and transnational approaches to the history of the Second World War have become more prominent. They contend that the war should be seen as a contested memory site in a discursive field in which various national discourses intermingle. As Stefan Goebel (2001) has argued, it will be the task of future research to determine more precisely how such 'intersecting memories' worked. However, to this day, there exists no Second World War equivalent for Max Lejeune's renowned museum of the history of the First World War in Péronne at the Somme, which is truly comparative and international (Winter 2000). There is hope that Europe might move out of its phase in which European events and caesuras are discussed primarily with reference to nation states.[23] But the dilemma would then be to decide which version of history to recount for the benefit of which formulation of Europe (Speth 1999; Stråth 2005).

History was a crucial ingredient in the construction of national identities in the nineteenth and twentieth centuries, and, as we have seen above, at the beginning of the twenty-first century the EU has attempted to harness the power of the past for its own purposes. So far, European symbols and myths have remained relatively weak, as has been a sense of a common European history. And yet it seems questionable whether the memory of the Second World War and of the Holocaust can be turned into a European foundational memory or *lieu de mémoire*. The Second World War had global dimensions which cannot be reduced to Europe, and the Holocaust has arguably become the paradigmatic case for all genocides and mass crimes worldwide. The US Holocaust Memorial Museum in Washington, DC, the USC Shoah Foundation Institute and even the conference of Holocaust deniers in Tehran in 2006 clearly demonstrate that concern about the Holocaust is global.

Yet it is perhaps possible to go one step further and question whether historical consciousness should be moved from a national to a European plane at all. History as an anchor of identity has done much harm in conjunction with the idea of the nation.[24] Could it not do still more damage in conjunction with the concept of Europe? It might be fitting to remember Ulrich Beck's warning (1998: 261f.): 'What Europe is or should be must … not be conjured up from the past, but politically drawn up as political answers to questions about the future.'

Notes

1. As I was unable to obtain sufficient materials discussing its memorialisation of the Second World War, Portugal is not included in this chapter. The final version of this article was produced in the spring of 2007, and therefore any literature from 2007 onwards has generally not been included.
2. This chapter is deeply indebted to the contributions on many of these countries included in Flacke (2004b).
3. For Germany, see Berger (2003: 41ff.); for Italy, see Bosworth (1998: 37ff.).
4. I am grateful to Benoit Majerus for sending me this unpublished paper.
5. On the many different ways in which the Second World War dominated memory discourses in Britain after 1945, compare Connelly (2004) and Weight (2000).
6. Dennis Mack Smith's *Modern Italy: A Political History*, published in 1959, presented this argument in its clearest form and was influential within Italy.
7. This argument is discussed in greater detail in Berger (2005).
8. On all aspects of the complex memorialisation of this massacre, see Farmer (1999). It would be intriguing to compare this incident with other 'martyred villages', especially in Eastern Europe. For a study of the Romanian village of Treznea, where Hungarian troops committed a massacre, see Bucur (2002).
9. See http://www.holocaustcentre.net/.
10. On French developments in the 1980s and 1990s, see also Jackson (1999).
11. On the link between debates surrounding fascism and the Second World War and Italian nationalism in the 1990s, see Patriarca (2001).
12. The literature on the *Historikerstreit* is legion. See, for example, Evans (1989) and Berger (2003). A good example of the neo-national newspaper coverage on the football world championships is Leinemann (2006).
13. See also http://www.kempowski.de.
14. Contrary to Niven, my own publications (Berger 2003, 2005) have been more critical of 'normalisation' nationalism in the united Germany.
15. A paradigm change from 'society' to 'memory' has been postulated by Confino (2005a: 7).
16. See http://elib.uni-stuttgart.de/opus/volltexte/2003/1409/pdf/Band01.pdf. On the close relationship between the idea of Europe and the idea of peace more generally, see also von Plessen (2003). On the importance of memories of the Second World War to all democratic polities of Europe, see Wood (1999).
17. The EU Presidency Statement on Holocaust remembrance can be found at http://www.europa-eu-un.org/articles/en/article_5224_en.htm.
18. Critical of such blatant functionalisation of the Holocaust was Amendt (1999), among others.
19. See http://www.gei.de/.
20. See http://www.eustory.org. For a programmatic publication, see volume 1 of the Eustory series (Macdonald 2000).
21. For EurhistXX, see http://www.eurhistxx.de/. For the ESF, see http://www.esf.org.
22. For an inspiring essay in this respect, see Woolf (2003). His article is one among many examples.
23. At the turn of the twenty-first century, an empirical study by Pingel (2000) confirmed that, in Europe, national history textbooks offer a European perspective only when and if the nation is perceived as having contributed something significant to Europe.
24. For a systematic comparison of the role of national histories in national identity formation, see the ESF programme 'Representations of the Past: The Writing of National Histories in Nineteenth and Twentieth Century Europe' (2003–2008). For details, see http://www.uni-leipzig.de/zhsesf.

Chapter 9

PRACTICES AND POLITICS OF SECOND WORLD WAR REMEMBRANCE

(Trans-)National Perspectives from Eastern and South-Eastern Europe

Heike Karge

The memory of the Second World War, it would seem, has not come to rest in Eastern and South-Eastern Europe.[1] It was not only during the wars in the former Yugoslavia in the 1990s that the media in this and abroad displayed images resembling the memories and symbols of the Second World War. Similarly, in other parts of Eastern Europe, depictions of the past retain a clear presence.[2] Although these findings may well allow for a perspective that is entirely concentrated on only one region of the European continent, namely, the East, I will argue that the developments which have shaped remembrance politics and practices in the whole of Europe should not be overlooked. The benchmark of 1989 was to have severe implications, not only for the remembrance of the Second World War in the former Eastern bloc, but also for that in the West.

However, the perspective of 1989–90 as a landmark for reinterpretations of collective memories of the Second World War is, at first glance, much more self-evident for Eastern European societies.[3] In most of these countries, the fall of the Iron Curtain was accompanied by a rapid delegitimisation of formerly state-sponsored national master narratives. Parallel to this, narratives that reinvented formerly hidden and suppressed aspects of the national past quickly spread into the public sphere elsewhere in Eastern Europe. Both processes often implied an uncritical reversal of formerly official memories, especially in the first decade following 1989. In terms of remembrance politics, this decade may therefore be characterised in terms of a 'dislocation' of collective memories by means of an exchange of ideologies and collective memories instead of a pluralisation of the latter.

Notes for this chapter begin on page 145.

The most obvious forms of dislocation and exchange of collective memories have taken place in the context of the phenomena of Second World War resistance and collaboration. During the Cold War period elsewhere in Eastern Europe, an official, 'purified' version of the past was communicated. This not only silenced those soldiers who had fallen onto the 'wrong' side but also externalised national collaborators – the pro-fascist autocratic regimes of the inter-war and war periods – as 'foreign class elements' or as singular, unimportant cases. After 1989, a new 'cleansing' of the past took place in which the formerly dominant class approaches of 'resistance' and 'collaboration' were to be replaced with a focus that often reflected revisionist tendencies.[4] A critical evaluation of collaboration with German SS and security police forces in the extermination of the Jewish population is a rather neglected public issue in the whole of Eastern Europe, with the significant exception of Poland.[5]

The public, non-scientific approach towards the legacy of the Second World War is thus, in most areas of Eastern Europe, subject to an inclination to see oneself and one's own nation solely as a victim. Within this context, uncritical or even absent reflections on one's own acts of perpetration during the Second World War are only one side of the coin. The other is composed of the memory of the Soviet war, the post-1945 occupation of the Eastern bloc and the communist takeovers in the newly founded 'People's Republics'. The Soviet Army, which in the decades immediately following 1945 had been portrayed as a 'liberator', was, subsequent to 1989, viewed primarily as an 'occupier', whereby Soviet policy was blamed for the installation of communist regimes in the immediate post-war period at the same time. The predominant tendency not to problematise one's own role in the process of the communist takeover corresponds well in a certain sense to the absence of 'negative memory' with regard to collaboration during the wartime period. What happens may be best described as an externalisation of both fascism and communism, of an imagination of one's own national 'non-responsibility' for what happened during 1939, 1941–5 and the ensuing Cold War period (Kovacs and Seewann 2006: 195). Here, one may be surprised by the continuity of interpretative patterns inherited from the post-war period, in which historical memory was instrumentalised to support a positive national self-image. While throughout Eastern Europe post-war collective identities had thus been constructed with the double image of heroes and victims – anti-fascist heroes, resistance fighters and victims of fascism – post-transformation societies after 1989 were to reinvent the very same images of heroes and victims, but out of a different, nationalised 'memory reservoir'.

Of course, Russia could not construct such images, since externalisation of the communist past to foreign forces was quite impossible for historical reasons. The propensity towards a more critical evaluation of the past, which came about at the end of the 1980s and the beginning of the 1990s, has today been replaced by, on the one hand, a growing public disinterest in the history of the Second World War and, on the other hand, a reawakened myth of the glorious, victorious past of the 'Great Patriotic War', which resembles the rhetoric and images of the Brezhnev period during the 1960s and 1970s. The cult of the war veteran and the pride taken in the victorious fighting of the Soviet Army goes hand in hand with the continuous marginalisation of certain victim groups, such as forced labour workers, deportees and prisoners of war (Kurilo 2006), and with overall ignorance towards the question of the high price paid by the population for the victory of the Soviet Army (Bonwetsch 2006).

Although it is under-researched, Europe finally seems to be a 'player' in the process of dealing publicly with the past in Eastern Europe. The very process of EU enlargement has had an impact on the modification and development of history textbooks in many Eastern European countries. Slovakia was expelled from the first round of EU candidate countries in 1995 because the government had approved a textbook in which the Holocaust was relativised (Haslinger 2005). The most notable example is probably Bosnia and Herzegovina, where, going beyond a commitment to history textbooks, international organisations such as OSCE and NATO, as well as European institutions such as the Council of Europe, have come to look on the 'management of memory' as an instrument of conflict prevention and regulation over the last decade (Price 2002).

Two decades after the fall of communism, scholars are more and more aware that there seems to be no linear process towards a pluralisation and democratisation of collective memories. Practices and politics of remembrance are not only manifold but open to reversals and detours, if one takes the democratisation of memories as a kind of 'European must' or 'DIN-norm'. Is, therefore, the East once again lagging behind in the sense that many of its regions will only very slowly arrive on the road to a free, plural discourse about Second World War remembrance, a path on which Western Europe embarked long ago?

The notion of a (Western) 'European memory standard' has become the subject of a fierce debate in the last few years. Following the cultural turn in the humanities, historical research has begun to question the post-1945 national master narratives that had dominated memory cultures and politics not only in Eastern Europe but also in Western Europe. Myths of victimhood, heroism and collective resistance against German fascist occupying forces, as well as the downplaying or professed ignorance of collaborationism, have dominated those master narratives of post-war societies in Europe. The scholar Tony Judt (2005: 829) has called this the 'amnesia of national experiences', which did not begin to erode until the end of the 1970s in Western Europe and after 1989 in Eastern Europe, with many detours on both sides. As for the topic at hand, these findings are important, although they do not at all imply a retrospective levelling of differences between the two bloc systems in Cold War Europe.

The partition of Europe after the Second World War was in many senses constituent. In terms of remembrance, it was one of the most important 'social general conditions' (Halbwachs 1950) for generating collective memories in the post-war era in both parts of Europe. Critical scholarship, however, emphasises that memory discourses after 1945 in European societies of the East and of the West can hardly be analysed as disengaged processes and discourses (Faulenbach 2006; Jaworski 2004; Troebst 2005a). Research has to acknowledge, with all necessary distinctions, a common European framework of 'coming to terms with the past' in the Cold War period and beyond. Such a perspective would have to centre on a historical period in which the landmarks of official and public war remembrance have been consolidated – namely, that of the Cold War. In no way did these landmarks become obsolete with the end of communism in Europe; rather, they seem to have become more comprehensible, with lingering consequences in analytical and empirical studies. However, research on Cold War practices and politics of remembrance currently faces two main obstacles. Firstly, there is a major historiographical research gap on forms of communication and on processes of transfer and its limits within a Europe which is politically divided. Secondly, a similar gap is apparent within the diverse relationships of practices and politics of remembrance in Eastern Europe, which is still all too easily identified as a 'frozen' space, that is, one in which change comes slowly.

The lack of interest in these studies might very well be the product of ideological screens or filters inherited from the Cold War period itself. Taking the screen of the totalitarian paradigm, there was little to 'negotiate' between the two bloc neighbours, nor were there identifiable actors with whom one could share a communication process about politics and practices of war remembrance on a wider European scale. In addition, such a dialogue could not take place anywhere other than politically controlled public spaces. In scholarly terms, the proclaimed absence of civil society structures in the East has made research on processes of communication and negotiation nearly redundant. With some valuable exceptions, the history of practices and politics of war remembrance in Eastern Europe during the Cold War period is still an under-researched field.

However, recent scholarly research has begun to approach common factors of remembrance politics and practices on the European continent across cultures (Niethammer 1992; Passerini 2003). In this sense, the historian Stefan Troebst (2005a) has already suggested replacing the obsolete, dichotomic templates of 'East' and 'West' with regard to memory cultures with a scholarly perspective that places them within the framework of a centre-periphery divide, or of a European patchwork (ibid.: 46). This would imply, however, an acknowledgement of the specific forms of public spaces of action and processes of negotiation in Eastern European societies after 1945.

Some significant studies have already developed an understanding of collective memory practices in Eastern European societies during the Cold War period that acknowledges the primacy of state politics in interpreting the past, but that is not content with doing so. Such studies have put analytical emphasis on mediation processes of remembrance practices, and, in doing so, they point towards two major aspects. The first touches upon processes of communication, which are seen to be a praxis of mediation of intellectual, political and cultural discourses about the past in a given society. The second deals with discursive approaches towards socialist *Vergangenheitspolitik* (politics of the past) and its adoption through diverse discourses that have been developed in recent years within some case studies (Sabrow 2000; Verdery 1991; Wertsch 2002). Such insight has gained in depth over the last few years, mainly due to ethnological fieldwork. The emphasis of these and the studies mentioned above is thus on the ambiguity of imposed *lieux de mémoire* such as state holidays (Merridale 1996; Tumarkin 1994) or official funerals and obsequies (Watson 1994a). Additionally, those latter studies centre on complex encounters of state-sponsored war narratives with local practices of remembrance – encounters that challenge any dichotomic picture of *Vergangenheitsaneignung* (adoption of the past) in the socialist period (Bax 2000; Bucur 2002).

Although these case studies are of enormous significance for future research, there is as yet no comprehensive study that investigates memory cultures and politics in Eastern Europe from a comparative perspective. A comparative study would not only suggest spaces of action and changes in remembrance cultures in a given society, but would also take into account the very similarities and differences that have marked Eastern European terrain in political, cultural and social terms. Notwithstanding important differences, certain common and comparable 'remembrance stimuli' may be identified here. Since, as emphasised above, empirical research has not yet fully addressed these issues, I can only try in the following to identify some benchmarks of Second World War remembrance that seem to be of greater importance for a dynamic understanding of the issue at hand. Without pretending to develop a kind of new chronology of Second World War memory in Eastern Europe, I will pick out three benchmarks that may nevertheless serve as a first step in this direction.

The first benchmark with regard to practices and politics of Second World War remembrance in Eastern Europe comes at the end of the 1940s – that is, the beginning of the Cold War in Europe. It is of importance for both Eastern and Western Europe and is well symbolised in the founding of the two German states. With it, repression and canonisation of Second World War memories were initiated on both sides of the Iron Curtain, although in different directions. From this point forward, the anti-totalitarian paradigm in the West served as the major interpretative scheme to downplay certain aspects of the anti-fascist resistance movements, especially those of communist groups. Accordingly, efforts were made in the East to marginalise the memory of non-communist resistance. However, it is interesting to consider the events of the short period before 1949. Academic literature indicates that at least in some parts of Eastern Europe these few years were marked by rather vivid, inclusive practices of war remembrance (Leo 1992). In Hungary, a brief 'period of discussion' with regard to Holocaust remembrance ended in 1948, that is, with the final communist takeover (Kovacs and Seewann 2006). Finally, in 1949, the founding of a common war veterans union in Poland, which was to replace the former 11 organisations for war veterans, prisoners of war, victims of fascism and resistance fighters, marked the cessation of a more plural and more diversified culture of remembrance.[6]

However, the most illustrative example, the history of the Day of Remembrance for the Victims of Fascism, comes from the two German states.[7] Celebrated for the first time on 9 September 1945 in Berlin, on the initiative of political survivors of concentration camps, this memorial day was a forceful demonstration of the will to remember, with participation from all political and confessional groups. The day was, therefore, held by an overall anti-fascist consensus. This unifying practice of remembering the victims of fascism on the second Sunday of September in every major German town came to a rather abrupt end with the founding of the two German states in 1949. From then on, in West Germany the day was to fall increasingly into oblivion, being replaced by an emphasis of the political public on 'Remembrance Sunday' in November, during which all victims of war and tyranny were to be officially commemorated. In the East German state, the Day of Remembrance for the Victims of Fascism was absorbed by the communist political elite. The event was made an official day of remembrance that celebrated only the communist anti-fascist resistance, thus changing the whole character of the memorial from the remembrance of victims to that of resistance fighters.

Interestingly enough, the partition of Europe into two distinct spaces of remembrance in 1949 did not mean the end of communication between the two. During the Cold War period, 'anti-fascist resistance' was one of the few issues that had been communicated across the Iron Curtain, even at common occasions such as historians' congresses. Resistance against the Third Reich was a topic upon which historians from both sides of the Iron Curtain could readily agree, since differences in defining who was to be identified as a resistance fighter did not impede the existence of similar narrative patterns.[8] Thus, the 'resistance that never happened' against the Holocaust within the German and European resistance movements was one of the topics neither expounded upon nor remembered in either part of Europe, at least up to the 1980s (Keval 1999: 239). Studies that focus on the dimension of gender have emphasised additionally that the remembrance of resistance and persecution has been shaped largely by male actors and their interpretative frameworks.[9] National organisations of war veterans, concentration camp survivors and their supranational federations, such as the International Federation of Resistance Fighters or International Camp Committees, have been major contributors in constructing the image of 'the heroic male', thus placing women predominantly into the memory frame of a suffering victim. Finally, remembering those persecuted during the Nazi period has been largely shaped by 'patriotic memory' in Eastern as well as in Western Europe (Hockerts 2005: 298). Individuals and groups who for any particular reason did not fit into the scheme of this memory system fell into oblivion on both sides of the Iron Curtain. This situation did not change appreciably until the beginning of the 1980s, and its consequences still linger today in terms of public acknowledgement and remembrance of certain persecuted groups.[10]

The second half of the 1950s represents a second major benchmark for the change and development of practices and politics of Second World War remembrance in Eastern Europe. The death of Stalin in 1953 and Nikita Khrushchev's 'secret speech' at the 20th Congress of the Soviet Communist Party in 1956 induced the, albeit brief, 'thaw period' in Eastern Europe, which had significant implications for the fields of fine art, culture and literature (Milcakov 2006). As for the Second World War memory, research on the impact of the thaw period has not yet been dealt with systematically. However, since memory is not only subject to politics but linked to the fine arts as well, a possible broadening of Second World War memories in the Eastern European public may be presumed here.[11] Some academic literature has suggested that developments in the arts have strongly influenced forms and practices of remembrance in the late 1950s. The end of the binding paradigm of 'socialist realism' in the cultural field was thus reflected in an, albeit brief, opening up towards more abstract styles in the fine arts, including Second World War monuments (Hein 1994; van Vree 2005). This is not to say that interpretative schemes regarding whom and how to remember changed entirely. But the application of more freedom in forms of artistic expression did facilitate spaces of interpretation and remembrance that so far had not been provided for. Most notably, the official image of the optimistic, victorious fighter – widespread elsewhere in Eastern Europe – had been, during that short period, at least partly counterbalanced by artistic image productions that exposed suffering, agony and disablement instead of 'blissful happiness' in the wake of war battles.[12] The period of 'rendering possible' forms and practices of remembrance in the public that transcended the otherwise one-sided, optimistic official versions in Eastern Europe was soon to come to an end with the dismissal of Khrushchev in 1964, if not before. However, the influence of the thaw period, as well as of other 'exceptional conditions' such as the Prague

Spring, should not be underestimated, since it was here that interpretative irruptions became visible and challenged the politically controlled terrain of memory in Eastern European societies.

Finally, the years from the mid-1960s onwards may be considered a third benchmark in the field of Second World War remembrance in Eastern Europe. In general, this period has been marked by an increased appropriation of the national past from the side of the political elites in most parts of Eastern Europe, far in excess of the narrower Second World War past. The imperative 'Ahead to the past!' (Milcakov 2006: 27) was thus the most important slogan of state cultural and educational policies in the following decades, mainly, but not only, due to the declining credibility of visions of prosperity in a communist future. The erection of huge war memorial complexes from the 1960s onwards in both the Soviet Union and in Yugoslavia, for instance, had rather been a poor reaction of state politics facing a generational change in society.[13] With it, the transmission of war memories to the younger generations born after the war was perceived as increasingly problematic. Solutions were sought in a kind of 'spicing up' of different forms of mediating war remembrance.[14] War memorial complexes such as Tjentiste/Sutjeska in Yugoslavia, built in the 1960s, or the largest free-standing monument in the world at the time, Rodina Mat (Mother Homeland) at Stalingrad's (now Volgograd's) Mamaev Kurgan, inaugurated in 1967, were thus designed to constitute 'places of contemplation' which should allow for a 'complex memorial cult ..., pilgrimages of several days' duration, even a true memorial tourism' (Kämpfer 1994: 334).[15] Following this conception, Sutjeska, for instance, was to serve not only as a place to commemorate a victorious battle of Yugoslav partisans in the summer of 1943, but also as a site of popular public performances. All-Yugoslav car rallies, organised regularly on the occasion of the Day of the Fighter on 4 July, have been one outcome of these methods aiming to revitalise narratives and memories about the Second World War past.

The process of reinforcing a rather traditional form of hero worship – the heroic image of those who had fallen on the battlefields – distinguished Eastern Europe two decades after the end of the war. Although in the West violence and death were understood as constituent and meaningful elements of the Second World War past, this traditional context of 'meaningful dying' was first and foremost to wither from the symbolic representation of the war in Western societies after 1945. War memorials in Western Europe therefore tend to produce the message of an absence of meaning, of the futility of dying in the war, thus reflecting both the horrible experience of mass destruction on the battlefields and in the concentration camps (Koselleck 2003). Questions about the actual impact of these and similar efforts in Eastern European societies on practices of war remembrance, however, remain open. Ethnological studies such as those of Tumarkin (1994) and Merridale (1996) on practices of celebrating state holidays in the Soviet Union point at the diversity of commemorating officially proclaimed days of remembrance by different actors, such as war veterans and surviving victims of deportation. The level of individual mourning can thus hardly be equated with state efforts to force memory onto a single track. Additionally, public rites in front of a state-sponsored monument may not be subsumed entirely under the label of politically controlled, official ritual in Eastern European societies. Current research on practices and politics of war remembrance in the socialist Yugoslavia has indicated that public rites would take place even beyond the authorisation of political elites. The gathering of people at the former concentration camp at Jasenovac, for instance, has been recognised by the political elite as having a remarkable capacity to accelerate solutions for certain memory spaces that had not yet found much consideration by official remembrance politics (Karge 2006).

Summarising these reflections seems to be rather difficult. The few examples of case studies discussed here point to a dynamic image of Second World War remembrance beyond state-controlled memory spaces. But since this is still a rather under-researched field, statements about the 'essence' of practices and politics of Second World War remembrance in Eastern Europe should be made with caution. I would rather close with a suggestion by Alon Confino (2005b: 58), according to whom a 'reshuffling of the meaning of victimhood, rights, and genocide remembrances has been at the heart of a remarkable turnabout in which the memory of the Second World War has become in the last sixty years not simply more inclusive of the victims of the war, but indeed dominated by them. The full story of this shift is still to be told'. As mentioned above, recent studies that develop Second World War remembrance as a story of both memory and oblivion, of political instrumentalisation, of adoption and negotiation of war memories by various actors both in Eastern and Western European societies have already begun to address this shift. Future empirical research that focuses on Eastern Europe while allowing for an analysis of the otherwise impenetrable Iron Curtain can certainly contribute to this intellectual endeavour.

Notes

1. Research for this chapter was primarily funded by the Ludwig Boltzmann Institute for European History and Public Spheres in Vienna, Austria.
2. For practical reasons, I will hereafter refer to Eastern and South-Eastern Europe as Eastern Europe.
3. Since 1989, the politics and cultures of collective memories in the Eastern European states have been well documented in numerous publications. See Corbea-Hoisie et al. (2004), Flacke (2004b) and Jaworski (2003). With regard to monuments, architecture and

memory after 1989, see ICOMOS (1994) and Neil (1999). For developments in historiography, see Brunnbauer (2004).

4. For the fierce controversies on resistance and collaboration in Croatia and Serbia, see Duhovski (2002), Ristović (2002) and Sundhaussen (1994). For recent debates in Slovenia, see Luthar and Luthar (2006).

5. In Poland, the main impulse for critical engagement with Second World War history and the Holocaust has been the work of Jan T. Gross (2001). See also Huener (2003), Steinlauf (1997) and Zaremba (2004).

6. Huener (2003: 96) has called this the process of 'streamlining' war remembrance.

7. See *Der zweite Sonntag im September: Zur Geschichte des OdF-Tages. Ausstellung* (http:// odf-tag.vvn-bda.org/ausstellung.php3) at a site maintained by the VVN-BdA (Vereinigung der Verfolgten des Naziregimes – Bund der Antifaschistinnen und Antifaschisten). After 1989, this day of remembrance was never to regain its high political prestige and is now celebrated primarily by German left-wing political parties and activists.

8. For a summary of historiographical research about resistance at the beginning of the 1980s, see Botz (1983). For new approaches towards resistance, see Geyer (1994).

9. See Wenk and Eschebach (2002), which focuses on gender-specific practices of remembrance of the National Socialist genocide: 'Memory loss, silence on and denial of specific and extremely painful experiences of suffering constitute … transnational phenomena of a nationally designed reconstruction of heroic masculinity' (ibid: 30; trans. by author).

10. The bitter debate of the last few years surrounding the opening of the International Tracing Service Archive in Bad Arolsen is particularly illustrative of the still highly sensitive topic of public and legal (non-)recognition of persecuted status for various persecuted groups (see Betz 2005). On the divide between the reality, definition and memory of persecution in the context of the compensation negotiations in Germany, see Hockerts and Kuller (2003).

11. In that sense, Niethammer (1992: 103) introduces the term *Gedächtniserweiterungen* (broadening of memory).

12. In his study on the fine arts and Second World War remembrance in the Soviet Union, Jahn (2005: 13) emphasises that suffering and pain have not been fully silenced in officially produced war narratives. Instead, they have been subordinated to an otherwise heroic, optimistic image of the past.

13. In the Soviet Union, 11 memorial complexes were built from 1945–59. In the 1960s, a further 59 and, in the 1970s, a further 67 Second World War memorial complexes were inaugurated (Jahn 2005). In his study on war memorial complexes in the Soviet Union, Kämpfer (1994: 337) highlights that these huge complexes were designed to 'bridge the gap that had evolved between the moral concepts of those who survived the war and those of their grandchildren'. With regard to history textbooks in the USSR, see also Wertsch (2002). For a brief discussion of similar developments with regard to war memorial complexes in Yugoslavia, see Knežević (1994).

14. Touching upon the methods of history education in the socialist Yugoslavia, see Karge (2008).

15. For the history of the coming into being of Mamaev Kurgan, see Arnold (1994). However, nothing lasts forever. In May 2009, it was reported that rising water levels have eroded the monument's foundations and that the statue is leaning to such a degree that it is in danger of collapse. It is thought that the statue is listing by around 20 cm.

Chapter 10

A VICTORY CELEBRATED

Danish and Norwegian Celebrations
of the Liberation

❧❧

Clemens Maier

The experience of war, occupation and liberation by a foreign force left deep wounds in Denmark and Norway. As with other European nations, there was an urgent need for patriotic memories to support the process of reconstruction (Lagrou 1997: 194), and the most widespread patriotic memory was one of a resistance that had defended the nation (Flacke 2004a: 8). Governments and political movements nationalised and glorified the resistance, claiming the merits of the relatively small proportion of the population that had actively resisted during the last years. This often required a denial of the actual experience of the majority of the population (Lagrou 1997: 195). The main objective of this chapter is to describe how a dominant version of the war history was established and perpetuated by means of anniversaries throughout the post-war period.

Anniversaries are central to the formation of narratives on the past. The values a society deems important to preserve become visible through connected celebrations (Eriksen 1995: 120). The celebrations of the liberation (*Frigjøringsjubileer* in Norway and *Befrielsesjubileer* in Denmark) belong to the sphere of semi-official public memory. These re-enactments not only are commemorative acts but also shape narratives by imposing specific interpretations of a given event. I will describe the arrangement of such commemorative processes at the central level in Oslo and Copenhagen on the occasion of the most important anniversaries conducted by the royal families and the governments in the two capitals. The aim is to show how, for a considerable period, certain interest groups have steered these processes.

Notes for this chapter begin on page 158.

Frigjøringsjubileer – the Lesson of the War Perpetuated

On 9 April 1940, German troops landed at a number of Norwegian cities. After two months of harsh fighting, the Norwegians were forced to surrender. During the next five years, a civil disobedience movement developed which, by means of slogans, directed the actions of a broad majority of the population that rejected the collaborating regime. This *Hjemmefront* (home front) was later complemented by a military resistance which built up a clandestine army – the *gutter på skauen* (the boys in the woods) – to be ready at the moment of a German defeat. For the next five years, the head of the Nazi government, Vidkun Quisling, became the symbol of collaboration, and a considerable number of people put themselves at the service of the Germans. As a result of this, the legal purge following liberation was comparatively severe in Norway. The resistance, on the other hand, had the backing of the government in exile and was composed of the ruling elites who would play a decisive role in Norwegian politics after the war.

The Early Celebrations

The summer was warm, and festivities celebrating the liberation, which had taken place on 8 May, were spontaneously arranged by the population. The following year, official arrangements were also few, and people began to celebrate on the evening of 7 May. The first sign of more extensive celebrations came in 1955 on the tenth anniversary of the liberation. Here we can observe features that would recur in all later observances. The government appointed a committee to plan the celebrations, and wreaths were laid at the Monument for the Fallen Norwegian Patriots, which had been erected at the Retterstedet, the point on the Akershus castle were the Germans had executed resistance fighters during the occupation.[1] On 8 May 1955, the liberation was celebrated with a repetition of the victory parade of June 1945. Around 1,500 veterans marched towards the castle in the knickerbockers which had, back then, been their 'battle dress'. That same evening, the government held a reception at the Akershus castle with representatives of the Allied Forces of 1945 and the royal family as guests (Hauge 1988: 38).

In 1965, another committee was appointed by the government to prepare the celebrations. It was affiliated to the Statsministerens Kontor (the office of the prime minister) and included important veterans and politicians.[2] The programme followed well-established lines. A special show in the national theatre was earmarked for invited guests on 7 May 1965. The next day, a parade of veterans moved through the city centre to the site of the main event at a sports ground, where the king and the crown prince welcomed 25,000 people and a military parade.[3] As in previous anniversary years, the Norwegian Parliament (Stortinget) arranged a ceremony in the chamber with the king and the leaders of the *Hjemmefront*.[4] The speech of Stortingspresident Nils Langhelle contained the basic elements of the dominant narrative on the war. After expressing his gratitude to the Allies, Langhelle talked about the different forms of resistance, evoking the motif of unity and of all Norwegians joining the struggle for freedom. The central figure for unity was the king, whose initials had become a symbol of resistance.[5] Apart from public events such as parades and wreath layings, the early celebrations were primarily arrangements for the elite of the political resistance.

Twenty-Five Years of Freedom – Forty Years of Peace

The next large-scale commemorative event was the twenty-fifth anniversary of the liberation. These celebrations included the unveiling of a national monument for the victims of war and the opening of the resistance museum, Norges Hjemmefrontmuseum, on 7 May 1970 (Kverndokk 2000: 40). The government again entrusted the coordination of the celebrations to a committee under the prime minister's office. For the first time, Dag Berggrav, who from this point onwards would play a decisive role in the preparations of the anniversaries to come, was made secretary of the committee.[6] Berggrav, himself a veteran of the struggle for liberation, had been imprisoned by the Gestapo. In December 1970, the committee produced a proposal suggesting that the expression of gratitude towards the Allies for the liberation should stand at the core of the celebrations. The committee also conveyed its belief that this goal would best be achieved by means of a memorial fund that would allow young people of other countries to visit Norway in order to promote mutual understanding. On 6 May – just two days before the anniversary of the liberation – the bill was discussed in Parliament. The minutes show that one representative expressed his misgivings about the fact that the fund would be accessible to young people of Norway's former wartime enemies, including Germany. Although he did not object to this, the representative felt that it would neither fit the theme of the celebrations nor the intention of the committee to make this anniversary an acknowledgement of the Allies. Yet after a short discussion, the bill was passed unanimously.[7] This illustrates, first, that the character of the celebrations, in fostering understanding with other countries, took on a new significance, and, secondly, that the fact that the Allies had been the decisive element in Norway's liberation was becoming more influential.

The rest of the programme followed the usual procedures. On 7 May 1970, the veterans and the state paid tribute to the resistance fighters and laid wreaths at the Retterstedet. The following day, the Norwegian Parliament had again arranged a commemoration ceremony. The programme was identical to that of 1965: the same guests were present, the same songs were performed and the military parade took place again in front of the Parliament.[8] The speech of the Stortingspresident Bernt Ingvaldsen also recalled to a considerable extent those of previous occasions. The expression of gratefulness to the Allies and the reinvocation of the spirit of unity were combined with appeals for a strong defence.

The fortieth anniversary of an event does not usually represent a typical occasion for sizeable festivities. Yet in Norway, the fortieth anniversary of liberation was celebrated with considerable vigour. One reason for this may have been the fear that the war generation might soon vanish. Again, a committee for the preparation of the celebrations was appointed, and its decisions and celebrations once again followed very much along established lines. The political agenda of the celebrations had not changed from that of 15 years before and remained very much determined by the fears of the Cold War. This was best expressed in a leading article of *Aftenposten* on the topic of the liberation day, which stressed that after the war all the 'great men' from the resistance agreed on the importance of a strong partnership with the Allies to safeguard the security of Norway. It further stated that the nation was still in danger and that security was an illusion.[9]

Although not a 'big anniversary', the administrative efforts for these celebrations were immense, and the veterans seem to have been highly involved, maybe out of concern that this might be the last common celebration. But this time, hitherto marginalised and smaller groups – veterans or victims of organisations less famous than the *gutter på skauen* – were included in the ceremonies. For example, on 8 May, Oslo police held a commemorative gathering for the members of the police force who had died in the resistance.[10]

The Fiftieth Anniversary – the Last Celebrations

A royal resolution of 8 November 1991 established a committee to prepare the celebrations on the occasion of the fiftieth anniversary of Norway's liberation. This time, preparations began four years before the actual event.[11] This was due to the widespread perception that this anniversary would be the last one for which that generation of the war would be present. Viewed as a 'last hurrah' for the veterans, it was therefore intended to represent a testament to the resistance and was accompanied by an extensive wave of publications and broad media coverage. The government's contribution was the brochure *Fritt Norge*, published by Forsvarets Forum, an organisation connected to the Ministry of Defence and the veterans' organisations (Berg et al. 1995). At not inconsiderable cost, this brochure had a print run of one million issues and was distributed free of charge to schools and households.

The planning committee, or Frigjøringskomiteen, also stressed the educational aspect of the celebrations. Schools and public libraries were asked to make special arrangements and exhibitions about the war.[12] A central part of the committee's work was the erection of a memorial. The Friheds-monument (Monument for Liberty) was planned for Narvik, which had been destroyed by the retreating German forces.[13] It was unveiled on 7 May (Sandberg 1995). The public was given a chance to pay tribute to the war generation when 3,000 veterans took part in a parade in front of the royal family in Oslo. Thousands of Norwegians applauded in the streets. It was to become Norway's biggest parade ever (Fuglehaug 1995).

Upon this occasion, too, the Stortinget had a commemoration ceremony which, at first glance, differed in no respect from the previous ones.[14] But this time the content of the two speeches of Stortingspresident Kirsti Kolle Grøndahl and King Harald VII differed from the hitherto cultivated repetition of the motifs of the master narrative. This time reconciliation was the central theme. The traditional motifs of struggle and unity were not completely excluded, but between the lines the speeches called for reconciliation, not only with the former external enemies, but also with those citizens who had chosen the 'wrong side' during the occupation. The addresses implicitly apologised for the treatment suffered by these groups and by the children of Norwegian women and German fathers. A further development was that for the first time a woman of the royal family played an official role in the festivities: Queen Sonja took part in some of the celebrations. During her speech in Trondheim on 7 May, she expressed dissatisfaction that the wartime efforts of women and their role within the resistance had not been sufficiently acknowledged in the earlier celebrations and in the literature on the war. She also expressed her gratitude to the planning committee for having considered women to a higher degree (Skjalg 1995). The fact that a member of the royal family had embraced the topic gave it the stamp of official recognition, and therefore the Queen's speech was important for the public recognition of an issue that had hitherto been neglected by both historians and society as a whole. For the first time, women were given significant attention within the official celebrations.

But despite these broad governmental efforts, public participation dropped, with only around 20,000 people taking part in the celebrations in total. This was a disappointing turnout compared to earlier years and when taking into account the overall sum of more than 16 million NOK that had been allocated for the celebrations.[15] One explanation might be the growing importance of television.

The fiftieth anniversary of the end of the war was generally seen as the last great celebration of the post-war era. Veterans were dying and the post-war world order was vanishing. And yet, 10 years later, some contemporaries of the occupation years were still alive. In 2005, celebrations in Oslo still took place on 7 and 8 May, albeit on a much smaller scale than previous anniversaries. The main reason – and the official one – was that 2005 was also the one hundredth anniversary of the peaceful dissolution of the union with Sweden. As the May events approached, there was already an abundance of special exhibitions, lectures and television programmes, culminating in festivities attended by both the Norwegian and Swedish royal families. The annual ritual of speeches and wreath laying at the memorial for the fallen patriots in front of the Hjemmefrontmuseum was nevertheless performed – albeit with just some dozen participants.

Befrielsesjubileer – the Celebrations of Denmark's Victory

Denmark's war had a very different trajectory from that of Norway. The main parties had formed a coalition government and had cooperated with the enemy until the situation became unbearable. Pressure from below and ever increasing German demands forced the government to resign. For most Danes, it is not the first three peaceful years of the occupation but rather the last two years of increasing terror and sabotage that have become the point of reference. One reason is that shortly before the end of the war, politicians and the resistance movement joined forces to secure the transition into peacetime. In a historic compromise, each of the parties involved assured one another that everyone had, in his and her own way, contributed to the liberation of the country.

As in Norway, news of Denmark's freedom came on the evening before the actual surrender of the German troops. The surrender of the German army units in Denmark came into force on 5 May 1945, but during the previous evening, the liberation had been announced on the Danish programme of the BBC. Therefore, the evening of 4 May is generally seen as the day when celebrations are of a more cheerful nature, whereas 5 May is the day of more sombre commemorations and official celebrations. Immediately after the news was broadcast, people went into the streets and celebrated, blackout curtains were torn down and burned in the streets, and some people lit candles in their windows. The 'return of light' after five years of darkness became the decisive theme of the night. As is discussed below, this iconography involving light was more strongly integrated into the Danish set of symbols referring to the war than in Norway.

The Early Celebrations

The division of the two days of commemoration – 4 May as the day of rejoicing and 5 May as the day of public mourning – continues in Denmark, as it does in Norway. It was along these lines that the different veterans' associations first celebrated freedom and commemorated their dead among themselves. State officials went to the meetings and gave speeches only when invited. One difference between the Norwegian and

Danish commemorations was the fact, that despite the compromise negotiated around the liberation days, the Danish trajectory held potential for
conflicts. Some veterans were very much aware of the fact that politicians
had joined the resistance reluctantly and that it was largely the active
resistance groups that had brought Denmark into the ranks of the Allies.
The politicians themselves were also aware of this and were cautious not
to provoke disapproval of the veterans. In their speeches, they confined
themselves to evoking the notion of unity and the resistance as a struggle of the whole Danish people. Successive governments only gradually
started to become more involved, planning events themselves in close
contact with certain groups of veterans, who were expected to maintain
the perception of consensus and unity (Bryld and Warring 1998: 155).

As in Norway, the twentieth anniversary of the liberation was celebrated
with nationwide events. In order to prepare the official celebrations, a committee under the prime minister's office was formed. It was composed of
several officials from different branches of the government as well as Svenn
Seehusen, the representative of the largest veterans' association, Frihed-
skampens Veteraner.[16] From this point onwards, Seehusen became the government's principal contact for the resistance movement. The committee
planned the central events and coordinated those where the presence of
the prime minister and the royal family was desired. On 4 May, there was
a street festival at Rådhuspladsen, the square in front of Copenhagen's
city hall, where, among others, Prime Minister Jens Otto Krag spoke to the
public. Despite the pouring rain, thousands took part in the march from
the memorial for the sailors in the district of Nyhavn to the square. The
speeches expressed gratitude to the Allies, and the mayor of Copenhagen
also reminded the crowd about the importance of international contacts
for the security of Denmark.[17] This was surely a reference to NATO, which
was seen then as the great legacy of the war. That the war was invoked to
legitimise Denmark's membership in NATO was a central element of this,
the first of the larger celebrations, and it should be seen against the background of the Cold War. The state took an active part in the organisation of
the commemorations in order to safeguard its political agenda.

Persistence and Change – Celebrations during and after the Cold War

The Danish prime minister appointed a committee for the twenty-fifth
anniversary of the liberation in 1970, this time well in advance, in order to
lay out the framework of the celebrations. Assuming that it might be the
last large-scale celebration, the committee recommended that the anniversary be celebrated in a spirit of harmony.[18] The celebrations were to
be nationwide, and the committee pointed specifically at the necessity of
involving the Danish State Broadcasting Agency to 'ensure, that [it] would

broadcast on a suitable scale'.[19] This was an acknowledgement that television had become so important that it could not be left out and also that it could be used to transport the message. The final programme had few surprises in store. On 4 May, the torchlight parade from Nyhavn to the Rådhuspladsen and the ensuing street festival took place.[20] Prime Minister Hilmar Baunsgaard and the prominent veteran Frode Jakobsen delivered speeches at the square. Jakobsen expressed his disappointment that the younger generation was occupied with a war in a country far away (Vietnam) and that they did not understand his generation and why the liberation was an event to celebrate.[21] The usual wreath laying took place on 5 May.[22] The spirit of unity was the main theme not only of the celebrations but also of the king's speech, which was broadcast on television. However, the initial programme of the traditional gala in the Royal Theatre apparently met with the veterans' disapproval. The originally scheduled piece, *År*, a play by Klaus Rifbjerg, was not an account of the heroic deeds of the resistance; rather, it portrayed everyday life during the war. After a massive protest by the veterans, the staging of *År* was cancelled, and Bertolt Brecht's *Svejk* was performed instead for around 1,000 veterans (Bryld and Warring 1998: 140). It seems that those responsible thought that these celebrations would be the last on such a grand scale and that their meaning should last beyond the actual days of the festivities. They therefore made an enormous effort to celebrate and to please the veterans. But it had become obvious that the general population was beginning to lose contact with the past.

Even if the government had thought that the twenty-fifth anniversary would be the last of its kind, the veterans' associations contacted the prime minister as early as 1983 to push for a new planning committee to recognise the fortieth anniversary of the liberation. However, some of the organisers felt that the younger generation was probably less eager to celebrate. It was also thought fitting to look on the arrangements as an educational programme geared towards the younger generation. The prime minister had sent out letters to mayors and governors in which he called the commemorations a national responsibility.[23] This indicates that there was a view that the celebrations could no longer be taken for granted. In addition to this, the committee seems to have had little confidence that the population would spontaneously light candles in their windows as a reminder of the first celebrations. Orders instructing public authorities to adorn their windows with 'living lights' as an example were published in the press prior to the days of commemoration (I. Pedersen 1985). In the end, the celebrations did not differ in any respect from those of previous years. The speakers at the central event on Rådhuspladsen were chosen carefully in order not to provoke anybody or leave anybody out. The goal was to reflect the spirit of consensus that characterised the liberation government. In addition to the conservative prime minister, Poul Schlüter, other speakers included a former minister in the liberation government and a communist, Alfred Jensen; a member of the resistance leadership Frihedsrådet and a Social Democrat, Frode Jakobsen; and the mayor of Copenhagen, Egon Weidekamp, likewise a Social Democrat (Warring 1987: 14–5). The Danish Communist Party (DKP) had agreed to participate in the official celebrations despite its criticism of previous anniversaries (Bryld and Warring 1998: 157).

Not everybody viewed the day with the same solemn feelings. The non-communist left used the event to demonstrate their dissatisfaction with the government. Around half of the 20,000 people present on the square were protesting against Schlüter's foreign policy (with regard to NATO) and because they felt that his appearance was an inappropriate attempt to 'usurp' the legacy of the resistance (Utzon 1985). Having remained silent during the speeches of the veterans, they booed and shouted during the Schlüter's address and even pelted him with tomatoes. Media reports were full of criticism for the protesters.[24] The prime minister's speech once more merely repeated the old themes of the necessity of a strong defence in international cooperation with friendly nations – that is, with NATO.[25]

With respect to setting and structure, the celebrations of 1985 were not at all different from those of previous years. Official agents followed the well-established patterns. Probably due to the veterans' wishes, little was changed. Yet the audience – the general public – *had* changed. The need to accompany the official rites with information shows how distant the experience of war, occupation and liberation had become for some Danes as a means of identity construction.

The year 1995 saw large-scale, worldwide celebrations of the fiftieth anniversary of the end of the Second World War. Denmark, too, was party to this enthusiasm. The budget for the celebrations was 15 million Danish Crowns, the largest sum to date. The governmental committee was advised by a secondary committee of veterans – the '5 maj udvalget' – to which veterans from the DKP and the right-conservative Dansk Samling were not invited.[26] The composition corresponded rather to current political realities than to the historical relative strength of the various parties in the period immediately after the liberation. This inadvertently directed the themes of the events, and the bulk of the money was allocated to initiatives represented directly in the committee.

The tradition of the *levende lys* (candlelights) was again evoked in a state-sponsored campaign which encouraged Danes to light candles, an apparent sign that the tradition was outworn and needed to be reintroduced. The candles also became the official logo of the celebrations and obtained a quasi-religious meaning when the 'light of freedom' was lit in Hvidsten on 4 May 1995 and brought to all parts of the country the following day (Olsen 1995). Ironically, in line with the hopes of veterans, the theme of light was taken up by the artist Elle-Mie Ejdrup Hansen, but not in the way that the veterans had wished. Hansen's piece *Linien – Lyset* or *Fredsskulpturen '95* (Line – Light or Peace Sculpture '95) was formed of a laser beamed from the most northern point of Jutland along the coast into Germany, connecting the German fortifications. The veterans unanimously opposed it. They perceived the bunkers as blots on Denmark's landscape and its history, and they did not wish to draw attention to them.[27] They even called on the public to sabotage the installation. Despite an intensive media debate on the freedom of art and the 'correct' way of memorialising, on 4 May the installation was inaugurated, accompanied by sound installations. As a result of pressure from the cultural ministry, Hansen's piece was funded by the committee, underlining that even if the Udvalg (the veterans' committee) perceived itself as the decisive institution in the planning of the celebrations, other agents were able to push their wishes through. The government was able to proceed with the controversial laser show because it had otherwise fulfilled the wishes of interest groups. The actual show reflected the preceding debate. More than 350,000 spectators gathered at the coast, but at the same time cables were cut at several points (Tobiesen 1995).

Military pressure groups such as Værn om Danmark (Defence for Denmark) and Atlantsammenslutningen (a group for the promotion of Danish involvement in NATO) were also represented in the Udvalg. Through a compilation of brochures, curriculum guidelines and videos, which they spread with the support of the committee, these groups tried to influence the interpretation of the war and its significance for contemporary Denmark. It is difficult to assess how this material was perceived, yet there are indications that it was not read at all. Teachers simply had enough good material at their disposal already.[28] In order to avoid protests that could spoil the celebrations, the critical leftist veterans' groups, which had hitherto been excluded, also received generous funding. However, they were not included in the committee (Bryld and Warring 1998: 152).

As in Norway, it is clear that over time the need to reinvoke the central themes of the master narrative was acknowledged, and anniversaries gradually developed from mere commemorations into a combination of commemorations and educational projects. The message had to be adapted to the present time so that it would appeal to the new generations.

The Sixtieth Anniversary – A Danish Historikerstreit?

In Denmark, the attention paid to the sixtieth liberation anniversary was far greater than in Norway, and the debate was far more intense. One reason was the contribution of Prime Minister Anders Fogh Rasmussen to the debate. Born after the war, Rasmussen was the leader of the Liberal Party (Venstre) and headed a centre-right coalition with the Conservative People's Party. He actively supported the US position on the war in Iraq and contributed troops to the US-led coalition, a move that was unpopular in Denmark. In 2005, Danish troops were still in Iraq, despite calls to bring them home, and Rasmussen's office was responsible for the celebrations.

The prime minister's words of welcome to the official digital portal to the festivities read: 'Under the Nazi occupation, many Danes were forced to take a decision between doing the right thing and taking a clear stance and exposing themselves to great risks or to bend to the threat ... and prioritise their own well-being and safety. This is a question that is equally important today.'[29] Not surprisingly, veterans and their organisations welcomed the Rasmussen's words and saw them as a late acknowledgement of their deeds in a time of relativisation.[30] Nobody denies that the prime minister's words were heartfelt; however, they should also be seen in the light of contemporary events. It is possible that Rasmussen was using the war narrative of the resistance to legitimise his foreign policy. This was certainly the perception of both veterans and historians.[31]

Otherwise the celebrations were as usual. Astonishingly, 60 years after the liberation, with almost nobody left who remembered the origin of the tradition, the government and the media again stressed the symbol of the living lights. Yet it is my perception that this tradition is about to die out. I personally saw few lights on windowsills during the celebrations in 2005.

Conclusion

Throughout the post-war period, the celebrations of the liberation in both Norway and Denmark displayed a great stability in their central topics and performances. All large events were well rehearsed, following the rituals and rhetoric of established traditions. The anniversaries became communications of a mythical message (Eriksen 1997: 12), and yet the message had to be adapted and made appealing to new generations that had not experienced the war. Its universal character had to be put into new contexts to prove its validity. Gradually, new groups were incorporated, and the history of the war was made subject to more intensive scrutiny. The message of the celebrations did not change considerably; rather, it was adapted to the present situation. The lesson of the war continued to identify the need for a strong military deterrent and for strong allies (i.e. NATO).

The rituals of remembrance consistently followed the same rhythm. This is most visible in the celebrations organised by the Norwegian Parliament, where organisers stuck to the exact same sequence of events and rituals with the exact same schedule. The increasingly professional nature of the celebrations is striking. The committees had their pool of manpower to draw from, and the veterans and others involved had no need to change what had previously proven so effective. One reason for this marked continuity was that the key agents – the government representatives and the veterans – did not change.

During the first three post-war decades, the celebrations and their narratives in both countries became totally detached from findings of historical research. More recently, this gap has narrowed, and spaces for discourse have now opened up. Those who resisted change were primarily the veterans and their lobby groups. Caught up in a process of self-legitimisation, they could not accept revisions to the dominant narrative communicated through the rituals. In the beginning, this was because veterans saw versions of the war that differed from their own as wrong and even fraudulent. Later, this may have been because any new narrative endangered the very basis of their existence within the memory culture. Tying central events to commemoration ceremonies over the fallen was a means to safeguard their influence. The connection to those 'who gave their lives' was a disincentive to putting events into perspective. We cannot ignore the dead (Eriksen 1995: 25). The coming years, when all the veterans will be gone, will show whether a development comparable to that which could be observed in other parts of Western Europe will also occur in Scandinavia.

Notes

1. P. Berg, letter to Regeringens Utvalg for feiringen av 10-årsdagen av frigjöringen, 26 March 1955, NHM.
2. K. Haugland, letter to Statssekretær Olaf Solumsmoen, 24 March 1965, NHM.
3. 'Fredsjubileet feiret med alvor og glede', *Aftenposten*, 10 May 1965.
4. Stortinget 1965. 'Programmet ved minnemøtet i Stortingssalen 8.mai 1965', Stortingets arkiv.
5. 'To minutters stillhet klokken 12', *Aftenposten*, 8 May 1965.
6. Komitéen til forberedelse av 25-års jubileet for frigjøringen, Stortingets Arkiv.
7. 'Opprettelse av et minnefond i anledn. 25-års jub: For feiringen av frigjøringen 8. mai 1945', *Stortingstidende*, 6 May 1970, 2634–7.
8. Minnemøtet i Stortinget den 8. mai 1970, Stortingets arkiv.
9. 'Da freden brøt løs', *Aftenposten*, 8 May 1985.
10. 'Politiet hedrer falne i krigen', *Aftenposten*, 8 May 1985.
11. Frigjøringskomiteen 1992. 'Delinstillingen', Statsministerens kontor.
12. Frigjøringskomiteen 1994. 'Innstilling', Stortingets arkiv.
13. Frigjøringskomiteen 1994. 'Instillingen', Stortingets arkiv: 7.
14. 'Kjøreplan for seremonien under minnemøtet i Stortinget 8.mai 1995', Stortingets arkiv.
15. Frigjøringskomiteen 1994. 'Innstilling', NHM, attachment 'Budsjett for frigjøringsjubileet': 16.
16. S. Seehusen, letter to Jørgensen, Eigil, 15 March 1965, Statsministerens kontor, København.
17. 'Mange samledes for at mindes den store dag for 20 år siden', *Politiken*, 5 May 1965.
18. Udvalget vedrørende 5. maj 1970, 1969. 'Indstilling', Statsministerens kontor: 1.
19. Udvalget vedrørende 5. maj 1970, 1969. 'Indstilling', Statsministerens kontor: 3.
20. Udvalget vedrørende 5. maj 1970. 'Notat om forslag til arrangementer i anledning af 25-året for Danmarks befrielse den 4–5 maj 1970, Statsministerens kontor, København.
21. 'Ingen må glemme kampen', *Berlingske Tidende* 5 May 1970.
22. '20 af de viktigste begivenheder I Storkøbenhavn 4. og 5. maj, *Berlingske Tidende* 4 May 1970.

23. P. Schlüter, letter to 'Til samtlige borgmestre og amtsborgmestre', 8 October 1984, Statsministerens kontor, København.

24. See, as just one of many examples, 'Foragt – Det Fortjener Demonstranterne', *Politiken*, 6 May 1985. The title roughly translates as 'Contempt – That Is What the Demonstrators Deserve'.

25. Statsminister Poul Schlüters tale på Rådhuspladsen lørdag den 4. maj 1985, Statsministerens kontor, København.

26. 5. maj udvalget, 1994, Referat Starsministerens kontor, København.

27. 5. maj udvalget, 1994, Referat af 2. møde, Statsministerens kontor, København.

28. Interview with historian Palle Roslyng-Jensen in Copenhagen on 3 May 2005.

29. See http://www.befrielsen1945.dk.

30. Interview with Jørgen H. P. Barfod in Frihedsmuseet on 2 May 2005. Barfod is one of the few surviving members of the resistance leadership and head of the veterans' association.

31. Besides the numerous commentaries in the newspapers that accused the prime minister of making use of the history of the resistance, historians such as Nils Arne Sørensen have supported that view of an instrumentalisation. For one example, see Sørensen (2005: 295).

Section 4

Towards a Europeanisation of the Commemoration of the Holocaust

Chapter 11

REMEMBERING EUROPE'S
HEART OF DARKNESS

Legacies of the Holocaust in Post-war
European Societies

◈

Cecilie Felicia Stokholm Banke

In his recently published book, *Postwar: A History of Europe Since 1945*, British historian Tony Judt (2005) argues that it is only now that Europe is recognising the horrors that took place during the Second World War, and that this phenomenon can be observed in the many memorials and commemorations instituted in European countries during the past one or two decades. Why did it take so long? What happened between the war and this recent recognition? And what has brought Europe closer to this part of its past – a part that was first neglected, then confronted and finally, at least in many countries, acknowledged?

This chapter examines Europe's relation to the Second World War and the Holocaust since 1945, and how this relationship has changed from initial neglect to the culture of remembrance, which exists, or is developing, in the majority of European countries. It discusses the ways in which this new culture of remembrance is related to political developments in Europe, the US and Israel, and asks whether we can speak about a 'Europeanisation' of the commemoration of the Holocaust. In other words, has Europe developed its own culture of memory around the Holocaust? Has it faced this historical trauma and transformed the experience into something creative, as something that needs to be addressed and remembered repeatedly?

If so, is this Europeanisation of the Holocaust related to the development of a union based on common or, more precisely, European values? Is there a relation between the increased interest in the Holocaust and political developments related to Europe? How can we understand the focus on the Holocaust in Europe, a focus that has resulted in the designation of 27 January

---

Notes for this chapter are located on page 174.

as a day of Holocaust commemoration in many countries, in the opening of new centres for research and information, and in the establishment of the Task Force for International Cooperation on Holocaust Education, Remembrance and Research (ITF)? Is this focus on the Holocaust part of a long process of coming to terms with history, which began with the reaction to the horrors of the concentration camps? Or can we identify a new political culture developing in Europe after the fall of the Berlin Wall?

To conduct such a study, we need to make an important distinction, that is, the difference between the culture of memory developed in Western Europe and that developed in Eastern Europe, and we need to consider the relationship between perpetrators, victims and bystanders. Based on better access to archives and sources and on new research, different interpretations of these relationships have emerged. During the last two to three decades, the once-accepted balance between them has changed. The questions at issue involve the relation that this change has to the official culture of memory and the extent to which the commemorations are influenced by political trends and developments.

Finally, it is necessary to consider the ways in which the Europeanisation of the commemoration of the Holocaust is part of a wider universalisation, which can be found not only in Europe, the US and Israel, but also in Latin American, Africa and Asia (Miles 2005: 371–93). For this reason, we need to ask whether the commemoration is specific to Europe, or if we are likely to see an increased focus on the Holocaust and the principles that have derived from it, such as the Universal Declaration of Human Rights and the Convention on Genocide, in other parts of the world. Is the universalisation of the Holocaust part of a new kind of moral order, based on the concepts of human rights and international humanitarian law? If so, what role does Europe play in this order?

Background

Since 1945, the Holocaust has been portrayed in European culture at first only sporadically, then more systematically and, in the last couple of decades, with an increased intensity. Most historians and experts would today agree that the intensification of global interest in the Holocaust started with the transmission of Marvin J. Chomsky's television series, *Holocaust: The Story of the Family Weiss*, in 1978 and 1979 (Cole 1999: 7). This mini-series was broadcast worldwide to 220 million viewers and had a huge impact (Zander 2003).

Another important explanation for the increased interest in the Holocaust was the trial of Adolf Eichmann in 1961. The same year saw the publication of one of the first, and now classic, studies of the Holocaust, Raul Hilberg's *The Destruction of the European Jews* (1961). As Hilberg later stated

(1988: 21), in the beginning there was no Holocaust. When the crimes of the Nazi regime became widely known by the end of the war, they were not understood nor were they fully grasped in the decades that followed. The story of the Holocaust was not a story to tell during the 1950s, a time when Europe was only just recovering from the war and the liberal-democratic culture of the optimistic West required development (Kushner 1994; Novick 1999).

From the 1960s onwards, however, there seems to have been what Pieter Lagrou (2000) has termed a 'reversal in remembrance'. Judt (2005) writes that the trigger for German self-interrogation was a series of trials prompted by investigations into German crimes on the Eastern front. The first case was in Ulm in 1958, with proceedings against members of wartime *Einsatzgruppen* (SS mobile killing units). This case was followed by the Eichmann trial in Jerusalem, and then came the Frankfurt trials of Auschwitz guards, between December 1963 and August 1965. During these proceedings, camp survivors had the opportunity to speak publicly for the first time about what they had witnessed. As Devin O. Pendas (2006) has described, the Auschwitz trial has to be understood as a political trial. Rendering justice on Auschwitz raised important contemporary political questions: 'The Cold War was a constant presence in the courtroom, but so too were questions about the nature of West German democracy and the relationship between the German past and the German present' (ibid.: 2–3).

The real transformation in Germany was motivated by a series of events in the following decades. The Six-Day War between Arabs and Israelis in 1967, Chancellor Brandt kneeling at the Warsaw Ghetto memorial in 1970, the murder of Israeli athletes at the 1972 Munich Olympics and the airing of *Holocaust* all contributed to a shift in the memory of the Holocaust. While in 1968, 471 school groups visited Dachau, by the end of the 1970s, the annual total was approaching 5,000 (Judt 2006: 811).

There are many ways of explaining this change. Some, like political scientist Norman G. Finkelstein (2000), would emphasise the changing role of Israel in world politics, starting with the 1967 war. The dramatic increase in the number of films, books, television programmes, museums and commemorations concerning the Holocaust since the Six-Day War in 1967 can be attributed to Israel having developed a partnership with the US. For this reason, it was no longer necessary to maintain silence about the Holocaust. Finkelstein (ibid.) suggests that the Six-Day War was the first element in the construction of a myth, within which the events of the Holocaust became part of a 'political game'.

Yet this is too simple an explanation. A complex series of events and social and political changes fostered the process towards a different public memory of the Holocaust and thus also of the Second World War. Some of these events and changes can be traced to the American Jewish community, to Hollywood and to Israel. But there are other ways to explain why

Europeans devote time and thought to the specific history of the Holocaust, and these factors have less to do with Jews and Israel. The suffering of European Jewry during the Second World War was a continental drama and fundamentally a European problem. To approach the Holocaust is also to approach important aspects of European history, culture and society.

This perspective points to the German *Historikerstreit* (historians' dispute) of the 1980s. The *Historikerstreit* clearly showed that for Germans the reality of dealing with the Holocaust was far more complicated than could be conveyed in an artistic film production. It was one thing to know what the Germans had done four decades earlier, but situating it in German and European history remained a very difficult and delicate task. How could Germany come to terms with this past? What would the relation of the next generation be to Nazi crimes?

Other Western European countries followed the same pattern. As Judt (2005: 812) describes it, 'the process of remembering and acknowledging had first to overcome self-serving local illusions – a process that typically took two generations and many decades'. In Austria, a serious and still incomplete investigation of the country's experience with Nazism began in the 1980s when the involvement of presidential candidate Kurt Waldheim in the Wehrmacht's brutal occupation of Yugoslavia was revealed. Switzerland, too, was late to admit the restrictive policy towards refugees before and during the war, and to acknowledge its use of 'J' passports as 'an intolerable racial discrimination' (ibid.).

For the Netherlands, facing the dark side of Dutch wartime behaviour began with the publication of Jacob Presser's book *Ondergang* (1965). This first full history of the extermination of Dutch Jewry was followed by television documentaries and other programmes about the years of Nazi occupation. During the same year, the Dutch government offered to contribute to the memorial at Auschwitz for the first time. As in Germany, the trials of the early 1960s triggered Dutch interest in Holocaust history. Every generation writes its own version of history, and the post-war baby boomers wanted to confront the silence of their parents. But even if the baby boomers shed new light on Dutch occupation history, it took a long time before the full implications of Dutch actions during the war would actually sink in. Not until 1995 did a reigning head of state, Queen Beatrice, publicly acknowledge the tragedy of the Dutch Jews. And it was perhaps only with the image of armed Dutch UN peacekeepers passively watching while Serbian militia groups rounded up and murdered thousands of Muslims at Srebrenica that the message finally got through: the Holocaust happened here, we did nothing to stop it and we may even have contributed to it. A long-postponed national debate about the price that the Dutch paid for their cooperation and obedience could finally begin.

As in the Netherlands, the Germans issued orders to deport and round up Jews in Austria, Switzerland, Norway and Belgium, but they could never have carried out these directives without the collaboration of local authorities, policemen and bureaucrats. In France alone, the Nazis did not have to issue orders: the Vichy regime did so itself. It helped the Germans by initiating discriminatory projects of its own, such as the introduction of 'Jewish laws' in 1940 and 1941, without being pressured by Germany to do so. The Vichy regime even rounded up Jews on French soil.

For this reason, it took the perspective gained by a generation with no direct relation to the Vichy regime before France could face its active role in the Holocaust. This affected not only France but the whole of Europe. As Judt (2005) writes, Europe's efforts to come to terms with the Second World War were overshadowed by France – not because France behaved the worst, but rather because, until 1989, France mattered the most in Europe. As long as the French refused to confront their past directly, 'a shadow would hang over the new Europe' (ibid.: 818–19). As in Germany, the changes in France came with a series of trials, which took place during the 1990s. The first was that of Paul Touvier in 1994. Touvier, an activist in Vichy's wartime Milice Française (a paramilitary force), stood accused of killing seven French Jews in June 1944. Touvier was not himself a major figure, but his trial served as a substitute for others that never took place.

The prosecution of another major figure, Maurice Papon, who served as a police chief in Paris under de Gaulle after the war, was also intended to set an example. Due to insufficient evidence, Papon was not punished, but the trial made it clear that Vichy France was not a closed historical parenthesis. Its spectre was indeed part of post-war France. Papon's trial showed that the Vichy regime was not an exception in French political history. People from the regime continued to serve in the French administration after the war, and their crimes went unacknowledged and unpunished. It was almost as if their behaviour was accepted.

The French president, François Mitterand, was himself an example of France's double standard. In his very person, Mitterand incarnated the national inability to speak openly about the shame of the occupation (Judt 2006: 819). Everything changed when Mitterand finally left office. In 1995, on the fifty-third anniversary of the round-up of Parisian Jews, France's newly installed president, Jacques Chirac, broke the taboo and acknowledged his country's role in the Holocaust. More than a decade later, the French historian Henry Rousso, commenting upon the death of the then 96-year-old war criminal Papon, stated that one of the principal effects of the Papon trial was the emergence of France as one of the most advanced European countries in its politics of reparation and recognition (Conan and Rousso 1998; Rousso 2007).[1]

In analysing these national cases, we can sum up some of the factors that account for the changes in attitudes towards the killing of European Jews during the Second World War. Modern culture and communication technology must be considered as important aspects in providing the Holocaust a central place in European public memory, as demonstrated by the interest in and success of the television series *Holocaust*. The impressive viewing figures not only were due to the quality of this production, but also underscored a resonance for the subject within the public. The trials and the many national debates that ensued, especially in France and Germany, were also important, primarily because they provided an opportunity to re-examine the past and to retell history, but also because the trials, in and of themselves, were signs of the political will to confront the crimes. Moreover, there was the influence of contemporary research based on new research questions, as illustrated by the Dutch case.

Holocaust in the Shadows of Srebrenica and a Unified Europe

If we look at the response to the Polish-American historian Jan T. Gross's book *Neighbors: The Destruction of the Jewish Community in Jedwabne, Poland* (2001), it becomes clear just how painful retelling the history of the extermination of the Jews remains in many European countries. This is the case not only in Western Europe but also, and maybe even particularly, in Eastern Europe. Gross describes how 1,600 Jews were slaughtered during the Second World War, not by the Nazis but by their Polish neighbours. The book prompted a heated debate in Poland about relations with the country's Jewish population. It also challenged the national myth about the war and provoked a painful process of reinterpreting Polish history – a process that involved acknowledging Polish anti-Semitism.

Gross's book is another example of how the focus on the Holocaust impinges on European society in a very specific way, raising a series of fundamental questions. As the Polish journalist and editor, Adam Michnik (2001) wrote, following the release of Gross's volume, it cannot be denied that guilt still hangs like a dark shadow over Europe and makes everyone (including Michnik himself) an accessory. Although a Jew and not personally involved in the events of the Holocaust, Michnik, as a European, is marked by the trauma that the Holocaust inflicted on Europe.

The various reactions to Gross's book in Poland are important in their own right. Although the Institute of National Memory had been established in 1998 to investigate precisely such controversial subjects as Poland's treatment of its Jews during the Second World War, the nation still finds it hard to confront its history. Yet Poland is not the only post-communist country that has difficulty coming to terms with this particular past. Since gaining independence, none of the Baltic states has prosecuted a single case against surviving national war criminals. In this sense, referring to the initial enquiry of this study, interest in the Holocaust is part of a grieving process. Such a process is not particularly pleasant and is even unwanted in some cases, but it does represent an immense potential to engage all Europeans in the same historical drama.

Some would say that nothing represents just how powerful and full of potential this drama is for developing a common European public memory than the newly opened Holocaust monument in Berlin. Here, the crimes of the National Socialist regime and their collaborators are remembered through the stories of six different European families from six different European countries, all with the same fate: murder at the hand of the Nazis. Walking around the exhibition connected to the monument, visitors learn about the number of Jews estimated to have been killed in every European country. For Poland, the number is between 2.9 and 3.1 million; Germany 160,000–165,000; France 76,100–77,100; Norway 765; Denmark 116. The figures, together with the family photographs – and, indeed, the exhibition as a whole – are a testament to a part of Europe that no longer exists.[2]

Every attempt to understand how this Europe disappeared contributes to the process of integrating the Holocaust into a specific European memory, centred around the same crime and the same history, with the same moral message – 'Never again!' In Europe, learning about the Holocaust through films, television dramas, documentaries, books and exhibitions is part of an attempt to understand this fundamental historical problem, this common legacy of European nation states.

It is by means of the 'other' that we can recognise all things European (Nabulsi and Stråth 2001). It is through negative examples that we can become aware of the characteristics of European civilisation. In this sense, the Holocaust acts as a benchmark for what Europe should be and for what it must avoid becoming. It sounds a warning against nationalism, xenophobia, ethnic cleansing and persecution on the grounds of culture, race or religion. In addition, it cautions against the direction in which rational thought, science and technology can take a society or an entire civilisation.

Although the Nazi genocide was carried out by rational means, when we look for a rational explanation for its cause, we find only the irrational (Y. Bauer 2002). The elimination of the Jews was the consequence of elitist politics, based on an ideal of a racially pure German nation into which the Jews did not fit and had to be removed. Not only did the Nazis attempt to remove all Jews from Germany, but they extended their persecution of Jews wherever they could, with the sole aim of eliminating them and solving Europe's 'Jewish problem' conclusively.

The notion that a community should be defined by a shared culture and history has been dominant in Europe since the beginning of the nineteenth century, despite Europe's own sense of itself as a civilisation defined by the principle of equality. With the Holocaust in mind, we can understand what European civilisation can give rise to and what such a view of community can spawn. Considering the Holocaust and its aftermath can also serve to draw attention to the kind of civilisation that is defined by fundamental rights and not by nation and culture. As the jurist Richard J. Goldstone (2001) writes, the Holocaust led to the creation of the international human rights movement and to the Universal Declaration of Human Rights in 1948, the same year that the United Nations adopted its Convention on the Prevention and Punishment of the Crime of Genocide.

In this sense, the murder of six million Jews during the Second World War gave rise to an international society based on the rule of law that places the individual above the state. Since the end of the Cold War, this legal order has established itself, not least because of the wars in the Balkans. In this sense, we are dealing with a view of community that prevails in the nation state and allows for the emergence of a new community, more fitting for the twenty-first century's ethnic and cultural diversity. This is the lesson passed on with stories of the Holocaust. As Hungarian writer Imre Kertész (2003) reflects, the Holocaust is a trauma of European civilisation, and the decisive question for this civilisation is whether this trauma will live on in European societies in the shape of culture or in the shape of neurosis, in the shape of creation or in the shape of destruction.

Imagining the Holocaust in Post-war Europe: Three Phases

Post-war modes of visualising the extermination of the Jews during the Second World War can be divided into three phases, which were, and continue to be, tied to a political context. The first phase, which occurred immediately after the end of the war, saw the worldwide dissemination of black and white photographs of the camps by the mass media. These photos were intended to say something about the winners and losers of the war. Nazism, in defeat, was to be shown in all of its horror. The photographs were thus part of a moral reconstruction which would lift not only Europe but also European values. Despite the genocide, good had ultimately prevailed, aided by the United States. Constructed around the Allied victory, this myth was, naturally enough, one to which European societies clung. Europe had survived, thanks to the US.

In the second phase, different artists reinterpreted documented images of the genocide. These artists had been in the camps themselves or, like the Italian Corrado Cagli, had been on the spot when the American soldiers entered Nordhausen and Buchenwald. Italian-American painter Rico Lebrun used photographs from Buchenwald in the 1950s to speak of the human condition – of pain, endurance and salvation. Pictures of naked and emaciated concentration camp inmates with shaven heads were used to say something about Western culture: its attitudes to death, the fragility of the individual, the myth of Christ, victimisation, redemption.

As early as Lebrun's work in the 1950s, the Holocaust possessed a symbolic value. A decade later, the Holocaust was the key to the iconoclastic NO!Art movement co-founded by the Russian-born Jew Boris Lurie. Himself a survivor of the camps, Lurie settled in New York after the war, where he established himself as an artist. In his work, he expressed the Holocaust as profound disillusionment with the West. His collages combined photographs from the camps with pornographic images. One of them, *Lolita* (1962), is composed of bits of the poster for Stanley Kubrick's film of the same name combined with images of three dead camp prisoners, whose shaven heads stick out from behind wooden barracks. In 1998, Lurie clarified what he had wanted to show with this particular arrangement: 'My pictures are less to do with the Holocaust than with discontent with the American way of life' (quoted in Liljefors 2002: 71).

During the 1960s and 1970s, the left frequently cited the Holocaust in its criticism of society, with Nazism symbolising all that was most degenerate in Western culture. Here was proof that capitalism led to perversion, barbarity, moral decline and the collapse of civilisation. This argument was shrewd indeed, for even if the attack was directed at the US, the Holocaust took place, after all, in Europe. During the Cold War, the US could portray itself as the civilisation that had saved Europe from the barbarians. The implication was that European civilisation would not have been able to do anything about the Nazi cancer itself, and this suggestion made it easy for America to occupy Europe morally. Europe had come to doubt its civilisation.

In the third, current phase, doubt has given way to confrontation, with a direct effect on the way in which European societies deal with the Holocaust. On the one hand, we have the culture of memory itself, of which Holocaust Remembrance Day on 27 January is a part. The Holocaust is remembered, genocide is acknowledged, the victims receive compensation. Events are analysed, and the guilty are named. The relationships between guilt and responsibility, victim and executioner are analysed anew. Some 60 years later, survivors and their children can confront the Holocaust in the same ways that perpetrators and their children can. Just as former German Chancellor Gerhard Schröder could, at the sixtieth anniversary of the liberation of Auschwitz, remind his audience that the Holocaust was a part of their life and memory as Europeans, we can now begin to address the question that is posed whenever pictures of the mounds of bodies appear: how was this possible?

In addition to its contribution to the culture of memory, the Holocaust has inspired a vast number of artistic and literary works. Like Sodom and Gomorrah or the destruction of Jerusalem, the Holocaust has assumed a significant cultural weight. Whether a memoir like Roma Ligocka's *The Girl in the Red Coat*, inspired by Steven Spielberg's film *Schindler's List*, or a historical study like that of Jan T. Gross, or artistic interpretations like those of Boris Lurie, these expressions are part of an attempt to answer questions that are vitally important to Europe and European history: Was the Holocaust an aberration or the natural result of European civilisation? Can Europe overcome the Holocaust?

These questions are also relevant to Europe's relationship with the United States. The Holocaust led to a decisive split between Europe and the US. This rift began with the First World War, when Europe woke up to the trauma of the trenches and at least ten million dead. This realisation was the first blow to Europe's self-image as the leading force of modern civilisation. The next and decisive blow came with the inter-war radicalisation of the political right and the advent of fascism and Nazism as dominant forces in European politics. The ethnic cleansing of the 1930s and 1940s in a Europe obsessed by nationalism gave the US a moral advantage, which was later strengthened by an increased focus on the Holocaust as the trauma of Europeans. The Holocaust was the dark side of European civilisation – its Janus face, as Zygmunt Bauman (1989) puts it.

With this characterisation in mind, we might shift the perspective and ask if, instead of being productive, all of the work on the Holocaust – the research, the literature, the films and television dramas, the art, the commemorations – serves instead to reinforce the conception of Europe as the 'dark continent', which is perpetually unable to overcome its monsters. We might also ask whether the Europeanisation of the commemoration of the Holocaust is actually European. Does Europeanisation mean that Europe faces this trauma on its own terms? How 'European' is this process, after all?

Acknowledging Europe's Holocaust Guilt

As the previous description of the visual representations of the Holocaust demonstrates, we can speak of three phases of the legacy of the Holocaust in Europe. The first phase was characterised by black and white photographs from the camps. The gravity of this crime, which occurred in the heart of the European continent, became known through these pictures taken by soldiers and camp survivors. The horrors were confronted, but no questions were asked. As in the French case, it took most European countries at least two generations to start doing this. The lesson of this phase was that Nazism had been defeated, and the guilty had been convicted at Nuremberg.

The second phase saw artists using the Holocaust to express something profound about Western civilisation, capitalism, consumerism and what was seen as a general decline of Western values. This artistic expression of the Holocaust embodies a great deal of political criticism on behalf of left-wing youths, both in the US and in Europe. Some say that this kind of art could be seen as intellectual abstraction, a way to deal with the Holocaust without really confronting it. During this phase, however, the post-war generation started asking questions, using the Holocaust as a reference for how far capitalism could go. This period also saw the publication of the first scholarly works about the Holocaust, which developed a more nuanced picture of the Holocaust and how it had happened.

During this second phase, the ideological battle about how to understand the Holocaust began. Similar to the anti-fascist discourse of the 1930s, the left wing conflated the Holocaust with colonialism and imperialism. To some extent, this way of interpreting the Holocaust relativised the crimes committed during the Second World War by comparing them to crimes committed by the European colonial powers. A clear example of this relativism can be seen in the Barbie case in France in the mid-1980s. The Nazi war criminal Klaus Barbie, also known as 'the Butcher of Lyon', was captured in 1983 and brought to trial in Lyon four years later. During the trial, the lawyer for the defence, Jacques Vergès, shifted the focus from the crimes of the Nazis and their collaborators committed in France during the Vichy regime to the crimes committed by France as a colonial power in Algeria and other former colonies. French philosopher Alain Finkielkraut (1992) noted that the 'relativism' of this trial showed how France again managed to avoid confronting the active role of the Vichy regime in the persecution and deportation of French Jews.

Figures such as Finkielkraut, for whom justice is the most fundamental principle of democracy, want France to face its own responsibility. Finkielkraut can be seen as representing a movement which advocates justice and the principles of international humanitarian law. This justice-orientated movement started to grow stronger in the years following the fall of the Berlin Wall and received a tremendous boost with the civil war in the former Yugoslavia during the 1990s. The movement, which has its roots in the human rights movement of the late nineteenth century, was institutionalised after the Second World War by the Nuremberg war crime trials, the Universal Declaration of Human Rights and the UN genocide convention. In addition to this, the 1980s also saw the emergence of Holocaust deniers, who question the Holocaust and the factual basis of new research. Initially a movement directed primarily by neo-Nazis, Holocaust deniers have now cloaked their bigotry, raising questions about the Holocaust in a way that may appear to be serious scientific critique. British historian David Irving is a clear example of this dangerous phenomenon.

The third phase saw the appearance of memorials, like that in Berlin by American architect Peter Eisenman, but also in France, Belgium and Norway. To be a member of the European club, a country has to confront and acknowledge its own Holocaust record. Or, as Alfred Pijpers (2006: 126–7) from the Clingendale Institute in The Hague recently stated: 'Now we should all acknowledge our Holocaust guilt.'

In closing, I would like to open the door to a fourth phase in the legacy of the Holocaust and the way it is being confronted and dealt with. Here I will refer to another visualisation of the Holocaust, Polish artist Zbigniew Libera's 1996 art installation at the international art *biennale* in Venice. Titled *LEGO Concentration Camp Set*, Libera's piece is a model of a gas chamber built from Lego plastic bricks. Unsure where I could fit this into my chronology, I recently showed a representation of this work to some of my students. Was this an example of the second phase or the third phase of the legacy of the Holocaust in Europe, I asked. One student answered: 'Maybe it is a warning. That there is a limit for how and to what end we can use the Holocaust.'

For students born around the fall of the Berlin Wall, the use of the Holocaust as a specific political symbol, as it was in the 1960s and 1970s, or as the background for a successful television series, as it was in *Holocaust*, or as a social critique, as it was in Zygmunt Bauman's work, is simply too much. Students of today see the Holocaust as the precedent for other ethnic cleansings and genocidal conflicts that are closer to their historical horizon, such as Rwanda and Darfur. Therefore, what we see in the fourth phase is a globalisation of the Holocaust – the Holocaust as a universal moral legacy.

The normative impact of the Holocaust in the post-war era has moved from something directed inwards to European societies to something directed outwards – a universal symbol of evil that is relevant not only for Europe but for the entire world. A general European law against Holocaust denial, suggested by the German EU presidency during the spring of 2007, is a sign of this impact, as was the reaction of the European Commission when Europe seemed to be haunted by a new wave of anti-Semitism at the beginning of the twenty-first century (Banke 2004; Prodi 2004). The Holocaust has thus assumed a dominating role in the political culture developed in Europe after 1989 as a historical reference against which European societies must constantly guard, both in Europe and elsewhere.

Notes

1. See also 'La France n'en a pas fini avec ces années noires', *Liberation*, 19 February 2007.
2. A special thanks to Stiftung Denkmal für die ermordeten Juden Europas in Berlin for explaining the idea behind the exhibition and the numbers as they occur in room 1. In most cases, the exact figures are not known and never will be. The countries are based on the 1937 borders.

Chapter 12

HOLOCAUST REMEMBRANCE AND RESTITUTION OF JEWISH PROPERTY IN THE CZECH REPUBLIC AND POLAND AFTER 1989

෧ᲒᎽᎶᎶᏏ

Stanisław Tyszka

The point of departure for this chapter is an observation of a close connection between the issue of restitution of nationalised property and processes of collective remembrance in Central and Eastern Europe after the fall of communism. On the one hand, the programmes of restitution adopted by the post-communist governments were an element of the reintroduction of private property rights into these societies within the general processes of denationalisation of their economies. On the other hand, they were meant as a means of redressing the wrongdoings of the previous regimes, and as such have become an important element of coming to terms with the communist past. But restitution was not only about the communist past. It quickly turned out that it was impossible to limit restitution only to the post-war nationalisations, because the communists had also taken over property previously seized by the Nazis. Thus, the issue of restitution of Jewish property that had been lost during the Holocaust appeared in the restitution debates. A characteristic of these debates is that they involved various historical narratives of victimhood presented both by groups of claimants and by those who opposed restitution.

The issue of restitution of Jewish property after the end of the Cold War was not limited to Central and Eastern Europe. It also appeared in countries such as Switzerland, Austria, France and Norway and can therefore be analysed within a broader European context. I would like to consider the problem of the so-called Europeanisation of the Holocaust memory. One of the proponents of the Europeanisation thesis is Dan Diner, who claims that the Holocaust is emerging as the foundational event for a common European collective memory, an event that can be

---

Notes for this chapter begin on page 189.

compared only to such historic turning points as the Reformation and French Revolution. In Diner's view (2003), the restitution of Jewish property has become one of the most important means of Holocaust remembrance, as the wave of restitutions since the 1990s has proceeded from the East to the West of Europe.

Taking this thesis as a point of reference, this chapter attempts to analyse two nationally specific cases of debates – in the Czech Republic and in Poland – on the issue of Jewish restitution and its relation to the processes of coming to terms with the past. I begin my examination of the restitution discourses with a discussion of two films, one Polish and one Czech, viewing both as symbolic representations of the problematics of Polish-Jewish and Czech-Jewish wartime relations. I believe that some important aspects of processes of collective remembrance of the Second World War and of the Holocaust that are particular to the Czech and Polish post-communist societies, and which can be identified on the basis of a comparative analysis of the films, will allow us to understand and explain better the ways in which the issue of Jewish restitution was approached, discussed and regulated in the Czech Republic and in Poland.

Comedy and Tragedy

The films I shall discuss are *Divided We Fall* (*Musíme si Pomáhat*) by Jan Hřebejk (2000, Czech Republic) and *Far from the Window* (*Daleko od Okna*) by Jan Jakub Kolski (2000, Poland). Both films tell a story of a Gentile couple who decide to hide a Jew during the Nazi occupation, and both are in part inspired by true stories. However, although their basic plot is strikingly similar, their symbolic meanings differ radically. Through the genres chosen to tell a similar story, these two films offer different answers to the question about the legitimate modes of representation for the complicated issues of Jewish-Gentile past relations in the Czech Republic and in Poland. Whereas the Czech film is a comedy interspersed with some dramatic scenes, the Polish film is a psychological drama with elements of a classical tragedy. Both films focus on a couple who are unable to have children because one of the spouses is infertile and who decide to give shelter to a Jew. Gradually, a complicated emotional triangle forms and threatens to split the marriage. The principal plot device hinges on the fact that a child is born as a result of this situation. But the similarities go even further. In both films, the hiding place of the Jewish individual is known to a local Nazi collaborator, with whom the couple has a complicated relationship and who tries to use his knowledge about the Jew to his advantage.

The main character of *Divided We Fall* is Josef, an ordinary Czech who wants to live a quiet life, enjoy his happy marriage to his beautiful wife, Marie, and survive the war. One day, however, he meets David, his Jewish friend from before the war, and, with some initial reluctance, takes him in. This decision sets in motion a chain of events that completely disrupt his peaceful existence. The couple receive frequent visits from Horst, an ethnic German and a Nazi collaborator, who suggests that, in order to protect his Jewish friend, Josef should become a Nazi collaborator himself. As a result, Josef loses his status in the Czech community. As in any good farce, things get more and more complicated. At one point, in order to avoid having to house a Nazi bureaucrat, Josef's wife has to declare that she is shortly to have a baby. But since Josef is sterile, they decide that she will get pregnant by David. A few months later, the town is liberated, and Josef is accused by the new authorities of being a Nazi collaborator. He is about to be executed when David appears to save him. Josef then rescues Horst from prison, saying that he is a doctor and is needed to deliver the baby. Thus, a Nazi sympathiser delivers a child of a Jewish father. When the child is born, the German shouts with joy, 'We have a baby!' In the film's final scene, Josef is proudly pushing a pram through a landscape of ruin when he sees the members of David's family, who perished in the Holocaust, now sitting at the table and drinking vodka together with a young German soldier, who also died during the war. Josef takes the baby out of the pram and holds it high above his head so that the child is visible to the group.

At the beginning of the Polish film, *Far from the Window*, we see Jan and Barbara as happy newlyweds. Their happiness, however, is soon overshadowed by the fact that Barbara cannot get pregnant and is increasingly obsessed with having a baby. One day, Jan returns home with a beautiful Jewish woman, Regina, and decides that they will hide her. The wife accepts Jan's decision, but treats Regina in an unfriendly manner. Soon Jan and Regina fall in love, and she becomes pregnant. Upon finding out about this, Barbara flies into a rage and wants to denounce Regina to the Nazis. Eventually, however, she decides to incorporate Regina and the baby into her marriage and starts pretending to be pregnant. When Regina gives birth to a daughter, Barbara takes the child away from her and brings it up as her own. As a result, the degraded, humiliated and helpless Regina runs away. After the war, two of Regina's acquaintances come to the house to ask for the child, offering a large sum of money. In this very dramatic scene, the envoys argue that it will break Regina's heart if they come back without the child, to which the Poles reply that if they let the child go, their hearts will be broken. The story continues into the communist period. The husband retreats into alcoholism and dies. The girl is raised unaware that the Polish woman is not her biological mother. Years later she discovers the truth, which inspires her to set out to find Regina in Germany. Regina, however, does not want to have a relationship with her daughter, desiring only to forget the suffering and humiliation that she has been through. In the end, everybody is miserable or dead, and the young girl is left to question continually who she is.

These two films can be viewed as retelling national history in the form of a family chronicle. In this perspective, the history of the nation is problematised by the changing relationships between the main characters. The shape of the historical narratives as reconstructed in the plot of the two films appears to a large extent determined by the particular genre chosen to tell the story: tragedy and comedy.

Each of these genres has a unique dramatic trajectory. While tragedy follows the protagonist from triumph to defeat, comedy charts the movement from repression to liberation (Frye 1957). We have seen above that both films follow these trajectories rather closely. Each of these genres also has its own dramatic focus. Tragedy is concerned more with the individual and his or her transformation, while comedy usually has a wider social focus. The plot of *Far from the Window* is indeed focused entirely on the psychological relationships between the characters, confined in a claustrophobic atmosphere. In *Divided We Fall* there are more characters and plot lines, and thus the historical context is depicted in more detail.

The Czech film was described in the reviews as a 'daring comedy of ethics' and was praised for its realism and for dealing with the moral complexity of wartime attitudes and relationships. Although the film does show that the relationships between the characters become complicated due to the war and the Holocaust, what is more significant is that it repeatedly highlights the issue of solidarity between the characters, with the birth of the child at the conclusion of the film becoming the ultimate symbol of reconciliation. Such an ending is another common characteristic of comedy, which often deals with the need for social regeneration, a process typically symbolised by the transfer of control from one generation to the next. At the same time, however, this happy ending overshadows any moral ambiguities concerning the previous behaviour of the characters. Even the film's title stresses the idea of solidarity and reconciliation, which is more evident in the Czech title, *Musíme si Pomáhat*, which means literally 'We must help each other'.

Northrop Frye's analysis (1957) of classic Shakespearian comedies is that they all share a three-stage development, moving from repression to liberation and, finally, to reconciliation. Such stages can also be identified in the plot of *Divided We Fall*. First, Josef's situation is complicated because he is hiding a Jew despite the fact that his house is often visited by the Nazi collaborator. Then, the occupation ends and the danger passes. Finally, after the 'settling of accounts', the story concludes with the image of reconciliation by the cradle.

It should be noted that the character of the Jew is clearly overshadowed by the character of the German. Although it is David and his situation as a Jew on the run from the Nazis that is the catalyst for the plot, the character of Horst and his relationship with the couple quickly becomes central to the story, the structure of which is determined also by historical events. The final symbolic reconciliation is made possible by the fact that the story ends at a very particular moment of Czech history. Significantly, this is before the Sudeten Germans were expelled from Czechoslovakia. Moreover, during the immediate post-war period it was usually impossible for the Jews to regain their property, which was taken over by the new Czechoslovak government.

In contrast, *Far from the Window* is a psychological drama that was frequently described in press reviews as reminiscent of a Greek tragedy. Indeed, as in a classic tragedy there is a deep and irresolvable conflict between the characters, which is best visible in the scene when Regina's envoys arrive to take the child back. In this tragedy, however, the power of fate is replaced by history, which had created the conditions for this conflict.

As far as the structure of the story is concerned, it is rather simple, beginning with a pair of happy newlyweds and then charting the gradual downfall of all characters into the post-war years. This extended time span of the narrative makes the ending quite significant, as it seems to raise the issue of Poland coming face to face with its Jewish past, which is symbolically represented through the meeting of the girl with her Jewish mother. At the end of the story, the tragic conflict remains unresolved and is passed on to the next generation.

These two modes of story development differ with regard to the possibility of providing or achieving justice. The idea of corrective justice presupposes the Aristotelian idea of normative equilibrium. Certain occurrences disturb this equilibrium, and justice consists of its restoration. In both stories we have the social equilibrium thoroughly disrupted by the war, which is reflected by the profound change of relationships between the main characters. However, the post-war resolution of this problem in the stories is very different.

The final reconciliation in the Czech comedy is made possible only by the symbolic settling of accounts. In both stories the necessity of hiding was presented as an extremely humiliating experience for the Jewish characters, who were stripped of their dignity. At the end of the Czech film, however, David is symbolically allowed to regain his dignity when he saves the life of his Czech friend. This impression is strengthened by Josef's behaviour: terrified that he will be shot, he hysterically kisses and hugs his saviour. Of course, this settling of accounts is much more visible in what happens to the German Horst, who is severely punished by the new authorities for his collaboration. It thus seems that comedy, as a genre, is compatible with – or even necessitates – providing some corrective justice.

In *Far from the Window*, on the other hand, there is no justice. The Jewish woman is stripped of her dignity permanently. In the scene when Regina finally meets her daughter, she is laughing hysterically and behaves like a mad person. The Polish family is miserable: the father drinks himself to death, the mother lives in a lie and the girl has no idea who she really is.

What we find in this case is a story of hopeless suffering for which there is no compensation, no reparation and no final redemption. The issue is captured well in George Steiner's definition (1961: 4) of tragedy as undeserved and irreparable human suffering, which excludes any compensation because 'where there is compensation there is justice not tragedy'.

The similarities between the plots of these films were sometimes noticed by their reviewers. The well-known Polish novelist Manuela Gretkowska (2002) praised the realism of the Czech comedy as opposed to the unnecessary symbolism and romantic rhetoric of the Polish film. Interestingly, some Czech reviewers recommended watching *Far from the Window* to those who did not appreciate the atmosphere of forgiveness and reconciliation of the Czech film. It seems, however, that the character of the films relates to the prevailing attitudes towards the war and the Holocaust in both societies. Such an opinion was expressed by the scriptwriter of *Far from the Window*, Cezary Harasimowicz, who claimed that in the Polish cinema this subject could not be dealt with in the manner of the Czech film due to what he called the 'taboo of national psychology'.[1] On the other hand, it is highly probable that a film presenting Czech-Jewish past relations as a tragedy would be regarded as out of place and would simply not sell in the Czech Republic.

The idea of the Czech film presupposes a certain closure regarding past Czech-Jewish conflicts. As we shall see, it is consistent with the fact that there are currently no Czech-Jewish issues that would evoke much interest in the wider circles of Czech society. As for Poland, although the Polish-Jewish dialogue is proceeding well, with the debate on Jedwabne as a significant breakthrough, any kind of symbolic closure of past issues would be mere wishful thinking at this point in time. I shall argue below that potentially the most explosive issue in Polish-Jewish relations is the unresolved restitution of Jewish property.

In the following paragraphs, I first discuss the regulations of restitution adopted or drafted in the Czech Republic and in Poland after 1989. I next set a theoretical framework for discussing restitution. Finally, I attempt to identify the most important characteristics of the two restitution debates with regard to Jewish restitution.

Restitution as a Means of Remembrance

As far as the general picture of property restitution in each country is concerned, it should be stressed at the outset that the Czech Republic has implemented the largest restitution programme in Central and Eastern Europe, returning property both to individuals and to some legal entities. Poland, on the other hand, despite numerous legislative attempts, has not yet adopted a general law on restitution to individual owners. It thus occupies the opposite pole of the spectrum of post-communist countries in the region, most of whom have, in one way or another, compensated individual former owners. Nonetheless, by means of a series of laws adopted during the 1990s, Poland did return property that had belonged to churches and other religious communities prior to the Second World War. Consequently, with regard to Jewish restitution, it can generally be said that the Czech state has returned property both to Jewish communities and Jewish private claimants, whereas the Polish state has returned property only to Jewish religious communities – not to individuals.

Because Jewish restitution has usually been linked to the issue of a general regulation of restitution, it should be examined within the broader picture of national restitution debates, in which different groups of former owners presented various restitution and compensation claims. In this respect, restitution is a very interesting example of how legal categories can collide with the categories that are typical for the politics of memory. Theoretically, as with any regulations adopted with respect to the rule of law, restitution laws should be determined by the principles of equality before law or non-discrimination. Although the Czech restitution laws, as well as some Polish draft laws, were formulated in neutral group language, in practice they favoured certain groups and excluded others from restitution schemes. This was done mainly by the adoption of provisions such as specific cut-off dates for restitution or by a requirement of citizenship and residency.

As a result, the discussions on restitution in both countries, which at the beginning of the 1990s concentrated on the question of whether to return property to the former owners at all, have quickly shifted their focus to specific claims of various categories of former owners, including the aristocracy, the former middle class, *kulaks*, the Catholic Church, German expellees, émigrés and Jews. In both countries, the adopted or planned schemes of restitution differed with regard to these groups, as did popular attitudes towards their claims.

As mentioned at the start of the chapter, restitution regulations in the Czech Republic and in Poland can also be seen as part of a wider European and global trend of amending past injustices through restitution and compensation. This trend is to a large extent rooted in the post-war West German response to the Holocaust through the politics of the so-called *Wiedergutmachung*, or reparations. Since the 1990s, however, the tendency to deal with past injustices by legal means has grown stronger, with still new groups asking for recognition of their past suffering and financial compensation. One of the authors attempting to identify the main characteristics of restitution in its global dimension is Elazar Barkan. In *The Guilt of Nations*, Barkan (2000) examines various cases of restitution, such as the Swiss banks affair, the claims of Australian aborigines and Native Americans, and the restitution in Central and Eastern Europe. Using these cases, he tries to construct a theory of restitution. Generally, the author conceives of restitution as a means of reconciliation, as a negotiation between the perpetrators and their victims leading to new interpretations of the past to which 'both sides can subscribe and from which each will benefit' (ibid.: 329).

I would like to argue that such a perspective on restitution does not capture the most important aspects of the restitution in the Czech Republic and in Poland. What distinguishes the post-1989 restitution in the examined countries from the other cases is that it is an attempt to redress only a small part of a multitude of various historical injustices suffered by their populations under two totalitarian regimes in the twentieth century. Moreover, as a result of the complicated history of the twentieth century, not only are there many categories of victims in both societies, but also drawing clear distinctions between the victims, beneficiaries and even perpetrators is sometimes difficult.

With regard to the changes in property relations in the Polish and Czech territories in the twentieth century, several waves of property revolutions can be distinguished: first under the Nazi occupation, then during the post-war population transfers and finally under the communist regimes. These interferences with property rights were often an integral part of – and sometimes a prelude to – general policies of persecution or discrimination that were motivated by various political, ideological and economic considerations. Above all, as concerns the situation of the Jewish populations under Nazi occupation, disregard for property rights represented only one aspect of a general process of abusive, discriminatory and ultimately genocidal treatment. What is most important with respect to restitution in the analysed countries is that all these confiscations and nationalisations of property belonging to various individuals, groups and institutions led to a very complicated situation with property rights, which after 1989 has often resulted in overlapping claims to property.

In view of the above, I shall argue that property restitution in the Czech Republic and Poland should be seen primarily as a discourse in which the status of victims could be recognised or denied, and in which a certain hierarchy of victims was established. The decision whether to return property at all involved defining victims, although the main argument of the opponents of restitution was that under communism 'everybody suffered' and that material suffering should not be treated as more worthy of compensation than other form of hardship.

At the beginning of the 1990s, when the general restitution laws were adopted in Czechoslovakia, the issue of Jewish restitution was not yet resolved. The first adopted restitution laws provided for the return of property nationalised after the communist takeover in 1948 – a cut-off date that was intended to exclude the claims of the Sudeten Germans who had been expelled in the immediate post-war period. At the same time, however, it made impossible restitution of property that was confiscated by the Nazis and was not returned to its former owners after the war. In addition, some Jews were denied the right to claim their property due to the requirements of Czech citizenship and residency. This form of restitution legislation was obviously criticised by the small Jewish religious community in the Czech Republic, but nothing changed until 1994. It should also be noted that the problem of Jewish restitution was rarely mentioned in Czech public discourse. Since 1994, however, these restrictions limiting Jewish restitution have been gradually removed. As the government began to transfer property to the Jewish communities through administrative channels, the general restitution laws were amended to provide restitution of some property confiscated for racial reasons during the war. Still, many issues remained open up until 1998, when the government established the Joint Working Committee on Mitigation of Some Property Crimes against Holocaust Victims to resolve all remaining problems.

As far as the popular perception of Jewish restitution in Czech society is concerned, the issue failed to raise strong emotions on either the national or the local level. This can be partly explained by the relatively low value of assets claimed by the Jews and by the rather modest and self-limiting demands on the part of the local Jewish religious communities who, for example, decided to leave many synagogues in the hands of other churches. More important, however, is that in the restitution debates, as they can be reconstructed from media reports and the statements of Czech politicians, the issue of Jewish property claims was completely overshadowed by other problems that were at the centre of public interest and shaped the dynamics of these discussions – namely, the property claims of the Sudeten Germans, of the Catholic Church and of the aristocracy. These issues attracted much more attention, evoking contentious and emotional disputes. I argue that it was the fact that the Jewish claims were of secondary importance for the Czech debates on the past and Czech national identity that made possible the eventual resolution of the problem of Jewish restitution.

The previously mentioned Joint Working Committee on Mitigation of Some Property Crimes against Holocaust Victims contributed to this resolution in 2000 when it proposed legislation that satisfied all remaining property claims and closed the issue of Jewish restitution. The committee was composed of representatives of the government and of local and international Jewish organisations, and its work was given high priority and considerable publicity. In 1999, the chairman of the committee, Pavel Rychetsky, who was at that time also a deputy prime minister, participated in 'The Holocaust Phenomenon', an international conference organised by President Václav Havel. The speech that Rychetsky gave there was particularly meaningful in the way it tried to justify historically the work of the committee.

Rychetsky began on a philosophical note, explicitly addressing the issue of trauma – understood as a subconscious memory displacement or an accelerated forgetting – which could result from being a non-Jewish witness to the Holocaust. While he acknowledged the possibility of such a trauma at the individual level, he denied it at the societal level. When a society assumes such a process, he asserted, it always amounts to a deliberate 'collective falsification of its own history'. Rychetsky continued as follows:

> During the Nazi occupation, a total of 67,000 of our Jewish sisters and brothers were carried off from the Czech lands to die in extermination camps, without any semblance of protest or resistance on the part of their respectable fellow citizens. And then, together with the majority of other European nations, we have been witness for many decades to the amnesia of our own disgrace.
>
> Immediately following its formation in mid-1998, the current Czech government resolved to become actively involved in the Europe-wide, perhaps even worldwide, efforts to finally and precisely give a name to that which the Holocaust signified for our nation and for mankind, and also to speak of how this carnival of monstrosity and horrors was actually organized in our country. In its programmatic declaration, the government pledged to resolve property claims raised by individuals and Jewish communities, insofar as previous administrations had failed to do so.[2]

The most important observation is that Rychetsky explicitly linked the issue of restitution with the Holocaust memory. As we shall see later, in Polish restitution discourse such a connection is by no means obvious. In the speech, the Czech minister first stressed the importance of the Holocaust for both European and Czech history. Next, he directly recognised the responsibility of the Czechs who did not protest enough against the deportation of Jews. Finally, he situated the Czech government's efforts towards restitution in the context of supposed processes of globalisation of the Holocaust memory. What is particularly striking about this speech is that it seems to confirm both the previously mentioned thesis on restitution as a means of Holocaust remembrance espoused by Dan Diner, as well as Elazar Barkan's ideas on restitution as a means of reconciliation.

However, we should bear in mind that the problem of Jewish restitution was not resolved in the Czech Republic until 10 years after the democratic transition and the adoption of the first general restitution laws. In addition, although a clear rhetoric of reconciliation is present in the speech, these statements cannot be related to any serious public debate on the issue. Thus, in the Czech case we cannot possibly speak of the processes of public negotiation of the past that are considered by Barkan as a condition for creating a new common interpretation of the past.

The Czech resolution of the problem of Jewish restitution in general and the manner in which particular related issues were addressed in Rychetsky's speech differ radically from the way that the problem is approached in Poland. In what follows I use examples of the major controversies concerning the question of Jewish property that have been reported in the media in recent years in an attempt to capture the general climate of the Polish discourse on the issue.

As mentioned above, in Poland individual Jewish property cannot be claimed due to the lack of a general restitution law, but Jewish communal property is being returned under a 1997 law. In contrast to the Czech Republic, however, this law was passed in Poland with little publicity. Moreover, it was only the last of a series of laws providing for restitution of property to various religious communities: the law returning property to the Catholic Church had been passed eight years earlier in 1989. From the legal point of view, we cannot speak of any discrimination against former owners of Jewish origin. However, because of the timing of the adoption of the relevant law, we could speak of a higher priority being given to the claims of the Catholic Church than to the claims of Jewish religious communities. Interestingly, we can observe here a certain similarity to the Czech Republic, where the Jewish claims were settled considerably later than the claims of Czechs whose property had been expropriated by the communists.

With regard to the perception of the issue of Jewish restitution in Polish society, there are significant differences with the Czech case. The importance of this question of Jewish property in post-war Poland is reflected even in everyday language. The word *pożydowskie* (literally, post-Jewish) has been coined and is used to refer to the formerly Jewish property. The meaning of this word transmits the memory of the former owners, but at the same time it indicates (by the prefix *po-*) that the item no longer belongs to the Jews. In the Czech language, we can find a similar construction in the expression *dům po Němcích* (a house left after the Germans), while *po Židech*, an equivalent for 'Jewish property', is rather uncommon, which is not surprising since there was much less property left by the Jews in the Czech Republic than in Poland.

An important characteristic of the Polish restitution discourse, and the main difference compared to the Czech debate, is that Jewish property claims since the 1990s have generated much public attention, often incurring some anti-Semitic reactions. One prominent example of the heated discussions is the 1999 case, in which 11 claimants – Polish Jews or their heirs – filed a class action lawsuit against Poland in a court in New York. The lawsuit contained stories of the claimants and an overview of the claims written by two famous American lawyers who specialise in restitution cases. This overview justifying the claims provoked the most controversy as it contained radical statements about the initial post-war period of Polish history. According to the authors, in post-war Poland a 'scheme of ethnic and racial cleansing designed to remove the remaining surviving 10 percent of

Polish Jews from Poland' was implemented by both the Polish state and ordinary Poles, who thus perpetuated the Nazi extermination of Jews in order to seize their property.[3] The lawsuit was published in Poland by *Gazeta Wyborcza*, the most popular Polish daily newspaper, together with a response by Adam Michnik, its editor in chief and one of the most important participants of the ongoing Polish-Jewish dialogue. In his article, expressively titled 'Kłamstwo w Cieniu Shoah' (A Lie in the Shadow of Shoah), Michnik (1999) criticised the ideas of the American lawyers as being clearly anti-Polish, claiming even that they could be compared only to cases of the most radical anti-Semitism. Importantly, he separated the memory of the Holocaust from the issue of restitution, a point also made by former anti-communist dissidents Jacek Kuroń and Karol Modzelewski (2001: 13), who declared that in these claims they saw 'neither sanctity nor the tragedy of the Shoah, only material interest'. Eventually, the most controversial part of the lawsuit was changed, but the New York court dismissed the claim for lack of jurisdiction.

In Poland, the determining factors that shaped the discourse on Jewish restitution were the most divisive and radical voices and opinions on both sides – in Polish public opinion and among the Jewish claimants and their representatives. It is important to note that these heated discussions and controversies were rarely initiated by the participants in Polish public discourse; rather, they usually appeared in reaction to statements or other activities of various actors in the international arena, as can be seen in the above example. A similar case, also widely and emotionally commented on in the national media in Poland, was a statement by Israel Singer, the general secretary of the World Jewish Congress (WJC), who declared at the 1996 meeting of the WJC in Buenos Aires that he had run out of patience waiting for the restitution of Jewish property in Poland. He threatened that if Poland did not take steps towards restitution, it would be 'publicly attacked and humiliated' in the international forum.[4]

This and other similarly radical statements have most often been met with aggressive reactions in the marginal far-right media in Poland, which frequently and willingly has spoken out on Jewish restitution. In March 2006, one such voice reached the national media and became the source of a scandal. A well-known commentator of Radio Maryja, a far-right Catholic radio station, attacked all Jewish restitution efforts, speaking of the attempts to 'exact financial tribute of 60 billion dollars in restitution claims' and referring to the 1997 law as a 'bribe' for joining NATO. The scandal arose, however, because of the anti-Semitic overtones in the language that was used ('the men from Judea'[5] who 'are trying to surprise us from behind'). The broadcast caused near-universal indignation, and some authorities voiced protests. A professional journalists' organisation, the Council for Media Ethics, immediately reacted, branding it an example of 'primitive anti-Semitism', while the papal nuncio in Poland wrote a letter to the Polish Episcopate demanding that it work to 'overcome difficulties caused by some views presented in Radio Maryja'.[6]

Another event which caused similar public indignation was reportage that appeared in 2004 in the Polish edition of *Newsweek* magazine (see Olecki 2004). The piece dealt with the possible claims of the Polish Jewish religious communities to some buildings in Jedwabne – the town about which Jan T. Gross (2001) wrote in his famous book *Neighbors* – and the fears of the local community that they could lose their homes. The main source of protest was the title of the article, which was supposed to express these fears yet was formulated in a controversial manner: 'Jews Return to Regain their Properties', read the cover of the magazine, which also showed a set of corroded keys found during the exhumation of Jedwabne Jews. A protest against the article, published in *Gazeta Wyborcza* and titled 'Restitution of Hatred', was signed by several well-known intellectuals.[7] It accused the *Newsweek* authors of anti-Semitism and asked the prosecutor to start an investigation into the case of an anti-Semitic poster, as they branded the cover of the magazine.

These examples show that Polish public discourse with regard to Jewish restitution remains extremely polarised. What captures the attention of the national media are some aggressive statements and property claims, usually made by international, rather than local, Jewish organisations, which then inspire anti-Semitic reactions to these claims and the ensuing condemnation of such voices by Polish intellectuals and authorities. However, it is striking – and I want to emphasise this fact – that none of the events mentioned above generated any serious and open discussion on the issue of restitution of Jewish property.

It is also significant that when the issue of Jewish property is brought up, it is frequently dismissed on the grounds that the Jewish claims will be dealt with together with the claims of all other expropriated owners in a general restitution law. Although this is obviously a valid argument from the strictly legal point of view, it does not explain why the issue of Jewish property is carefully avoided in public discussions on Polish-Jewish past relations. In light of this, it seems that the issue of Jewish restitution remains a taboo subject in Polish public discourse. In what follows, I shall discuss some plausible explanations for this phenomenon.

Numerous public opinion surveys have shown that the very idea of restitution is rather unpopular in Polish society. There seems to be a general unwillingness on the part of the majority of the population to return property to the minority, regardless of who the previous owners were. This can be explained in part by the diminished respect for private property rights as an enduring legacy of communism and its anti-private ownership propaganda.

This general unwillingness to return nationalised property to its former owners is, however, not enough to explain the lack of willingness to deal with the particular problem of 'post-Jewish' property. With regard to the declared reasons for opposing restitution, the argument most frequently employed is that under communism 'everybody suffered'. In the case of Jewish property claims, this argument has sometimes been extended to include the period of war and occupation. A good example of this position is an article by the former foreign affairs minister Adam Rotfeld (2007), himself of Jewish origin, which was written in reaction to the claims of the WJC. In the piece, titled 'It Has Not Occurred to Me to Claim Compensation', Rotfeld wrote that during the war 'millions of people were murdered, their property confiscated and houses destroyed'. He continued that 'probably the view of the destroyed Warsaw and of thousands of burned villages … was the reason why it had never come to my mind to claim compensation for the apartment buildings my family had owned in Warsaw and the property they had left beyond the Bug River' (ibid.: 2). Rotfeld's argument amounts to the claim that the enormity of tragedy that took place on Polish territories in the twentieth century excludes any possibility of bringing justice to the victims of history.

The issue seems to touch large parts of Polish society on a very emotional level due to the still vivid memories of Polish wartime suffering. This memory of victimhood has for many years been constructed as exclusively 'Polish'; for example, communist propaganda branded Jewish victims of the Holocaust exclusively as 'Polish citizens'. It is this distinctive Polish memory of victimhood that has often resulted in friction with the Jewish memory of victimhood. In the post-1989 period, this rivalry has been additionally fuelled by a generally prevailing feeling that Polish wartime suffering has not been appropriately recognised by international public opinion. The negative responses to Jewish property claims discussed above should also be perceived within this broader context.

The issue of the so-called victimhood rivalry between Poles and Jews is, however, a much more complex phenomenon, and to help explain it we can consider the psychological perspective as proposed by Jan Błoński ([1987] 1990) in his famous essay, *The Poor Poles Look at the Ghetto*. Błoński asked why, after the war, Poles were unable to come to terms with the Polish-Jewish past. In his view, the reason is the feeling of guilt resulting from the often passive and silent witnessing of the Jewish Holocaust. This feeling of guilt is accompanied by the fear of accusations of being 'counted among the helpers of death' (ibid.: 42). Surprisingly, Błoński's words, written two decades ago, express precisely the nature of contemporary reactions to the issue of Jewish property claims as described above: 'We read or listen to discussions on the subject of Polish-Jewish past and if some event, some fact which puts us in a less-than-advantageous light, emerges, we try our hardest to minimize it, to explain it away and make it seem insignificant. It is not as if we want to hide what happened or to deny that it took place. We feel, though, that not everything is as it should be' (ibid.).

In this perspective, Jewish restitution claims seem to be perceived by Poles precisely as these feared accusations, while the decision to return property would mean admitting some guilt. And while nobody can reasonably claim that Poles as a nation took part in the genocide of the Jews, merely agreeing to discuss the issue of Jewish property would mean facing the fact that some Poles benefited from the Holocaust.

Conclusion

This brief discussion – first, of the two culturally specific artistic representations of the Holocaust and then of the debates on Jewish property restitution in the Czech Republic and in Poland – leads to the conclusion that in these societies we observe two diametrically different patterns of coming to terms with the Czech-Jewish and the Polish-Jewish pasts. Neither, however, supports the idea of restitution as a means of creating a common European collective memory with the Holocaust as the central historical event and the main point of reference. Restitution of Jewish property in both the Czech Republic and in Poland was to some extent determined by the general shape of restitution legislation and the principle of non-discrimination. As far as it was influenced by the memory of the Holocaust, we observe two culturally specific approaches.

The politically arranged closure of the problem of Jewish property in the Czech Republic, with its strong rhetoric of reconciliation, was accompanied by widespread societal indifference. As the above analysis of the Czech film and of the restitution discourse has demonstrated, in the Czech public debates on the past, the issue of Czech-Jewish past relations has been overshadowed by other issues, especially that of Czech-German relations. In contrast, 20 years after the fall of communism and over 60 years after the end of the Second World War, the problem of so-called post-Jewish property still generates strong emotions in Poland, but no serious discussion on the issue has yet taken place.

Notes

1. Interview with Cezary Harasimowicz, 5 March 2002, http://www.stopklatka.pl/imprezy/impreza.asp?ii=844.
2. P. Rychetsky, speech to the Joint Working Committee on Mitigation of Some Property Crimes against Holocaust Victims, 'The Holocaust Phenomenon' conference, Prague, 6–8 October 1999, http://old.hrad.cz/president/Havel/holocaust/speeches/prychetsky_uk.html.
3. See '11 Żydów skarży Polskę', *Gazeta Wyborcza*, 3 August 1999, 9.

4. See 'World Jewish Congress Demands Prompt Action on Restitution', PAP news wire, 21 April 1996.
5. The Polish term was *Judejczykowie*, a word coined by a Polish poet of Jewish origin, Julian Tuwim. It was used by the commentator in such a way, however, that it could also be translated as 'kikes'.
6. See 'Do Przewodniczącego Konferencji Episkopatu Polski', *Gazeta Wyborcza*, 7 April 2006, 8.
7. See 'Restytucja Nienawiści', *Gazeta Wyborcza*, 6 April 2004.

Chapter 13

A Europeanisation of the Holocaust Memory?

German and Polish Reception of the Film *Europa, Europa*

❧✦❧

Małgorzata Pakier

Holocaust Memory – Beyond Narratives and Images?

Can it be said that narratives abuse events in the mere act of telling them? The idea that our knowledge of the past is largely conceived of as a text/narrative – as we have learned, for example, from Hayden White – touches on the most problematic issue in the study of cultural representations and remembrance of the Holocaust: the (im)possibility of conveying a traumatic event like the Holocaust within narrative frames. The Holocaust is said particularly to resist integration into narrative stories since narratives imply some sort of 'mastery' over the event, while it is precisely this traumatic event that 'masters' one's individual memory. The cultural theorist Mieke Bal (1999) juxtaposes what she calls a 'traumatic non-memory' with a more common 'narrative memory'. Particular to the former is that it has no social component and is not addressed to anybody. In other words, it cannot be said that trauma is socially framed, whereas narrative memory fundamentally serves a social function (ibid.: x).

Theodor Adorno's dictum about the impossibility of writing a poem after Auschwitz has, over the years, been interpreted and analysed by historians, artists, theorists and critics, while the conception of Shoah as something unrepresentable and infinite has become a commonplace in the literature on the theme. The crisis of representation inherent in the experience of the Holocaust has been connected both to the fact that those who should bear witness to it are those who have been murdered – the

---

Notes for this chapter are located on page 203.

idea of the vicarious witness (Levi [1986] 1993) – and to the unspeakable, traumatic memories of those who survived.

At the same time, however, since and despite Adorno's dictum and prohibitions regarding representation of the Holocaust formulated by other authors, the Holocaust has frequently been represented in literature, theatre and film, popular genres and media included. In the history of filmic representations of the Holocaust, two films – the nine and one-half hour documentary *Shoah* by Claude Lanzmann from 1985 and *Schindler's List* by Steven Spielberg from 1993 – have become the subject of extensive discussions. Most often, however, the two have been placed at opposite poles. Lanzmann was one of the most vociferous opponents of Spielberg's film, criticising it as a violation: 'A certain ultimate degree of horror is intransmissible. To claim that it is possible to do so is to be guilty of the most serious transgression' (Lanzmann 1994; my translation).

The controversies provoked by various representations of the Holocaust – with the discussions about the 1978 television series *Holocaust*, Roberto Benigni's 1998 Holocaust comedy *La vita è bella* and the 1996 art installation *LEGO Concentration Camp Set* by Zbigniew Libera serving as additional examples – have derived from the fundamental dilemma inscribed in the post-Holocaust culture. On the one hand, there is a belief that the propagation of the memory of the Holocaust to a mass audience is necessary to ensure that this event is never repeated. On the other hand, there is obedience to radical formulations about the impossibility of representing Auschwitz. This is expressed in the words of Holocaust survivor and author Elie Wiesel (1991: 682): 'I have not told you something about my past so that you may know it, but so that you know that you will never know it.'

For many, to give the memory of the Holocaust a more universal character has equalled trivialisation of this event. In her article '*Schindler's List* Is Not *Shoah*', Miriam Bratu Hansen (1996) summarises the discussions around Spielberg's film and the representation of the Holocaust in popular genres. Hansen's analysis describes the critical reactions to the film, especially the harsh criticism of Claude Lanzmann, as the echo of an old debate on modernism versus mass culture. The film was mainly criticised for being a Hollywood product, circumscribed by the economic mechanisms of the culture industry (in the sense of Adorno and Horkheimer), with its unquestioned and supreme values of entertainment and spectacle. *Schindler's List* was usually compared to Spielberg's previous mega-productions, especially to *Jurassic Park*, and was accused of trivialising the meaning of the Holocaust.

Hansen agrees that Lanzmann's *Shoah* has been rightly praised for its unique and radical film language. However, she states that *Schindler's List* does not seek to negate the representational, iconic power of filmic images; rather, it exploits this power, deliberately relying on familiar tropes and common techniques to narrate the extraordinary rescue of a large group of individuals. Hansen concludes that the critique of *Schindler's List* 'in high-modernist terms' reduced the problem of representing the Holocaust to the dialectics of showing and not showing it, rather than casting it as a question of competing modes of representation.

The issue raised by Hansen touches on the paradox of the need to shout 'Never again!' while proclaiming the impossibility of representing what happened. For some scholars, however, Adorno's sentence about the barbarity of a poem after Auschwitz can be read differently. According to Shoshana Felman (1992: 34), the implication is not that poetry should no longer be written, but that it must be written 'through' its own impossibility. This would mean that the Holocaust spelled not the end but rather the onset of new and greater difficulties in the field of memory. There was no choice but to remember, Susannah Radstone (2000) stresses, and this was 'the founding equivocation of post-Holocaust memory' (ibid.: 6).

Cultural rituals and narratives have played a significant role in constructing the memory of the Holocaust. Today, more and more scholars are turning their attention to the fact that the memory and our imagination of the Holocaust have become, to a large extent, created by the media. Marianne Hirsch (1997) has coined the term 'post-memory' to describe a 'second-generation' memory that is characterised by belatedness and, most of all, by displacement, in which personal memory is dominated by cultural images. Importantly, Hirsch uses the term 'post-memory' as a means to understand the complexities of the memories of the children of survivors, as well as broader processes of cultural remembrance. In her analyses, she refers to well-known images of the Holocaust – children being deported to concentration camps, the gate to Auschwitz, piles of bodies in the liberated concentration camps – which have over the years gained the status of icons in social knowledge of this event.

Art Spiegelman's comic book *Maus* (1986) is one of the most frequently cited examples in works discussing the phenomenon of post-memory. *Maus* tells the story of the author's father, a young Jew during the Second World War. One frame presents a variation on the famous photo by Margaret Bourke-White of the survivors of Buchenwald from 1945. A small arrow marked 'Poppa' points to one of the prisoners in the picture. In Hirsch's interpretation (2001: 219), this is a sign of the narrator's inability to perceive his father's story in any way other than through emblematic images. In a similar way, Manuel Köppen (1997) discusses the intertextuality of *Schindler's List*, arguing that both documentary film material from the war period and popular representations such as the television series *Holocaust* served the director in the same measure as reference points. From the perspective of cultural practices of remembrance, both of these kinds of footage may be considered legitimate.

Narratives and Images, and What Audiences Make of Them

What is most interesting for me about Hirsch's concept of post-memory is that it emphasises the cultural processes of imagining the Holocaust. To acknowledge the importance of cultural representations of the Holocaust is the first step in moving from normative formulations about the limits of such representation towards concentrating on the ways in which particular representations interact with their audiences and shape social knowledge and memory of the Holocaust. This leads to the next step, the question of social reception. How does a particular work of art, a story or a film dealing with the Holocaust influence its recipients? How is it interpreted by different audiences? What is the spectrum of various meanings attributed to it, dependent on different historical, political or cultural contexts?

With regard to whether we can speak of a development towards a more universally framed Holocaust memory – for example, a common European memory of the Holocaust – a focus on the reception of particular cases of Holocaust representation seems crucial. The claim can certainly be made that there already exists a kind of 'Holocaust canon' that embodies some common social knowledge and memory of this event, to which both *Shoah* and *Schindler's List* would belong. However, a study of how particular representations have been received by different groups of recipients at different times and in different places would give new insight into whether these canonical images are indeed so universal that they would be understood everywhere in the same way.

My aim in this chapter is to discuss the reception of a particular case of Holocaust representation, the film *Europa, Europa*[1] by Agnieszka Holland, a German-Polish-French co-production from 1990, in the national contexts of Germany and Poland. Scholars studying reception agree that every cultural representation is ambiguous and needs recipients to give it particular meaning. Individual readings vary, depending on many factors, such as the reader's historical or social situation, interests or experiences with a genre (Weckel 2003: 65–6). I want to repeat after Alon Confino (1997: 1397–9), who stresses the importance of reception analysis when studying processes of public remembrance, that different interpretations by different groups of recipients not only constitute knowledge that can be added to our previous assumptions about particular representation, but are an integral part of it. They are indeed what constructs its meaning.

In the literature of what can be generally termed collective memory studies, James Wertsch's concept (2002) of public remembrance understood as a 'mediated action' is particularly interesting for the purposes of this chapter, as it emphasises a dynamic relation between an artefact and its recipient. This concept can be useful to understand better the role of cultural representations of the Holocaust as media of memory. Human beings think and act – and also remember – by using cultural tools that are made available by their particular socio-cultural settings (Wertsch 1998, 2002). Within this understanding, Wertsch's notion of collective remembering is located as textually mediated action. His investigation of the nature of collective remembering is mainly concentrated around the usage of broadly defined textual resources in mediating between the past and the present.

Importantly, there are two poles of mediated action: the cultural tools and the active agent, that is, the reader or interpreter, who uses them. At this point, it is important to note that Wertsch's analysis is based on a clearly defined notion of cultural text derived from the writings of M. M. Bakhtin. With Bakhtin (1986), Wertsch (2002: 14) defines text as a 'basic organising unit that structures meaning, communication, and thought'. However, although our perception of past events is here understood as deeply entrenched in culture and language, Wertsch's idea of collective remembering, together with the Bakhtinian notion of text, leans towards the perception of a more autonomous position of the reader or the interpreter. The utterance is produced not only through the text's structural properties. Rather, the 'equally defining moment of text is its use by a concrete speaker in a concrete setting' (ibid.: 15). The text exists only when the reader fills it 'with his own intention, his own accent, when he appropriates … [it], adapting it to his own semantic and expressive intention' (Bakhtin 1981: 293–4).

The concept of mediated action draws our attention to the processes of interpretation. When considering the issue of representation of the Holocaust, the dilemma of how to remember and not to represent at the same time is important. But also important is how particular representations are actually received and interpreted by various audiences, and this consequently raises the question of the shape of the Holocaust memory in different national contexts.

These subjects will be discussed in the remainder of this chapter, which contains an analysis of the film *Europa, Europa*. In what follows, I will briefly describe the plot of the film, indicating also those aspects that might be of particular interest to either the German or the Polish audience. Then I discuss some strategies that the film uses in its attempt to 'represent the unrepresentable' and thus how it actively takes a stand in the debate about the (im)possibility of representing the Holocaust. The second part of the analysis will concentrate on the reception of the film in the press in both Germany and Poland, and on some controversies that the film has provoked.

Europa, Europa – a Holocaust Film

Based on an autobiographical account of events that took place during the Second World War (see Perel 1992, 1993), *Europa, Europa* tells the story of Salomon (Solly) Perel, a teenage German Jew. When separated from his family, Perel accidentally ends up in a Soviet orphanage in Grodno, where he is subjected to communist indoctrination and becomes an exemplary member of Komsomol, the youth wing of the communist party. When German troops reach Grodno, Perel is taken prisoner and, using his perfect knowledge of German, passes himself off as a *Volksdeutsch*. Solly quickly manages to win the sympathy of the German soldiers and is enrolled in the German army as a translator. Adopted by a Nazi officer, he is sent to an elite school for the Hitlerjugend. But since he is circumcised, he may easily be exposed as a Jew, and he lives in constant fear that his secret will be discovered at any moment.

For the Polish audience, the first part of the film, which takes place in the Soviet orphanage, could have been particularly interesting. At this point, a Polish pupil, Zenek, is introduced as a supporting character. Presented as Solly's antagonist, Zenek epitomises the most radical tradition of Polish patriotism, in which love of the fatherland, which is strongly linked to the imperative to defend the Catholic faith, often turns into hostility towards the Jews. In the film, Solly's loyalty for the communist ideology is juxtaposed with Zenek's strong resistance to it. This could be read as the film's critical reflection of a view that prevailed in the immediate post-war period in which Jews were seen as traitors allied with Poland's worst enemy, the Soviet empire – the stereotype of the so-called Judeo-communism.[2]

The second part of the film, in which Solly joins a German unit fighting on the Eastern front and is then sent to a Hitlerjugend school in the Reich, presents a broad and diversified spectrum of German characters. Solly is shown first among the German soldiers in the scenery of the battlefield and then among his peers, teenagers who grew up and were socialised under National Socialism. With some of the Germans Solly forms meaningful relationships, including friendship and love.

Europa, Europa retells Salomon Perel's autobiography in a particular manner. The director Agnieszka Holland claimed that she had found the form of a 'philosophical tale' most appropriate for telling such an incredible story of survival in a twentieth-century Europe controlled by two totalitarianisms (*Dziennik Lubelski*, 12 February 1992). Although the narrative is highly tragic in its essence, there are numerous ironic and humorous scenes in the film in which the absurdities and internal contradictions of the totalitarian ideologies are ridiculed. But above all, the very fact of Perel's survival is so amazing that it almost becomes absurd. Holland highlights this absurdity of Perel's fate in an ironic manner, which is reflected, for instance, in the Jewish character's concise comment, after he had been located in the Soviet orphanage and his parents had been moved to the ghetto in Łódź: 'Thanks to the agreement between Hitler and Stalin, I could receive mail directly from home.'

However, since Solly's story is by no means typical of European Jews during the Second World War, while we are watching it, we remember the fate of the millions of other Jews who did not survive. By choosing what remains unsaid and unseen, the film often conveys its message in specific ways. In a scene set in the vicinity of Grodno, where the Soviet orphanage is located, we hear remote bursts of machine gun fire, which means that executions are taking place in the nearby forest, but the camera shows only the terror on the prisoners' faces. Maybe the cruellest scene of the film is the one in which Solly, now a member of the Hitlerjugend, is searching for his family and crosses the ghetto in Łódź in a tram. Through Solly's eyes we witness the terrifying world of the ghetto, but the view is severely limited by the painted tram window.

What becomes noticeable is the difference between what the movie tells at the level of the plot and the message that it communicates by meaningful silence. This silence is also a constitutive element of the tragic irony that is omnipresent throughout the film. For example, at one point Solly reads a letter from his father, who, after expressing joy that his son is safe in the Soviet orphanage, asks him: 'Are you eating kosher there? Do you observe Shabbat? Never forget who you are!'

The Reception of *Europa, Europa* in Poland and Germany

While press reviews and articles cannot be seen as fully representative, they can give us considerable insight into how audiences reacted to the film. The analysis below is based on German and Polish reviews that appeared in major national newspapers and film magazines and in the local press and various cultural magazines after the premiere of *Europa, Europa* at the beginning of the 1990s.

The Polish premiere of *Europa, Europa* took place in 1992, and the film met with a generally favourable response. Several meetings with the director and with Salomon Perel were organised. Numerous articles about the movie, its director and its international success appeared in the national and local press. It is interesting to observe how these articles defined the genre of the film. The majority of the reviews noticed the fundamental importance of the absurd and the irony in the movie. *Europa, Europa* was classified as a 'philosophical tale' (which was consistent with how it was described by the director in numerous interviews) or as a 'picaresque story'. One magazine even called it a 'comedy about the Holocaust' (*Obserwator*, 7–8 March 1992). The genre of comedy or philosophical tale was generally considered appropriate to highlight the tragic fate of the main character and to portray both Nazism and Stalinism as absurd and foolish (*Dziennik Polski*, 21 February 1992; *Obserwator*, 7–8 March 1992). In many reviews, the film and the director were praised for the intelligent and sensitive manner in which Perel's story was told.

In general, the Polish press reviewers responded enthusiastically to the unconventional way in which this particular Holocaust story was told.

Interestingly, no scene was criticised as being inappropriate, in spite of the fact that various moments in the movie, including those focusing on the sexual experiences of the main character, provide scope for controversy. Among the unmentioned scenes there is also a potentially very controversial surrealistic dream sequence in which Zenek, the Polish pupil at the Soviet orphanage, is presented ironically as a suffering Jesus Christ.

However, this favourable reaction to the film by the majority of the Polish audience entailed a specific interpretation of the story of the Jewish survivor. It was frequently argued that the film presented not only the life story of Salomon Perel, but also a more general depiction – a metaphor for twentieth-century European history. Most often, it was the history of Europe that was regarded as the main subject of the movie, as is made clear by article titles such as 'The Maliciousness of History' (*Gazeta Lubuska*, 11–12 April 1992) or 'The Vagaries of History' (*Gazeta Poznańska*, 4 January 1991). Consequently, the main character, Perel, was described as a tragic hero in the world of two totalitarianisms and as a pawn in the hands of history (*Film*, 9 February 1992; *Gazeta Lubuska*, 11–12 April 1992; *Gazeta Poznańska*, 4 January 1991). In these articles, the film's 'Polish' sub-plot and the issue of complicated Polish-Jewish relations, along with the myths and stereotypes dominating them, were hardly discussed at all. The enthusiastic reviews focused almost entirely on the absurdities of totalitarian regimes and the perverse history of twentieth-century Europe. Such a 'universal' interpretation dominated the reception of the film. The main character was most often viewed in abstract terms, as if the film told the story of Everyman – an average European and his fate in the Second World War – and not the story of a European Jew in the time of the Holocaust.

It is worth mentioning that there were also a few exceptions to the positive responses to the film, mainly in the far-right press. Typically, these reviews paid considerable attention to the way in which Polish history and Polish characters were presented. For example, in the magazine *Najwyższy Czas!* (7 March 1992) the film was considered 'not objective', especially due to the way it portrayed Poles and because it linked Catholicism with anti-Semitism. In this review, neither the symbolism nor the irony of the movie was taken into consideration: the sole criterion of evaluation was the film's historical 'accuracy'. From this perspective, *Europa, Europa* provided an unrealistic and unjust image of Poland during the war, mainly because it described Polish behaviour in purely negative terms and neglected the fact that some Poles had risked their lives to help Jews.

Even before the film was screened in Poland, the Polish press wrote extensively about its international success and also about the 'scandal', as it was described, surrounding the nomination of *Europa, Europa* for the Academy Awards. The German Export Film Union, which was entrusted with proposing German films in the category of Best Foreign Film, decided not to enter *Europa, Europa* as the official German entry, even though the film had already been a major success in the United States. In Germany, differently than in Poland and the US, the film received a very unfavourable response. For German film critics, Holland's work was viewed most often as 'unsophisticated' and 'melodramatic'. Equally unpopular with German audiences, the movie was quickly taken off cinema screens.

The decision of the German selection committee prompted a strong and emotional reaction from the director of the film, Agnieszka Holland. In an interview published in the *New York Times* (14 January 1992), she accused all Germans of an unwillingness to be confronted with the past: 'They really hate this subject', she said. 'I have many German friends, but I was really shocked at how the minds of the people changed after unification. The arrogance and xenophobia which was hidden is now official. They felt guilty many years after the war, but it was official guilt. This time is over. This generation hates all those people who put them through the official guilt.'

Holland's generalising statement, linking the decision not to enter *Europa, Europa* for the Academy Awards with German collective unwillingness to be confronted with the past, was given specific significance in the Polish comments on this event. A belief similar to Holland's conviction – that the Germans took the fall of the Berlin Wall and unification as a 'thick line' under the past and as an exemption from responsibility to deal with it – was fairly widespread (e.g. see the liberal Catholic weekly magazine, *Tygodnik Powszechny*, 23 February 1992). It was pointed out that for the German public the film was 'a pill too bitter to swallow' (*Gazeta Lubuska*, 9 March 1992). However, the arguments of the German film critics regarding the form of the film were scarcely ever taken into consideration by Polish commentators.

Appearing under a different title, *Hitlerjunge Salomon*, the film was screened in Germany a few months earlier than in Poland. Therefore, even before the controversy over the German selection committee's decision began, the movie was reviewed in the German press. Although there were some positive reactions to the film, with similar comments as in the majority of the Polish reviews discussed above, in general the film met with either negative criticism or indifference. Holland's work was deemed unsophisticated, melodramatic and embarrassing. It was often underlined that the film mixed sex and nakedness with genocide. The critics most often concluded that the movie was a commercial product for the world market rather than an appropriate representation of Salomon Perel's tragic biography.

What needs to be emphasised is that the reviews often represented relatively high levels of theoretical sophistication with regard to the question of the possibility of representing the Holocaust in artistic and popular genres. The objections raised with regard to what was shown in the film and to how it was done often referred to theoretical discussions about other filmic representations of the Holocaust, such as the television series *Holocaust* or the movie *Shoah*. It can therefore be said that the film was condemned not only for putting a Holocaust story into a genre considered insufficiently serious, but also for doing it, in the critics' view, in a superficial way that failed to provoke reflection.

A major part of the criticism against the film revolved around the fact that, according to the critics, it did not show the 'inner truth' of the story of Salomon Perel. It was argued that had more consideration been given to the psychological aspects of the protagonist's experiences, the film would have been much more comprehensive and believable. According to one reviewer, the rapid sequence of episodes distorted the real meaning of Perel's biography and made the story excessively superficial, neglecting inner experiences like those related to the loss of his family and the necessity of hiding disguised as the enemy (*Süddeutsche Zeitung*, 8 February 1992). It was argued elsewhere that the film neglected the issue of Perel's inner transformation, as well as the psychological impact of the events in which he had participated. It was often stated that the film was excessively and unnecessarily preoccupied with the main character's sexuality. Some critics wrote that instead of highlighting the tragedy of Solly's fate or focusing on the fear of being a Jew in a uniform of the Hitler Youth, *Hitlerjunge Salomon* reduced the character's 'Jewishness' to his circumcised penis and the necessity to hide it.

Is the film's focus on the connection between Solly's wartime experiences and his sexuality indeed a distortion of Perel's biography and thus only the director's unnecessary creation? When compared to Perel's memoir and his statements in interviews, the film seems rather a detailed and meticulous account of his story, with its variety of tragic, terrifying, and also absurd and perverse situations and events. For example, the scene of Solly in the toilet at the Hitlerjugend school, which shows him trying to 'undo' his circumcision, is a faithful translation of a detailed depiction of this situation in Perel's memoir (see Perel 1992, 1993; see also an interview with Perel in *Spiegel*, December 1992).

During the discussion about the unwillingness of the German selection committee to nominate the film, doubts were also raised as to whether the film should be regarded as a German production at all. The committee attributed its decision not to nominate the film to its failure to conform to the regulations of the Academy Awards. Many commentators expressed serious reservations about whether the film could be considered German, stressing that important artistic components of the film came from Poland: the director, the composer, the cinematographer and many of the actors were Polish. In some comments it was even wrongly claimed that English was the language of the movie. These voices, however, seem to testify less to the possibility that the selection committee's negative decision was motivated by xenophobia, as the producer Artur Brauner and Holland had argued, than to the fact that there was little interest, and consequently little information, about the movie in Germany.

The reason that German audiences found it difficult to acknowledge the 'Germanness' of the film does not appear to be the nationality of the crew and the language of the film (which was in fact German). Different arguments raised in discussions about the film seem more relevant. It is useful to focus on the criticism of the form of the film, as it contains an important message about the reviewers' expectations regarding how such a story of survival from the Holocaust should be told. Significantly, the German critique paid considerable attention to the film's neglect of the lead character's inner experiences while recounting his story.

Several months after the film's first screening in Germany, Salomon Perel published his memoir in German, under the title *Ich war Hitlerjunge Salomon* (1993). The book was widely commented upon in the German press and was received very positively. Perel appeared in numerous interviews and was frequently invited to participate in various meetings. One of the articles reviewing the book started by quoting Perel's statement: 'I can understand the war better than other Jews.' The article then asked rhetorically whether someone would be able to understand Salomon Perel, who was 'a subject of experiment in the totalitarian laboratory of psychology of the masses', as were all Germans at that time, it could be added. The main thesis of the article was that Perel's biography could be read as a metaphor and an answer to the question of how 'that' was possible (*Frankfurter Allgemeine Zeitung*, 26 June 1991). In another article, Perel was quoted as saying that he and his comrades from the Hitlerjugend were all victims of National Socialism, which filled their brains with its ideology.

Thus, it was not Perel's story but the film itself that met with such an unfavourable response. The general argument against the movie was that it 'wasted a good subject'. What was observed and criticised in many reviews was the film's failure to show the extent to which Perel had actually identified with the National Socialist ideology; instead, the movie suggested that most of the time Perel had been able to put up some kind of inner resistance to this ideology. Indeed, there is just one scene in the film that suggests Perel's identification with the Nazi ideology – the scene in which he weeps with other Hitlerjugend cadets on receiving the news of the German defeat at Stalingrad. We can learn much more about the extent to which Perel empathised with his role as a *Hitlerjunge* from the memoir and the interviews. For example, Perel admitted that he was in such deep mourning after the defeat at Stalingrad that he wrote a poem about it. From the memoir we also learn that he was a diligent student in the Hitlerjugend school and studied race ideology with great interest.

It is also notable that in one interview Perel uses the word *Vergangenheitsbewältigung* to describe his personal reckoning with his wartime experience. Upon being asked why he did not reveal his story until 40 years had passed, he answered: 'Such a process of coming to terms with the past [*Vergangenheitsbewältigung*] needs more time' (*Spiegel*, 16 March 1992). German newspapers very willingly cited this kind of confession.

Conclusion

Both in Germany and in Poland there was a strong tendency to read Perel's biography as a meaningful parallel of their own national histories. In the German reviews, the film was criticised for not reflecting on the crucial issues concerning the susceptibility of ordinary people to totalitarian ideologies. The critics reproached the director for not highlighting the problem of Perel's authentic and deep identification with National Socialism, which was recounted in his memoir. Although the Polish audience assessed the quality of the film in a radically different way from the German audience, the attempt to appropriate Perel's story was equally strong. The Polish reviewers compared the protagonist's experiences to the tragic fate of Poland, emphasising the fact that both Salomon Perel and the Polish nation were victims of two totalitarian regimes, Nazism and communism. The critical tone of some examples of negative Polish wartime behaviour that Agnieszka Holland directed towards the Polish audience did not register, and the Zenek-Christ reference, along with the whole sub-plot of the conflict between the young Pole and the young Jew, remained almost unnoticed.

Interestingly, in both cases of the reception of the film, concepts of the universalisation of the Holocaust and of the memory of the Second World War appeared, although in two very different versions. The German reviewers pleaded for a more nuanced depiction and analysis of the past that would go beyond nationally ascribed roles of victims and perpetrators. The critical assessment of the one-dimensional and stereotypical mode in which the German characters were portrayed in the film can be seen as a consequence of this perspective. On the other hand, the 'universalised' interpretation of Polish critics referred to a depiction of twentieth-century European history as a history of two totalitarianisms. The fact that the excessively optimistic and 'European' reception of the film in Poland paralleled a very critical and emotional reaction to the reception of the film in Germany should not be disregarded. Most Polish critics linked the film's lack of popularity in Germany with German unwillingness to deal with the National Socialist past, which was presented in Poland in terms of a threat that Polish suffering during the war would be forgotten.

In the reception of the film, two different concepts of remembering the past clashed. The film theorist Gertrud Koch has rightly suggested that the discrepancy between the ways in which the film was received in Germany and in Poland can be read in terms of conflict between two different kinds of national historical experiences and, resulting from it, cultures of remembrance. Referring to the negative reactions to *Hitlerjunge Salomon* in Germany, Koch has underlined the fact that the film's message was directed more towards Eastern European societies, with their experience of occupation by two totalitarian regimes, and thus might have been more comprehensible for Eastern Europeans than for the German audience (after *die tageszeitung*, 21 March 1992).

When debating the Europeanisation of Holocaust commemoration practices, it is useful to concentrate on particular case studies. Depending on what sources we are using and what areas of cultural production we are investigating – ranging from official, political acts of public commemoration to more spontaneous, everyday acts of evoking the past – we will find different results. The history of *Europa, Europa* in Germany and in Poland is an interesting case study with regard to the possibility of the development of more universal, European frames for Holocaust memory. The study of the reception of the film in these two countries and of the controversies that its screening provoked shows that, instead of a common memory, there was a conflict of different nationally defined cultures of remembrance. To talk about a European memory of the Holocaust is problematic. Rather, the normative long-term goal would be a mutual understanding of just how different the European experiences are.

Notes

1. Details about the film *Europa, Europa* are as follows: German title, *Hitlerjunge Salomon*; director and screenplay writer, Agnieszka Holland; editor, Christina Undritz; producer, CCC-Filmkunst GmbH, Berlin, and Les Films du Losange, Paris; release date, 1990; running time, 111 minutes.
2. For a more detailed discussion of this film in the Polish context, see also Pakier (2007).

Chapter 14

ITALIAN COMMEMORATION OF THE SHOAH
A Survivor-Oriented Narrative and Its Impact on Politics and Practices of Remembrance

Ruth Nattermann

In July 2000, the Italian Parliament unanimously welcomed the establishment of a Giornata della Memoria in commemoration of the Shoah. The date of the liberation of Auschwitz-Birkenau in 1945, 27 January, was chosen as a suitable day of remembrance. At first sight, the decision to commemorate the Shoah on the date of the liberation of the largest National Socialist extermination camp (where most of the deported Italian Jews were murdered) seems obvious and convincing. Why, then, did Law 211 of 20 July 2000 meet with considerable criticism on the part of Italian public opinion and, in particular, on the part of the press linked to the Italian centre-left? Upon closer consideration, the seemingly suitable date for the Giornata della Memoria posed at least two problems. Firstly, 27 January is associated with German guilt. It is not a date central to the crimes of anti-Semitic politics in Fascist Italy. According to the law's official wording, the Giornata della Memoria is intended to remember not only the extermination of the Jewish people by the Germans but also Fascist anti-Semitic legislation and persecution. Furthermore, it is explicitly meant to commemorate other, non-Jewish Italian victims of National Socialism, namely, deportees and soldiers who were interned by the German Wehrmacht. And herein lies the second problem: there is the danger that the Giornata della Memoria may also become a day of 'exoneration of an Italian culprit's memory' (Klinkhammer 2006b: 661).

The establishment of the Giornata della Memoria expresses much about Italy's politics of commemorating the Shoah and, more generally, about the official attitude towards the country's own past. Especially significant is the fact that the Italian Parliament refused to accept the initial suggestion

---

Notes for this chapter are located on page 216.

from some left-wing members to set the date of the Giornata della Memoria as 16 October, the date of the deportation of Jews from Rome's ghetto in 1943 (Focardi 2005).[1] This date would have involved painful memories of Italy's Fascist past, as it would have required that Italians face and remember the collaboration of the Italian police with the German occupying forces, the denunciations made by Italian informers and perhaps even the attitude of Pope Pio XII (Klinkhammer 2003). In comparison, 27 January provided a far more neutral point of reference that was politically and emotionally less problematic.

However, the tendency to marginalise or even to silence debate about collaboration and the anti-Semitism of the Final Solution must by no means be regarded as a recent phenomenon within Italian politics of commemoration: it has deep roots that can be traced back to the post-war period (Focardi 1999). It should be understood as the result of various narratives that culminated in an image of Italy as 'a safe haven where Jews could find a secure place to reside without being persecuted' (Nidam-Orvieto 2005: 158) and of the Italians as *brava gente* (good people), instinctively opposed to anti-Semitism. Interestingly, the construction of this rather one-sided and mythical tradition of Italian attitudes and politics towards Jews not only developed out of the – often apologetic – narratives of non-Jewish Italians but also was supported to a considerable extent by the memories of Shoah survivors themselves. Additionally, scholarly research both in and outside of Italy has long reflected and perpetuated the image of Italian humanity towards Jews. This perspective was endorsed not least by the eminent Italian historian Renzo De Felice (2001: 372), who stated that 'even in 1939–1943 the great majority of Italians remained ... opposed to racism and anti-Semitism'. In 1987, De Felice asserted in an interview that 'Fascism had stood outside the shadow of the Holocaust'.[2]

My aim in this chapter is to analyse how the image of a general Italian humanity towards Jews was constructed. I focus on the memories of Jewish survivors and their influence upon this process. Without trying to discredit the testimonies of the survivors or to deny the existence of many courageous and humanitarian efforts undertaken by Italians in order to help Jews, I attempt to offer a more differentiated picture of the construction of memory. I intend to explain the underlying motives and patterns of behaviour that led to a survivor-oriented narrative and to discuss the effect of this on the Italian self-image and on the politics of commemoration of the Shoah after the Second World War. My contention is that, for many years, the positive image of Italian humanity towards Jews helped to eliminate – or at least to silence in public memory – the discussion of Italian anti-Semitism and Italian war crimes.

My focus will also be on the transition from survivor-oriented narratives towards critical research. Only recently has a younger generation of Italian and non-Italian historians begun to question the traditional narrative of

Italian humanity towards Jews and to examine critically the anti-Semitic course of Fascist Italy and the denunciation, persecution and deportation of Jews by Italians. I explore whether this 'new' and increasingly critical investigation of Italy's past has already led to a more differentiated way of commemorating the Shoah and, indeed, whether it has had an impact on current Italian politics and practices of remembrance.

The Memories of Jewish Survivors

Two recurring elements characterise testimonies and memoirs of Italian Jews who survived the Shoah. The first is that memories of everyday life under the anti-Semitic legislation during the years 1938–43 are either blurred or glossed over, and are thus represented as a period in which Jews 'didn't really suffer'.[3] In contrast, the German occupation of Italy from 1943 to 1945 is remembered with all its horrors and existential fears. In the face of the extreme cruelty of German annihilation politics and the shift from the 'attack on Jewish rights' to the 'assault on Jewish lives' (Sarfatti 2006: 178f.), memories of survivors are often split into two phases: 'before' and 'during' the German occupation. Compared with the extremely traumatic experience of their eventual deportation by the Germans, the prior conditions under the Fascist legislation seemed quite acceptable (Collotti and Klinkhammer 1996). Silva Bon's interviews (2005) with Italian Jews who had suffered through the phase of National Socialist persecution in camps such as Risiera di San Sabba, Auschwitz, Ravensbrück or Bergen-Belsen also revealed a striking 'flattening' (*appiattimento*) of memory regarding the reconstructed image of the Fascist period. In extreme cases, this progressed almost into a grateful, comforting sensation of amnesia, which clouded the deepest and most painful memories (ibid.: 18).

In particular, during the immediate post-war period, Italian-Jewish survivors often chose – either consciously or unconsciously – to forget or even to deny what had happened to them under Italian Fascism. They did so in order to reintegrate themselves socially and psychologically into Italian society as quickly as possible. In most testimonies and studies that appeared shortly after 1945, the responsibility for the persecution of Jews in Italy was attributed exclusively to the Germans. Thus, the limitations of rights and liberty enacted before September 1943 were silenced or eliminated from memory, as was the fact that the conditions prepared by the Fascist regime in the years 1938–43 enabled and facilitated the transition to the phase of the Final Solution.[4]

Two fundamental problems have contributed to the construction of a survivor-oriented narrative: firstly, accounts by people who did not survive are exceedingly rare or have been widely neglected within relevant research and, secondly, the existing memoirs and oral testimonies of those who did survive are mainly retrospective and have thus been influenced by complex mechanisms of remembering, transforming and forgetting. Only if other materials from the period itself, such as diaries, letters and official documents, are taken into account can a differentiated picture of the characteristics of Fascist anti-Semitism – as well as the response it found within Italian society and its impact on the lives of Italian Jews – be gained. A recent study by Iael Nidam-Orvieto (2005) has analysed letters written between 1938 and 1941 by Jews to the Italian authorities. The results reveal the considerable pain, distress and suffering imposed on the Jewish community as a result of anti-Semitic laws in Italy.[5]

Similarly complex processes of memory can be observed in the testimonies of Jews who survived the Shoah in Italian-occupied zones in Yugoslavia, Greece and France. Having escaped deportation and death in German extermination camps, Jewish survivors have represented the treatment by Italians and the conditions in Italian internment camps in an almost exclusively positive way. This applies especially to the case of the Italian-occupied zone in Croatia, where approximately 3,500 to 4,000 Jews managed to survive when Italian military commanders and diplomats refused to hand them over to the Germans for deportation (Nattermann forthcoming).

This case contributed to the development of a survivor-oriented narrative in the immediate post-war period. As early as 1946, the Jewish historian Jacques Sabille published one of the first studies on the Jews in the Italian-occupied zone in Croatia. On the basis of Jewish testimonies and German documents from the foreign office, Sabille concluded: 'Individually or in groups, Italian officers and their soldiers did everything possible to keep the Jews out of the territories of terror and to hide them in secure places … their wonderful work of help deserves the highest respect and admiration' (Poliakov and Sabille 1956: 134f.). In 1962, Sabille's study was supplemented by a new publication, a collection of documents relating to the 'persecution of Jews in Italy, Italian-occupied territories and in North Africa', which was edited by the United Restitution Organization (URO), an international Jewish organisation offering legal assistance to survivors of the Shoah. The text presented Italy as Germany's victim with regard to the former's policies towards Jews. The introduction stated that the anti-Semitic legislation in Italy had been initiated by the Germans, who had also tried in vain to force upon Italy the politics of the 'Axis' towards the Jews (URO 1962: ii, xi).

In 1977, the Milan-born Israeli historian Daniel Carpi, the descendant of a traditional and patriotic Italian-Jewish family who had survived the Shoah and emigrated to Israel in March 1945, showed on the basis of newly discovered sources that issues of prestige and territorial power politics had been driving forces for the Italian actions in favour of the Jews in Croatia. In his final conclusion, however, even Carpi (1977) endorsed the thesis that had dominated the discourse on Italians and Jews since 1945:

Italian soldiers and civilians had regarded the attitude towards persecuted Jews as a 'humanitarian' problem and had tried to solve it out of reasons of conscience, regardless of all political considerations.

The 1987 documentary film *The Righteous Enemy* by Joseph Rochlitz and the volume *Un debito di gratitudine: Storia dei rapporti tra l'esercito italiano e gli ebrei in Dalmazia (1941–1943)* (A Debt of Gratitude: The History of the Relations between the Italian Army and the Jews in Dalmatia, 1941–1943) by the Israeli historian Menahem Shelah (1991) are important examples of works with an even more obvious autobiographical motivation. The starting point of Rochlitz's film is the story of his father Imre, who survived the Shoah in the Italian internment camp Kraljevica and later on the island of Rab (Rochlitz forthcoming). Although the director's personal commitment is understandably evident, his carefully researched representation nevertheless manages for the most part to keep a critical distance, combining oral history with the findings of written sources and research. Rochlitz's main aim is to show the rescue actions of Italian individuals without denying the opportunism, injustice and crimes of the Fascist regime as a whole.[6]

The historian Menahem Shelah (1991) adopts another emphasis: his study is based on the gratitude of a survivor. Born in Yugoslavia, Shelah fled as a young boy into the Italian-occupied zone of Croatia, where he was picked up by Italian soldiers. Interned first in Piedmont and later transferred to the concentration camp of Ferramonti in Calabria, he was liberated from the camp in September 1943 by the Allies. Shelah's work is probably the most significant example of a survivor-oriented narrative in which the conditions in the Italian sphere of influence appear downright positive in comparison to the extreme cruelty and determination of Nazi persecution. As Enzo Collotti and Lutz Klinkhammer (1996), as well as Carlo Spartaco (2004), have stated elsewhere, this memory pattern can at times even result in the representation of a notorious camp like Ferramonti as a kind of oasis in comparison to the camps of the Germans or the Croatian Ustasha. As a result of this 'filtered' memory, Ferramonti appears as a model of humanity and the Italians as nothing but rescuers.

These examples of Italian politics towards the Jews in occupied territories reveal similar problems to those found in the representations of anti-Semitism in Fascist Italy mentioned above. The existing testimonies and several key scholarly works have been influenced by the perspective and the memories of those who survived. The image of an innate Italian humanity, which this particular perspective has hereby created and reproduced, is based on feelings of gratitude and, to a considerable extent, is the result of comparison with the Germans. Yet it remains a fact that many Italians tried to offer help to persecuted Jews. In general, the Italian military commanders and diplomats did not pursue a politics of persecution with the ultimate aim of the Final Solution, as the Germans did. While

Jews in German-occupied zones awaited deportation and death in the extermination camps, under Italian occupation there was a realistic chance of survival. For those who were persecuted, imprisonment or internment represented the lesser evil. Naturally, most survivor accounts do not recall cases in which Italians behaved indifferently towards the plight of the persecuted or even contributed indirectly to the Final Solution by denying sanctuary to Jews who arrived at the Italian border and by returning those who were captured back to the German-occupied zone (Burgwyn 2005; Rodogno 2003). As in the case of anti-Semitic politics in Italy before 1943, most of the available testimonies in which Jews describe their fate in Italian-occupied territories were written after the actual events had taken place. Jews who had been deported and killed in German camps after having been denied sanctuary or who had been expelled from Italian-occupied zones could not bear witness.[7]

The result of the predominance of testimonies and studies which bear the grateful perspective of survivors, on the one hand, and the general disregard of Jewish testimonies which offer a less positive image of Italian attitudes towards Jews, on the other, was the construction of a narrative that emphasised and sometimes even celebrated the great humanity of the Italian occupying forces. In the extreme case, this resulted in a stylisation of all Italians as *brava gente*, a move that automatically diminished the efforts of those Italian soldiers, military leaders, diplomats and others who actually did help, sometimes even risking their lives for Jews. Nor did this stereotypical and rather anthropological interpretation of Italian behaviour leave room for an in-depth enquiry into the political and military context of the Italian refusal to hand over the Jews to the Germans for deportation. Only recently has the re-examination of relevant sources, the discovery of new documents and the contextualisation of events led to a far more differentiated picture. This has shown that it was above all political calculation that motivated the apparently humanitarian Italian actions: at a time when the military, political and economic competition between the partners of the Axis was growing heavily in the Balkans, the debate on the handling of the Jews developed into an argument concerning power and prestige which offered the Italians the chance to openly demonstrate to the Germans their sovereignty (Collotti 2003; Mantelli 2000; Nattermann 2009; Rodogno 2003).

The humanitarian image of the Italian occupying forces that the survivor-oriented narrative had highlighted also became doubtful when historians finally began to shed light on Italian war crimes in the Balkans (Collotti 1997; Di Sante 2005; Focardi and Klinkhammer 2004; Mantelli 2004; Rodogno 2003). Evidence of ethnic cleansing – the brutal fight against the Slavic population and the Partisan movement – did not square with the traditional narrative of a benevolent Italian occupation that had emerged from the majority of Jewish survivor testimonies. Thanks to these new critical incentives, relevant research displays a growing awareness of the necessity of analysing the complex processes of memory in survivor accounts, as well as the importance of re-examining Italian politics towards Jews within their military and political context.

Commemorating the Shoah in Post-war Italy

For decades, the Italian politics of remembering the Shoah was based on the traditional narrative of Italian-Jewish relations, dominated by tales of humanity and heroism on the part of Italian soldiers, civilians and clergy. From the end of the Second World War onwards, knowledge of the refusal of the Italian occupying forces to hand over Jews to the Germans and of the truly courageous behaviour of Italian individuals who hid and saved Jews inside Italy, together with the symbolic importance of the Italian partisan resistance, shaped configurations of memory to the extent that Italy's long alliance with the Nazis and its own anti-Semitic persecutions were minimised or even silenced, both in Italian public discourse and the politics of remembrance (Ben-Ghiat 2005).

Significantly, Italian practices of commemorating the Shoah during the post-war period were basically limited to one location: the Fosse Ardeatine in Rome. In March 1944, the German occupiers, led by SS officers Erich Priebke and Karl Hass, killed 335 people (most of whom were Italians) in the Ardeatine caves, following the killing of 33 German soldiers by members of the Italian resistance on via Rasella (Klinkhammer 2006a; Portelli 2003). The largest cohesive group among the murdered in the Fosse Ardeatine were members of Bandiera Rossa, a communist military resistance group, and it was for this reason that the commemoration of the massacre gained considerable significance for the memory of the Italian resistance in general. Of the victims, 75 were Jews awaiting deportation to the extermination camps (Klinkhammer 2006a). Because the massacre involved several 'victim groups', the Ardeatine caves quickly developed into a kind of 'unifying symbol' (Portelli 1999: 105) for the suffering and the efforts of the Italian people as a whole. This has been clearly reflected by Italian practices of commemoration in the post-war era. Every year around All Saints' Day, the mayor of Rome and a leading representative of the Jewish community went to the Fosse Ardeatine in order to hold a ceremony in memory of the victims of the National Socialist occupation in Rome (Klinkhammer 2003). In this way, the commemoration of the Shoah was embedded, or absorbed, into the memory of the persecution of Italians by the German occupying forces in general and was even held on a day that was central to Christianity. The remembrance of the Shoah became 'merely a religious or ethnic subheading within the general framework of the repression of the Resistance and anti-fascism' (Bravo 2005: 311).

Certainly, the Ardeatine caves were not a suitable place to remember the Shoah in Italy; sites such as Risiera di San Sabba would have been far more significant. But what is even more characteristic for Italian practices of remembrance in the post-war period is that the commemoration of the Shoah at the Fosse Ardeatine took place in the context of remembering Italian resistance against the German occupying forces and the crimes committed by the latter towards Italian Jews and non-Jews alike, thereby excluding Italian anti-Semitism and collaboration in the Final Solution. Commemorating the Shoah at the Fosse Ardeatine was a way of avoiding the painful truth that only half a year prior to the massacre, on 16 October 1943, the arrest and deportation of more than 1,000 Roman Jews to Auschwitz had been considerably facilitated by the collaboration of Italian police and informers (Osti Guerrazzi 2005). In this context, it is all the more significant that by sending one of their representatives to the commemorative ceremony at the Ardeatine caves, the Jewish community in Rome accepted and indirectly even supported the official version of the young Italian Republic's memory regarding the Shoah. As we have seen, the predominant Jewish narrative that emerged from the memories of grateful Jewish survivors and the lack of critical records supported the collective memory of the newly born Italian democracy, in which anti-Semitism was represented as alien to the Italian people, and the Germans were depicted as the real and sole persecutors and murderers of Jews in Italy (Focardi 1999).

The joint commemoration of the Shoah at the Ardeatine caves continued to foster this narrative since it was Germans alone who had murdered Jews at the site: Italians had themselves been victims of the Germans in the atrocious massacre. In the post-war period, the Fosse Ardeatine commemoration was neither complemented nor confronted with other symbolic places or dates, such as 16 October, which would have rendered the memory of the Shoah more painful for an Italian audience and might have fostered a more critical confrontation with the Italian past. This corresponded not only to the prevailing memory discourse of the young republic, but also to the predominant Jewish narrative in which the Italians appeared mainly as good people, themselves victims of the Germans, who had been forced by the Nazis to adopt anti-Semitic measures. The survivor-oriented narrative was an important support for the maintenance of Italy's post-war practices of remembrance since it was based to a considerable extent on the memories of those who had themselves been persecuted. Similarly, the participation of a Jewish representative in the commemorative ceremony at the Fosse Ardeatine seemed to confirm the one-sided version of Italian humanity and victimisation versus German brutality and *Machtpolitik* (power politics). The widespread tendency among Jewish survivors to forget or even deny Italian anti-Semitism, along with the missing voices of those who had been murdered, encouraged the general atmosphere of 'amnesia' and suppression, in which a critical examination of the Italian attitude towards Jews during Fascism had no place.

From a Survivor-Oriented Narrative
towards Critical Research

If we return now to the initial considerations concerning the Giornata della Memoria and the problems involved, it becomes clear that the overall narrative, as it has been outlined above, had not changed significantly well into the 1990s. In fact, the refusal in July 2000 of the Italian Parliament to choose 16 October as a suitable day for the Giornata della Memoria and the choice of 27 January instead reflect the tendency to marginalise within the official memory discourse an in-depth discussion of Italian responsibility for the tragic fate of Jews during Fascism. At the same time, the fact that the parliamentary decision was not supported by all groups of Italian society – and indeed was met with criticism, especially in the press – shows that at least in some parts of society there was a growing awareness of the need for a more critical approach towards Italian politics and practices of commemorating the Shoah. Two main factors initiated this change of consciousness. Firstly, the survivor-oriented narrative began to lose part of its weight because of generational changes, with few firsthand witnesses still alive at the end of the twentieth century. The second factor is closely linked to the first: research on Italian politics towards Jews during Fascism was increasingly carried out by scholars who had a greater temporal and emotional distance from the events.

In 1988, the fiftieth anniversary of the anti-Semitic legislation sparked a revival of interest in Italian-Jewish history in general and in the history of Jews during Fascism in particular. A younger generation of scholars began to approach well-known documents with new interpretations and made use of sources that had previously been inaccessible or neglected. They also began to consider the complex mechanisms of remembering and forgetting in the accounts of Jewish survivors, and to question the traditional image of an innate Italian humanity. Susan Zuccotti's *The Italians and the Holocaust* (1987) was key to this shift. Zuccotti pointed out how the tales of heroism and rescue in wartime Italy had distracted attention away from negative aspects of the relations between Italian non-Jews and Jews, leading to generalisations about the 'good character' of the Italian people. Similarly, in his study on exile in Italy between 1933 and 1945, the German historian Klaus Voigt (1989–98) argued that the Fascist regime's attitude towards Jewish refugees was considerably less benevolent than previous studies had claimed. One of the first to examine the anti-Semitic legislation in Italy more closely was Michele Sarfatti (1994, 2000), who refuted the thesis that the legislation had been adopted by the Italians only for the sake of their German ally. In her now classic study, *Il Libro della Memoria*, Liliana Picciotto Fargion (1991) pointed to the direct involvement of the *Repubblica sociale* in the persecution, capturing and deportation of Jews. Other important contributions from the 1990s that supported the existence of an 'internal project' of anti-Semitism within Fascism – its pseudo-scientific character and its embodiment in bureaucracy and institutions – came from Giorgio Israel and Pietro Nastasi (1998), Roberto Finzi (1997) and Giorgio Fabre (1999). In his pioneering study, *Il Mito del Bravo Italiano*, David Bidussa (1994) distanced himself from the traditional image of Italian humanity and condemned the tendency to represent Fascist anti-Semitism as a mere copy of the German model. There were also portrayals that had a considerable impact on the general public, such as the autobiographical and critical account of anti-Semitism, *La Parola Ebreo*, by Rosetta Loy (1997), as well as Roberto Begnini's now famous film from the same year, *La vita è bella*, an unconventional Holocaust narrative which dealt with the experience of anti-Jewish discrimination and persecution in Italy (Ben-Ghiat 2005).

All these works played a fundamental role in the slow transition from the tales of rescue and humanity towards an increasingly critical examination of the anti-Semitic course of Fascist Italy. Even still, innovation and development in research, along with updated literary and cinematic portrayals, have been unable to replace completely the old narrative. Near the end of the century, Filippo Focardi (1999: 140) stated that, in spite of various new contributions, old stereotypes about an 'inefficient' anti-Semitism that was generally unappealing to the Italian people maintained a considerable degree of power and influence.

Recent Tendencies in Italian Politics and Practices of Remembrance

The history of Jews during Italian Fascism is still a topical issue, both within and outside of Italy. The studies from the 1990s have been an important incentive and base for numerous recent works that provide in-depth research on a wide range of aspects of the matter in question. Especially relevant has been *Il Fascismo e gli Ebrei* by Enzo Collotti (2003). In this astute portrayal of the genesis, application and consequences of the anti-Semitic legislation, Collotti also discusses the belated compensation of Jews in Italy after 1945. Other examples are Giorgio Fabre's recent study (2005a) on Mussolini's ideological development and his personal influence on Italian anti-Semitic politics, and Amedeo Osti Guerrazzi's *Caino a Roma* (2005), which gives evidence of the direct involvement of ordinary Italian individuals in the persecution, deportation and murder of Jews who had been their neighbours for decades. Davide Rodogno's comprehensive study (2003) on the Italian occupation of France and the Balkans has been particularly important for the discussion of the attitude of the Italian occupying forces towards Jews. On the basis of numerous previously unpublished documents, Rodogno reveals the brutality of Italian occupying politics and points not only at the opportunistic motives for the allegedly 'humanitarian' efforts on behalf of Jews, but also at cases of indifference and refusal to help. His work is a passionate, well-documented plea against the myth of the *bravo italiano*.

The question remains as to whether these studies have been able to reach public consciousness. Sarfatti (2006: xi) wrote that 'today Italian society has accepted Fascist Italy's responsibility for the anti-Jewish legislation, the arrests and deportations'. If this is true, it would mean that the intense research that has been carried out in recent years would have escaped from the halls of academia and found its way into the public. In fact, Italian practices of commemorating the Shoah have already begun to show signs of a changing, more self-critical attitude towards the past.

One of the most significant examples of this is the Museo della Shoah in Rome, which originally was set to open in 2008 (De Roche 2006; Fabre 2005b; Moretti 2005; Pradarelli 2006). However, due to financial and other reasons, the opening was postponed, with 2010 set as the new opening year.[8] The driving force behind the ambitious project has been Walter Veltroni, Rome's mayor from 2001 to 2008, but the proposal goes back to the Jewish community of Rome, which turned to Veltroni for support in 2001. Today, the Fondazione Museo della Shoah di Roma and representatives of the city of Rome, the Italian Jewish community, the Associazione Figli della Shoah and the Spielberg Shoah Foundation are taking care of the financing and realisation of this first Shoah museum in Italy. The museum will include a permanent as well as changing exhibitions, a library, a conference hall and rooms for educational use. There will be a particular focus on anti-Semitism in Fascist Italy, including Italian anti-Jewish legislation and the deportation of Jews from Italy. In order to encourage visitors to perceive the acts of discrimination as 'materially' as possible, the intention is to reconstruct the atmosphere of an Italian assembly hall and show how Jewish pupils were expelled from Italian schools in 1938 (Fabre 2005b). A special area will be dedicated to the October 1943 raid in the Roman ghetto (De Roche 2006).

The appearance of a newly self-critical tendency in Italy's practices of remembrance is reflected not only by the representative and instructive content of the museum. Especially characteristic has been the choice of the location as well as the original inauguration date: the Museo della Shoah will be built in the park of Villa Torlonia, Mussolini's private residence until 1943. In this way, the memory of the Shoah in Italy remains closely connected to the memory of the crimes of the Fascist regime and its *Duce*, as well as the collaboration of Italians in the Final Solution. The choice of the original inauguration date of 16 October 2008 was significant because it took up a previously rejected parliamentary suggestion from 1997 for the day of remembrance, Giornata della Memoria. It is thus a visible sign of a change in public consciousness.

Looking back at the way that the Shoah was remembered in Italy during the post-war period, it becomes evident that the transition from a mainly survivor-oriented narrative towards an increasingly critical examination of Italian politics towards Jews has had a considerable impact on the development of Italy's politics of remembrance. The concept of the Shoah museum in Rome reflects the beginnings of a tendency to face the negative aspects of Italian-Jewish relations during Fascism without covering them up with stereotypes about an innate Italian humanity. Hopefully, Italian politics of remembrance will continue in this direction, motivating and supporting a critical confrontation with the past. It is imperative that the opening of the Shoah museum is not understood to represent the final point of a process, as if the museum's completion signifies that Italy has fulfilled its political and cultural duty. Nor should the Museo della Shoah become an object of political correctness or a means of flouting national pride in an international 'competition' of Shoah museums. Especially in view of the current debate on a common European commemoration of Auschwitz, it is unclear whether in the Italian case a Europeanised memory of the Shoah would contribute to an increasingly critical examination of history. The danger is that it might instead result in a 'de-Italianisation' of the events, leading to a relapse into old stereotypes and the avoidance of Italian responsibility.

The politics and practices of remembrance in Italy, but also in other countries, should aim not only at preservation but also at the transmission and discussion of history. In order to achieve this, it is not enough to found museums and establish commemorative dates, places and ceremonies. Italy, like many other countries, must above all stimulate research and open its archives, many of which have been inaccessible or are only partly accessible to date.[9] Especially in the case of the Shoah, there is still need for serious investigations regarding the compensation of victims, the tracing of family members and the return of plundered goods. Not least, the examination of relevant sources may offer justice to those Italians who truly behaved with humanity towards Jews, and whose individual courage and integrity have been dissolved into and obscured by the narrative of *italiani brava gente*.

Notes

1. The suggestion was made as early as 1997.
2. See Giuliano Ferrara's interview with Renzo De Felice, titled '… il fascismo è al riparo dall'accusa di genocidio, è fuori dal cono d'ombra dell'olocausto', in Jacobelli (1988: 3–6).
3. Testimony of Giulio Levi Casellini in Coslovich (1997: 10).
4. This interpretation was by no means adopted only by Italian Jews but was shared by the majority of the Italian population. In the post-war period, it became part of the collective memory of the democratic and republican Italy (Focardi 1999).
5. The more than 1,000 letters that Nidam-Orvieto (2005) analysed are addressed to Mussolini or to King Emmanuel III, showing a strong, general adherence of Italian Jews to both fascism and the royal house.
6. In this context, it is significant that the film has never been shown by an Italian public broadcasting station.
7. One of the few existing texts from the period itself is the testimony of the lawyer Edo Neufeld (Loker 1993). Having succeeded in escaping from the concentration camp at Gospič to Switzerland, in November 1943 Neufeld delivered a long talk at the Swiss reception camp about his experience under Italian occupation. His testimony calls into question the view that the Italian occupation in Yugoslavia was exclusively benevolent towards the Jews.
8. Tommaso Martini, 'Il Museo della Shoah', 27 January 2008, http://www.sindromedistendhal.com/Alzheimer/Memoria-08/museo-shoah-roma.htm.
9. Significant examples of Italian archives that are still barely accessible are those of the *Carabinieri* and the Vatican. Regarding archives abroad, Italy has only recently shown a striking (if rather passive) opposition to the opening of important Shoah archives in Bad Arolsen, Germany (Del Vecchio and Pitrelli 2007).

Section 5

Coming to Terms with Europe's Communist Past

Chapter 15

MANAGING THE HISTORY OF THE PAST
IN THE FORMER COMMUNIST STATES

◈

Arfon Rees

An assessment of the communist legacy in those countries that were part of the Soviet Union and those that were its satellites in Central and Eastern Europe reveals many paradoxical and differentiated reactions. These variations indicate very different responses, both at the level of governments, corresponding to different strategies of regime legitimisation and different priorities concerning state and nation building, and with regard to public opinion and popular memory. The perception of the communist past has changed over time and, to a significant measure, has been shaped by the post-communist experiences of these countries. These highly significant differentiations contradict in important respects the expectations for these nations, expressed at the time of the anti-communist revolutions in Eastern and Central Europe in 1989 and at the dissolution of the USSR in 1991, regarding their prospects of transition into liberal democratic states.

Mikhail Gorbachev's election as general secretary of the Communist Party of the Soviet Union in 1985 inaugurated a new openness (*glasnost*) in public debate. Gorbachev explicitly spoke of the need to fill in the blank pages in Soviet history. By the end of the 1980s, the system of state censorship in the USSR had collapsed. A deluge of articles, analyses and memoirs exposing the dark side of communist rule were published. Different publications sought to outdo one another in exposing the crimes of the past. Public interest in these revelations was intense, and this led to a huge expansion in the circulation of these journals and newspapers. Significantly most of these revelations came not from the pens of historians but from those of journalists or individuals trained in the social sciences and the arts (R. W. Davies 1989).

This revolution in the writing of Soviet history and the unfettered debate on the past were associated with a dramatic shift in public attitudes

---

Notes for this chapter are located on page 232.

and with the emergence of a genuine public opinion. The uncovering of the crimes of the past went much further than the controlled revelations inaugurated by Khrushchev's 'secret speech' at the 20th Congress of the Soviet Communist Party in 1956. The revelations made after 1988 covered a number of highly sensitive issues which in the past had been suppressed or treated in a propagandistic manner: the conduct of the 1918–20 civil war and the use of terror by the Bolsheviks; the famine of 1921 and the suppression of peasant resistance to the Bolshevik regime; collectivisation and de-kulakisation; the famine of 1932–3 and the Great Terror of 1937–8; the conduct of the Second World War; the post-war repression under Stalin and the size and nature of the Gulag system.

The public debates during the 1980s served to subvert the official historical discourse that had been maintained until that time. Facts that were well known in the West were now made available to a Soviet audience, and they had far-reaching implications within the USSR, including the open questioning of the Communist Party's moral authority and its right to rule. A far broader discussion centred on historical alternatives – whether there had been an alternative socialist path of development available in the late 1920s (the Bukharinist option), whether the October Revolution itself had been historically necessary (or 'law governed') or whether, by following Finance Minister Witte's policy of industrialisation of the 1890s and Prime Minister Stolypin's policy of agrarian reform after 1906, there had been alternative capitalist patterns of development available to the country before 1917.

In the communist states of Central and Eastern Europe, this new frankness regarding the past allowed open discussion about the way that Soviet rule was imposed on these states after 1945, the scale of repression during the most intensive period of communisation in 1948–53, the experience of these countries under communist rule, the history of the major challenges to communist rule (in East Germany and Poland in 1953, in Hungary in 1956, in Czechoslovakia in 1968) and the question of the relationship between Moscow and the military government of General Wojciech Jaruzelski, which attempted to crush the mass movement of Solidarność (Solidarity). In each of these countries, the debate on the past was associated with the delegitimisation of the system of communist rule. This was associated with a rather critical evaluation of the role played by the Western Allies in ceding these countries to the Soviet Union after 1945 as part of the deal between the Great Powers at Tehran and Potsdam.

In those republics annexed by the Bolshevik regime, the experience under Soviet rule was reappraised. In Ukraine, the means by which the republic was incorporated into the USSR was critically analysed, and the adverse impact of Soviet modernisation policies, especially collectivisation and the ensuing famine of 1932–3, was widely discussed. In Estonia, Latvia and Lithuania, the process whereby these Baltic states had been incorporated into the USSR under the terms of the Nazi-Soviet Pact of 1939 and their Sovietisation after 1945 were critically discussed. Associated with this was the argument that as this had been unlawful, the citizens of these republics could no longer be held subject to the laws of the USSR. In these republics we see the clearest repudiation of the Soviet past. A questioning of the Soviet order, in varying degrees, was seen in the other republics of the former USSR, including those of the Caucasus and of Central Asia.

By 1991, in the states of the former USSR and the Soviet bloc there was a general repudiation of the communist past. The anti-communist revolutions that followed ushered in governments that were in most cases strongly anti-communist. In the Russian Federation, President Boris Yeltsin, rejecting Gorbachev's 'third way', embarked on a new course, aiming to achieve a rapid transition to a liberal democratic free market system that would be able to draw support from the West in the restructuring of the country. In almost all the post-communist states, the system of communist rule was depicted as totalitarian and as an evolutionary dead end that had isolated these countries from broader social and economic changes. All post-communist countries experienced strong trends to ground their newly created states within national traditions and to re-establish connections with their non-communist past.

The legacies of communism, with regard to the problem of democratic consolidation in Eastern Europe and the transition to capitalism and liberal democracy, became matters of intense debate (Hollis 1999; Kovacs 1994; Rév 2005; Rosenburg 1996; Rousso 2004b). In Russia, as in other countries, the reappraisal of the past was bound to the task of redefining national identity in the post-communist era (Tolz 1998) and became part of contemporary political struggles.

In the 1990s, these states underwent dramatic transformations, which in all cases imposed large social costs. But the experience of the countries concerned varied considerably. For most of them, the difficulties of the transition period proved more onerous than anticipated, and the West provided far less assistance than expected. The acute social costs of the transition, and the inequalities generated by it, stimulated a mood of nostalgia for some aspects of the communist system. Among the middle-aged and elderly in the USSR, there was even an idealisation of the Stalin era as a period of common endeavour and shared suffering (Paxson 2005).

As political debates in these states became more fractious, the discourse on the past became more heated. For the Central and Eastern European countries and the Baltic states, membership in the European Union and NATO promised an economic and security framework. In these fledgling states, the debate on the communist past inevitably became embroiled in the drive to establish responsibility and to ascertain who had collaborated with these regimes. In Poland and Hungary, the debate has been politicised by the struggle for power between those in favour of liberalisation and those who derive their origin from the old communist parties. In the Baltic states, the effort to assert the rights of the indigenous population and to restrict the rights of those from the settler community of Russians and Ukrainians has been bound up with the debate concerning the illegal incorporation of these states into the Soviet Union.

In the successor states of the former Soviet Union, the evaluation of the communist past has thus produced clearly divergent approaches. These disputes are intimately tied to current debates as regards the path that these countries propose to follow in terms of domestic reconstruction and external relations.

In the Russian Federation in the 1990s, there was a sense that the past had been absorbed. The passage of time also meant that these past events were seen as no longer having a bearing on the present. The main revelations concerning the abuses of power under Stalin had been divulged before 1991. A commission into the crimes of the Stalin era, headed by Aleksandr Yakovlev, whose work was continued under Yeltsin, determined that the sentences handed out by the Stalinist courts over political offences lacked any proper legal basis. The victims were posthumously rehabilitated. Yakovlev (2004) himself saw this work as exposing the criminal nature of what he characterised as the communist totalitarian regime. Under Yeltsin's government, small sums of compensation were paid to the victims of these crimes.

The detailed and scholarly study of the Soviet past has been left largely to professional historians. Russian historians, such as V. P. Danilov (1999–2001), A. N. Dugin (1999), N. A. Ivnitskii (1995, 1996) and V. M. Zemskov (2005), undertook enormous labours to determine precise figures for the number of victims of the famines, de-kulakisations and purges, as well as the size of the Gulag population and the number of victims of the Second World War. A great number of books, articles and archival documents detailing the darker aspects of the Stalin era were published. A new generation of historians, such as O. V. Khlevniuk (2004), has provided detailed accounts of the inner workings of the Stalin government, the history of the Gulag and studies on Soviet culture and society. This rewriting of history profoundly influenced school textbooks published in the 1990s, which on the whole provided objective and balanced accounts of the Stalin era. In this period, collaboration with Western scholars and the publication of translated editions of Western historical research on Russia became a normal practice.

In the Russian Federation, revelations regarding the crimes of the past were quickly depoliticised. Disclosures regarding mass executions and the imprisonment of millions of people in prison and concentration camps had few political repercussions. The initial ban imposed on the Communist Party in 1991 was lifted, and proposals to bring it to trial as an illegal organisation came to nothing. Nobody was charged with crimes committed in the name of the state, and no one was brought to trial. No truth and reconciliation commission was established. Detailed documentation of the repression of the Stalin era was undertaken primarily by the independent organisation Memorial, which published details of individual cases and identified prisons and mass burial sites (Adler 1993; A. White 1995). Memorial's work was facilitated with assistance provided by the FSB and its archivists.[1] This indicates how the process of revelations was managed, and how it served to rehabilitate those agencies involved in the perpetration of these crimes.

The same depoliticisation of the past can be seen in other areas. In 1990, Memorial erected a small stone monument to the victims of the Gulag in Lubyanka Square on the traffic island where the statute of Felix Dzerzhinsky, the first head of the Cheka, then stood.[2] Plans for a more conspicuous monument remain unfulfilled. Similarly, projects discussed in the early 1990s to transform some Gulag camps into sites of commemoration were never realised.

Even during the Yeltsin years, the attitude towards the Soviet past evinced a certain ambiguity. Although Yeltsin himself often used the crimes of the Stalin era as a stick with which to beat his communist political opposition, he was constrained by what he could do (R. W. Davies 1997). Proposals to remove Lenin's body from the mausoleum on Red Square and plans to relocate the mausoleum elsewhere met with strong opposition and were never acted upon. Although the statues of prominent Bolshevik leaders were removed from public view and re-erected in museums, several statues dedicated to Lenin remained in situ. Place names have been changed, usually reverting back to pre-revolutionary days, the most notable example being the reversion of Leningrad to St Petersburg. The de-communisation of symbols coincided with the efflorescence of advertising posters and the emblems of commercial culture.

The defusing of the past as an issue of political controversy can also be explained in terms of vested interests and political culture. The political elite that established itself after 1992 was, to a large extent, derived from the ranks of the communist elite, and it had no interest in raking over the past. The victims and their descendants from the Stalin era were not an organised force and also lacked means of articulating their views. The institution that was the main victim of the Stalinist repression – the Russian Orthodox Church – became one of the main beneficiaries of de-communisation and was turned into an important prop of the state (Bacon 2002). Popular opinion regarding the past reflects a strongly authoritarian current in Russian political culture. In opinion polls, Lenin and Stalin are still rated highly: alongside Peter the Great, they are viewed positively as renowned leaders, modernisers and defenders of national sovereignty. Moreover, there are no clear, current political agendas associated with reassessing the past.

In the Russian Federation, the evaluation of the communist past underwent a very significant shift at the end of the 1990s. The strongly anti-communist line taken by President Boris Yeltsin was reversed by his successor Vladimir Putin, who was elected president of the Russian Federation in May 2000 (Bacon and Wyman 2002; Bacon et al. 2006; Sakwa 2004). The change was reflected not only in the official pronouncements of government figures, but also in public history. While academic inquiries into the dark side of the communist era were not impeded, neither were they strongly encouraged; there was no attempt to dwell on or to confront the past. This is now also evident in the teaching and research on history in most Russian universities. The mass media as well tends to highlight the positive aspects of the past, particularly themes of a patriotic nature.

A number of reasons can explain this transformation of attitude. It is undoubtedly related to the economic collapse of the early 1990s, which was extremely painful for the great majority of the population and was widely seen as a national humiliation. Another factor was Russia's loss of international prestige following the dissolution of the USSR. By the late 1990s, other figures had come to occupy the role of public enemies: the beneficiaries of privatisation, the so-called oligarchs, and the Chechen separatist movement, whose members were branded as 'terrorists'. These developments served to galvanise public opinion and strengthen the hand of the government.

The depth and duration of the experience of Sovietisation explains in part the stress on the positive achievements of the Soviet regime, both domestic and international. Already under Stalin, Soviet patriotism and Russian nationalism had in many ways been fused (Rees 1998). The crimes of the Stalin era therefore tend to be relativised, regarded as part of the cost of modernisation. Moreover, only a small proportion of the population has any direct experience of the Stalin era. Most middle-aged people experienced the Soviet system during the Brezhnev years (1964–81), when the country enjoyed a period of unprecedented stability and prosperity. This accounts for the very negative assessment generally held by Russians of the Gorbachev years, which are seen as a period of disintegration that heralded the social and economic debacle of the early 1990s.

Under Putin as president and then prime minister, a determined attempt has been made to reassert the importance of the Second World War as the central legitimising myth underpinning the traditions of the Russian and Soviet state. Under Yeltsin, the Victory Day celebrations were muted, partly soured by the revelations of the scale of the human cost of the victory. During the Second World War, the USSR suffered a staggering population loss of 27 million people out of a population of 194 million, about 15 per cent. Most of the dead were civilians, many of whom died of starvation. Seen as the product of Nazi aggression and its racial ideology, the war is still viewed as an anti-fascist crusade that resulted in the liberation of the

USSR and of Eastern Europe from Nazi tyranny. This is a crucial aspect of Russian self-identity. Consequently, attempts to equate Nazism and Stalinism as two totalitarian regimes were increasingly frowned on. The scale of Soviet losses in part explains the reluctance to address the plight of particular victims – such as those of the Holocaust – and the tendency to stress common suffering instead. The war experience also acts as a taboo on any discussion about the conduct of the Red Army or of Soviet occupation policies in Eastern Europe. Russian sensitivity on this issue is illustrated by the Kremlin's indignant response in April 2007 to the Estonian government's relocation of the Soviet Second World War memorial in Tallinn.

In the Russian Federation, unlike in Poland, the Czech Republic and the Baltic states, there has been no movement for the restitution of property confiscated by the communist state. State ownership of industry and agriculture still commands high levels of public support. The privatisation of state assets and the loss of savings through hyper-inflation in the 1990s is a more controversial issue than the dispossession of landowners, financiers and industrialists after 1917, or the dispossession of peasants through the collectivisation of agriculture after 1929. The debate on property rights is partly offset by the granting of the right to tenants to buy their apartments.

Under Putin, the increased role of the state in economic management and moves towards greater restrictions on the media and political association have been presented as a return to strong government. Since 1999, the Russian oil-fuelled economic boom has provided the basis for a reassertion of national pride, which is manifested in a more forceful foreign policy that plays on a deep popular mistrust of the West and the outside world. The promotion of people drawn, like Putin himself, from the federal security agencies – the so-called *siloviki* (men of power) – into senior positions of power in the federation's centre and in the regions confirms the noticeable trend towards greater authoritarianism.

These changes correspond with important ideological shifts. The strong support that the Putin-Medvedev partnership enjoys in the Duma underlines the large consensus around official policy.[3] The fringe far-right nationalist and hard-line Stalinist groups have been marginalised. The Russian Communist Party has shifted to a more nationalist position, based on a programme of reasserting state intervention in the economy and protecting vulnerable groups, such as pensioners (March 2002). This shift is also reflected within the intelligentsia. One highly significant indicator of this was the endorsement of Putin by historian Roy Medvedev (2000), the most prominent socialist critic of Stalinism since the 1960s, with his outspoken attack on the oligarchs, liberals, westernisers and separatists who threatened the integrity of the state.

Russian political culture has always emphasised respect for strong leaders, collective solidarity and patriotism, combined with a high tolerance of infringements by the state on individual and group rights and a low level of toleration of those construed as dissidents. This is clearly reflected in the lack of any effective opposition to the government's two wars in Chechnya, apart from the anti-war protests of the Committee of Soldiers' Mothers, and in the absence of any great public outcry at the murder of critics of the Putin government (see Politkovskaya 2004, 2007). The weakening of democratic institutions and practices, and thus the shrinking of the public sphere, means that the government is increasingly reliant on symbolic legitimation. To this end, the government itself, both in its domestic and foreign policies, fosters the growth of national chauvinism.

At a symbolic level, there is an explicit attempt to reconnect the present regime with the past. The trend could be seen in Putin's own proclaimed regret for the loss of the USSR, his reluctance to unequivocally condemn the crimes of Stalin (although in an interview with the German newspaper *Bild* in 2005, he referred to Stalin as a tyrant) and his refusal to criticise the KGB and its predecessor organisations. The 9 May Victory Day celebration in 2005, on the sixtieth anniversary of the defeat of Nazi Germany, marked a new stage in the commemoration of the military achievements of the USSR. Under Putin, the Soviet national anthem, which had been rejected in 1991, was reinstated, albeit with new words to the old tune, evidencing a determination to see the Soviet period as marked by positive as well as negative aspects. With opinion polls giving Putin approval ratings of over 70 per cent, it can be seen that his policies commanded widespread consent.

The positive assessment of the Soviet past in the Russian Federation is seen also in Belarus, under President Aleksandr Lukashenko, and in Moldova. In sharp contrast, in other former communist states the internal debate between different parties concerning the communist legacy is connected to the question of past and present relations with Moscow. It is shaped by the availability of alternative courses of development and by external factors such as the geo-political rivalry between Russia, on the one hand, and the US and NATO, on the other. The intensity of the debate is inflamed by what Russia sees as NATO encroachment into its sphere of influence and by the establishment of US military bases in the Caucasus and Central Asia.

The conflicts have been dramatised by the Georgian Rose Revolution, the Kirgizhian Tulip Revolution and the Ukrainian Orange Revolution.[4] In each case, the establishment of pro-Western governments that sought to distance themselves from Moscow and were critical of the Soviet heritage has had implications as regards the official view of the historical past. US involvement in these events, as in the successful ousting of Slobodan Milošević as president of Serbia in the wake of the NATO military campaign in Kosovo, highlights this geo-political rivalry. It is also associated with US pressure against the authoritarian, pro-Russian government of President Lukashenko in Belarus. The resurgence of Russia economic power, based on oil and gas exports, has reshaped its relations with its immediate neighbours and with the countries of the European Union.

In the case of Ukraine, geographically split between a pro-Russian, largely Russian-speaking population in the east and a pro-Western Ukrainian-speaking population in the west, differences in the appraisal of the Soviet past divide political parties and the Ukrainian Parliament. This is connected to crucial choices as regards the course of economic development that the state should follow – whether to draw on its traditional links with Russia and its heavy reliance on Russian oil and natural gas supplies, or whether to develop its autonomy by strengthening economic ties with the European Union. This situation is also compounded by disagreements regarding foreign policy and defence priorities – whether to build on ties with Russia or to forge new links with NATO as a counterweight to Russian influence.

The conflict between the two camps climaxed in 2005 in the presidential election campaign between two candidates, the pro-Russian Viktor Yanukovich and the pro-Western Viktor Yushchenko. The campaign was marred by an assassination attempt on Yushchenko by dioxin poisoning. Yanukovich, who claimed victory in the election, was forced to accept a rerun of the election as a result of prolonged, mass demonstrations in the capital Kiev. The new elections gave the victory to Yushchenko in what became known as the Orange Revolution. However, in the succeeding months, Yushchenko's position as president was weakened by the defection of the Socialist Party, which had previously supported him. This gave both a parliamentary and Cabinet majority to those supporting the defeated candidate Yanukovich, whom Yushchenko was obliged to appoint as prime minister.

In this tense situation, the question of the past and of Ukraine's relationship with Russia was again brought to the fore. One of the main issues of contention was the highly emotive question of the Ukrainian famine of 1932–3. This matter has long been the subject of prolonged and extensive debate. Immediately following the declaration of Ukrainian independence in 1991, a monument commemorating the victims of the famine was erected in Kiev. Leading historians have argued that the famine (*Golodomor* in Ukrainian) was the result of Stalin's deliberate policy, which aimed at breaking the power of the peasantry. Robert Conquest (1986) describes it as a 'terror-famine', and James E. Mace (Heretz et al. 1986) calls it a policy of genocide (see also Graziosi 1996). Many Ukrainian nationalists argue the case that the famine was an act of 'genocide' against the Ukrainian nation.

Other historians challenge this view. The most detailed analysis to date is that by R. W. Davies and S. G. Wheatcroft (2004), who argue that the famine was the product of collectivisation, de-kulakisation and forced grain extraction from the peasantry, and was also due in part to severe drought conditions and problems of weed infestation that affected the principal grain-growing regions of the USSR. They contend that the famine was a product of miscalculation and mismanagement. Not only Ukrainians, but Kazakhs and Russians also suffered. The economic costs were great, and Stalin himself experienced a loss of authority as a consequence of the crisis. In this view, the Stalin government was guilty of gross negligence and inhumanity in its handling of the famine, but the evidence that it perpetrated a deliberate act of genocide, specifically targeted at the Ukrainian people, is lacking, Davies and Wheatcroft conclude (ibid.; see also Davies and Wheatcroft 2006). Their interpretation has been challenged by other historians, such as Michael Ellman (2005, 2007), who argue that Stalin was intent on using starvation as an instrument of policy to break the peasants, and that the outcome can be construed as genocide.

The issue remains extremely contentious among serious historians. Notwithstanding the problems of interpretation and definition, for many participants in the debate, the matter has been resolved: the famine was pure and simple an act of genocide against the Ukrainian people. These views are advanced particularly on many web sites that have a strong nationalist orientation, such as that of the Ukrainian Genocide Famine Foundation. Moreover, the governments of 10 countries, including the United States, Canada, Austria, Hungary and Lithuania, have endorsed the view that the Ukrainian famine was an act of genocide.

In October 2006, a meeting of political figures and 'scientists' in Kiev called on the country's Parliament to recognise the famine as genocide. On 28 November 2006, Ukraine's Parliament (Verkhovna Rada) passed a bill labelling the famine of 1932–3 an act of genocide. It authorised the release of KGB documents, which purported to prove that the famine was part of a deliberate policy, aiming to cleanse ethnic Ukrainians from the territories of Ukraine and parts of Russia. The resolution was advanced by President Viktor Yushchenko and his then prime minister, Borys Tarasyuk. Their goal was to attack the so-called Ukrainian famine-genocide deniers (the attempt to equate the terms 'famine' and 'genocide' is significant), to gain UN recognition of the famine as genocide and thus to open the door for possible compensation for the survivors of the victims.

As part of the power struggle between President Yushchenko and his chief rival, Yanukovich, these moves were intended to whip up Ukrainian nationalist feeling and to heighten anti-Russian sentiments. The resolution was hotly debated in the Ukrainian Parliament. The pro-Russian Party of the Regions and the Ukrainian Communist Party criticised the use of the word 'genocide'. The Party of the Regions, Yanukovich's party, proposed a softer formulation of 'tragedy' and 'crime against humanity'. The two opposition parties also proposed that the famine be described as a crime directed against the 'Ukrainian people' and not the 'Ukrainian nation', signalling that its victims were not only ethnic Ukrainians.

Following the debate, the Ukrainian Parliament approved a resolution describing the famine as a 'genocide' against the 'Ukrainian people', but the clause in the original resolution that criminalised famine denial was dropped. With these changes, the resolution was carried by 233 votes to 1, in a house of 450 members. The resolution was supported by the Tymoshenko bloc, Our Ukraine and the Party of the Socialists. The members of the Party of the Regions (except for two members who supported the resolution) and the Ukrainian Communist Party abstained (*International Herald Tribune*, 28 November 2006). On 8 December 2006, the lower house of the Polish Parliament unanimously passed a supportive resolution: '[J]oining in pain with the relatives of the victims of the great famine in Ukraine, which cost the lives of millions of residents of the Ukrainian countryside from 1932–1933, the Polish Parliament condemns the totalitarian regime responsible for the genocide' (*International Herald Tribune*, 9 December 2006).

The voting along party lines in the Ukrainian Parliament mirrors the highly politicised nature of the debate on the famine. The attempt to shore up President Yushchenko's position continued in the succeeding weeks, and in April 2007 he dissolved the Parliament, ignoring opposition claims that he was exceeding his constitutional powers. This discord corresponds to a wider division within Ukraine – between those who condemn the communist era and those who still emphasise its positive achievements. While for Ukrainian nationalists, acknowledgement of the famine as genocide is the touchstone of national allegiance, some communists still deny that a famine occurred. This bitter dispute revolves around the question of who has the right to speak in the name of the Ukrainian nation and whether others, because of past associations, have forfeited that right. Yushchenko stated this explicitly: 'Those who deny the *Golodomor* today loathe Ukraine deeply and resolutely. They hate us, our spirit and our future. They deny not only our history but deny Ukraine' (*International Herald Tribune*, 28 November 2006).

Ukrainian society is deeply divided, and this poses serious problems for forging a common national identity. Yushchenko sought to use the famine ('genocide') as the basis for such identity formation and as a moral issue with which to attack those who espouse an alternative conception of what Ukraine was and is. In this view, Stalinism is depicted as 'absolute evil' and the Ukrainians as victims of Soviet oppression. By contrast, in Russia Putin employed the argument of continuity with the pre-Soviets and Soviet past in an attempt to forge a common identity, based particularly on the theme of patriotism and commemoration of the Second World War. In both cases, official history is used to mould public opinion and public memory in the process of state building and nation building.

The significance of the Ukrainian famine debate is lent support by the debate on Holocaust denial, with other groups and peoples staking claims for their suffering to be recognised. This not only reflects the domestic political pressures but also corresponds to the desire of former communist states to gain accession to the European Union: they seek to establish their democratic credentials by fully repudiating their totalitarian past. In July 1993, in preparation for its accession to the EU, the Czech Republic passed an act condemning its Soviet-era government. In 2001, Bulgaria's Parliament, again in anticipation of accession to the EU, passed a resolution condemning the former communist regime.

But reappraisals of the past are also shaped by domestic political considerations. In Budapest in February 2002, the House of Terror museum, documenting the crimes of both the Hungarian Nazi Party and the Hungarian Communist Party, was opened. The launch of the museum was authorised by the conservative government headed by Viktor Orbán. The initiative was criticised by the opposition Socialist Party as a political ploy to sway public opinion before new parliamentary elections in April 2002. It was also criticised by historians for trying to use the memory of the past for purposes of political propaganda.

In December 2006, in preparation for Romania's accession to the EU, but also in a move to strengthen his domestic position, President Traian Băsescu of Romania formally condemned the communist regime that had ruled his country for four decades, declaring it to have been criminal and illegitimate. His pronouncement was based on a lengthy report compiled by a presidential commission charged with analysing the country's communist past. The parliamentary session which approved the report was attended by King Michael I of Romania,[5] who had been forced to abdicate in 1947, and Lech Wałęsa, founder of Solidarność. Băsescu pledged to establish a national day commemorating the victims of communism and to erect a museum of dictatorship. Also in 2006, the Council of Europe's Parliamentary Assembly passed a resolution condemning the region's former communist regimes and called on all the former communist states to 'reassess the history of communism' and to condemn those regimes 'without any ambiguity' (*The Guardian*, 16 February 2006).

With regard to the reappraisal of the past, an important issue concerns citizens' right of access to files that were compiled on them by the secret police during the communist era. In so far as it provides insights into the extent and nature of the system of surveillance and informing carried out during communist rule, this constitutes one of the most sensitive issues for governments in the post-communist era. The degree of access provides a benchmark for the degree of liberalisation and the extent of openness with regard to the repression of the past. In the Russian Federation and most of the states of the former USSR, the files of the KGB on individuals and on collaboration remain closed. The exceptions are the Baltic states, reflecting their more liberal regimes.

For the countries of the former Eastern bloc, the pattern has varied. In 1991, Germany passed a law opening the files of the German Democratic Republic's Stasi (internal security force). Granting individuals access to secret police files compiled about them was made a specific condition of

EU accession. Thus, Hungary allowed access to these files in 2003, the Czech Republic in 2003, Slovakia in 2004, and Romania and Bulgaria in 2005. In Poland, the opening of files has been combined with a policy of lustration, that is, the exclusion of those who collaborated with the communist regime from public employment and from elected public office. The resignation in January 2007 of Stanisław Wielgus, designated archbishop of Warsaw, and Reverend Janusz Bielański, rector of Wawel Cathedral, may presage a more general programme of expulsions that carry important political implications. In Albania, no law on access has yet been enacted. In the states of former Yugoslavia, the most controversial issue is access to the files of the post-communist regimes.

On 19 April 2007, the European Union approved legislation that made Holocaust denial punishable by imprisonment, but it gave the 27 member countries the right not to enforce the law if such a prohibition did not exist in their own laws. In the weeks preceding this decision, demands were advanced by the Baltic countries that the proposed law should criminalise the denial of atrocities committed by the Soviet regime under Stalin. This demand was rejected, although the EU's justice commissioner, Franco Frattini, said that the EU would organise public hearings on the 'horrible crimes' of the Stalin regime in the following months (*International Herald Tribune*, 20 April 2007).

In Russia, attempts by the government to control the use of the historical past have been most evident with regard to the use of school and university textbooks. Since 2004, pressure has grown to remove books that are critical of the Soviet past and to promote works that highlight the achievements of the country. The argument advanced is that books should foster national pride and patriotic feeling, rather than induce feelings of shame and humiliation. These pressures, coming from the presidency and the Ministry of Education, have been complemented by initiatives from below, that is, from veterans' organisations and some teachers. In an address to a conference of teachers in July 2007, then President Putin called for a new approach to the teaching of the country's history, aimed at inspiring patriotic feeling, and announced his intention to have the government commission and authorise history textbooks that would serve this purpose. Those works, supposedly influenced by external organisations and outside opinion, that allegedly denigrate the country's past would be excluded (*The Independent*, 20 August 2007). On 15 May 2009, President Dimtri Medvedev signed a presidential order (*ukaz*) establishing a commission of high-ranking government officials and historians for the purpose of 'counteracting attempts to falsify history to the detriment of Russia's interests' (Griffiths 2009). Speculation concerning possible differences between President Medvedev and Prime Minister Putin on economic reform clearly do not extend to any serious differences as regards the treatment of Russia's past. In the course of

2008–9, moves in the Russian mass media towards an effective rehabilitation of Stalin continued unabated.

The experiences of the former communist states reveal different dangers with regard to the use of the past. In the case of Russia, discussion of the past has been stifled to assist in fostering patriotic feelings in support of an increasingly authoritarian state which caters to a public that wishes to be relieved of the tendency to dwell on the dark side of its history. This imposes serious impediments to attempts to analyse the past dispassionately. In the former communist states that were under Soviet sway, there is the tendency by politicians to appropriate history as refracted through the memory of trauma and suffering. This is allied to a notion of easy moralising, where the crimes of the past have to be atoned for and absolution for past sins sought. In serious historical analysis, the plight of the victims always deserves particular attention and respect. Yet the prospect of a memory culture that turns history into a morality tale of good versus evil carries its own dangers.

In both Russia and its former communist neighbours, the battle over the past poses a threat to academic freedom and to mature and open political discourse. History as an academic discipline is eroded by the way that governments and politicians – of quite different political ideologies – seek to use the past and to shape popular memory and public history as part of their nation- and state-building projects. But it is also eroded where public attitudes are deeply polarised, where individuals and groups see the past only as a source of pride or resentment, and where their view of the past excludes from consideration the perspective of others who shared that past.

Notes

1. FSB is the Federal Security Service, the successor of the KGB, or Committee of State Security.
2. From 1917 to 1922, the Cheka (Chrezvychaynaya Komissiya, Extraordinary Commission) was responsible for investigating counter-revolutionary activities in the Soviet Union.
3. A form of Russian governmental institution, the Duma is the legislative body in the ruling assembly.
4. These conflicts include the 2008 military operations in Georgia under President Medvedev.
5. Born in 1921, His Majesty Michael I King of the Romanians ruled from 20 July 1927 to 8 June 1930 and again from 6 September 1940 until being forced to abdicate by the communists on 30 December 1947. He is one of the last surviving heads of state from the Second World War.

Chapter 16

EUROCOMMUNISM

Commemorating Communism in
Contemporary Eastern Europe

❧

Péter Apor

On 25 February 2002, the Hungarian prime minister Viktor Orbán inaugurated the House of Terror museum. The government at the time was led by the Fidesz-Magyar Polgári Párt (Fidesz-Hungarian Civic Party), which had originally been a radical anti-communist liberal party and later became a radical anti-communist conservative party. It was claimed that this museum was built to commemorate the victims of dictatorial rule in the country. The spectacular opening ceremony preceded the general elections by just two months and was part of the electoral campaign of the ruling conservative party. The personal presence and inauguration speech of the prime minister, the appointment of his personal consultant in 'historical matters' and the establishment of a public foundation from huge state subsidies to manage the museum indicated that the event was considered a highly important political step. In his address, the prime minister stressed the eventual realisation of a true representation of the history of the twentieth century in Hungary, which would teach future generations the meaning of the fight for freedom.[1] The House of Terror immediately became the subject of fierce criticism. Public intellectuals, including many respected historians, pointed out the ambiguity of historical interpretation in the museum, the controversial nature of the comparison of fascism and communism, the unclear distinction of victims and perpetrators, and the ignorance of the longer-term historical roots of political terror and violence in Hungary.

While the Hungarian debate was somewhat dramatic and the House of Terror benefited from an exceptional amount of taxpayers' money, the significance attributed to a historical museum devoted to the representation of the communist past was far from being a uniquely Hungarian phenomenon.

Notes for this chapter are located on page 246.

The president of Romania, Traian Băsescu, who initiated a presidential commission to investigate the crimes of the communist regimes in Romania, proposed setting up an official, state-sponsored Museum of Communism in the capital in December 2006. Likewise in Poland, the cultural programme of the conservative-nationalist government of the Law and Justice Party emphasised the necessity of establishing a Museum of Freedom that would include the break-up of the communist regime. Similar to the controversial reception of the central initiatives, the foundation in the Baltic republics, Poland and Romania of private museums devoted to the history of the communist dictatorships also triggered passionate debates and exchanges (Knigge and Mählert 2005).

Antiquarianism is certainly not the first term that comes to mind when considering the relationship towards the contemporary past. Collecting and displaying strange and alien objects regularly recalls the image of archaeological exhibitions that demonstrate the richness and fascinating nature of distant and different pasts, such as ancient or mediaeval periods of human history (see Bann 1990). Nonetheless, the strange yet characteristic obsession with relics, including communist medals and images of 'great leaders' (Boym 1994: 225–38), and the frenzied demolition of old statues, the erection of new monuments and the mushrooming of museums dedicated to the terror of tyranny suggest that physical objects play a significant role in the relationship to the recent past. The relationship between the present – here understood as the period after 1989 – and the recent past is established through a peculiar, practical activity that is simultaneously concerned with the construction and destruction of things. The fate of themes in the public discussion of contemporary history seems to be bound to the assignment of objects. Why are historical museums and exhibitions so important in the current politics of commemorating the communist past in Central and Eastern Europe?

The exhibition in the House of Terror capitalises on a shocking and depressing atmosphere of violence. Immediately, the entrance hall with its dark, mystical design weighs heavily on the visitor. The inner courtyard of the building is dominated by a Soviet-made tank and a huge board displaying a vast selection of photographs of the victims of Soviet terror. For the average visitor, a crucial part of the impression formed by the experience is the depressing descent in an elevator while an old man – formerly a cleaning attendant present at executions – provides a detailed description of the routine hangings. The journey underground ends in the cellars of the museum, where a torture chamber of the communist secret police has been reconstructed.

The exhibition of communist prison cells plays a central role in postcommunist museums. The reconstructed communist execution chamber in the Museum of Genocide Victims in Vilnius (Lithuania), dominates the exhibition, which is situated in the building that formerly served as KGB and Gestapo prisons. In spite of the lack of evidence for its alleged previous uses, curators here opted for the conspicuous display of marks of violence of the Soviet political police. Bullet holes in the walls were carefully covered with glass, and a chute, which was claimed to have been used to drain out the blood of executed victims, was also left in place. Two other Baltic museums of occupation in Riga (Latvia) and Tallin (Estonia) emphasise horrible aspects of the Soviet era, including deportations, national subjugation and mass executions. Both built their historical representations on the remnants and reconstructions of former communist prisons, particularly underground cells (Mark 2008).

Similarly, the major site of encounter with the history of communism in Romania is the impressive building of a former political prison in the small provincial town of Sighetul Marmatiei. Constructed as a barracks during the Austrian-Hungarian Monarchy, the building later became a border town next to the USSR. In the 1950s, it was used to house important prisoners, major figures of the inter-war Romanian political and cultural elite, many of whom died in captivity. The museum opened in the early 1990s, first with one room, which was claimed to be a torture chamber and was called the Black Room. Subsequently, other cells of former captives were reconstructed. Today, the museum continues to preserve the original prison structure and atmosphere through its renovated iron stairs and walks and its tiny exhibition spaces, transformed directly from the previous small cells. The aim is to provide a comprehensive display of the history of Romanian communism in the context of the Cold War. In fact, it represents only the terrorist aspects of the regime, such as forced collectivisation, labour camps, political police, persecution and the tyranny of Ceauşescu. Other significant topics are the anti-communist resistance and revolutions throughout East-Central Europe. Although the prison stopped accepting political prisoners in 1955 and was closed in the 1970s, the museum claims to symbolise the entire communist regime, thus compressing the latter into an abstract, ahistorical period of violent clashes between oppression and resistance (Cristea and Radu-Bucurenci 2008).

The most well-known museum of communism in Poland, initiated by the Socland Foundation, which is paradoxically still under construction, also emphasises the violent nature of the regime in its representation of the communist dictatorship. The foundation behind this very ambitious initiative focuses on the demonstration of the inhumanity and cruelty of the communist system and insists on depicting a history of profound brainwashing, subsequent revolt and the final collapse of the dictatorships (Main 2008).

These museums, which depict violence, martyrs and terror within their walls, are the direct descendants of the anti-communist imagination. When anti-Stalinist insurgents occupied the party headquarters in Budapest in October 1956, they immediately began to search for the secret underground cellars that were believed to hold numerous captives of the communist secret police. When no entrance was found within the building, the freedom fighters started to dig up the square with excavators to access the hidden prison of the communists. Despite the fact that exploratory wells dug 20 metres deep failed to reveal any underground constructions, the search continued. It was stopped only when the Soviet troops crushed the revolution. The museums that eventually succeeded in establishing these underground prisons were thus the antitheses of Stalin's utopia realised beneath the surface in the Moscow metro system (Rév 2005: 249–65).

The emphasis on instances of terror and violence in this interpretation is not accidental. The intention is not simply to demonstrate the brutality and barbarity of communist rule in these countries, but rather to represent these regimes as if they had been founded and maintained exclusively by force and profound systems of coercion. The rule of the communist parties thus appears alien to these societies, a result of outside or foreign forces for which the respective nations bear no responsibility. It follows that the dictatorships contradicted the true spirit of these nations, since the communist regimes were imposed on them by means that were impossible to resist. Communism is presented as the result of fate, a tragic historical event caused by uncontrollable forces: the Soviets, the Great Powers, the Communists. The history of communism acquires mythical qualities in these museums as a catastrophe, a disaster that remains beyond the limits of human (national) capacities and comprehension. Instead of providing historical explanations for the origins of the communist dictatorships, these exhibitions seek to moralise more generally about the significance of human suffering.

At the meeting of the Romanian Parliament on 19 December 2006, President Băsescu formally condemned the communist regime in the country and declared its existence illegitimate. The president's statement was based on a report of almost 700 pages, compiled by a group of 22 contemporary historians led by the internationally renowned political scientist and sociologist, Vladimir Tismăneanu. Members of the Civic Academy Foundation, the initiator of the Sighet Memorial Museum, played a prominent role in the construction of the report. The document focused on the genesis of the communist dictatorship in Romania and revealed its subsequent crimes and killings. For the first time after 1989, the persons responsible were named. The president declared:

> The Commission's conclusions, which I espouse, confirm that the totalitarian communist regime in Romania was imposed by foreign dictate. Indeed, it was a case of an illegitimate regime, founded upon a fanatical ideology, an ideology that systematically cultivated hatred, an ideology for which the 'class struggle' and the 'dictatorship of the proletariat' symbolised the essence of historical progress. Imported from the USSR, the communist ideology justified the assault against civil society, against political and economic pluralism; it justified

the annihilation of the democratic parties, the destruction of the free market, extermination by assassination, deportations, forced labour, and the imprisonment of hundreds of thousands of people.[2]

However, instead of a historically accurate analysis of the reasons for and the social and political context of the horrific crimes, the report simply attributed these to a vaguely defined, undifferentiated conglomerate – the 'communists'. This distanced the terror, portraying it as an abnormal phenomenon that originated from outside Romanian society. This theory was grounded in extremist reasoning like that of Stelian Tănase, a member of the historians' commission. Tănase claimed that communism was ultimately a materialisation of abstract, ahistorical forces of evil. Communists in power, he wrote, 'remained hidden in a bunker, far away, alien to society, continuously conspiring against it. They failed to come to the surface, to obtain legitimacy, not even for one day during the almost half a century when they were running the Romanian world. They remained confined to their condition of eternal beings of darkness' (quoted in Cristea and Radu-Bucurenci 2008: 278).

Băsescu's condemnation of the communist regime was embedded in a characteristic trajectory of post-1989 Romanian anti-communism, while, in turn, his subsequent actions provided recognition for and made official previously marginalised ways of representing the communist system, supported mainly by various civic and church organisations. This anti-communist representation, which builds extensively on Christian symbols, articulates a quasi-religious interpretation of the martyrdom of the nation. Various monuments to the victims of communism and exhibitions in institutions such as the Romanian Peasant Museum present the fallen as fighters for national dignity. The victims of communism are regularly incorporated into a broader historical continuity of the struggle of all Romanians for the state, since they are associated with the image of the inter-war Greater Romania and are linked to the fallen soldiers of the First and Second World Wars. The unveiling of the majority of these monuments was accompanied by a religious service, and the symbol of the Cross was strongly present. Thus, the essence of the nation is defined in close connection to the (Orthodox) church and the (all-Romanian) state. The Romanian Peasant Museum transforms these national virtues into eternal principles: the exhibitions display an image of the peasantry as profoundly Christian, permanent and unchanged since antiquity. The museum claims that this atemporal and ahistorical peasant life was destroyed by communism. The communist dictatorship thus appears as a brutal rupture in the harmonious history of the nation, its state and its church (Cristea and Radu-Bucurenci 2008: 279–95).

Historians Robert Kostro and Tomasz Merta (2005) recently published a collective volume titled *Pamięć i odpowiedzialność* (Memory and Responsibility) in Poland. Merta, the ideologist behind the volume, was also the author of the cultural programme of the Law and Justice Party, the governing force of Poland that had been elected in October 2005. In the introduction, the authors argued for the necessity of a 'memory politics' for the Polish government. They suggested that this new politics of commemoration would be a proper means to raise the self-respect of Polish citizens and the appreciation of national heroes who fought for the freedom of the country throughout its history, including the period of the communist regime. In this understanding, the communist dictatorship was nothing but another device in the history of the repression of the Polish nation (Górny 2007: 131). The idea of a museum dedicated to freedom was at the core of the related measures of the Polish government to develop this 'memory politics'. The Museum of Freedom was to represent the history of the Polish nation as constant manifestations of its essence – the love of freedom and the readiness to fight for it. The Ministry of National Cultural Heritage suggested that the exhibitions should focus on the 'unique aspirations for freedom during the period of the First Republic (sixteenth to nineteenth centuries), the struggles in the nineteenth century, and the successful fight against two totalitarian dictatorships of the twentieth century: the Polish victory over communism and Nazism' (Main 2008: 389).

The House of Terror in Budapest was inaugurated on 25 February 2002, the Day of the Victims of the Communist Dictatorships. This commemorative day was created on 16 June 2000, when the Parliament of the Republic of Hungary passed Resolution 58/2000. There were 201 yeas, 24 nays and 87 abstentions. This decision expressed the conviction of the Parliament about the necessity of establishing a particular day for commemorating the victims of the communist dictatorships in Hungarian secondary schools (*Magyar Közlöny*, 16 June 2000, 3360). On 25 February 1947, the Soviet Red Army had carried away Béla Kovács, the general secretary of the Smallholders' Party and one of the most ardent critics of the communists' aspirations to power. In 1947, this violent action clearly marked the boundaries of Hungarian democracy: the Hungarian communists could count on the support of the Soviet military forces to resolve crucial political conflicts.

The date on which the national assembly passed the decision in 2000 – 16 June – was the same as that of the execution of the Hungarian prime minister, Imre Nagy, in 1958. In 1989, the reburial of the prime minister of the failed Hungarian Revolution of 1956 on the anniversary of his death constituted the core symbolic event of the demise of the communist regime. This parliamentary act depicted the continuity of communism – from its takeover in 1947 through its fundamental crisis in 1956 to its fall in 1989 – and the communist dictatorship as a state of undifferentiated repression. The resolution touched on isolated historical facts and blurred the personal fate of the communist prime minister, who had remained true to his convictions, consciously accepting the death penalty, and that of the persecuted Smallholder oppositionist politician, who had become a member of the Parliament in 1958 in the post-revolution Kádár regime. The history of communism was represented as an abstract entity identified with political terror.

The relatively recent action of the Hungarian legislative assembly to establish a memorial day for the victims of communism marked the first post-1989 commitment towards a systematic politics of commemoration related to the communist past in the country. The anniversaries of the October 1956 revolution had been celebrated annually with remarkable pomp and publicity, bearing the marks of the typical contemporary political context. Nonetheless, they failed to express any coherent intention to interpret systematically the history of the communist dictatorship. Although the members of the first conservative government (1990–4) demonstrated considerable interest in historical matters and did not decline to make statements on particular historical questions, these were individual undertakings rather than part of a comprehensive political will to remember. Immediately after 1989, the general disorientation of history produced a variety of interpretations, yet the self-identity of the first socialist-liberal coalition (1994–8) was based largely on the priority of the current economic and social problems and appeared rather indifferent to issues of the past. The then still largely post-communist socialists found it extremely inconvenient to face their fairly dubious late-communist legacy, while liberals considered questions of historical identity a lesser issue compared to the pressing need for restructuring the economy and public administration.

However, the second conservative government (1998–2002), led by the Fidesz-MPP, managed to formulate a strongly historically orientated conservative nationalist ideology. In the struggle for votes in the post-communist elections, the Fidesz-MPP realised the importance of identity politics, embedded in an imaginary history of the nation. The party, which had already laid great emphasis on its intention to 'give back Hungarians their national self-esteem' in its campaign, began to inundate the electorate with historical interpretations immediately after its victory in the general elections.[3] The Fidesz decided to build 'national pride' on a mythical series of events reflecting *grandeur et gloire* that were connected to the history of the Hungarian state and (Christian) church(es). The first element of this politics of history was the establishment of the new Ministry of National Cultural Heritage, which was commissioned to define aspects of cultural heritage considered worthy enough to be integrated into the imagined historical-national identity (Erdősi 2000).

This initiative culminated in two controversial events. The first of these was the centrally organised celebration of the 1000th anniversary of the foundation of the Hungarian state in 2000. Common historical understanding held that on Christmas Day in the year 1000, Stephen, the apostle of the Magyars, was crowned as the first king of Hungary. This millennium was clearly modelled on a previous 1000th anniversary in 1896, when the modernising Hungarian state had celebrated the conquest of the Carpathian basin by Magyar tribesmen. At that time, national pride had been embedded in the achievements of civilisation and modernity connected to the active involvement of the state, whereas in 2000 the millennium provided an opportunity for the government to distil a historical continuity of the Hungarian state grounded in a Christian-clerical historicisation and in national particularism (Gerő 2006: 153–70). The intention to set the point of departure of the history of the modern Hungarian state in the symbolic foundation of the mediaeval kingdom was demonstrated by the transfer of the Sacra Corona from the National Museum to the building of the Parliament. In the late Middle Ages and early modern period, and closely related to the fact that the actual ruler of the country resided outside the territory of the kingdom, in Vienna, the sacred crown of Saint Stephen had begun to be looked on as the ultimate representation of the Hungarian political body. The crown had been removed by the US Army at the end of the Second World War and was given back to Hungary in 1978. It was kept in the National Museum until 2000, when the Fidesz-led government decided to place it in the hall of the Parliament as the symbol of Hungarian statehood, thereby designating the contemporary Hungarian state as the subject of the supra-personal Sacra Corona (Radnóti 2001). Hence, the subject of this particular Hungarian history – the Christian state – became an ahistorical and eternal abstractum whose essence was not subject to temporal change but remained the deepest desire of the nation.

The museums of communism play a special role in these politics of commemoration of national pride. The politics of history in contemporary Eastern Europe, which also embraces the interpretation of the communist dictatorships, represents the nation as an eternal entity, a set of virtues and values, whose history is described as a success story of the realisation of these qualities. Shameful periods of national history are regarded as regrettable historical accidents caused by various external forces. Representing the communist regime exclusively as a terrorist rule imposed by such external forces and maintained solely by violence is a crucial means of implementing this concept-rooted historicist understanding of nationalism. If the communist dictatorships in these countries can be successfully isolated as events of non-national history, it is possible to claim that a range of resilient qualities and features characterise the nation and that these remained unchanged despite and during communism. From such a basis, it is possible to state that there is an eternal national identity despite temporal changes and that the former manifested itself in the periods of genuine national history.[4]

Historical museums established in the course of the nineteenth century have played a crucial role in the formation of national consciousness throughout modern history. In the museums of classical historicism, the value of the exhibited objects was derived from the fact that they were able to represent and preserve authentically the meaning of the past. For this purpose, exhibits were normally richly contextualised and situated in accurate historical periods. In this way, historical museums could demonstrate tangibly the origins of nations in the past and the notion of unbroken historical continuity since that time (Korff and Roth 1990). It is precisely this 'touch of the real' that makes historical exhibitions so attractive for various politics of history and memory. Museums, which are able to re-present the past, that is to say, to make the past once again present, provide the perfect commemorative means and serve as 'connective structures' towards history. In contemporary Eastern Europe, museums are frequently employed as a means of creating historical authenticity to render communist terror tangible and the related interpretation of the recent past credible.

When exhibitions of atrocity began to be connected to the image of communism, the same concepts and understandings had already been strongly identified with Nazism. After the Second World War, during the Nuremberg trials, Nazi atrocities and crimes were represented as signs of senseless, unintelligible barbarity. Atrocities committed with special ruthlessness emerged as a characteristic feature of the Nazi system. The judges at Nuremberg argued that the specificity of the newly formulated concept of crimes against humanity was not the enormous size or industrial mode of killing, but rather its connection to atavistic practice. Nazi violence was seen as a return of primitivism in the heart of modern civilised Europe. To illustrate this point, the prosecution exhibited a shrunken head of a former prisoner of war that was found in the Buchenwald camp. The head shocked the audience, reminding them of the practice of head shrinking carried out by the Latin American Jivaros, which had become widely known in the Western world a few years before the war. This depiction of primitive violence was accompanied by a constant description of instinctive and uncontrolled anti-Jewish atrocities that invoked a conscious reference to mediaeval pogroms. The spatial (Latin American) and temporal (mediaeval) distancing of uncivilised barbarous violence allowed for these Nazi atrocities to be described as unexpected and unimaginable in modern Europe. This remarkably tangible relationship between uncivilised and unlimited atrocities and the historical understanding of the Nazi regime successfully binds the icons of violence and barbarity to the notion of Nazism (Douglas 1998).

Many of the museums that depict the history of communism identify themselves as exhibition sites dedicated to the representation of the horrors of the modern totalitarian dictatorships: fascism (Nazism) and communism. These institutions are designed to display and demonstrate the equally horrendous nature of these regimes. The museums in Tallinn and Riga, which are called the Museum of Occupations and the Museum of the Occupation of Latvia, respectively, claim to represent the history of these countries from the Second World War to the dissolution of the

USSR. Hence, they contain images, objects and installations depicting the Nazi occupation of these countries. Similarly, the History Meeting House in Warsaw titled its recent major show, arranged by the KARTA Centre, the 'Faces of Totalitarianism: Twentieth-Century Europe'.[5] Designed to introduce visitors to the history of modern dictatorships, the exhibition interpreted the history of Europe in the 'short' twentieth century. Although the presentation stopped at the beginning of the communist regime in Poland, it portrayed in parallel the genesis and functioning of the Bolshevik system in Russia and the Nazi dictatorship in Germany. The last boards depicted the German and Soviet occupation of Poland and the defeat of Nazism versus the triumph of communism. The House of Terror in Budapest also claims to represent the history of two terror regimes in Hungary. It provides first an overview of the rule of the Hungarian fascist party, the Arrow Cross, and then a long and labyrinthine presentation of the communist dictatorship.

These exhibitions illustrate a very important agenda. The depiction of communism solely as a terror regime, situated conspicuously next to the already established icon of violence, Nazism, is an attempt to associate the Gulag with Auschwitz, to construct an understanding of the history of communism as the twin of the ultimate horrors of Nazism and as the Eastern double of the ultimate catastrophe of European civilisation. This understanding represents an effort to increase the fatally misunderstood significance of communism for a pan-European history of the modern period by claiming that it was equally as destructive and merciless as the Nazi regime. The promoters of this present-day 'Eurocommunist' interpretation falsely believe that their actions are able to establish the history of East-Central European communist dictatorships as a genuine European event.

In the West, since the early 1960s, and especially in the wake of the publication of Hannah Arendt's report on the Eichmann trial, the history of the Nazi regime – understood as the ultimate manifestation of barbarity and violence and evoked by the images of Auschwitz and the Holocaust – has functioned as a powerful means to prevent similar crimes. In spite of the various dilemmas it embraces, the historical memory of the Second World War, based on notions of moral and political responsibility, serves as an effective obstacle to the repetition of state-sponsored genocide (Arendt 1963; Friedländer 1993; J. Young 1993).[6] The Eastern European post- and anti-communist revisionism of fascism offers a radically and dangerously different interpretation. The exhibitions in the House of Terror represent the history of twentieth-century Hungary as the site of the violent clash of two equally barbarous but opposing ideologies. Germany and Russia, the exemplars of totalitarian fascism and communism, were fighting for global dominance. By chance, Hungary became the battleground of this conflict. According to the museum, however, Hungary had nothing to do with either of these two ideologically motivated great powers. The Hungarians remained the suffering subjects and victims of the war (see Frazon and Horváth 2002: 338–46). Critics have already pointed to the dubious implications of these exhibitions, which appear to use the cataloguing of communist crimes to build up and convey nationalist ideological messages and to mitigate or even exonerate Nazi crimes and criminals retroactively. Indeed, the House of Terror fails to raise questions concerning the role and responsibility of the nationalist authoritarian regime preceding the Arrow Cross takeover in assisting Nazi aspirations or to document the legal and social exclusion and subsequent deportation of Jewish citizens of Hungary. The museum similarly fails to address the impact of the inter-war social and political system on the discrediting of non-communist alternatives in the post-war period and its contribution to the eventual communist takeover. In addition, the exhibition consciously manipulates the comparison of the short-lived and fairly insignificant episode of Arrow Cross rule, isolated from its historical context, and the tangibly longer communist system, which is represented as an undifferentiated terror regime.

The House of Terror is typical of attempts in contemporary East-Central Europe to provide a historical understanding of the recent past. Such an approach situates the struggle between fascism and communism outside of the history of the nation and fosters an interpretation that emphasises the similar terrorist essence of these regimes while ignoring their contradictory ideological claims. This is clear in the example of the museums in the Baltic republics, which depict these periods of the past as the culmination of the tragedy of a nation suffering two consecutive occupations. This approach towards representing the past is in clear and definite opposition to the Western interpretation of national responsibility: instead of raising a barrier against the possibility of committing similar crimes in contemporary societies, the Eastern European offer is an 'unbearably light' attempt to divert this responsibility.

Nonetheless, before leaning back in the comfort of the notion that these issues are but another manifestation of familiar post-communist Eastern European nationalism, it is important to take note of the genuinely pan-European nature of this construction. The Sighet Memorial Museum is affiliated with the International Centre for the Study of Communism, the executive scientific board of which reflects a truly all-European composition. The members of the board are Thomas Blanton (National Security Archives, George Washington University), Vladimir Bukovsky (Cambridge University), Stéphane Courtois (CNRS, Paris), Dennis Deletant (SSEES, London University), Helmut Müller-Enbergs (Federal Office for the Study of Stasi Archives, Berlin) and Pierre Hassner. Furthermore, in 1998, the Council of Europe granted the Sighet Memorial Museum the status of being among the most significant monuments of the continent, together with the Auschwitz Museum and the Peace Memorial in Normandy. The Twentieth-Century Institute that is associated with the House of Terror in Budapest has received visits from such illustrious guests as Ernst Nolte, the controversial German historian of fascism. The History Meeting House in Warsaw and its backer, the KARTA Centre, have close links with the Institute of National Memory, members of which contributed to the Polish sections of *The Black Book of Communism*.[7] The honorary members of the board of the Socland Foundation include Zbigniew Brzeziński, a former US national security adviser, and the well-known French historian Alain Besançon.

The participation of Western scholars and policy makers in the process of shaping the historicist-nationalist memory of communism and its identification with fascism can be explained by benevolent ignorance and a sincere will to condemn the communist dictatorships as a Soviet phenomenon. The principal reason that the public tends to disregard the problematic implications of this interpretation of communism based exclusively on a comparison with totalitarian violence is general indifference. The West, which has already succeeded in containing fascism, is reluctant to give up its convenient position and to face the challenge of once again coming to terms with its dictatorial past. It would be discomforting to understand communism as the consequence of European modernity, instead of attributing it to an imagined Eastern European anti-modernity. In general, there is no incentive to reopen these issues, which allows Eastern European politicians of history or *The Black Book* to shape the discussions about communism.

However, exactly this general indifference might provide the opportunity to resist the historicist-nationalist revision of the history of the recent past. Nazism as a historical phenomenon has been clearly and powerfully associated with Auschwitz. The spectacle of the crematoria, gas chambers and mass graves unambiguously marks the historical identity of Nazism. Auschwitz, as an authentic site of mass extermination, successfully localises, connects to credible evidence and, hence, renders tangible the interpretation of the genocide and war crimes. On the contrary, the image of communism as terror, as a dictatorship characterised exclusively by violence, is an essentially abstract argument. The propagators of this historical view ordinarily base their reasoning on certain carefully selected historical facts that demonstrate their claims. The cited instances of atrocities, cruelty and terror are usually cautiously isolated from other sources of historical evidence. They are thus presented in a profoundly decontextualised environment that is stripped of any accurate historical reference and localisation. Because of this, the authenticity of statements on the historical nature of communism as terror and violence is based largely on a comparative evocation of fascism.

The House of Terror is probably the most eloquent example of this manipulation. At the same time, it contradicts the conditions of museum representation based upon the relationship of the authenticity of the artefacts and their narrative contextualisation. The exhibition displays three different categories of objects: the first covers authentic historical materials, the second consists of copies of original articles and the last includes objects from contemporary everyday life, whose role, meaning and place remains unclear in the context of the exhibition. In general, the museum uses its authentic materials in a way that further increases uncertainty concerning their interpretation. Typically, there is so little information attached to even authentic objects that it is often very difficult to decide whether these are the genuine remnant of an actual historical moment or simply objects that might represent a historical interpretation authentically if contextualised properly. This transforms the exhibited material into merely illustrative accessories of a dramatised story. In addition, the museum constantly blurs the distinction between real and fabricated objects since it displays them in the same way and eschews further explanation. The profound lack of historical contextualisation, the ambiguity and the methodological inconsistency eventually undermine the credibility of the displayed representation of the past. The entire museum thus resembles an installation referring to an imagined world rather than an accurate representation of an actual historical period. The exhibition uses its objects to refer to previously established abstract ideological tenets, to illustrate and hence to evoke these allegorical meanings (Frazon and Horváth 2002: 311–25; Rév 2005: 278–90).

Techniques of blurring the distinction between fabrication and authentic representation have been employed in other museums. The Museum of Genocide Victims in Vilnius uses the same level of information – or rather, the same lack of evidence – to justify very different claims of authenticity. On the one hand, it reconstructs a Soviet-era torture chamber based on insufficient and very dubious proof, stating that it is exactly the lack of information that signifies the authenticity of the reconstruction, since it proves the efficiency of the communist secret service in eliminating all evidence. On the other hand, the museum staff do not dare to use historical imagination in the same way in relation to the Nazi past. They refuse to reconstruct a Gestapo prison cell in the museum building, despite the fact that there had also been a prior Nazi presence, arguing that the tiny available evidence precludes any speculation on the actual use of the chamber in question (Mark 2008: 355–9).

The considerable corpus of previous scholarship on memory and history in East-Central Europe usually recorded the disorderly status of evocations of the recent past and tried to explain this by arguing that historical interpretations in this region are politically driven and usually supported and maintained by various political groups. The malfunctions of historical consciousness were understood as the distorting consequence of politicised projections. In this context, history (historical studies) increasingly came to be seen as a reflection of ideological intentions and as a means of politics; accordingly, it has been viewed with suspicion (Bartetzky et al. 2005;

Bucur and Wingfield 2001; Todorova 2006; Watson 1994b). This reasoning gradually undermined the importance and relevance of assessing the problems of evidence, authenticity and truth. Nonetheless, as demonstrated by this survey of the contemporary politics of commemoration with regard to communism in Eastern Europe, the present deep and peculiar disorientation in historical matters is intimately connected to the conspicuous uncertainty about the authenticity of historical representations in the region. The credibility of abstract political projections of history, which have very little – if any – connection to the actual embedding of their sources in their respective historical contexts, is attributable to the growing demise of the evidential criteria of historical narratives. To understand the current state of post-communist politics of commemoration, it is necessary to raise questions about the historically and socio-politically generated conditions and standards of conceiving historical facts – of factuality, realism, credibility and acceptability in historical representation.

Notes

1. The speech of the prime minister is available at http://www.orbanviktor.hu.
2. The address of the president is at http://www.presidency.ro/?_RID=det&tb=date&id=8288&_PRID=ag.
3. The context of this politics of history in historiography proper is described in Apor and Trencsényi (2007: 45).
4. On the formation of the historical identity of nations, see Mosse (1975: esp. 47–99).
5. The KARTA Centre in Poland is a non-governmental organisation and publisher whose mission is to document the history of Poland and Eastern Europe. Originally founded as an underground organisation during martial law in 1982, it was legalised in 1990.
6. The special German case is discussed in Lüdtke (1993).
7. *The Black Book of Communism*, edited by Stéphane Courtois, was originally published in France in 1997 as *Le Livre noir du communisme: Crimes, terreur, répression*. It is published in the US by Harvard University Press.

Chapter 17

THE MEMORY OF THE DEAD BODY

❦

Senadin Musabegović

The disintegration of Yugoslavia as a socialist federation can be interpreted through the political use of symbols. In uniting the former country, communist symbols drew inspiration from war motifs. In destroying the communist order, nationalist symbols also fed on fantasies of war. This begs the question: in what way did the symbols of the powerful totalitarian body create a new consciousness about society and the future?[1]

The communist body was represented through the figure of the 'warrior-worker'. This line of representation implied that the new society of workers was created through war, but also that class enemies were defeated through labour. In the crisis-utopia relation, as described by Koselleck (2002), the 'monumental' communist body possesses a dual character. The communist body (warrior-worker) denotes war and conflict (crisis), but also promises harmony in the future (utopia). Within this configuration, each individual is in harmony with the collective, spurred on, as if in a symphony of labour, by victorious war enthusiasm. This in turn begs another question: in which way does the pagan 'cult of the fallen fighter' acquire significance for the myth of the formation of the 'new man'? The fallen fighter gives himself over to a new future by means of the logic of symbolic reciprocity between the gift receiver and gift giver. As Marcel Mauss (1997) explains, on the symbolic level, if the receiver does not reciprocate the gift, he will be 'burnt, scorched'. Consequently, on a symbolic plane, gift receivers were obligated to reciprocate the gift of life from fallen heroes by building communism.

The relationship between the nationalist and communist bodies in the former Yugoslavia is constituted upon different temporal perspectives. Unlike the communist body, the nationalist body does not speak about the future but rather about returning to 'one's own homeland', the 'golden age' and the 'faith of our ancestors'. By abolishing the international labour

---

collective, it introduces the archetypal pre-political collective, which, like an organic body, unites blood and faith, community and territory, memory and history, space and time. Through the cult of the victim, it also establishes new meanings: the victim calls on the entire nation to return to the past – to the womb of mother earth. While the communist body signified acceleration, workers' action and construction for the future, the nationalist body insists on the myth of a return of the ancestor cult, permeated by the spirit of the Holy Cross, and upon the rediscovery of ancestral faith in which there is communication with mother earth and within which the entire national memory is inscribed.

However, if the differing temporal perspectives of the communist and nationalist bodies are evident, it could equally be argued that there are similarities between nationalism and communism. Many believed that during communism, nationalism was hidden from the official discourse and fostered in private narratives and that when the communist system began to crumble, nationalism exploded and came out into the light. Since every system is complex, and the transition from one system to another still more so, it is certain that there must be an element of continuity in the 'transitional discontinuity'. Thus, the collective narrative of war as one of the main mechanisms through which a community is formed is common to both nationalism and Josip Broz Tito's communism.

Communism presented the myth about the construction of a new man through war and through the NOB (National Liberation Movement of Resistance). Nationalism also used war to present its myth about the return to the golden age. For both the communist and the nationalist projects, war offered the means to reshape society and collective consciousness and to form new mechanisms of organising political life. Nationalism championed the return to the lost golden age, but it derived its utopian expectation from the disintegration and collapse of communist expectations. In essence, the communist vision for a utopian future was turned inside out and transformed into the nationalist call for a return to old values. In the 1990s in Yugoslavia, a growing sense of nationalism came about, not because people no longer believed in communist values, but because those beliefs were disrupted – and from the disintegration of unfulfilled communist expectations issued nationalism. The latter promised a new collective myth based on the incestuous tendency to return to the familial identity. In effect, nationalism is nothing but an autistic process of self-isolation. It digs its own grave (through which the identity myth is constructed) in the hope of entering it to touch the centre, the womb of its own birth. The process of self-isolation is thus perceived as a maternal embrace of limitless freedom.

This chapter deals with symbolic representations of bodies from organised ritual exhumations of mass graves of Serb victims of the Second World War, who had been killed mainly by the right-wing Croatian Ustasha, and the attempts to rebury them in accordance with the customs of ancestral faith. Following the experience of communism and 'brotherhood and unity', I am particularly interested in the question of how these rituals served to unify the national community, and how the suffering inscribed into the bodies of victims (termed 'martyr relics') legitimated a war propaganda in which the national collective was united through an explosion of violence.

In the language of Nietzsche, I should point out at the very beginning that the mass graves are a form of atrocity that reflects an excessively human face of man himself. Hannah Arendt's stipulation that Nazi concentration camps reflect the shame of humanity is also applicable. However, the intention of the nationalist discourse was not to bury the bodies of the victims properly, but rather to proclaim them as 'our victims' and to construct an identity in the graveyard of the past. The belief in the relics of saints, however, does not in its original religious context denote national mobilisation or exclusivity. On the contrary, this meaning was ascribed when religious symbols began to be used for the purposes of national unification and homogenisation.

The reason I deal primarily with Serb nationalism is that examples of constructing a national identity through the cult of the dead body are most evident in Serb culture and because Serb nationalism, through its numerous concentration camps and mass killings during the war in Bosnia and Herzegovina, made the greatest contribution to the disintegration of Yugoslavia. My decision was also influenced by my own experience of living for four years in besieged Sarajevo – a city whose siege and destruction was the direct result of Serb nationalism.

The Use of Symbols and Myths

In the late 1980s, the myth about 'holy places' was emphasised in Serbia. Together with the Serb Democratic Party of Bosnia and Herzegovina, the Serb Orthodox Church organised the exhumation of Serb victims killed as the result of racist policies of the Independent State of Croatia, which implemented the laws of the Third Reich from 1941 to 1945. The victims of these fascist policies included Jews, Roma, Serbs, communists and sympathisers of the partisan movement. An organised genocide of the Serb people was conducted in Bosnia and Herzegovina and Croatia.[2] Its goal was stated in lapidary terms by the author Mile Budak, a minister of the Independent State of Croatia: 'A portion of the Serbs we shall kill, another we shall relocate, and the rest we shall convert to the Catholic faith and thus assimilate into Croats.'

However, the Yugoslav Communist Party did not broadcast the fact that one fraternal nation had committed genocide against another, nor did it allow haggling over which nation had caused more harm to the other.

Instead, it insisted that all people had domestic traitors who committed crimes against other nations, which was, in a sense, true. It is for this reason that the exhumation of mass graves became charged with the political intent to point out directly and irrefutably which nation was the greatest victim and which was the perpetrator of the greatest crimes during the Second World War. More precisely, this was part of an attempt to demonstrate that members of the Serb nation were the greatest victims of the Second World War and that the perpetrators of the crimes committed against them were members of other nations – in particular, that they were Croats. According to this reasoning, since the greatest victims of the Second World War were Serbs, they – as victims – had the greatest right to speak on behalf of history and on behalf of the political will within Yugoslavia.

The haggling over victims contained the political objective of forming vengeful war iconography, using the bodies of victims to promote national unification and to demand new sacrifices on the basis of old ones. In this way the mass graves were transformed into weapons to fight the enemy. Explicit confirmation of this appears in a text by one of the leading ideologists of Serb nationalism, Professor Nikola Koljević. When asked why the exhumation of the 'relics of new martyrs' from 'bottomless graves' was spiritually important, Koljević (1991: 8) responded:

> With this redemptive act, the Serbs were newly Serbianised and Christianised. Our innocent martyrs, whom we had relegated to the darkness of oblivion and political falsehood, we justly proclaimed our victims. Thus, their death became imbued with the meaning of our awareness and our care, for their relics brought us back to the roots of our culture, which has for time immemorial taken care of ancestors and the deceased and always saw the greatest meaning of life in sacrifice. And always with the hope that the graves may grow flowers for generations yet to come.

While in communism the cult of the fallen fighter aimed to point out the sense of the struggle and ways to create the many new men who would construct brotherhood and unity among the nations, the nation state has tended rather to bring about a disintegration of such fraternal harmony among nations. The suffering of a national victim does not build unity with other nations. The nationalist cult of the victim does not use the suffering of the body to talk about a new unity among nations. Instead, it uses the cult of death, fragmentation and sacrifice to communicate with its own national essence and belonging, from which all other perspectives and nations are excluded as adversaries. The logic of fragmentation and disintegration of the body, sacrifice, death, wounding and suffering is not aimed at creating new unity after the war. Indeed, in contrast to the goal of the communist ideology to create a 'new proletarian man', here the intention is to revert the nation back to its ancestral faith. This return takes place at a time when the communist body of the new proletarian man is in fact collapsing: as the outer body falls apart, the national body is revealed within, signifying the return to national unity and the Orthodox faith.

Consequently, the national body finds itself in a paradoxical relation towards the 'new' and the 'old' body. It represents the old body, with the national essence containing the very beginnings of history, which, according to nationalists, existed before modern ideas such as liberalism and communism. At the same time, it is also the new body because it issues from the collapse of the body of communism and in this way reveals and creates itself. The nationalism arising after the disintegration of communism is thus constituted out of the fragments and destroyed body of communism.

In the former Yugoslavia, the exhumation of graves was accompanied by a church liturgy, and the exhumed bones, laid out on blankets, were consecrated by an Orthodox priest. There were also instances of victims' relatives kissing the bones. After 50 years, bones dug up from the earth were honoured by church services and nationalist assemblies.[3] Such events served to unite the bodies of the living with the bodies of the dead. However, in this case, in contrast to communism, the dead do not herald the future but rather signal the past. Their theme and expectation is that the living are supposed to 'return' to them, that is, to their own tradition, to the past. Therefore, the exhumation of graves as a ritual served to return national unity to itself. While the communist victim is imbued with the intent to form consciousness of a 'debt' to construct a new society, a new system, the victims belonging to the fantasies of nationalism signify a return to tradition. The exhumation of remains from mass graves aimed to exhume the national community out of the forgotten past, to discover in the memories of the earth a forgotten and repressed national self.

The cult of the dead also implies a feeling of guilt. As the living remembered the dead after 50 years, the implication was that in the meantime the dead had been forgotten.[4] As their memory came hurtling back, the dead appeared as bones to warn the living of their lost homeland and their forgotten national unity. Thus, the exhumation of the dead was accompanied by the idea of a return to the homeland and to a forgotten and mythical national unity. It was also a call to return to the primary community and the land of the ancestors. Feelings of guilt towards the dead signify feelings of guilt about forgetting one's own national unity. The ritual exhumation of dead bodies and bones thus sought to rediscover traditions long forgotten.

But is such a return really possible? Returning to tradition is illogical in and of itself. The presence of tradition in everyday life is evident, so no collective rituals such as the exhumation of graves should be necessary. Although nationalism embraces the corpse and the skeleton in order to discover tradition within it, the corpse is precisely the reflection of the part of tradition that cannot be possessed – the graveyard. It could be said that nationalism constructs its identity upon the graveyard of its own tradition and that the tradition towards which it strives is dead – it does not exist. This is why tradition is being invented through the corpse: the aim is to uncover and reconstruct the so-called golden age marked by the glory of the 'heavenly people'.

In Serb nationalism, as in most other nationalisms, there is a nostalgic myth about the golden age. In the Serbian case, it is represented by the image of Dušan's kingdom before the Battle of Kosovo and Ottoman occupation. However, this myth contains a certain ambivalence. According to legend, Prince Lazar was offered a choice: to accept the earthly kingdom, meaning victory at Kosovo Polje, or to opt for the heavenly kingdom, implying defeat by the Turkish army. Lazar chose defeat, thus allowing the Serb people to enter the heavenly experience. This legend enabled church ideology, which participated in forming the new national iconography, to launch a myth about the heavenly people. Lazar's decision to accept the heavenly kingdom was interpreted by many as a substantiation of the Christian belief that through sacrifice, as related to the figure of Christ, resurrection is achieved. Hence, these two myths work together. The first is that of the golden age, during which all was harmonious and unified as in heaven and as before the creation of the world. The second stipulates that collective redemption is achieved through sacrifice, or a 'Golgotha'. The symbolic presentation of the body relies on these two principles. The dead preserve both the heavenly glory of the golden age, a unity that is akin to that of a mother's womb, and the Golgotha, the sacrifice and crucifixion which leads to heavenly truth (Bandić 1997; Milosavljević 2002; M. Popović 1977). Yet exhumation does not uncover a new tradition, nor does it resurrect a forgotten tradition: all it does is uncover the corpse, or dead tradition, which is then proclaimed sacred.

The fear of the dead is more apparent and noticeable in the case of national unification than in the case of communism. According to the Serb national idea, the living give themselves to the dead so that the latter may return to the heavenly kingdom, the forgotten homeland of 500 years ago. Of course, the dead are those killed 50 and not 500 years ago. But in every cult of the ancestors, the cult of the dead marks the unity between the people and the land in which the bones of the ancestors reside.

But how are the living to return to the dead, and in which way are they to continue their work? It has already been said that in communism, the dead – those who died building the foundations of the revolution – embodied the debt that the living had to constantly repay through constructing the new proletarian man and collectively creating a new future. In nationalism, the living give themselves to the dead, not figuratively, through the construction of a new society, but literally, by giving themselves. Through the 'spirit of revenge', they are united with the dead and return to heavenly unity, to the homeland. The debt which they repay to the dead is not, therefore, one to be paid by following in the footsteps of the hero, or by constructing a new society. Instead, it is repaid through the logic of sacrifice and revenge, whereby the living will be united with the dead.

The spirit of revenge and the possibility of giving in the form of self-sacrifice arise from a fear of the dead. According to mythological thought, if the dead are not repaid through sacrifice, they will avenge themselves against the living. In other words, if the living do not return to their national unity, the dead will have their revenge, and their own tradition will punish them. That is why the living must avenge themselves against those guilty of the killing, in other words, the enemy. In the case of Serb nationalism, the enemy was the Ustasha or, in nationalist terms of generalisation, all Croats as a collective, that is, as a nation.

According to the mythical precepts of nationalism, the perception of the enemy is easily transferred and extended to include other nations. Through the elimination of the enemy, one's own self-purification and enlightenment can be achieved. This also constitutes a unification with one's own tradition, with the ancestral faith, which is opposed to the changeable logic of the intentions of an adversary. The face of the enemy, the symbol of subversive, irrational and diabolical forces that negate the spatial and temporal coherence of the eternal national essence, is always masked – it is the impostor. It can even act as a benefactor, as did the faces of all our nations in the embrace of brotherhood and unity when they shared the common fate of constructing a new society, although in this case by signifying those to be looked on as enemies.

Revenge in Communism and Nationalism

The communist ideology did not foster the myth about revenge against the enemy to the extent that the nationalist ideology did, despite the fact that in partisan communist films, for instance, the hero would be shown shooting an enemy even after the latter had surrendered. Although the black and white representation of war on film enabled the absolute eradication of the enemy and his perspective, this contrasts with partisan communist mythology, which interprets conflict with the enemy as the formation of a new consciousness and a new class affiliation, as the creation of a new man. In this view, conflict heralds collective emancipation and the final utopian form that is communism – or, as Isaiah Berlin interprets Marx, the consciousness of conflict is consciousness of progress. Therefore, according to communist logic, the new man, formed through the struggle with the enemy, is to be constructed not through the cyclic pagan myth of the spirit of revenge, of eternal regeneration of time, but instead through the vertical, linear rise of history towards the utopian paradise.

The cult of revenge in nationalism is connected with the cyclic consciousness of returning a debt to the past, to the dead and to lost national unity – a belief that makes opening up towards the future impossible. By repaying a debt to the dead, the living return to them and subject themselves to their laws. The living identify themselves by the laws of tradition that the dead represent and are thus determined by their will, which for the nationalists represents tradition, a fixed essence. Related to this, the anthropologist Dušan Bandić (1980) discusses the often taboo status of the body of the deceased in folk belief. Corpses were often considered unclean and even dangerous. There was also a belief that contact with a dead body could taint the living with the spirit of the dead. Thus, the relationship of the living to the bodies of the deceased consists at the same time of various fears and of an emotional connection.[5] Indeed, one such fear relates to the mythic belief that there is no accidental death and that if a man 'is not killed by real, he is killed by imaginary weapons – magic or conjuring'. Bandić points out in particular the perception of the grave as the home of the human spirit and the notion of the grave as a symbol of the deceased. Since the grave is the house of the deceased, the graveyard is the city of the dead, and all those who would desecrate the grave or graveyard should be punished, according to folklore. To return to the case of the former Yugoslavia, it was the Ustasha who symbolically desecrated a graveyard by throwing the dead into mass graves. For this reason, the exhumation of the dead appears as an activation of the old belief that whoever desecrates a grave must be punished.

Well-known anthropologist Veselin Čajkanović (1973) noted that the Serb religion can be reduced to the cult of ancestors, as is evidenced by various customs, folk poetry, proverbs, etc. For instance, Serb customs related to Christmas Eve include the feast for ancestors, in which ritual acts, such as setting the tables and eating off the ground, are performed to attract the souls of the deceased. This could be interpreted as offering various gifts as a sacrifice because, according to Serb folklore, every deceased person has his own table in the beyond. And if the dead eat with the living, might there not also exist an unconscious fear that the living will be eaten by the dead, that the transition from this world to the next is like the process of being chewed by the jaws of the wolf (which in Serb mythology symbolises the ancestral soul) and swallowed?

Bishop Dr Irinej Bulović has asserted that 'our nation rests on the relics of saints', and that perhaps Serbs 'shall be in the face of God, before His judgement, in a more difficult position precisely because we have so many saints' (*Javnost*, 14 December 1991, 8). When Bulović lists figures such as Saint Sava, Prince Lazar or national heroes (Sinđelić, Karađorđe or Major Tepić) as belonging to the Serbian tradition in which 'humanity and heroism' are based on 'eternal human and Christian spiritual values', on 'faith' and 'on honour', then despite insisting on the Christian faith, Bulović invokes the pagan, pre-Christian cult of ancestors, according to which warriorship and heroism are the basis for unifying the living and the dead. Thus, in the ritual of exhuming graves, the debt to the ancestors paid through revenge and in blood is combined with the suffering of the relics soaked in Christ's blood as the symbol of love and forgiveness.

At the inauguration of the memorial at the site of the Prebilovci mass grave, the history professor Milorad Ekmečić proclaimed that graves 'have become the new Kosovo epic of the Serb people, the ashes from which new life is born'. In this speech, he too was combining two cosmologies about the victim: the first, a pagan understanding of time renewed through sacrifice, the second, the Christian notion of resurrection.[6] Of course, the protagonists of these ritual gatherings did not acknowledge this. Their emphasis was exclusively upon Christian symbolism: redemption of the soul, purification from past sins, and God's forgiveness, mercy and love in the image of Christ. Yet these rituals also revived and exhumed pre-Christian beliefs, relics of the past. Such conclusions about the cult of the ancestors are important for understanding the genealogy of the ritual of exhuming graves as well as the unconscious and conscious meanings of folk beliefs during exhumation.

In the case of nationalism, the cult of the dead body and the skeleton also serve to fix tradition. This contradicts several notable perspectives. According to Elèmire Zolla (1998), for example, tradition is never stable but rather a constantly changing flux. In Marcel Proust's *In Search of Lost Time*, the return to lost time is never identical; it is always different and always appears within a new perspective. When arguing in favour of a return to ancient gods, Nietzsche knew that the modern era, as opposed to the heroic Hellenic age, is marked by decadence and the deterioration of values, and that it is impossible to return to a specific time in the past. In the same way, Giorgio Agamben (2000) talks about the 'incomplete past', which is being completed in the present, and the 'incomplete present', which is being completed in the past. Borrowing a term from Heidegger, Agamben sees time as 'ecstatic'. It does not posses a vertical line in which every individual moment is separated from every other; instead, each moment, as in a rhythm of poetry or music, contains another moment in which it is reflected. As the return of the eternal circle is always the creation of something new for Nietzsche, so for Agamben, time does not have a centre or a beginning to which we may return. The essence of time is in the non-identical, in the constant difference that creates unity. In contrast, the exhumation of graves strives to fix tradition and to imbue it with a physiognomy through the image of the corpse in order to find its place, a body in which it is located, and in order to discover its centre, its womb. The dead signify a tradition that is fixed and unchangeable, inscribed in the land and into mother earth by the blood of victims.

In national mythology, therefore, the corpse not only signifies fragmentation, rotting, sacrifice. It also signifies immortality, the fixing of a tradition within a body that is unchangeable, that is, in effect, a skeleton which can no more be transformed. Firm and immoveable, like Plato's immortal ideas, it belongs to the heavenly people, and it is through the discourse of those killed and buried in mass graves that the national mythology formulated the myth about the latter. Every victim belongs to a heavenly truth, and immortality is constructed through the image of the corpse. Thus, the idea of a return to the heavenly homeland, to national unity, is realised. Propagating the idea of the heavenly people, a chosen people belonging to God, the national mythology places its ancestors on a heavenly throne from which they are to rule the living. The dead belong to the heavens, and the national idea of the Serb nation is constructed through the figure of the heavenly people, its heavenly affiliation. This leant gravity to the national idea and fortified the discourse on a return to the mediaeval kingdom and the cult of ancestors.[7]

But what does national ideology mean when it speaks about the victim? The first association that nationalism used in responding to this question was the idea of Christ's crucifixion: that which connects the dead and the living is the symbol of the cross. National ideology mainly used the symbol by incorporating it into the national body; consequently, the history of the Serb nation is often represented as the history of the cross. The logic of the cross implies the idea of sacrifice and of suffering, which makes necessary internal individual and collective redemption in the name of the idea of the 'man-god'.[8] The very figure of the cross rests on a dual signification of guilt and sin. This guilt is to be borne not merely by the perpetrator of the crime, but also by both its victims and those who survived it. Indeed, the sin belongs not solely to those who perpetrated the crime; it is disseminated throughout the entire national body. What, therefore, is the relationship towards guilt and sin within nationalism? It could be said that collective feelings of sinfulness and guilt offer a possibility to enlighten the national body, so that it may recognise itself again in the Divine presence. In such a view, the significance of the relationship between crime and punishment is not the potential to redeem a crime through punishment, but rather the capacity to transform the individual and collective soul and send it on its way to a heavenly experience. This redemptive transformation is impossible without a sinful act, without some form of crime. In this sense, the irony is that the crimes committed in the war of 1991–5 made repentance and enlightenment possible.

What then, we may ask, is the basis for the relationship between the dead and the living? Beyond doubt, it is based on some archetypal symbol capable of uniting the living and the dead. As mentioned above, one such representative symbol is the cross, whose meaning in this case is not directed towards universal human suffering but rather towards national suffering. In its archetypal symbolism, the cross represents a circle, ahistorical perfection, the unity of heaven and earth, or the relation between vertical and horizontal paths, in which one line represents man's vertical growth and the other connotes man's tendency towards expansion. Yet the metaphor of the perfect circle and of horizontal and vertical growth is also marked ambiguously by the symbol of suffering, implying a focus point, a closing up and narrowing down in the manner of Christ's body, whose sufferings testify to a transformation and transcendence in order to reveal the soul. At the heart of national unity, the essence of archetypal symbols uniting the heavens and the earth, the past and the present, the living and the dead, is fear. Archetypal symbols do not usher in Jung's collective unconscious, manifested through constant creation, in which the individual self is transformed through mythological images and symbols. Instead, these symbols dig deep, uncovering subterranean fears in the face of which life itself crumbles.

The fear at the heart of the collective enthusiasm of national unity is dissipated and submerged within the entire national body. There is no fixed centre to instigate that fear, such as a despot. The exhumation of the dead and self-recognition in religious symbols – based on narratives of national unity as the eternal divine temple, the cross as the fated unifier, saints' relics and the cult of the ancestors with its implications of ahistorical time – served to unearth the fear of the dead. This was the fear of supernatural cosmic forces responsible for the dead that could potentially bringing new threats and even a new crucifixion. Fear, disguised within archetypal symbolism, swallowed up the collective and ceased to be controlled by it, forming instead, the basis for a new, imaginary, national sacred centre, which in effect equals the entire collective national body.

Thus, the experience of mystical unity of all cosmic forces in the national body is based on fear. Fear is at the very heart of unity and of the workings of symbolic power. With the cult of revenge against the enemy, nationalism strove to delineate the border between 'our' body and 'their' body, between the inside and the outside, between friend and foe. It sought to tame its own fear. The war that took place immediately after the exhumation of the mass graves confirms that it is impossible to draw such a border.

Nationalism relies on the impossibility of establishing a border, the impossibility of separating off from another nation and the impossibility of controlling one's own fear. And it is precisely through that impossibility that the power of nationalism surges, for the best food of war is fear and, in turn, war is the best way to preserve national unity. Therefore, by exhuming graves, Serb nationalism was actually unearthing its unconscious collective fears, creating them and elevating their torches to the heavenly heights of war.

As a result, like the human body in wartime, the national body fell apart (see Kristeva 1982). It was outside its own borders, containing life and death, matter and anti-matter, the organic and the inorganic. It is due to such contradictions that a border is desperately sought – in order to confine one's own fear. All that nationalism attempted to expel from itself was its own reflection, carried on the wings of a narcissistic lamentation of its own imaginary sacrifice, from which it tried to escape. Destroying the lives of others in the war of 1991–5, Serb nationalism exulted in its image as the victim, expelling other nations from its territory as impure. Yet it was actually expelling something from itself, proclaiming its organic body immortal. With its internal cancer gnawing at it, in its own disunity it recognised unity. In short, the total logic of violence during the war was manifested in the impossibility of nationalism to set a border between itself and another nation and to use that border to control the 'other' within itself.

René Girard (1989) points out that communities find scapegoats in order to wash away their internal discord. But how does discord enter the community in the first place? Is its source to be found among unknown dark forces, or does it reside within the community? Although it implicated an external enemy, the nationalism that exhumed graves in fact uncovered the discord within itself. It dug up the fear of itself and of its own death, as symbolised by the exhumed corpses. The best way to overcome the fear of death is to yield to it, and this was done during the war that was precipitated by the exhumation of mass graves.

What, then, is the image of the enemy in the nationalist fantasy? Undoubtedly, it is just like the image of the corpse – anonymous – for only as such can it represent an entire people without individual properties and characteristics. By exhuming mass graves and identifying with the skeletons therein, nationalism came up with an image of the enemy – and it is identical to the image of death. Thus, the dead body denotes eternity, coherence and unity, and yet, at the same time, signifies the enemy's decay, the disintegration of closeness, and the invisible, destructive force emanating from the depths of the grave. The dead body transformed into a skeleton is the ultimate image of the very nature of the fear that incites and reinforces national unity. In the emptiness winding around its bones, we can discern the echo of the elementary primal horror of the body facing death. In contrast to Nazism, Serbian nationalism does not advocate a body which, in conflict with its own forces, creates the myth of a new man, a new future. Rather, through the dead body it finds its narcissistic reflection in the primal fear of the victim, which echoes the horror of the primordial consciousness at the moment when it faces the disunity of earthly and cosmic forces inscribed in the depths of graves. And it is precisely from that cosmic loneliness that the need for collective unity is born. This unity is perceived as the only foothold, the only security, and although it is like a bag of stones pulling a drowning man to the bottom, it is nevertheless seen as the only salvation at the moment of one's own shipwreck. In its own death throes, nationalism finds redemption.

Notes

1. I have dealt with this issue in a recent publication (Musabegović 2008).
2. The exhumation of mass graves took place mostly in Bosnia and Herzegovina, which is predominantly multi-ethnic. The many mass graves in Serbia were not exhumed in order to give the dead a 'proper burial' because the population of those areas was mononational, that is, Serb. Since fascist Croat military units of the Ustasha had never been there, there was no need – in terms of war propaganda – to exhume those graves. Also there was no exhumation of mass graves of Muslim victims of Serb quisling groups, such as the Chetniks, during World War II in eastern Bosnia (see Tomanić 2001). The exhumations had a ritual character and were attended by many poets, painters and professors from Bosnia and Herzegovina and Belgrade, as well as members of the leadership of the Serb Democratic Party in Bosnia and Herzegovina, led by Radovan Karadžić.
3. In her essay 'Plombiranje memorije', the Sarajevo author Alma Lazarevska (1993) recognises in the television images and photographs of exhumed bones from mass graves sorted in plastic bags a grotesque intention to mask the actual tragedy of the past with a veneer of politicised memories.
4. However, it cannot be said that communism definitively prohibited the commemoration of the dead; examples are the commemorations of Jasenovac and many other crimes of Ustasha and Chetnik terror. This said, fearing that the commemoration ritual might turn into mono-national exclusivity, communism did repress the national generalisation of commemoration and the possibility of equating Ustasha and Chetnik crimes with the Croat and Serb people, respectively.
5. For a discussion of the belief, common to many tribal communities, that at the moment of death even previously benevolent members of the community undergo a transformation and become a threat to the living, see Levy-Bruhl (1965). On the animatist and the animist perceptions of death in Serb folklore, see Bandić (1980).
6. See 'Prebilovci: Povratak kući', *Javnost*, 1 December 1990, 1.
7. Ivan Čolović (2000: 49) notes that, according to this perspective, the fatherland is also present in heaven: 'In the beyond as well, Serbs, and especially innocent Serb victims, live in an organised society. This is the Heavenly Serbia, the greatest country in the heavens.'
8. The formation of the myth about the 'man-god' in the Serb Orthodox Church owes much to the works of Dostoyevsky. Justin Popović (2003) has written that this figure cannot be grasped by a Western European mindset because the path of the man-god is that of faith, in contrast to the materialistic egocentrism of the European. According to Popović, Orthodox culture is 'primarily a culture of the soul', and in line with this, the 1990s saw ongoing discussion of the mystical suffering of the Serb soul.

Chapter 18

NEITHER HELP NOR PARDON?
Communist Pasts in Western Europe

෴

Kevin Morgan

'History to the defeated – May say Alas but cannot help nor pardon', read the closing lines to British poet W. H. Auden's poem *Spain* (1937: 12). Auden's sentiments are worth revisiting in the context of communism and the politics of remembrance, since his poem exemplifies the compulsion felt by many in the 1930s to 'take sides' in what seemed a battle of epic simplicity. Spain was the crucible: Europe's front line between progress and reaction, democracy and fascism, culture and barbarism – every human value and its antithesis. The international resonance of the Spanish Civil War (1936–9) was symbolised by the 32,000 volunteers of the International Brigades, whose cause Eric Hobsbawm (1994: 160) described 60 years later as being one which uniquely 'even in retrospect, appears as pure and compelling as it did in 1936'. This was not the collective memory of communists like Hobsbawm alone. Rather, this memory of Spain symbolised the identification of communism with a broader movement of anti-fascism which, at one level, has been foundational in the modern idea of Europe. In countries like France and Denmark, with their own experience of occupation, the moral significance of this memory was to some extent subsumed in a national memory of resistance to which communists could justifiably stake their own claim (Skoutelsky 2000: 51–2). In Hobsbawm's Britain, on the other hand, almost the only public memorials to communists are dedicated to volunteers who fought in Spain, and these have most commonly been the initiative of Labour-controlled local authorities. Embedded in the collective memory of the left, communism in this context represents a combative commitment to a cause that now seems vindicated by history. François Furet (1999), acknowledging this as part, but only part, of the picture, characterised

---

Notes for this chapter begin on page 271.

communism as a 'democratic form of heroism' moved by what he conceded was a genuine 'passion for liberty' (ibid.: 261, 264).

Spain, however, has also been accorded a very different place in the European memory of communism: by some it is viewed as the closest that Western Europe came to the establishment of an authentic Soviet police state. In part, this may be traced to a left-wing counter-narrative of disillusionment in the Second Spanish Republic. Epitomised by George Orwell's contemporaneous *Homage to Catalonia* and latterly by Ken Loach's film *Land and Freedom* (1995), this was perhaps most authoritatively voiced in *Les communistes contre la Révolution espagnole*, the account of the veteran Spanish Marxist Julien Gorkin (1978).[1] However, whereas Orwell (1966) rather discountenanced the bogey of a 'Russian dictatorship' in Spain, in the wider pathology of Stalinism that has since developed, the possibility is taken altogether more seriously. Stéphane Courtois' introduction (1999a) to *The Black Book of Communism* (first published in 1997 as *Le Livre noir du communisme*) provides a classic text of remembrance as indictment, and this is precisely how Spain is remembered. If a passion for liberty played any part in the Moscow-instigated International Brigades, it does not register here. Certainly, it is not identified with the communism professed by so many of the volunteers and the vast majority of their organisers. Spain instead points once more to a starker moral – 'the impossibility of separating the legal and criminal enterprises of the Communists in their pursuit of their political objectives' (Courtois and Panné 1999). In *Le Livre noir*, Spain provides the one sustained attempt to catalogue communist misdeeds in Western Europe (see also Radosh et al. 2001).

Here, anti-fascism and totalitarianism provide two very different perspectives within which one might locate Europe's communist past. The issue, in terms of a Europeanisation of commemorative practices, is not just whether these two perspectives can be reconciled, or whether one can be extended a legitimacy that is denied the other. Even if both the heroic and anti-heroic view have ample foundation, this does not mean that the experience is the same everywhere. Within the context of a Europeanisation of remembrance, an obvious issue is the congruence of East and West. In particular, if Spain, in all its ambiguity, remains the closest to a Western European experience of communism as delivery or as repression, this only underlines how different this experience is from that of the East. In recent discussions of the communist past, and certainly in recent historical scholarship, the significance or otherwise of this difference has been a central issue. Either communism represented a single, indivisible phenomenon, whose primary function everywhere was as the client or instrument of communism in power, or else it was more complex, diverse and even contradictory in its values and its practices, and thus implicitly equally contradictory in the forms of remembrance which are now appropriate to it. Translated into nearly 30 languages, *Le Livre noir* has been the most provocative and internationally successful expression of the first view. Providing a sort of counter-narrative that acknowledges the social and political complexity of communism, another French publication, *Le siècle des communismes* (Dreyfus et al. 2000), as indicated by the plural form of its title, replies to Courtois' perceived reductionism. Whether it lends itself so readily to conventional forms of commemoration is another matter.

Variations on this debate can be traced throughout Western Europe. However, the French case more than any other has been of genuinely European scope. On the one hand, books like *Le Livre noir* and Furet's *Le passé d'une illusion* have had a remarkable resonance internationally, and writers like Furet and Alain Besançon have provided a reference point for discussions of the communist past in countries such as Poland and Romania (see Laignel-Lavastine 2004: 172, 191n66). By the same token, the prestige of numerous French intellectual sympathizers with communism has again attracted wide attention internationally (e.g. see Caute 1964; Judt 1992). Emigrés like Tzvetan Todorov and Jorge Semprun have made influential interventions in the discussion of memory and totalitarianism in France itself (see Todorov 2003). In respect of the communist past, Paris thus remains a sort of capital of Europeanisation. At the same time, France has its own historical memory of communism, with which only that of Italy and, more remotely, Germany can be compared in Western Europe. Not only was the French Communist Party (PCF) a notable player in the pre-war popular front and the French resistance, but in the early post-war period, it was actually the largest political party in France and had the largest communist electorate in Western Europe. Since the late 1970s in particular, the PCF has suffered a precipitate decline. Nevertheless, unlike the majority of its Western European counterparts, it continues to describe itself as a communist party and self-consciously deploys a sense of the past as a source of political capital (Lavabre 1994). It is for these reasons that the French case provides the basis for the present discussion.

A Communist *Historikerstreit*

In discussions around these rival perspectives of anti-fascism and totalitarianism, the central issue has been the alleged equivalence – or, alternatively, antagonism – of communism and fascism.[2] The idea of such equivalence was strongly asserted in early expositions of the concept of totalitarianism by writers like Hannah Arendt. As Cold War anxieties abated during the post-Stalin era, the stronger variants of totalitarian theory prevalent in the 1950s came in for increasing academic criticism. Nevertheless, it was intrinsic to the terms of the debate that fascist and communist regimes at least made for appropriate comparison.[3] Differences should not be overlooked, not only between these types of regime, but between the different manifestations of communism in power. In retrospect, too, remembrances of communist rule can range from outright repudiation to considerably more ambivalent responses – to say nothing of the singular case of Germany, where the East German socialist state, the GDR, was reabsorbed into a unitary state that was firmly located in the West, both culturally and ideologically. Nevertheless, in each of these cases communism primarily represents a delimitable past, a specific period of government, a particular phase in the national history – or else the interruption or appropriation of the latter. With the possible exceptions of Czechoslovakia and the GDR, where Weimar-era communists enjoyed considerable real and symbolic authority (Epstein 2003: 262), communism in Eastern Europe had little prehistory as an oppositional movement. As Andrzej Paczkowski (2004: 253) writes of Poland, its 'real experience' began only with its establishment as a system of government. If its memory is thus coterminous with the divisions of the Cold War, its crimes and achievements alike can be traced through the relatively clear lines of accountability, if only to the past, of a party in power. Whether sites such as the Berlin Wall or Budapest's House of Terror tell the whole story of this past can be left for others to debate. What is undeniable is that such phenomena lend themselves to, and perhaps demand, relatively conventional forms of commemoration in which victims and perpetrators are clearly delineated.

Viewed in Paczkowski's terms, communism in the West was a real experience that never actually happened. Its memory is one, not of the past, but of a contested present, an unrealised future, and of the much debated connections to the 'actually existing' socialism of the East. Practices of remembrance have inevitably reflected this. It has become a commonplace to refer to the asymmetrical character of the European memory of totalitarianism. Alain Besançon has even alleged a sort of 'amnesia' regarding communist crimes, which he contrasts with the 'hypermnesia' respecting those of Nazism (see Rousso 2004a: 5). Overlooking the element of exaggeration that might be forgiven in such a statement, within a Western European context it would be grotesque to liken the victims of communism to those of fascism. Essentially, there are no sites lending themselves to the sacralisation of the communist system's victims, nor are there obvious counterparts to the resistance and anti-fascist museums that can be found in Western Europe. Communist power, however it is judged, was more like colonialism than the First World War or the Holocaust; its sites and symbols of oppression were located elsewhere. Unlike colonialism, this also applied to its centres of power and decision making. In the case of communism, there is not even the kind of direct material legacy that is increasingly being linked to the proceeds of colonialism and African slavery. The asymmetry of remembrance is thus in part a refraction of the asymmetry of lived experience. Its prevailing practices have been those involving the vaulting of geographical distance through the mobility of film crews, artefacts or texts. Amnesia and hypermnesia – exactly as in the case of African slavery – are partly a question of location.[4]

There has also been a sort of *Historikerstreit* (historians' dispute), but of a distinctive kind. Marc Lazar (2005: 13–4), a frequent collaborator of Courtois, has noted that critics of the *Livre noir* approach have not, by and large, sought to deny or minimise the crimes of communist regimes. In *Le Livre noir* itself, the longest, most powerful and arguably most authoritative section is Nicolas Werth's meticulous documentation of Soviet political violence, 'A State against Its People' (1999). Nevertheless, it was not this section that gave rise to controversy, but rather Courtois' slighter and more polemical observations (1999a, 1999b) seeking to assimilate the experience of Western communists to this wider campaign of repression. It is therefore not revisionist accounts of the origins and extent of the Soviet terror that are the principal issue here. Instead, it is the validity of a sort of counter-memory, epitomised by Spain and 'anti-fascism' but extending to the oppositional activities of communists on issues ranging from anti-colonialism to social and economic rights, that is the issue at stake.

The idea of coming to terms with Europe's communist past is thus spatially as well as politically ambiguous. The centrality of the Holocaust to European remembrance lies not just its moral enormity, but in the fact that it took place within and across Europe. Extended more generally to the victims of fascism, observers remain confronted with a pan-European experience that – with certain exceptions, such as Mussolini's attack on Abyssinia – was confined within Europe's borders. Communism, on the other hand, as represented in *Le Livre noir*, was not an exclusively or even a predominantly European phenomenon. According to Courtois' calculations (1999a: 4), only 1 per cent of its victims fell within Europe outside of the former USSR, and only 1 per cent of *this* figure – Courtois suggests some 10,000 deaths – through 'the international communist movement and communist parties not in power'. Although Courtois says little regarding his methods of calculation, it appears that this includes the deaths of foreign communists and sympathisers in the USSR, which certainly ran into several thousand and should not be minimised.[5] Nevertheless, adopting the crude statistical measures by which Courtois provoked such controversy, the figure is a fraction of that of a single conflict such as the Algerian War of Independence or the current war in Iraq. In Courtois' international inventory of such losses, Western Europe is not an item.

The same is true of North America, Australasia, South Asia and (if we exclude Afghanistan) the Middle East. Nevertheless, the paradox of the European memory of communism is that communism is seen as representing a development of European ideas and aspirations in a way that was not true in its other, secondary theatres of action. 'Europe, mother of communism, was also its principal arena', Furet (1999: x) proclaimed, justifying his own exclusively European focus. Europe was 'the cradle and the heart' of communist history, and, in the view of its inventors, it was specifically in Western Europe that its destiny would be decided (ibid.). The focus of *Le Livre noir* was geographically wider and less concerned with the idea (or illusion) that communism could be traced back to the Enlightenment. Nevertheless, Courtois (1999a), too, wrote within an avowedly Western European context. If Europe, as he put it, had 'set itself the task of reconstructing popular memory', then a memorial to communism's victims was necessary as part of this enterprise (ibid.: 28). Citing Todorov, Courtois urged this as a way for Western Europeans in particular to move beyond preoccupations with their 'own' national misfortunes (ibid.). Superficially calling forth an expansive regard for human suffering, the injunction was at the same time circumscribed in an intensely political way. Not only were the examples of European misfortunes that Courtois provided exclusively those of right-wing dictatorships, but the device of *Le Livre noir* – one borrowed, be it noted, from the communists[6] – meant that other regions like Latin America and Africa were depicted as if principally afflicted by dictatorships and insurgencies from the left.

While global in its frame of reference, the argument thus derives from political divisions within Western Europe itself. Courtois, significantly, is an established historian of the French Communist Party. Furet acquired his international scholarly reputation through his work on the French Revolution. Both wrote out of their own experiences as supporters of communist systems: Courtois as an ex-Maoist and Furet as a former PCF member. In this, they may be grouped with an influential roll-call of ex-communists, including Annie Kriegel, Edgar Morin, Philippe Robrieux and Pierre Daix, whose literature of disillusionment greatly influenced French intellectual circles in the 1980s and 1990s. Seeking a reckoning with the communist past, which was also their own personal past, these individuals saw in Stalinist crimes the material for an indictment. Nevertheless, its primary target was that of the complicity and extenuation of those crimes by sections of the European left. In contrast to the positive associations of communism with anti-fascism and other grass-roots mobilisations, these were anti-anti-fascists who argued for the indivisibility of communism as a political phenomenon, linked, as Courtois (1999b: 754) put it, by a 'sort of genetic code' that was rooted in 1917. How, Courtois (2003–4: 256–7) argued on another occasion, could one concede any positive aspects to the PCF's history 'when these were established on 15 million zek corpses, deaths from famine and victims of the Great Terror in the USSR, or the extermination of a fifth of the Cambodian population'? This 'established on' suggests a certain imprecision in such writing, as when Courtois (1999a: 28) simultaneously suggests that Europe 'played host to the twentieth century's many tragedies' and yet produces figures indicating that more people were killed under Mao than under Stalin and Hitler combined. Even so, it is the character of this relationship between Europe, and more specifically the European left, and the acknowledged tragedies of Stalinism that constitutes the crux of the debate regarding the communist past.

Complicity and Teleology

The argument of communism's indivisibility rests on two foundations: that of complicity, or its international character, and that of teleology, or the unrealised communist future. The notion of complicity was based on the strong codes of discipline that united the world's communist parties and on the acceptance of a political command system centred in Moscow. The close, continuous and unequal character of the relations between ruling and non-ruling communist parties was a central theme in popular studies deriving from hitherto closed archives. French examples of a voluminous literature include *Les aveux des archives, Prague-Paris-Prague, 1948–1968*, by Karl Bartošek; *L'argent de Moscou*, a documentation of financial links introduced by the veteran Comintern historian Branko Lazitch (Loupan and Lorrain 1994); and *Hôtel Lux*, a translation of the exposé of the Russian journalist Arkadi Vaksberg. From this perspective, Western communists lay somewhere between the categories of perpetrator and bystander, which were familiar from discussions of Nazism, and it was on this basis that Courtois (1999a: 11) invoked the Canadian legal code to include as crimes against humanity 'providing encouragement for de facto complicity' and 'being an accessory after the fact'. However, few went this far. Werth, Courtois' most important contributor, publicly dissociated himself from the reduction of communism to criminality.[7] Jean-Louis Margolin, who urged prosecution of crimes committed by the Khmer Rouge in *Le Livre noir*, took care to distinguish between different communist parties and even regimes. In Finland, home to a relatively successful communist party but also to a far larger number of victims of Stalinism than Italy or France, proposals for the trial of communist crimes provoked considerable public discussion. Here, too, however, no serious suggestion was made that such a process should be extended to include accessories after the fact.[8]

Linked with the notion of a genetic code, the argument of teleology was that every communist movement represented a different stage of advancement along a fundamentally common line of development. This, for example, was the significance of the Spanish Republic, which was viewed as a 'pre-totalitarian' laboratory for the methods of rule that were elsewhere to be carried out under the direct protection of the Red Army (Courtois and Panné 1999: 356–7; Furet 1999: 256–7). Following Annie Kriegel, communist parties themselves were also seen as displaying the classic features of totalitarian movements; and the PCF's own codes of discipline and denunciation were considered to be lacking only the death penalty (Lazar 2005: 106, 108ff., 116). Through this teleology, two distinct aspects of the communist past were rejected. One was that of dissenting communist currents positing an earlier period of revolutionary principle, which was to be betrayed by Stalin. In Martin Amis's *Koba the Dread* (2003), a vulgarised Anglo-Saxon variant of *Le Livre noir*, caustic assessments of Stalin were thus incongruously intermingled with a sort of score-settling with Amis's Trotskyist student acquaintances – who, whatever their shortcomings, can have had very little time for Stalin. The second aspect referred to communists' oppositional activities. In this teleology, the idealisation or even recognition of these activities was vitiated by the latent totalitarianism of communism. If communists had sometimes defended democracy, Lazar (2005: 106) suggested, it was simply better to destroy it in due course. Memory was thus not only actively constructed but teleological and even prophetic. According to Mao's most chilling adage, it was on the blank page that the most beautiful poems were written. In this teleological view of the communist past, every page was already written, and it was only a question of how far the story was allowed to unfold.

While communism retained some credibility as a possible future, both positive and negative readings were identified with their realisation under communist regimes. As Lazar (2005: 210) again points out, however, communism no longer represents this future, and the PCF's retention of an overt communist identity is based on a powerful sense of collective memory. Even in their heyday, communists in countries like France and Britain saw the past as a field of struggle in which they made some of their most effective intellectual interventions (Schwarz 1982). However, with the marginalisation of communism, an increasing preoccupation with the historical memory of communism itself became apparent (Mischi 2006). The belief and insistence that a positive legacy remained extricable from the memory of communism in power were not confined to communists themselves. The sentiments of French Prime Minister Lionel Jospin, a socialist who in 1997 was reliant on the support of communists, are often cited in this connection, and Lazar (2005: 10–16) expresses unease at how its status as a party of opposition lent the PCF an appearance of innocence and incorruptibility.[9] In fact, the emphasis was more on the irreducibility of communism simply to its negative features and to its characterisation essentially as thwarted totalitarianism (Vigreux and Wolikow 2003: 9–10). Neither innocence nor incorruptibility in any absolute sense was usually claimed. Yet in a Western European context, the counter-suggestion of responsibility for crimes committed only counterfactually again serves to problematise the notion of a simple equivalence between communism and fascism. Writing about communism in power, Alain Besançon, who has published extensively on the Gulag, asks quite plausibly how much it really matters if the intentions according to which a victim is killed are good or evil (cited by Malia 1999: xv). However, where only the intentions existed, and not the killings, the distinction is a basic one.

Memory and Amnesia

Rather than the issue of memory or amnesia, communism's intensely polit-icised character raises questions about what should be remembered, by whom and, in particular, by what public or semi-public agencies of Euro-peanisation. In the Furet-Lazar presentation, communism itself is pre-emi-nently a *lieu de mémoire*, while amnesia, as Furet (1988: 19) once observed, is a virtue of democracies. It is true that there is often a defensive and introspective aspect to communist forms of remembrance. Chastened by seemingly definitive setbacks, communists in a country like Italy used the memory of Spain to reaffirm the movement's humanitarian credentials. Extensive media coverage of the fiftieth and sixtieth anniversaries of the Soviet repression in Hungary was counterbalanced in communist circles by celebrations of the International Brigade. Such efforts could also provide a counter-narrative to orthodox national histories containing their own blank spots. Simplified accounts of wartime resistance, for example, have tended to write out or downplay the involvement of communists, just as they have de-emphasised the extent of quiescence or collaboration on the part of other political movements and the state itself (Lagrou 1997). Within a domestic political context, the Popular Front alliance, which won the 1936 legislative elections, could also be reclaimed as part of this radical counter-narrative. In France, one of the first publications to receive the imprimatur of the Fondation Gabriel Péri, initiated in 2004 and named after a famous communist resistance martyr, was devoted to the reclamation and vindica-tion of this legacy on its seventieth anniversary (Vigna et al. 2006).

The issue of colonialism and colonial wars is especially significant in light of its potential to present crimes in exactly the sense used in texts like *Le Livre noir*, but with the difference that they were perpetrated by or on behalf of liberal democracies. One might imagine that Besançon's univer-salist categories might equally be extended to these conflicts. In practice, however, influential treatments like Tony Judt's discussion of French left-ist intellectuals seem to refute any possible equivalence between these acts of killing and torture and those committed under Stalinism. Indeed, it is characteristic of the ideological interdependence of remembrance and amnesia that Judt in this account simply passes over these crimes as if they were irrelevant to his subject.[10] In the work of Todorov (2003), the possibil-ity of such extensions is clearly indicated. Nevertheless, in the contempo-rary politics of memory, it is often those most indulgent to the memory of the French left, notably communists themselves, who are among those most committed to remembering the victims of French colonialism. At the same time, in so seemingly comprehensive an exploration of the national memory as Nora's *Les Lieux de mémoire*, scathingly described by Perry Anderson as a 'union sucrée', Algeria and Indochina barely even figure (*London Review of Books*, 23 September 2004).

Where communism has had a significant political and intellectual presence, its memory represents not just an unrealised vision of the future, or the compromising associations of a sometime communist present, but an alternative version of the national past. Even in Britain, historians emerging from the Communist Party exercised an influence unrivalled by communist intellectuals in other fields. In France, where the revolutionary origins of the republic offered more than just the radical counterpoint of history from below, communism embodied an affirmation of the Jacobin legacy, whose plausibility or otherwise is central to the very identity of the nation. That these issues are interconnected is especially evident in Furet's work. Leaving the PCF in 1956, Furet's whole professional career was to be founded on the attempt to wrest France's revolutionary legacy from a Jacobin-socialist reading, of which communists had become the recognised standard-bearers. Furet was not concerned to challenge the communists' credentials to carry this legacy but rather the reverse. Unlike a good deal of international communist historiography,[11] Furet had no desire to extricate a purer ideal of the left from its entanglement with Bolshevism or Stalinism. Instead, rather after the fashion of J. L. Talmon's *Origins of Totalitarian Democracy* (1952), communism provided the sequel which could be used to bury or delegitimise a much longer radical or republican tradition. Seen in this context, Furet's *Le passé d'une illusion* was a final exorcism of the ghosts of 1793. Perhaps this can be linked with the anti-Marxist revisionism of his works, such as *Penser la Révolution française* (1978). More certainly, it provides a sort of sequel to the co-authored *La République du centre* (Furet et al. 1988), in which Furet depicted the fate of communism and of the republican tradition in France as almost inextricable. In announcing the simultaneous ending of the 'long' cycle of revolution that began in 1789, the shorter cycle of Bolshevism that commenced in 1917 and the still briefer ascendancy of the recent 'union of the left', Furet dispatched at once the idea of the left, of socialism and of the revolutionary republic. All that remained was *la République du centre* itself. Although Furet (1988) took care to distinguish this from pure neo-liberalism or the end of ideology, it was clear that the passing of this twentieth-century illusion meant the passing of what he called the 'French exception', and thus of a whole package of ideas linking egalitarian values with the activist state (ibid.: 9–12).

This was also the message of Lazar's *Le communisme: Une passion française*. A nuanced example of history as autopsy, on its first publication in 2002 the book dismissed the illusion of an egalitarian modernity, at least as something capable of generating the economic benefits of capitalism. Reissuing the book with a new foreword in 2005, Lazar did not retract this position, but he did acknowledge the resilience of what he saw as communist values and mentalities as transmuted by a new generation of anti-liberal and anti-globalisation activists. With the French rejection of the draft European Constitution,[12] in large part in preference for a 'social' Europe, *la République du centre* seemed more fragile than it had once appeared. Perhaps by extension, *l'Europe du centre* suffered a setback, too. Ironically, it is 'capitalist modernity' which is now taken to represent a sort of historical inevitability to which politics is seen as representing a necessary form of accommodation. Embedded in and legitimised by the past, it is the alternative social agendas of the left that serve as a reminder of values and culture as profoundly rooted in European history as the notions of pluralism, diversity and contestation on which they depend and to which they give expression.

In this respect, the idea of a Europeanisation of the politics of remembrance is ambiguous. As representing a wider frame of reference for these debates, and in particular as an antidote to the amnesia that supports collective memory on both sides of the ideological divide, it is both salutary and necessary. However, Europeanisation can also suggest a parallel with the forms of economic or institutional harmonisation with which the concept has hitherto largely been identified. In this it recalls an earlier wave of nation building, including the selective national myths whose potential proved so destructive and which today require critique and transcendence, not 'enlargement'.

Todorov (2003: xxi) has wisely counselled: 'Memory ... should not be used only to celebrate one's own heroes, to mourn one's own dead, and to stigmatise the wrongs committed by others.' More than that, it should prompt reflection on the very notion of one's 'own' versus the 'others', whose uncritical acceptance lay behind so many twentieth-century tragedies. While the European remembrance of the Holocaust obviously meets Todorov's criteria, even this depends on a willingness to construct these wrongs in such a way that they are not the sole responsibility of others. The British need to remember the Holocaust as a European phenomenon. Elsewhere, collaboration and collusion may need most to be remembered. But for a German historian like Ernst Nolte – whose *European Civil War* appeared in France with a preface by Courtois – the Europeanisation of the Holocaust at the expense of its German character amounts to moral and political apologia. Memory, like every other relationship – in this case that between ourselves and the past – depends on position. Remembering Europe's civil war through wrongs that are always committed by others is simply to employ memory as a tool for forgetting.

Amis (2003: 10) suggests that the pioneering historian of the Soviet terror, Robert Conquest, should have entitled his memoirs *I Told You So, You Fucking Fools*. Furet, for all his sophistication, elaborated the same basic theme, and Courtois was missing only the expletives. There are three possible dangers with this approach. The first is that the example of communism may be used to delegitimise a wider oppositional politics of the left, which has played, and continues to play, an important role in the development of a democratic political culture. Recovering this legacy in *Forging*

Democracy, Geoff Eley (2002: xi) concludes: 'During the 1990s new amnesias brought some essential histories under erasure.' A second danger is that this amnesia extends, not only to the oppositional movements with which Eley is concerned, but to the less than heroic attributes of our 'own' heroes, be they European empires or the authoritarian or collaborationist regimes which predated communism in many parts of Eastern Europe. A third danger, perhaps cutting deepest, is that the dichotomous construction of one's 'own' and the 'other' is left undisturbed, exactly as in Amis's recent fiction, where the theme of the Soviet labour camp is addressed almost interchangeably with the contemporary threat of Islamic extremism (Soar 2007).

Remembrance of the victims of communism is a moral and political imperative. In the spirit of Todorov's dictum, I have suggested that this responsibility falls particularly on those who identify with the socialist project in whose name these crimes were perpetrated and condoned (Morgan 2001). In an imperfect world, they – which in the present author's case means we – cannot simply be left to get on with it. On the other hand, the institutionalisation of a particular, generalised memory of communism, whose role in European history is as complex as that history itself, may well appear as an instrumentalisation of history in the name of remembrance. Neither help nor extenuation is as much an issue as that of who gets to play the role of History.

Notes

The author wishes to express thanks to Constantin Davidescu, Stephen Hopkins, Steve Parsons and Tauno Saarela for comments and/or information. The usual caveats regarding responsibility apply.

1. Gorkin was a partisan of the POUM (Party of Marxist Unification).
2. Fascism is here used indiscriminately to include all its variants, including Nazism.
3. See, for example, the broadly anti-totalitarian interpretations presented in Kershaw and Lewin (1997).
4. From the author's perspective of a British schooling of the 1970s, there was no obvious amnesia regarding Stalinism, which was studied both as history and through literary texts such as *Animal Farm* and *Ivan Denisovich*. Regarding African slavery, for which Britain bears a somewhat more direct responsibility, it was an altogether different matter.
5. See, for example, the estimates provided in Agnew and McDermott (1996: 148–9) and Panteleiev (1994–5). Even where relatively few individuals were involved, their fate has naturally attracted wide attention. See, for example, Beckett (2004) and Sohn (2000).
6. Probably the first example, which aimed at 'keeping alive the memory of the criminal acts of the Nazi Government' was *The Brown Book of the Hitler Terror and the Burning of the Reichstag,* prepared by Otto Katz for the World Committee for the Victims of German Fascism and published in 1933.

7. For Werth, see 'Le communisme, entre analyse scientifique et vision policière de l'histoire', *Le Monde*, 21 September 2000.
8. Thanks to Tauno Saarela for information about the debate in Finland.
9. More recently, the current French president Nicolas Sarkozy aroused considerable controversy shortly after his installation in office when he decreed that the final letter of the communist resistance fighter Guy Môquet should be read in all French schools 'to explain what it is to be young and French'. See, for example, the commentary of Rosa Moussaoui in *L'Humanité*, 1 June 2007.
10. See, for example, Judt (1992: 173), where he refers to 'the crude "distributive justice" which placed on an equal footing mass murder and wage labor, political trials and the contradictions of liberalism'. Had Judt borne in mind the injunctions of Orwell's *Politics and the English Language*, he might have been less inclined to write of the 'contradictions of liberalism' and readier to refer, for example, to torture in Algeria or the use of napalm.
11. Classic examples are Kendall (1969), Weber (1969) and, more recently, Broué (2003).
12. Ivaldi (2006) describes the PCF as the 'linchpin' of the left-wing campaign against the European Constitutional Treaty.

Section 6

Coming to Terms with Europe's Colonial Past

POLITICS OF REMEMBRANCE, COLONIALISM AND THE ALGERIAN WAR OF INDEPENDENCE IN FRANCE

&

Jan Jansen

Since the final wave of decolonisation in the 1950s and 1960s, 'colonialism' and 'imperialism' have been considered part of a European – as well as worldwide – historical heritage.[1] But unlike the two world wars and the Holocaust, they have not yet found their place in the various national or shared European cultures of remembrance. This relates not only to the fact that colonialism ended relatively recently but also to its spatial distance. The 'great events' of colonial history did not take place inside Europe; rather, colonialism left its most significant marks in remote and 'exotic' regions. Despite great efforts to transmit the 'colonial experience' to the metropole via cultural media and its impact on everyday life,[2] for many Europeans colonialism remained an abstract concept. Its presence in the public space has been dependent on a strong political will, a will which abruptly decreased after decolonisation, when colonialism no longer contributed to national glory. By simply abandoning existing commemorative and propagandistic efforts, it was thus quite easy to deterritorialise colonial history from Europe. A critical remembrance of colonialism was (and still is) even more unlikely, as colonial history after decolonisation was a history of loss and defeat, undermining the generally 'narcissistic' politics of national identity.

Nevertheless, since the 1990s, in countries such as France, Italy and Germany, it is possible to identify a 'rediscovery' of colonial history in academic, public and sometimes even political discourse. Working against the deterritorialisation of the colonial past, researchers are beginning to revisit its residues and reflections within Europe. They rediscover these traces inside European cultures, shaped by cross-cultural influences and

Notes for this chapter begin on page 292.

'colonial cultures'; inside urban spaces, replete with manifold abandoned colonial vestiges; and on the level of immigration and migration politics, linked with debates about the non-European 'other' (Aldrich 2005; Andall and Duncan 2005; Blanchard et al. 2005; Hargreaves 2005; Henneberg 2004; Heyden and Zeller 2002).

Even so, most of these debates tend not to consider colonialism as a common European experience and remain encased within a national framework. Moreover, the recent increase in public discourse on colonialism is not a Europe-wide movement. This is demonstrated by the huge gap regarding official and public remembering of colonialism in Great Britain and France, the two main European colonial powers during the nineteenth and twentieth centuries. There seems to be no or very little public debate regarding the Empire in Great Britain. French colonialism, however, and especially the history of French Algeria (*Algérie française*), has since the 1990s become the subject of increasingly fervid academic and public debates and has resulted in hurried commemoration activities by state and non-state actors.

Given these differences, the current public remembrance of national colonial pasts in some parts of Europe cannot be explained simply by general mechanisms of 'collective memory', such as a delay of three or four decades that enables a dramatic event to be 'remembered'. For a massive and nearly 'obsessive' wave of remembrance to occur and for colonialism to become a first-rank political issue, as it is in present-day France, these general trends have to coincide with other factors. The evolving treatment of the colonial past in the French public sphere therefore constitutes a prominent case for examining the making of official and public memories of colonialism. This chapter outlines the main stages of this process from the Algerian War of Independence to the present, focusing on the public and political remembrance of French Algeria.

In the first part of the chapter, I argue that the period from Algeria's independence until the 1980s was characterised by an antagonism between the attempt to conceal the colonial past by the French state and the constant pressure to remember that past, which was felt by other historical actors. Focusing on the period since the 1990s, the analysis deals with the subsequent increase in public memories of Algeria and with the first steps of 'officialisation' by the French state. In both periods I argue that, in spite of state efforts to conceal colonialism and, in a later period, to shape the remembrance of it, remembering French Algeria and the colonial past has always been a complicated, embattled and contested process outside the purview of any single actor. Taking the perspective of European politics, the scope of the discussion will not include the important aspect of post-colonial remembrance in Algeria, which has been studied abundantly elsewhere (Branche 2005; Kohser-Spohn and Renken 2006; Manceron and Remaoun 1993; Stora 1991). The conclusion will sum up the essential lessons from the French case and expose some obstacles to the 'Europeanisation' of these forms of remembrance.

Politics of Concealment and *Lobbies de Mémoire,* 1960s to 1980s

The recent debates and conflicts in France arise from a specific historical context. They are closely related to the political constellations of remembrance that evolved in France after its last war of decolonisation, the Algerian War (1954–62). The decade-long contradiction between official politics of concealment and the historical actors' practices of remembrance has had wide repercussions on current debates.

The Algerian War of Independence constituted a dramatic turning point in twentieth-century French (and Algerian) history. With around two million French soldiers fighting in Algeria between 1954 and 1962, it was the third violent war that France experienced in the twentieth century. Yet its significance went deeper, marking the dramatic agony of the French colonial empire and catalysing a crisis of the political system that led to the fall of the Fourth Republic. It was no accident that the Algerian struggle for independence produced such a deep national crisis. As France's colonial 'masterpiece', French Algeria (1830–1962) had been considered an integral part of French national territory and the homeland of the settler community of *Français d'Algérie,* which by far outnumbered those in other French colonies. Despite worldwide decolonisation trends and the dissolution of the French colonial empire, for a long time a non-French Algeria seemed inconceivable to many French citizens and the French political elite. Thus, the Algerian War, unlike the Indochina War (1945–54), attracted great public attention, producing deep fissures and intense debates about decolonisation, colonial violence and the reassessment of French history and identity (LeSueur 2001; Shepard 2006). Hence, for the French state, the colonial era, which had come to a bloody end as a result of the war, was a sensitive and disagreeable issue that needed to be concealed.

The politics of concealment started immediately after the conclusion of the Evian agreement (18 March 1962), which put an end to the fighting in Algeria. Two main tools were supposed to prevent a remembrance of the conflict: control of the official language and a broad amnesty (Renken 2006; Stora 1991). Since Algeria was considered part of France, events had to be represented as a conflict inside French territory rather than a war. Thus, until the end of the 1990s, expressions such as *événements, opérations* and *mesures pour le maintien de l'ordre* were substituted for the term 'war'. Even more than language, the backbone of the state's politics of concealment was unarguably the general amnesty on crimes committed during the war. This began with the first decrees on 22 March 1962 and was consolidated with further measures during the 1960s. This politics of broad amnesty closed the door on any potential judicial aftermath.

No public 'update' or revision of French colonial history was carried out. In general, street names and memorials, which remained unchanged, were slowly abandoned and neglected. In some cases, attempts were made to cover the tracks of the colonial past. The previous *Ecole coloniale*, in former times a virtual 'temple to French Expansion' (Aldrich 2005: 34), was used as a school for Third World students. The building's facades, bearing the names of French colonial heroes, were sandblasted, busts of colonials and colonialist wall panels were removed, and in the foyer a false ceiling was installed to hide the colonial ceiling paintings from the new occupants.

Today, these decades of official concealment are often referred to as a period of collective 'repression', keeping up a tradition of collective psychoanalysis dating from the 1960s. The Algerian War and the loss of the cherished object empire thereby appear as a historical 'trauma', which produces a collective 'neurosis' or 'syndrome' (see Raybaud 1997; Schalk 1999; Stora 1991). In this view, the painful process of remembrance – and especially the creation of a reconciliatory official memory – corresponds to a type of collective therapy. Yet although it may be of heuristical value, this essentialist Freudian interpretation raises serious problems. In particular, the personification of the French nation as a single 'psyche' seems inappropriate. National remembrance, in contrast, emerges from communication and interactions between different social actors.

Hence, French Algeria and the Algerian War – although not officialised – were continuously commemorated within families and by several groups. During the period of official repression, approximately 2,000 titles about French Algeria and the Algerian War were published (Branche 2005: 18–23). The discrepancy between the official version and the public debate also became obvious in the fact that everyday language never adopted the artificial wording *opérations* to describe the war; instead, the term *guerre d'Algérie* remained in use. Despite the general public interest, it was, first of all, the historical actors of the colonial period and the war who, in quite different ways, kept alive and diffused the memories. The two largest *lobbies de mémoire* were 'repatriated' *Français d'Algérie* (the *rapatriés*) and veterans of the Algerian War.

The end of French Algeria led to a mass exodus of almost one million French and other European citizens from the colony. Despite their mostly successful economic integration in mainland France, many of the repatriates were left with a feeling of discontent and bitterness. This feeling found expression in their self-designation as *pieds-noirs*, marking a specific group identity based on shared experiences of the year 1962 (Leconte 1980).[3] The creation of a *pied-noir* identity was accompanied by specific forms of nostalgic remembrance, cultivated within families and a dense network of associations and *Amicales* that emerged after 1962. Yet looking at southern French urban landscapes with a high percentage of *pieds-noirs* strongly suggests that, on a local level, memories related to French Algeria quickly entered the public space via street names or objects and ceremonies dating back to the times of *Algérie française*.

The second set of decisive non-state actors on the scene after 1962 were veterans of the Algerian War. Numbering around two million, they challenged the official doctrine of oblivion, which had far-reaching consequences for them. They were denied the status of veterans and thus the corresponding symbolic honours and material benefits. In response, the largest veterans' organisation of the Algerian War, the Fédération Nationale des Anciens Combattants en Algérie, Maroc et Tunisie (FNACA), claimed the right to equal treatment with the veterans of the world wars (Renken 2006: 270–325). The FNACA thus entered the politics of remembrance. As early as 1963, it started to lobby for the creation of a commemorative day for soldiers killed in Algeria, choosing 19 March, the date of the ceasefire in 1962. During the following decades, their annual ceremony at the Arc de Triomphe gained public recognition, although it was rejected by rival organisations and repatriates' associations and was not officially recognised by the French state. The FNACA has also been successfully campaigning to name public spaces after 19 March and to erect memorials to the Algerian War. By September 2002, over 3,000 *communes* (and in 2004, also Paris) named a square, a street, a park or a bridge after the date (FNACA 1999; Renken 2006: 317–18).

These two examples of the *pieds-noirs* and the veterans demonstrate that French Algeria and its bloody decolonisation had not been forgotten in post-1962 France. While they were kept out of official memory, they found their way into the public space of many *communes*. Far removed from the state, certain forms of remembrance, front lines and conflicts emerged that have had decisive impacts on current debates.

Processes of Remembrance since the 1990s

Since the 1990s, the issue of the colonial past, and particularly the Algerian War, has found a wider public audience in France. Efforts to create an official memory have produced new monuments, commemorations and restructured museums. Hence, the colonial past and the 'extra-European' legacy of French history have become part of a wider and more in-depth process of redefining France's national identity and history since the 1980s. Furthermore, this process has been affected by growing international conviction about the necessity of coming to terms with negative aspects of the national past.[4]

The politics of concealment have fundamentally affected these recent processes of remembrance. Once the state and the wider public entered the debate, they encountered a multi-structured, occupied and embattled territory. The non-state purveyors of memory have also increased their activities in recent years, trying to pass on their historical experience and to influence the official culture of remembrance in the process. New actors, such as migrant groups or the *harkis*, the Algerians who had fought for France during the Algerian War, have also entered the historico-political stage.

Given this complexity, the following portrayal can elucidate this debate only by focusing on its most important factors and stages. The first of the next five sections examines the central steps in the state's commemoration and recognition of the Algerian War, followed by two sections focusing on two important public debates, the so-called torture controversy and the debates about colonialism in the context of immigration. The fourth section deals with the law of 23 February 2005, which tried to establish the 'positive role' of colonialism in the school curriculum. The fifth section deals with the most important events and changes that have taken place during Nicolas Sarkozy's presidency, starting in May 2007 to the present.

From Vichy to the Algerian War: The Official Politics of Remembrance during the Chirac Era (1995–2007)

Until the 1990s, the Vichy past and collaboration during the Second World War had preoccupied the French public, research, courts and politics. The steady decrease in these debates enabled a revisionism of French colonial history and the Algerian War (Cohen 2002). In general, the coming to terms with Vichy is often cited as a model for dealing with French colonial history. Thus, demands to apply the central juridical tool against Vichy – the category of 'crimes against humanity' – to French colonialism are a common feature of the debate.

Since the late 1980s, historical research and public interest have increasingly focused on the Algerian War.[5] A generational change at the helm of French politics further enabled a greater focus on the French Algerian past. After the death of François Mitterrand in 1996, two members of what one may call a *génération algérienne* stepped into the limelight: Jacques Chirac, who had participated in the war, and Lionel Jospin, who had opposed it. In the initial years of Chirac's presidency, starting in 1995, the first cautious attempts were made to incorporate the legacy of the Algerian War into the French culture of commemoration. On 11 November 1996, Chirac unveiled the first Parisian monument to the conflict at the Square de la Butte du Chapeau-Rouge. However, the precise function of this monument – commemorating all 'victims and combatants killed in North Africa, 1952–62' (*Le Monde*, 12 November 1996) – was somewhat vague (see also Cohen 2002; Schalk 1999). The remote location of the memorial also reflects the slow, hesitant and difficult nature of these first steps. Before and during the inaugural ceremony, special attention had to be paid to the strict representative balance of all affected groups – veterans, *rapatriés* and *harkis*. Not surprisingly, the monument failed to establish itself as a public site of memory. A few months after its unveiling, it had been partially covered by graffiti and seemed to be neglected. Apparently, as a result of its vague 'oecumenism' (*Le Monde*, 12 November 1996), the monument had not met the expectations that had been placed on it by very different groups of actors.

Nevertheless, one finds in this first step an attempt to remember the Algerian War and the colonial past within the categories of national honour, dignity and duty, a pattern characteristic of the official policy in the following years. A crucial first effort was thus made to recognise on a national level the people who had fought and worked for the French colonial empire – a recognition that had been withheld from them for a long time. This was primarily a political response to the various historical actors, in particular the veterans, and to the increased pressure to be remembered that they had built up in the previous decades. Chirac purposely addressed his speech to the 'troisième génération du feu' and opposed the disuniting dimensions of the war with a unifying act of recognition: 'I do not want to return to either the causes of these often fratricidal confrontations or to the tragedies these battles produced.... That is the reason why we are here, to collect our thoughts, to honour those combatants who gave their lives for France, along with those men and women who died on French soil, soil enriched, for 130 years, by their parents' work.'[6] Concluding his speech, Chirac acknowledged the 'incontestable achievements' accomplished by French citizens overseas, citing 'pacification', economic development and the spread of instruction, medical knowledge and administrative institutions.

Another crucial step was taken in 1999. On 10 June, the French National Assembly unanimously replaced the term *opérations* with the expression *guerre d'Algérie*.[7] Thus, almost 40 years after the war, official language was adjusted to the public discourse. From the year 2000 onwards, Chirac's commemoration in accordance with national *grandeur* moved on to the *harkis*. Since 1962, the French state had denied any responsibility towards them. Most were not allowed to flee to France, exposing them to bloody acts of vengeance and massacres after the ceasefire. Those who had managed to relocate to France were housed for decades in camps under miserable conditions. A revolt of *harki* children in 1991 and actions such as hunger strikes drew and augmented public attention to their situation.

In 2001, Chirac intervened in these debates by organising a Journée Nationale d'Hommage aux Harkis on 25 September (Branche 2005: 37–8, 54). On this occasion the eternal flame was ignited at the Arc de Triomphe, a commemorative plaque was unveiled at the Hôtel des Invalides and 150 Muslim veterans were decorated by Chirac. Furthermore, a presidential message was read in all French *départements*, acknowledging the honourable effort of the *harkis*. Chirac's address at the Hôtel des Invalides was couched in careful words of recognition and sympathy for the *harkis'* destiny. However, Chirac did not offer any apology for the French state's responsibility in failing to prevent the massacres following the ceasefire, a step required by many *harki* associations.

On 5 December 2002, the French president unveiled a Mémorial National de la Guerre d'Algérie et des Combats du Maroc et de la Tunisie, 1952–1962 (Aldrich 2005: 150–5; Schalk 2002). The monument was built at the Quai Branly, located prominently next to the Eiffel Tower and the newly opened Musée des Arts Premiers, a much more accessible and central location than the 1996 memorial. The monument's deliberate simplicity contrasted with its solemn inauguration on 5 December. In his speech, Chirac emphasised that the soldiers of the Algerian War were firmly established 'in the glorious line of France's sons distinguishing themselves on all continents and serving our country during the most tragic moments of its history'. Chirac largely avoided the term 'war' and talked about Algerian 'separation' instead of 'independence'. The 'French overseas achievements' were also mentioned.

In 2003, the government declared 5 December, the day of the memorial's unveiling, the annual Journée Nationale d'Hommage aux Morts des Combattants d'Afrique du Nord. The government thus tried once again to end the still smouldering conflict over the date on which to commemorate the Algerian War (Branche 2005: 106–8). In January 2002, the socialist government under Jospin had sought to declare 19 March the national day of commemoration. After heated debates, the law was passed with a small majority on 22 January; however, the government had previously declared that it would act only if a large majority supported the law. In 2003, the FNACA immediately rejected the date of 5 December, arguing that it had no relation to the historical events it was supposed to commemorate. Hence, the search for a fitting day of commemoration continues, revealing the limitations of any attempt to find a consensus on official memory.

The final step in the politics of national recognition during the Chirac era came about as a consequence of Rachid Bouchareb's 2006 film *Indigènes* and the response it produced among the French public. The film deals with the history of French colonial troops during the Second World War. It both celebrates the 'indigenous' veterans' 'patriotic' contribution to the liberation of France and deplores the overt discrimination they experienced in comparison to their French counterparts. On 27 September 2006, the day the film was released, Chirac announced a law, aligning 'indigenous' pensions with those of 'normal' French veterans (*Le Monde*, 26 and 27 September 2006). However, these raises referred only to basic retirement and disability pensions and did not concern the more significant military retirement pension for those serving at least 15 years.

The Torture Controversy, 2000–2002

On 20 June 2000, *Le Monde* published an article on its front page, which, in the words of a French journalist, provoked a virtual 'earthquake' (*Le Monde des Livres*, 15 June 2001). In the article, the journalist Florence Beaugé described the suffering of Louisette Ighilariz, who had been tortured for three months by French soldiers during the Algerian War.

By this point, the issue of torture during the war had been a generally known fact.[8] The article about Ighilariz nevertheless ignited an unprecedented debate in the French public sphere.[9] The daily newspaper *L'Humanité* published 47 articles concerning torture in the course of less than seven months (June–December 2000). On the one hand, the intensification of the debate, in comparison with earlier discussions, pointed to a greater willingness on the part of the French public to deal with an issue as sensitive as torture and with the suffering of its victims. At the same time, several new factors became involved in 2000, adding to the intensity of the debate. Ighilariz's attitude, for example, was quite unusual. Her remarks implied less of a desire for vengeance and focused more on her gratitude towards her saviour, a French military doctor (*Le Monde*, 20 June 2000). Moreover, Ighilariz named and accused high-ranking officers of having attended the torture sessions. The reactions of those officers, who had previously unanimously denied or justified any wrongdoing, now became more diverse. Upon the enquiry of *Le Monde*, one of the accused, General Massu, acknowledged the use of torture and even questioned the necessity of interrogations under torture (*Le Monde*, 22 June 2000). Numerous interviews with high-ranking officers and soldiers followed. In November 2000, the remarks of the hitherto relatively unknown General Aussaresses shocked the public. In an interview with *Le Monde*, he confirmed torture practices and admitted, without emotion or regret, to summary executions. Aussaresses emphasised that 'there was no need to repent' and that he would do it again, if necessary (*Le Monde*, 23 November 2000).

The French government and the head of state witnessed the growing debate as neutral spectators. On 31 October 2000, 12 prominent anti-war activists went public with a manifesto in *L'Humanité*, asking for official recognition and condemnation of the torture practices. Shortly afterwards, the Parti Communiste called for a parliamentary commission of enquiry into torture (*Le Monde*, 24 November 2000). A poll from March 2002 revealed that 50 per cent of the public approved an official condemnation of the use of torture (*L'Humanité*, 19 March 2002). Prime Minister Jospin and President Chirac reacted evasively and cautiously to the public pressure and media enquiries. Chirac's commemorative acts during these years showed that he was not willing to integrate the issue of torture into the official remembrance of the war. He even asserted that he would 'never do anything damaging the image of French soldiers who fought in the Algerian War or besmirch their honour' (quoted in Aldrich 2005: 145). Jospin endorsed the *Appel des Douze* in principle, but he understood that the reassessment of the Algerian War should fall within the purview of historians rather than political actors (*Le Monde*, 28 and 29 November 2000). It was only when Aussaresses presented his version of events – in all their brutal detail – in his book *Services Spéciaux* in May 2001 that politicians were forced to take a clear moral stand and condemn Aussaresses' cynicism (*Le Monde*, 5 and 6–7 May 2001). Aussaresses was fully retired and stripped of his Cross of the Legion of Honour. However, throughout the debate, the French government and president avoided assuming any official responsibility for 'individual' acts of torture.

In the meantime, the debate had already reached large parts of the French public. Leading military officials aggressively questioned the credibility of Massu and Aussaresses. At the same time, many of the participants in the war felt the need to speak out. Editors of leading newspapers and historians were swamped by a flood of individual confessions and testimonials admitting to (or denying) acts of torture and violence. Newspapers such as *Libération* and *Nouvel Observateur* now jumped on the bandwagon.

Yet by mid-2002, the torture debate had receded and almost disappeared from newspapers and television screens. The two-year-long public focus on violence and the suffering of its (mainly Algerian) victims has failed to elicit any official commemoration or recognition from the state. Significantly, the most important public act remembering torture since then was made by the Paris city council – and it referred to a prominent French victim. On 26 May 2004, a square in Paris's fifth *arrondissement* was named after Maurice Audin, an anti-colonialist mathematician at the University of Algiers who was tortured and killed by the French army on 21 June 1957 (Aldrich 2005: 20). The torture controversy has nevertheless left behind lasting effects. Its pressure led to 'a quiet revolution … in archival access and research' (MacMaster 2002: 455) and to greater public awareness of torture as a commonplace during the Algerian War. Furthermore, it awoke passions and intensified certain divisions that influenced subsequent processes of remembrance. The law of 23 February 2005, discussed below, and increased initiatives aimed at the construction of pro–French Algeria monuments (e.g. in Toulon, Nice and Perpignan) can be seen as a backlash against a primarily negative discourse about the French opposition to Algerian independence (Liauzu 2005).

To date, the torture controversy is the most intense encounter of the French public with its colonial past. The most prominent feature of this debate is its focus on a particularly bloody aspect, a pattern of remembrance that is present in other metropoles. Similar instances of public debate include, in Germany, the wars against the Herero and Nama peoples of south-west Africa of 1904 and, in Italy, the use of poison gas during the Second Italo-Ethiopian War of 1935–6. Whether the torture debate represented a hidden discussion about the whole of French colonialism – and whether it will revise the picture of the colonial 'civilising mission' in general – remains to be seen. Some views voiced during the debate did purposely make a connection between torture in Algeria and the colonial context as a whole (Cohen 2003: 235–7). Yet both official and public memory tends to dissociate the Algerian War and torture as *le mal absolu* from the history of colonialism in general (Manceron 2003: 286; Stora 2005). In a 1990 poll, at a time when a majority of the French people believed that torture had taken place during the Algerian War, three out of five respondents stated that the French presence in Algeria was a 'pretty good' or a 'very good' thing and thus exhibited a clean colonial conscience (Rioux 1993: 16–17).

Racism and 'Repressed' Colonialism

The contemporary debates about migration, integration, racism and ethnic segregation in French cities have created fertile ground for yet another remembrance of colonialism. Immigration presents a potential site of colonial memory in France in so far as the majority of the immigrants originate from former colonies in the Maghreb, sub-Saharan Africa and Asia. Furthermore, racism in France is very strongly influenced by an anti-Algerian sentiment (MacMaster 1997; Renken 2006: 389–408).

Since the 1990s, younger immigrant societies and anti-racism organisations have entered the historico-political stage against this backdrop. In novels and plays, public events and music, one finds an increasing focus on the colonial problematic (Derderian 2002; J. Gross 2005; Ireland 2005; Oscherwitz 2005). An often-mentioned theory in this context concerns the connection between the repression of the colonial experience, which has not yet 'found closure', and the racism towards immigrants in present-day France.[10] According to this theory, the official silence, which perpetuated the existence of colonial racism and the desire for revenge after the loss of Algeria, is now projected on those migrants living in France: 'Collective amnesia and the *non-dit* covering this painful period foster anti-Maghreb racism.'[11] Thus, an Internet manifesto, published in January 2005, proclaimed: 'Nous sommes les indigènes de la République' (*Le Monde*, 22 February 2005; *Le Monde*, 17 March 2005). Written against the background of the public controversy surrounding the 2004 law banning conspicuous religious signs from public schools (mainly targeting Muslim headscarves), the manifesto referred to these political issues in historical terms. The deliberate use of the colonial term *indigènes* equates the treatment of the immigrants in France with the colonial situation. Following its manifesto, the Mouvement des Indigènes de la République has continued to link its political activities with historical references by commemorating, for example the anniversary of the massacres by French troops in Sétif and

Guelma (Algeria) on 8 May 1945 (*Le Monde*, 10 May 2005).[12] The discourse surrounding the French 'post-colonial situation' also shaped the public perception of riots by youths of foreign origin that broke out in French suburbs in October–November 2005 and that have regularly resurfaced since then (Bertrand 2006: 123–46).

The official processes of remembrance are most clearly affected by the successful struggles concerning the memory of 17 October 1961, the day on which the Parisian police bloodily repressed a demonstration of about 25,000 Algerians, organised by the FLN (National Liberation Front), against a curfew. More than 11,000 people were arrested and between 50 and 200 dead bodies were thrown into the Seine. While the authorities kept silent about the event, since the 1980s, and even more so since the 1990s, it has become an occasion of systematic remembrance (House 2001; House and MacMaster 2006: 265–334). In 1990, an organisation titled Au Nom de la Mémoire was established. Together with other associations, it holds annual commemorations on 17 October and fights for access to the relevant archives. A great deal of media attention surrounded a symbolic march held along the path of the demonstration on the thirtieth anniversary of the event. As a first official act of remembrance, the socialist mayor of Paris put up a commemorative plaque at the Quai du Marché for the victims of the massacre on 17 October 2001 – the fortieth anniversary of the demonstration.

The current conflicts and debates concerning racism and xenophobia have thereby perpetuated and further complicated the processes of remembering the colonial past. However, they might also cause certain confusions and reductions. Thus, with regard to the commemoration of 17 October, the conflict appears less as a demonstration within the framework of the Algerian struggle for independence and more as an example of a deeply rooted tradition of racism in France (Branche 2005: 43–9). Even if one can find certain personal and ideological continuities from *Algérie française* and the colonial empire to the New Right in France, the xenophobia in the metropole is hardly a result of the 'repatriation' of racism after decolonisation. France has experienced waves of xenophobia since the late nineteenth century, and one can trace anti-Maghreb racism back to the 1920s (MacMaster 1997). These simplifications put aside, it is clear that the issues of immigration and racism in France cannot be entirely detached from the colonial past.

The 'Positive Role' of Colonialism

The arguments around the *loi portant reconnaissance de la Nation et contribution nationale en faveur des Français rapatriés* (Law on Recognition by the Nation and National Contribution in Favour of the French Repatriates) of

23 February 2005 show how hotly contested, chaotic and often contradictory the state's attempts to establish an official memory really are. Initially in 2003, the official Année de l'Algérie, France offered Algeria a series of conciliatory gestures. The highlight was Chirac's visit to Algeria on 2–4 March, which included some 'risky' symbolic acts; for instance, Chirac returned the ceremonial seal of the Dey of Algiers, which the French Army had taken to Paris after the conquest. The most crucial moment was Chirac's public handshake with two historic leaders of the FLN, Yacef Saadi and Zobra Drif (Renken 2006: 146–52).

The trip came only shortly after the torture debates had subsided, and pictures of such events caused a political backlash in France. As a reaction to Chirac's journey, the interfactional parliamentary Groupe d'Etudes sur les Rapatriés managed to gain the support of several younger deputies for a new law.[13] The latter would focus on the question of material reparations for the *rapatriés* and the *harkis*. Yet the *exposé des motifs* to the law clearly showed that the law was also intended to influence current processes of remembrance in favour of the repatriates and their 'civilising mission': 'Recognising the positive achievements of our compatriots on these territories is an obligation for the French state.'[14]

When the law was first read in the National Assembly on 11 June 2004, the historico-political dimension was expanded through modifications that would later lead to public scandal.[15] During the debate, amendments of a firmly politico-educational nature were introduced. The representative Christian Vanneste, of the Union for a Popular Movement (UMP), introduced the decisive amendment, stating that school programmes should 'introduce all young French to the positive role France played overseas'. Without any resistance from the socialist and communist opposition, the amendments were accepted and became Article 4 of the law: 'The university research programmes accord the history of French overseas presence, in particular in North Africa, the place it deserves. The school programmes particularly recognise the positive role of the French overseas presence, especially in North Africa, and accord French Army combatants originating from these territories the prominent place to which they have the right to claim.'[16] Neither in the Senate nor in a second reading in the National Assembly did the wording of a 'positive role' and the demand for political influence on historical research encounter any opposition.

Only when Chirac signed the law on 23 February 2005 did an intensive public debate take place about Article 4 of the law. In a petition in *Le Monde* on 25 March, Claude Liauzu and five other prominent historians demanded the removal of the article and the refusal of an apologetic *histoire officielle* (*Le Monde*, 25 March 2005). Other daily newspapers quickly addressed the issue (*Libération*, 26 March 2005). Anti-racism activists linked the discussions about the law to the November 2005 riots. The scientific community demonstratively organised a colloquium in Lyon from 20 to

22 June 2006, attracting an impressive number of participants (Abécassis and Meynier 2008).

Public pressure eventually stimulated political change and conflict. A motion for removing Article 4 was rejected by the UMP faction in Parliament. The issue even became part of the inner UMP power struggle, between Minister of the Interior Nicolas Sarkozy and Prime Minister Dominique de Villepin, to succeed Chirac. While the former claimed in an interview with *France 3* that one had to stop 'the permanent repentance' (7 December 2005), the latter was to declare a day later on *France Inter* that it was 'not up to the Parliament to write history'. On 4 January 2006, Chirac demanded a reconsideration (*Le Monde*, 6 January 2006). Since this could not be done by parliamentary means, it took a request before the Conseil Constitutionnel on 25 January 2006 to find a way out of the blockade. The Conseil Constitutionnel declared that the expression *rôle positif* had only a *caractère réglementaire* and could thus be eliminated by governmental decree.[17]

The conflicts surrounding the law of 23 February 2005 demonstrate that different antagonistic forces continue to influence the construction of an official memory of colonialism in France. Only an intervention 'from above' brought an end to the struggle over Article 4. Such conflicts also indicate that the strategy of remembrance within the category of national honour can be used by various actors with various intentions. The debate around the law, moreover, has given rise to further broad discussions within the public and the academic sphere about the role of the colonial past in French school programmes, the relationship between history and legislation, and the difference between 'repentance' and official recognition of responsibility (e.g. Jahan and Ruscio 2007; Lefeuvre 2006).

The Post-Chirac Era

Many other areas of French public life, such as museums, with their representations of historical events, have been affected by the current encounter with the colonial legacy (Aldrich 2005; Stora 2007). Given its connections with problems of present-day France, this complex and chaotic encounter will continue over the next years. It was during the Chirac era that the French state started to deal actively with its colonial heritage, but many conflicts surrounding the colonial legacy have remained unsettled. Thus, Chirac chose not to yield to the various demands for an official recognition of the French state's responsibility for acts of violence perpetrated during colonial rule (such as torture or the 8 May 1945 massacres) and during the massacres of the *harkis*. Moreover, several official measures did not settle the existing conflicts, but instead gave rise to new struggles. This has, for example, been the case with the partial alignment of military pensions and Article 3 of the law of 23 February 2005, which provides for an official memorial foundation for the Algerian War. Moreover, the situation of immigrants in France and the social unrest in French *banlieues*, another important factor in the remembrance of colonialism, continue to occupy the French public and the state, reinforced by the focus of the current president, Sarkozy, on the topic of 'national identity' in this age of immigration.

President Sarkozy therefore continues to address the colonial legacy. While he still commemorates the Algerian War within the categories of national honour, he has adopted a line which is different from that of his predecessor. During his presidential campaign, Sarkozy took a stand against what he saw as an overly self-critical approach to French national history, equating demands for official recognition with 'repentance' and 'expiation' (e.g. *Le Monde*, 21 April 2007). During his first trip to Algiers on 10 July 2007, Sarkozy rejected Chirac's project of a Franco-Algerian friendship treaty and clearly refused to make any official 'apology' for Algerian suffering during colonialism (*Le Monde*, 12 July 2007). Only some weeks later, a speech Sarkozy made in Dakar on 26 July 2007, on his first official trip to sub-Saharan Africa, led to public scandal in France and several African countries.[18] The speech did not omit the colonial legacy and its violent aspects. Yet Sarkozy made it clear that 'nobody could ask today's generations to expiate this crime', and he refused to consider the significance of the colonial legacy in Africa today. The most conspicuous feature of the Dakar speech was that it largely drew upon nineteenth-century colonial stereotypes of the ahistorical state and the 'mysterious' nature of the African continent and its inhabitants.

While the Dakar speech perfectly fits into Sarkozy's 'anti-repentance' discourse, the fear of a general revisionist and pro-colonialist backlash in the treatment of the colonial past seems to be exaggerated. Even if Sarkozy more aggressively rejects a self-critical discourse on national history than his predecessor, who tended simply to ignore it, he will hardly be able to turn back the current state of the debates. Even the purveyors of nostalgic memories increasingly feel the effects of the rising public awareness and, paradoxically, their own fight for national recognition. Whereas dozens of monuments erected in commemoration of French Algeria were given relatively little attention during the first four decades after Algerian independence, new pro–French Algeria projects such as the Mur des disparus (inaugurated on 25 November 2007) and the subsequent *pieds-noirs* museum in Perpignan have met nationwide, sometimes even international, protests, not least from critical *pieds-noirs* and *harki* organisations.[19] Also, in view of Sarkozy's first long trip to Algeria on 3–5 December 2007, a group of French and Algerian historians initiated a petition, 'France–Algérie: Dépasser le contentieux historique', which called upon the French state to publicly recognize its responsibility for the 'traumatisation' experienced by the Algerian society under colonialism.[20] In a speech at Mentouri

University in Constantine on 5 December 2007, Sarkozy tried to downplay the importance of the colonial legacy in favour of a common future within his vision of a 'Mediterranean Union' (*Le Monde*, 4–6 December 2007). However, he clearly condemned the violence and injustice of the colonial system. In doing so, he nevertheless avoided any 'excuse' or official recognition, pointed to the 'sincerity' of many colonisers and vaguely mixed Algerian and French suffering.

In its uneasiness and ambiguity, the speech shows how contradictory and embattled the French public remembrance of colonialism continues to be. Similar to Chirac, Sarkozy has to manage different conflicting visions of how to deal with the colonial past. While in late 2007 the government confirmed the creation of the controversial and supposedly biased memorial foundation of the Algerian War, the French ambassador in Algeria, Bernard Bajolet, on 27 April 2008, publicly recognised the 'huge amount of responsibility' of the French authorities for the massacres of 8 May 1945 (*Le Monde*, 5 October 2007, 28–29 April 2008). French Algeria and particularly the Algerian War remain crucial to these ongoing processes of recognition and national discourse. Whether the memory of Algeria serves as a driving force for the remembrance of colonialism as a whole is, however, unclear.

Conclusions

The colonial past is among the neglected or even 'forgotten' aspects of Europe's history. In some countries, however, and especially in France, an atmosphere has emerged since the 1990s in which the issue of colonialism – and of French Algeria in particular – is intensely discussed and remembered. Yet this 'boom' in remembrance followed a period of official silence. As in many other European countries since the 1960s, the colonial past had been excluded from official memory. However, in the aftermath of the Algerian War, the official process of forgetting came to contrast dramatically with the emergence of informal and popular memory. Several non-state actors – especially the repatriates and the veterans – created an enormous pressure to remember. The remembrance of Algeria and the Algerian War had thus already begun to enter the local public space despite being kept out of national memory and the Parisian cityscape.

Beginning in the mid-1990s, the state's first attempts to create an official memory seem, after the long period of inactivity, cautious and disorganised. They are obviously meant to meet, negotiate and balance the demand of the various *lobbies de mémoire* by recognising those who made their contribution to French Algeria and the Algerian War. Despite clear, conciliatory gestures to independent Algeria, the violent aspects of colonialism and the numerous Algerian victims are still largely excluded from this official remembrance. In contrast, beginning in June 2000, fervid public debates about torture during the Algerian War focused on one of the darkest chapters of French colonial history. The law of 23 February 2005 exemplifies the political backlash that occurred due to a primarily negative public discourse on colonialism. Finally, a younger generation of immigrants and anti-racism organisations have appeared as new actors on the historico-political scene, making a connection between 'repressed' colonialism and racism today.

All these events make clear that the current boom in the remembrance of colonialism in France is not simply an automatic mechanism in collective memory, starting after a delay of a few decades. More likely, the process is driven by heated conflicts, struggles and negotiations about the past, and by various factors that are not at work in other countries, for instance, Great Britain. France's two colonial wars rendered its process of decolonisation particularly bloody and dramatic. In contrast, the dissolution of the British Empire is often referred to as a rather smooth process. The Algerian War made the fall of France's colonial empire an agonising mass experience, producing the crucial pressure group of around two million *anciens combattants*. Issues of commemoration were thus closely related to issues concerning financial compensation by the state. Furthermore, the number of repatriates returning to Britain was considerably smaller and more prosperous than the dispossessed mass of *Français d'Algérie* who returned to France. In addition, the integration of immigrants from former colonies has been more explosive in France than in the UK.[21] These factors may explain the waves and conflicts of remembrance in France, but they should not be misunderstood as a type of *Sonderweg*. Their absence does not necessarily imply the lack of any remembrance of colonialism. Germany and Italy have recently engaged in public debates on the colonial past with some similarities to the French, despite the fact that in these cases there was no bloody war of decolonisation, no great number of repatriates and no considerable immigration from former colonies.

Presently, a cross-national memory of Europe's colonial past would appear to be unattainable, and not only because of the differences mentioned above. Remembering the Algerian War is of a high national importance for several actors in France, and heated controversy is often the result. Thus, the war almost appears in the current debates as a domestic French (and not a colonial) issue. Even the related but more general issue of French colonialism as a whole tends to fade into the background by comparison. The national and international challenges which affect the remembrance of colonialism are partly grounded in the subject itself. Despite its huge importance in European history, imperial expansion cannot be considered as a specifically European fact. In addition, European expansion itself is a multi-dimensional phenomenon: the colonial empire of a single nation could include various forms of colonial possession. There is a reason French Algeria still evokes constant waves of remembrance in France, while French Indochina is located more at the 'outskirts' of French memory.

In principle, the international trend during the last several decades to come to terms actively with negative aspects of national histories might be favourable for a common European and international remembrance of colonialism. Nevertheless, a common remembrance would have to start with the quest for a common denominator. The increasingly critical survey into deeply rooted colonial patterns of thinking, the concept of a European 'civilising mission' or the condemnation of slavery might serve as points of departure. The challenge for a lasting remembrance of colonialism is to include all parties involved – not only Europe, but former colonies as well (Thénault 2005a).

Notes

For their substantial help and critical readings I would like to thank Robert Aldrich, Michael Anklin, Simon Creak, Henning Diedler, Jürgen Osterhammel and Kirsten Schüttler. Any errors are the responsibility of the author.

1. If not otherwise mentioned, the words 'colonialism' and 'imperialism' used in this chapter refer to the last period of European expansion in the nineteenth and twentieth centuries. The Algerian War of Independence (1954–62) will be referred to as the 'Algerian War'.
2. For colonial propaganda and colonial (popular) cultures, see, for instance, August (1985), Bancel et al. (1993), Chafer and Sackur (2002) and MacKenzie (1986).
3. See Baussant (2002: 396–411) for different theories about the origin of the term *pieds-noirs*.
4. The increasing number of truth and reconciliation commissions and of international trials worldwide is the most important indicator of this process.
5. For the changes in this historiography, see Branche (2005: 255–314).
6. All quotations from Chirac's and Sarkozy's speeches are taken from the archives on the web site of the French presidency: http://www.elysee.fr.
7. See Journal Officiel de la République Française, Assemblée, débats, 11 June 1999, 5710–33).
8. Shocking reports had already been published during the war itself: Henri Allegg's memoir of 1958, *La question*, influenced a whole generation of anti-war activists. Even after the Algerian War, the issue was addressed in books and films and regularly debated in public. A poll, conducted by the University of Paris VII in 1991, revealed that 94 per cent of the French population aged 17–30 assumed that torture had occurred during the Algerian War (Branche 2005; Thénault 2005b).
9. For the main features of the controversy, see Cohen (2002), MacMaster (2002) and Quemeneur (2001).
10. This thesis has also been raised in academic debates, for example, by Bancel and Blanchard (1999) and Stora (1999). Similar theories have been proposed for other former colonial powers, for example, by Paul Gilroy (2004) for the British case.
11. The source is a flyer produced by an anti-racism organisation, dated March 1993 (quoted in House 2001: 364).
12. The organisation has recently tried to become an 'anti-imperialist' and 'anti-Zionist' political party. Within the French Left it is regularly accused of propagating 'anti-white racism' and 'communitarist' (non-integrationist) ideas and is criticised for its proximity to the controversial Muslim intellectual Tariq Ramadan.

13. For the law's genesis and debate, see Bertrand (2006), Liauzu (2005), Liauzu and Manceron (2006) and Renken (2006: 449–57).
14. Projet de loi no. 1499. Exposé des motifs, 10 March 2004. See also Christian Kert, Rapport no. 1660 sur le projet de loi (no. 1499), 8 June 2004.
15. See Journal Officiel de la République Française, Assemblée, débats, 12 June 2004, 4819–71. See also *Libération*, 26 March 2005.
16. See Journal Officiel de la République Française, Lois et décrets, 24 February 2005, 3128–30.
17. See Journal Officiel de la République Française, Lois et décrets, 16 February 2006, 2369–70.
18. The speech was written by Sarkozy's special advisor, Henri Guaino. For the speech, its content, and public reactions and criticism, see *Libération*, 27 and 28 July 2007, McDougall (2007), Gassama (2008) and Chrétien (2008).
19. Among the *pieds-noirs* and *harki* associations that fight against revisionist and nostalgic visions of the colonial past, one can cite the Association des Pieds-Noirs Progressistes et Leurs Amis and the Association Harkis et Droits de l'Homme. For the Perpignan monument, see *Libération*, 26 November 2007.
20. The petition was published on 1 December 2007 in *Le Monde*, *L'Humanité*, *El Watan* and *Al Khabar*. Rejecting the polemical terms of 'repentance' or 'official excuse', the text asks for a public recognition of acts of violence as the basis for a future trans-Mediterranean writing of Franco–Algerian history.
21. This does not mean that imperialism and its dissolution did not have any significant impact on Great Britain. For a survey of its various and often subtle repercussions, see Thompson (2005).

Chapter 20

MEMORY POLITICS AND THE USE OF HISTORY
Finnish-Speaking Minorities at the North Calotte

❦

Lars Elenius

With the shift of focus from history production to memory production, there has also been a shift of initiative from professional historians to amateur historians. This has signalled not only a change of positions within the field of history, but also an epistemological change: new kinds of groups create new kinds of memory places (Nora 2001: 365ff.; Wertsch 2002: 30ff.). One example of this phenomenon is the Sámi and Finnish-speaking minorities in the North Calotte region.[1] Neither of these groups dominated ethnically in the Scandinavian kingdoms of the early modern period. Subordinated to the Scandinavians, they had little influence on the building and form of official monuments and memory places during the modernisation process.

The few towns on the North Calotte are either costal or in the newly industrialised inland mining areas. In both cases, the memory places of the towns are connected either to the merchant class or to the working-class movement, made up by the majority of the population. As a result of the assimilation policy directed at the national minorities in the twentieth century, the language of official commemorations and memories became the official Scandinavian languages. The language of the minorities was used only in local or private domains.

In spite of this, the Sámi and Finnish-speaking minorities preserved much of their cultural heritage and collective memories in connection to dwelling places in the countryside or names and memories connected to nature. This kind of collective memory was very much related to genea-logical narratives. Indeed, narrations in the vernacular about the present connection to the chain of previous generations constituted *lieux de mémoire* (Elenius 1995).

Notes for this chapter begin on page 306.

With the change in policy towards the national minorities, which started at the end of the 1960s, the vernacular languages of the Finno-Ugric minorities received a new status as 'home languages' (*hemspråk* in Swedish). The minorities were now allowed to learn their vernacular languages in school. In the late twentieth century, the status and language of both of these minorities were codified within a European legal framework. This coincided with a strong political mobilisation among the Finnish-speaking minorities in the 1980s and 1990s and the strengthening of the legal rights of the Sámi people in a global indigenous context (Elenius 2006a).

The revitalisation of vernacular languages coincided with a media revolution which challenged not only the media monopoly of the state, but also the political monopoly of established elite groups. For many decades, public discussion about the memory of history had been carried out between elite groups in well-organised media settings or in easily controllable educational contexts. Through its relative control over the production of knowledge in media and education, the state also exerted a relative control over the construction of the historical space. The nation state was the obvious framework of identification within which historical remembrances were embedded. The national identity was the standard from which other forms of identifications took their starting point.[2]

In creating a communication system that is both globally effective and decentralised, the Internet has contributed in a dramatic way to the undermining of centralised communication structures. It has led to a democratisation of the media structure and, at the same time, has created a forum for non-democratic forces. Parallel to this development, the influence of the nation state has declined in favour of transnational macro-regions, such as the European Union. The result of these changes is that history, as a collective memory, is now created by new kinds of public groups.

In combination with global changes in minority legislation and the decolonisation process, this has led to unpredicted consequences among the national minorities on the North Calotte. Conflicts about different kinds of local resources have developed between different ethnic subgroups. One such conflict is that between certain Finnish-speaking minorities and the reindeer-herding Sámi people about the right to use land and water. As an indigenous people, the Sámi group has special rights to use these resources on territory where they herd reindeer. Over the last few decades, other groups have contested these rights, both internally within the Sámi population and externally by Finnish-speaking minorities. This conflict makes evident the struggle over the historical interpretation of the origins of certain groups.

There are several officially recognised minorities in the Nordic countries, although in this context only those relevant for the North Calotte are mentioned. There is no common basis in the states on the North Calotte for deciding which groups will be recognised as national minorities. This decision is specific to each nation state.

The Sámi people are recognised as an indigenous people in Norway, Finland, Sweden and Russia. In addition, the Sámi people, the Torne Valley people and the Sweden-Finns (all of whom use Sámi and varieties of Finnish as their native language) are recognised as national minorities in Sweden. In Norway, the northerly Finnish-speaking Kven population is recognised as a language minority.[3] This new kind of recognition has given rise to a new kind of memory production among the minorities. The new narrations of collective memories are made in the vernacular languages, either in order to communicate in a better and more genuine way or for symbolic reasons. Not least, the vernacular communication functions as a protest against old power structures, which can be regarded as a kind of 'internal colonialism'.

The Connection between Colonialism and Internal Colonialism

We are living in an exceedingly post-colonial world, but the post-colonial perspective is not a geographic perspective separating the industrialised Western world from the rest of the world of colonised nations, peoples and cultures. In a post-colonial context, colonialism refers above all to how power structures influence relations between dominating and subordinate groups. These relations are determined within a global system which is economically, politically, ideologically and culturally coherent.

In such a context, the subordination of national minorities within the Western European states can be understood as a manifestation of internal colonialism. The peripheral territories of the Western states, which in many cases were inhabited by ethnic minorities, were colonised by the majority of the population in the state. The minorities have more or less been integrated and assimilated into the political, cultural and economic framework of the majority population. In the discourse of internal colonialism, one could understand this as a cognitive power system of dominating and subordinate groups. In such a system, the cultural norms of the dominant part of the population have been used for the creation of national identification.

Michael Hechter (1999) has used theories about internal colonialism to explain how a cultural division of labour has occurred in the nation state. The result is a system of stratification of the structure of professions within which objective cultural differences gain advantage before class differences. Hechter and others with him have further tried to qualify the theory by asserting that the cultural division of labour leads to an ethnic mobilisation and revitalisation from below. The theory has been used to explain the ethnic revitalisation in the Celtic territories, in the meaning of 'ethnic class antagonism' (Hechter 1999). The concept has, however, been criticised for territorial reductionism. Hechter later modified the model of the cultural division of labour to a more 'segmented' type, but even this revision has met with criticism (Smith 1981: 32ff.).

The discourse on internal colonialism can also be applied to the national minorities in the Scandinavian countries. Indeed, this discourse has been applied to the Sámi people in many contexts – from religion and school policy to commercial and tax policy. In connection with this, it is interesting to note that in Sweden both the Sámi people and the Finnish-speaking Torne Valley minority have protested against being regarded as colonised groups. They have dissociated themselves according to different standpoints, but there has been a clear ethno-political indication that they regard themselves as citizens in democratically ruled countries.

The politically organised Sámi, for example, did in 1960 oppose being compared with colonised peoples in the Third World. This happened at the UN, when the South African apartheid regime accused the Swedish government of having a double standard of morality. The Swedish Sámi policy was criticised as discriminatory with regard to racial issues. This caused the Congress of the National Federation of Swedish Sámi People to dissociate themselves from the accusations of the deeply discriminating apartheid regime (Lantto 2003: 59). In the viewpoint of the Sámi people, this was a way to avoid being used by the South African apartheid propaganda.

The Torne Valley people also protested in 2002 when the social democratic minister of culture then in charge compared the situation of the Torne Valley people with that of the Kurds. This caused a number of prominent persons of the Torne Valley to deny the comparison in a jointly written letter to the local press. In light of their political status and citizenship, and offended by the comparison between Kurdistan and the Torne Valley, they protested against being compared with colonised people in the Third World.

However, the national minorities in the West also have a colonial past from which to liberate themselves. The post-colonial process of decolonisation within the former colonies in the Third World is not a simple one. It consists of a two-way process in which decolonisation influences the internal conditions in the dominating Western countries in a corresponding way.

Decolonisation has affected the global legal system with regard to the relation between the colonies and the colonial powers, and this has influenced the rights of the indigenous people in a positive way. It has also strengthened the position of the national minorities in an increasingly international context. At the same time, the nation state has been weakened in favour of new transnational global structures.

The Era of Neo-tribes and Particularistic Narratives

History has moved its focus from universal narratives and big stories to particularistic narratives and small stories. This move to particularity is related to efforts to avoid a kind of false objectivism, which, in turn, is related to the deconstruction of history after the Second World War in the discourse of post-colonialism (Hettne 1999, 2004; Loomba 2006). The shift in focus within history research during the last 30 years, which has come to be known as the cultural or cognitive turn, could as well have been labelled the particularistic turn.

In sociological terms, the development of an urban, postmodern society of the masses, with a mass culture, mass media, mass consumption, etc., has come to a point at which we see deliberately formed micro-groups present in everyday life. The sociologist Michael Maffesoli (1996) has referred to such groups as 'neo-tribes'. Neo-tribes are not rational groups in a normative modern way. Driven by the aim to socialise in local and sub-cultural contexts, they are motivated more by empathetic than rational arguments. Maffesoli calls them neo-tribes because they tend to be counterparts to the organisational, national projects of the Enlightenment era that were based on individuation and separation.

As opposed to being rational 'social' individuals in a civic sense, neo-tribes are devoted to an empathetic context of everyday life, within which sociality is more important than being a social citizen. In the context of mass societies of mega-policies, the neo-tribes take the form of sub-cultural groups, qualified in terms of 'trans-' or 'meta-definitions'. Outlined in various sexes, appearances, lifestyles and ideologies, they do not correspond to the typical logic of identity or binary logic (Maffesoli 1996: 11). The arena in which these new kinds of identity projects take place is not the national arena of political parties, parliaments or other well-known organisational forms of modern society. Instead, it is the arena of everyday life, which, in an era of rapid urbanisation, stabilises the social world of individuals (ibid.: ix; see also Tierney 2002).

The present mass culture is both national and international in its content, and it affects every part of each nation state. Therefore, the purview of neo-tribes is not restricted to urban settings; it is as vital in a countryside as it is in a metropolis. The common denominator is that people with the same lifestyle and affinity of habitus may share the same politics of everyday life. Examples of neo-tribes can be taken both from youth sub-cultures and from various interest-based collectives (Maffesoli 1996: 61ff.). These kinds of collectives do not express a wish to identify what is universally right or wrong, but rather try to express their particularity in the discourse of quotidian life. This may explain why neo-tribes are regarded as odd and backward in the eyes of elite groups in society: they do not fit into the rational matrix of the Enlightenment paradigm.

In this postmodern discourse of neo-tribes, it is helpful to talk about the kind of 'ethnicity without groups' discussed by Rogers Brubaker. Brubaker (2004) stresses the use of a cognitive perspective as a new means of conceptualising ethnicity. He argues that by treating ethnicity as a way of understanding, interpreting and framing experience, it will be easier to avoid stereotype analyses of group experiences. To do so may also help attempts to link phenomena like culture and cognition to each other, or to consider the relation between macro- and micro-levels in society. Cognitive perspectives may also help to correct the elite bias present in much constructivist research and to direct interest to the activities of common people in their everyday lives (ibid.: 86). Many non-professional history projects and books tell the story of how particular histories, in an everyday context, are replacing professional historians as the legitimate tellers of a universal history. This particular use of history is present among ethnic minority groups and pressure groups of different kinds, such as feminists and other sub-cultural groups. Taken together, they undermine the rational, hierarchical modern narrative of the Enlightenment era. The outcome is a choir of particular interests and narratives.

The North Calotte as a Historically Borderless Area of the North

When applying the discourse of memory production and remembrance production to the territory of the North Calotte, the particular social and cultural features of the region must be considered. From the early Middle Ages until the nineteenth century, Norway, Sweden and Russia each enjoyed a certain influence in the most northerly part of Fenno-Scandinavia. In some areas, the Sámi people had to pay taxes to all three kingdoms. The frontiers between the states were established in 1751 between Sweden and Norway, and in 1826 between Norway and Russia. In the treaty of 1751, the Sámi people were granted the right to cross the national frontier and to use land and water in both Norway and Sweden for their reindeer herding. This right remains in use to this day (S. Pedersen 2006).

During the early Middle Ages, the area was inhabited by the Sámi people, while in the Torne Valley there was an early Finnish settlement, dating from at least the eleventh century. The territory of the North Calotte was colonised by Swedish, Finnish and Russian (on the Kola Peninsula) settlers. During the colonisation of the inland area of the North Calotte, the Sámi and Finns came to live in close connection with each other, and, until the nineteenth century, they made up the majority of the population.

The Sámi and the Finns differed significantly, both politically and culturally, from the Scandinavians. Neither the Sámi nor the Finns had any kind of state organisation at the time that they were integrated into the Norwegian and Swedish states. The Finno-Ugric language family, to which Sámi and Finnish belong, is totally different from the Indo-European language family from which Swedish and Norwegian derive. There is also an affinity between the Sámi and the Finns regarding their cultural status within the Norwegian and Swedish nation states. This became very clear during the period of the assimilation policy. In primary schools, both the Sámi and Finnish-speaking minorities were forced to renounce their native tongues, causing them to feel inferior to the dominant Swedish population (Elenius 2006b).

Ethnicity and Collective Memories of the Nation

There is always a struggle within nation states about the ethnic dimension of the collective memories of the nation. This struggle is more or less explicit during different stages of the nation state project, and its content usually shifts over time (Smith 1986). The ethnic dimension of national myths is blurred by the fact that the dominant ethnic group of the nation state is always the primary 'myth maker'. It is taken for granted that the creation of myths by the dominant ethnic group is the myth of the nation, not of a particular ethnic group.[4] This was the case in the old kingdoms of Sweden, Norway and Denmark, which were established during the early Middle Ages on the basis of dominant Scandinavian ethnic groups that had very close cultural relations with each other. Over the years, these ties resulted in many arranged dynastic marriages and political unions of different kinds. The national myths of these Scandinavian kingdoms derived from narratives about brave Vikings, figures of Nordic mythology and genealogically constructed chronologies of royal lines, based on noble families of Nordic descent.

Four main stages in the evolution of the remembrance production of the heritage of the Nordic nations can be tentatively described: first, the pre-national heritage of the Viking Age (which is transferred into the mythology created in later stages of the nation state); second, the Christian national heritage during the establishment of the kingdom in a culturally diverse nation state; third, the monocultural construction of a national heritage and national remembrances during the breakthrough of modern democracy; and fourth and finally, the particular and multi-cultural construction of differentiated ethnic heritages in the era of the post-colonial framework of the European Union. In the context of this description, the focus will be on the national heritage during the eras of monoculturalism and multi-culturalism and on the Finno-Ugric national minorities in particular.

It was the establishment of Christianity which created the first Nordic mythologies for the purpose of ethnically formed kingdoms. It is not by chance that the national saints of Sweden and Norway were created at the same period in history. Both St Eric of Sweden and St Olof of Norway mythologised the connection between the establishment of state power and the Christian framework of its ideology. There are numerous memory places, such as sculptures and inscriptions inside churches and pilgrim paths, that refer to the holy saints as cradles of the nations.

For the subordinated ethnic minorities there was no such direct ethnic connection to the early myths of the growing nation state, since the memory places were connected to the majority population. In the accounts of the Swedish Christianisation of both the Sámi and the Finnish people, it is the Swedes who are the ethnic group in power, and thus Swedes are the 'holy group' of the nation.

During the long period up until the nineteenth century, the Christian faith was the most significant element in the myth of the nation. The transformation from the Catholic to the Protestant faith strengthened the cultural position of the Sámi and the Finns within the kingdom, because Lutheranism emphasised the use of the native tongue in church services, and therefore also the production of religious texts in vernacular languages (Elenius 2006a).

The Polarisation between a Scandinavian and Finno-Ugric Culture

The Napoleonic wars at the beginning of the nineteenth century changed the national frontiers and the ethnic constellations in Fenno-Scandinavia. When Finland was ceded to Russia in 1809 and Norway was forced into a union with Sweden in 1814, a stronger cultural unit of Scandinavian culture was established within the joint Norwegian and Swedish states. Stimulated by the ideology of Scandinavism, it encouraged the Scandinavian elements in the myth of the nation (Elenius 2001).

Together with the growth of a monocultural minority policy, this led to an East-West polarisation between Scandinavians and the Finno-Ugric peoples. The latter were regarded as inferior ethnic groups and also as cultural threats against the nation. This led to a monocultural minority policy towards the Sámi people and the Finnish-speaking minorities in both Norway and Sweden (Elenius 2001, 2006a).

In Sweden, the polarisation became apparent around the turn of the century in 1900, as historians debated the role of ethnic groups in the history of the nation state. One such debate was about which ethnic group had inhabited Finland from the very beginning – the Swedes or the Finns. An associated debate was about the role of Finns and Swedes in the colonisation of the Torne Valley. In the discourse of cultural polarisation, the history of the Torne Valley was reinterpreted in 1919 by a state commission, whose real interest was educational issues in the Torne Valley. The official report stated that the Torne Valley was from the beginning inhabited by Swedes, who had later been assimilated into the Finnish immigrating population. Reservations expressed by one of its members effectively accused the commission of falsifying history (Elenius 2001).

Another kind of reinterpretation concerned the historical roots of the Sámi people. In the eighteenth and the beginning of the nineteenth centuries, the prevalent opinion was that the Sámi people were the original inhabitants of the entire Scandinavian Peninsula. In the late nineteenth century, the dominant theory came to be that the Sámi people had arrived as immigrants from the East and thus were invaders of the Swedish nation (Lundmark 2001).

The official version of the histories of minorities was challenged through the political mobilisation and organisation of the national minorities. It followed roughly the same line and chronology in Sweden and Norway. The Sámi people began efforts to organise themselves at the beginning of the twentieth century. In both countries, minorities had managed to establish a national association after the Second World War. The Sweden Finns, who are regarded as a national minority only in Sweden, founded a national association in the 1950s. However, the Torne Valley people and the Kven people had not been able to do so before the 1980s (Elenius 2006a).

National Minorities: From Outsiders to Insiders

An alternative kind of collective memory created by the national minorities consists of a gradual reinterpretation of the minority policy. During the decades up to the 1990s, two parallel stories were told – one about the segregation and assimilation policy towards the Sámi people, and one about the assimilation policy towards the Torne Valley people and the Sweden Finns. In these accounts, the minorities were represented as repressed and homogeneous, existing under the pressure of the state.

At the beginning of the 1990s, this approach changed dramatically to a more particularistic way of interpreting the minorities from the inside. This did not follow the old structure of a dichotomisation between the minorities and the state. Instead, new kinds of intra-ethnic antagonisms occurred, as well as more overtly expressed internal conflicts within the minorities. One of the most confusing examples of such a conflict is that between the North Calotte pan-Kven movement and the reindeer-herding Sámi. The dispute has its roots in legislation designating the Sámi as an indigenous people, especially ILO Convention 169 of the United Nations, which regulates the right to self-determination of indigenous people over the natural resources within their area of residence.[5]

One striking feature of the pan-Kven movement is that the Finnish speakers involved are organised across the national boundaries of Sweden, Finland and Norway. Another factor is that the movement mobilises through Internet home pages and web-based discussion forums. In this sense, the system of organisation breaks with the traditional pattern of political minority organisations.

The ethnonym 'Kven' is the Norwegian word for the Finnish-speaking minority in northern Norway. It has at least three different meanings for different contexts. The first meaning originated with the Viking chief Ottar from Hålogaland in northern Norway. Ottar's account of different tribes and peoples on the North Calotte was written down by the scribe of King Alfred in England in the late ninth century. It is the first account of ethnicity in northern Fenno-Scandinavia and the original meaning attributed to the ethnonym. Most scholars have identified the Kvens as an ancient Finnish-speaking tribe in the area of the Gulf of Bothnia, but the statement is disputed.

The second meaning ascribed to 'Kven' is the Finnish-speaking minority in northern Norway, which was established by the migration of Torne Valley people from northern Sweden and of Finns from Finland during the eighteenth and nineteenth centuries. In northern Norway they came to constitute a Finnish minority, called 'Kvens' by the Norwegians. The third meaning of the notion 'Kven' is the postmodern creation of a Finnish-speaking, pan-Kven identity that cuts across the boundaries of Sweden, Norway and Finland.

The pan-Kven movement was founded just three months after the Swedish government presented its report on ILO Convention 169 in April 1999. The report stated the implications of the convention for the Sámi people with regard to particular collective proprietorship and right of occupation, the right to maintain their own language and institutions, and the right, under certain circumstances, to solve internal disputes in compliance with common law.[6]

At a constituent meeting in Pajala, in Swedish Torne Valley, the Kvenland Association (Kvänlandsförbundet) was founded. The association demanded recognition as an indigenous people in Sweden. After the initial meeting, the basis for mobilisation spread rapidly over the North Calotte (Lundmark 2005). The aim was widened to embrace the entire North Calotte region (except the Russian Kola Peninsula), and the Kvenland Association demanded recognition as an indigenous people for the region, as well as indigenous rights associated with that status. From the very beginning, the tone of the Kvenland Association was very aggressive towards the politically organised Sámi people, especially the reindeer-herding Sámi (Kvenangen 2002; Kvist 1999; Lundmark 1999, 2001; Ryymin 2003).

To a large degree, the pan-Kven movement has established its identity and collective memory on historical written sources. This must be looked on as a deliberate way of gaining legitimacy for its political claims. As mentioned previously, the Finnish minorities in northern Sweden and northern Norway had never built up any strong official monuments of remembrance or any salient official memory places. Official buildings connected to the state, such as churches, school buildings or museums, were constructed within the framework of the majority language and culture. Private buildings were connected to the memory of family and kin, and a large proportion of the collective narratives either described the struggle against a harsh climate or linked individuals to an eternal chain of descendants, thus forming a narration of collective memory (Elenius 1995).

The Political Strategies of the Pan-Kven Movement

With regard to interpreting history, the strategy of the pan-Kven movement has followed two general paths, the purpose of both being to legitimate the claim of Finnish-speaking minorities to the status of an indigenous people. The first of these has been to argue from historical accounts that the Kven people, interpreted as Finnish speakers, had a long history related to the territory before the state established its power. The second approach has been to show genealogically that the present Finnish speakers are descendants of Sámi people and thus have been deprived of their rights.

The most striking example of the first argument is the account of the Viking chief Ottar from the ninth century. The pan-Kven movement refers to this historical written source in order to support its claim that the Kven people are descendants of the Finnish-speaking Kvens of that time. They also claim to have been residing all over the North Calotte before the states of Sweden and Norway were established in this part of Fenno-Scandinavia and assert that they thus have indigenous rights. The creation of memory is deliberately chosen to fit the political agenda, which is the legal framework of the UN declarations on the rights of indigenous peoples.

An example of the second argument is the reasoning used by the association Suonttavaara Lappby (Suonttavaara Lap Village, in Swedish) in northernmost Sweden and Finland. Its members deliberately employ the old ethnonym 'Lap' (*lapp* in Swedish, *lappalainen* in Finnish) to infer that the word 'Sámi' as it is currently used is a more recent construction by ethno-politically organised Sámi people. The association claims that its members are descendants of the real Sámi people, the Laps, and therefore should be recognised as an indigenous people. In their argumentation, they point to the fact that they have Sámi ancestors but have lost their indigenous rights because their forebears left the reindeer-herding profession to become farmers.[7] Unless it stresses the ethnonym *lapp*, the association can be placed under the umbrella of the pan-Kven movement. The Swedish Suonttavaara Lappby association has a 'mirror organisation' on the Finnish side. Many of the members are also parallel members of the nation-crossing Kvenland Association.

The common denominator for what is referred to here as the pan-Kven movement is that its evidence draws on the kind of obscurity about ethnicity that is apparent in even the oldest historical sources. History is used to prove certain roots and the long continuity of residence within a specific territory. However, the historical method used by the movement is unprofessional and eschews scientific examination (Wallerström 2006). During the early Middle Ages, the Finnish-speaking minorities in Sweden were integrated into the Swedish state. It is therefore difficult to stress moments in the national history when the Torne Valley minority, for example, made a history of their own. The only way for this minority to separate themselves from the present state is to claim kinship with the Kvens mentioned in the ninth century by the Viking chief Ottar.

Arguments are also frequently levelled by the pan-Kven movement against the attempts of the Scandinavian states to legitimate historically the Sámi as the only indigenous people on the North Calotte (Ryymin 2004). Early in the history of these nation states, the Sámi people were recognised as an ethnic group with special rights. This was codified in 1751 in the so-called Lap Codicil, an addendum to the frontier treaty between Sweden and Norway.

The Lap Codicil gave the Sámi people the right to move freely with their reindeer across national boundaries. The Swedish government's step towards recognising the special status of the Sámi people as a specific group – with particular and immemorial rights to the use of land and water – was taken with the legislation of reindeer herding in 1886, which tied the right of reindeer herding to the Sámi population. The ethnification of reindeer herding became even clearer with subsequent modifications of the reindeer-herding legislation (Lantto 2000). With the recognition of the Sámi as an indigenous people in 1977, the Swedish government reconfirmed the distinguishing legislation that had been initiated more than 200 years earlier.

The pan-Kven movement is not homogeneous, but it can be said that it argues for its demands within the framework of the post-colonial redistribution of rights, which indigenous peoples have attained after the Second World War. The dialogue about indigenous rights is therefore held, not within the limited power sphere of the nation state, but within the extended international and global domain of EU and UN politics.

Conclusion

The consequences of decolonisation are incalculable, but one obvious effect is the outcome for national minorities within the European states (Bhabha 1990; Childs and Williams 1997; Said 1997). This is connected to two related processes. One is the problematisation and deconstruction of the ethnic content of the nation state, which has led to changes in power relations between different ethnic groups. The other is the postmodern problematisation of the cultural content of the state, which has allowed for the recognition of the nation state as a multi-cultural unit. As a result, cultures can be regarded as mixed instead of monolithic units, and in this way different kinds of hybrid identities have obtained normative status. At the same time, the large narratives of the nation state have been challenged by the accounts of ethnic groups and national minorities, making possible new kinds of identifications and constructed identities for political purposes (Castells 1997; Harrison 2003: 99ff.; R. Young 2001).

An important consideration is the use of history as a form of collective memory for the purpose of ideological and moral aims. As an aspect of this, present needs are to a great extent guided by the creation and formulation of a history consciousness out of the goals of distinctive groups (P. Hall 2000; Hobsbawm and Ranger [1983] 1992; Karlsson 1999). In this regard, the ethnic mobilisation on the North Calotte demonstrates how influences of globalisation have an effect on ethnic relations and collective memory production from below in stable nation states, such as the Nordic ones.

Notes

1. The North Calotte region (in Swedish, Nordkalotten) was formally created in 1957 as a northerly sub-region within the transnational region of the Nordic countries, created some years earlier. The purpose of establishing the North Calotte region was to emphasise the special living conditions of the people living in those subarctic parts of Fenno-Scandinavia and also to identify a common ground for policy making. The North Calotte consists of the northernmost counties of Norway, Sweden and Finland, and sometimes also the Russian Kola Peninsula. The term 'northern Fenno-Scandinavia' is used to depict this northern area of Scandinavia and Finland, but in a broader context than the North Calotte. For research about minority issues at the North Calotte, see Lars Elenius (2009a, 2009b, 2009c).
2. Identity is a notion that captures our personality in a holistic way. It can be described as occurrences, episodes and activities that influence our way of reflecting about ourselves. It consists of different parts which we can strengthen or weaken, and it changes over time. Identity can thus be described as a process through which we identify with different parts of our personality (see Jenkins 2004).
3. The Sámi people are resident all over the North Calotte in all four countries. The Torne Valley people have their traditional settlement area in a territory in northernmost Sweden, close to the border between Sweden and Finland. The Sweden-Finns are Finnish speakers, originally from Finland. They are mainly resident in the middle and southern parts of Sweden, but many also live in the northernmost part of Sweden. The Kven people are a Finnish-speaking minority in northern Norway. Through descent and kinship ties, they are related to the Finnish speakers in northern Sweden and northern Finland (KU Rapporter från riksdagen 2004/05: RFR3). For a discussion about the indigenous status of the Russian Sámi population on the Kola Peninsula, see Paul Fryer (2007, 2009).

4. The dominant ethnic group in a multi-ethnic state does, in another way, have a disadvantage in identity creation because it is not always seen as a distinct ethnic entity with an ethno-political programme, but instead as the ethnic core of the state. Consider, for example, the debate about the role of Russians in the former Soviet Union. The Russians were associated with the new 'socialistic man' who, in theory, should not have any ethnic features but only class features.
5. See Statens Offentliga Utredningar (Swedish Government Official Reports), 'Samerna – ett ursprungsfolk i Sverige', 1999, 25.
6. Ibid.
7. See http://www.suonttavaara.se/.

NIGHTMARES OR DAYDREAMS?

A Postscript on the Europeanisation
of Memories

Konrad H. Jarausch

In an era enamoured by technological futurism, the extent and intensity of the current memory boom have come as somewhat of a surprise.[1] Eyewitnesses to historical events, who previously bemoaned the lack of interest in their suffering, now appear constantly on talk shows or in documentaries. Business people have discovered that money can be made by hawking memorabilia or sponsoring heritage tourism. More and more politicians are justifying their policies by appeals to their own sanitised versions of the past. Many countries recently liberated from dictatorship are renationalising their collective recollections. Other states see themselves forced to apologise for prior misdeeds or to compensate their former victims. Due to the immediacy and availability of images and sound bites from earlier times, the past appears to be present to an unparalleled degree. Accustomed to benign neglect, many historians are disorientated by all this attention.

It is therefore not surprising that pro-integration intellectuals and Brussels bureaucrats should have discovered a lack of collective memory in Europe, which they now seek to remedy. No longer content with economic utility alone, engaged Europeans want to overcome the frustrations of insufficient political progress by grounding their efforts in the inevitable logic of history – thereby rediscovering to some extent the original motivations of the founders of the Common Market. As Klas-Göran Karlsson suggests, this trend is part of a general process of cultural Europeanisation that tries to create a shared culture, transcending linguistic and national differences. As a response to the pressures of globalisation, the creation of a European cultural space, capable of resisting popular Americanisation or radical Islamicisation, may seem appropriate. But in the struggle over the

Notes for this section are located on page 320.

preamble of the European Constitution, the search for common roots has had the opposite effect of raising tensions and fostering disagreement.

The quest for a shared European memory should, therefore, be considered a normative discourse that, in combining two problematic projects, compounds some of the difficulties. The call to Europeanise memory aims not just at inspiring a more profound understanding of the European dimension of the past in its component regions, but at creating a transnational public memory that can legitimate the transformation of the European Union into a super-state. As the French and Dutch referenda have shown, this goal is opposed by many European citizens and resisted by countries like Britain and Denmark. Although the availability of funding from Brussels makes it tempting to join in the project of providing a historical justification for such a transformation, historians ought rather to demythologise it, deflate its rhetoric and deconstruct its subtext. Hence, the following reflections will attempt to delineate several memory regimes, discuss the degree of their Europeanness, probe their value structure and explore ways to create a more open-ended appreciation of European pasts.

Memory Regimes

The very proliferation of terms and approaches dealing with memory suggests that for all the newfound attention, the issue remains rather elusive in academic debate. Frederick Whitling's valiant effort to create some order points to the French roots of the concept, which extend from Maurice Halbwachs's emphasis on social construction via Pierre Nora's nostalgic notion of *lieux de mémoire* to Paul Ricoeur's philosophical reflections. In the German discussion, the emphasis of Jan and Aleida Assmann on cultural memory predominates, although a group of political scientists around Peter Steinbach focuses instead on the politics of history, or *Geschichtspolitik*, in order to get at the uses of historical references in the public realm. In US practice, the term 'memory' is usually conflated with Holocaust observance, as the 'Lessons and Legacies' conferences show, narrowing its meaning to a single, albeit crucial, issue. To reduce this conceptual confusion, the following remarks will begin by exploring the question of which memory regimes currently dominate public observances in Europe.

Following Wolfgang Schieder's suggestion, three clusters of narration and commemoration that represent differing historical experiences can roughly be distinguished. The first is Western memory, sometimes referred to as 'an Allied scheme of history', which has an understandably self-congratulatory tone (Nützendadel and Schieder 2004; cf. N. Davies 1996). Especially prevalent in the United Kingdom, it focuses on the Allied victory in the Second World War, seeing it as proof of the superiority of the democratic system. In occupied but then liberated countries such as

France, the emphasis is instead on the struggle of the resistance against the hated Wehrmacht and on celebrating its martyrs, as in the Paris museums on Leclerc and Moulin. Critics might ask embarrassing questions about elite appeasement in England or popular collaboration in Vichy, but on the whole, a united front – ranging from veterans' associations to leftist intellectuals – continues to celebrate the heroic defence of freedom as a successful enterprise that was both intensely national in motivation and potentially European in its transnational cooperation.

A second group of more troubling memories, located in Central Europe, revolves around the crimes of Nazi Germany and its allies. Not only does a shattering defeat prevent displays of national pride, but the unprecedented extent of atrocities perpetrated and abetted by Germans, Austrians, Hungarians, Slovaks, Croatians and Romanians, to name a few, requires public contrition – even if the populace does not want to admit its own guilt. Here the historical sites are not memorials to victorious battles or courageous acts of resistance; rather, they are places of terror and annihilation, such as the remains of the concentration camps for which Auschwitz and Buchenwald may stand as examples. Since efforts to relativise tend to raise an international outcry, the only escape from the burden of guilt is the attempt to submerge one's own responsibility in a sea of universal suffering, as at the Neue Wache memorial in Berlin, thereby joining the privileged status of victim. The result of this memory regime is a politics of regret and material restitution which must seek to undo the damage of the past by symbolic or tangible *Wiedergutmachung* (reparations).

The third and final collection of memories resides primarily in Eastern Europe, which is preoccupied with coming to terms with decades of communist repression. Although Stefan Troebst points to internal differences, the countries of the former Soviet bloc share the task of reconstructing their memory culture after regaining self-determination. In all of them, the long hoped for liberation from Nazi domination turned, after a brief interval, into new subjection to Soviet rule, which imposed upon them a Marxist view of history with a set of working-class-centred commemorations. Toppling Soviet monuments and recovering a sense of national independence were exhilarating experiences, although there were national variations in the extent to which governments were willing to expose their collaboration with the secret police. While East Germany was the most open, the negotiated nature of the revolution swept much of the previous dirt under the rug in Poland and elsewhere. As Péter Apor points out, memory culture is deeply divided between hard-line anti-communism, such as in the Hungarian House of Terror, and post-communist apologetics, such as those in Slovakia.

This overview suggests that European memory culture remains divided into regional regimes because different Europeans experienced the catastrophes of the twentieth century in distinctive ways. Due to the recovery of the nation state after the defeat of National Socialism and the collapse of communism, public memories remain intensely national. Once the Iron Curtain dissolved, the coming together of the divergent memory regimes was bound to arouse fierce controversies. In the West, joint school textbook commissions, media debate and conversations of politicians have succeeded in gradually reconciling the Central European version with the dominant view, allowing Chancellor Gerhard Schröder to be asked to attend the sixtieth D-Day anniversary in Normandy, an invitation his predecessor, Helmut Kohl, coveted in vain. But the Eastern European suffering under communism is too recent to subordinate itself readily to the emerging memory consensus on the primacy of the Holocaust. At the same time, Western intellectuals are not ready to condemn communist crimes with the same vigour as their counterparts in the East.

Carriers of Memory

Among the different carriers of memory, the salience of the European dimension remains rather weakly articulated at present. As I have suggested in *Shattered Past*, an actor-centred approach that focuses on the actual bearers of recollections can distinguish between individuals, groups, national governments and, in addition, transnational institutions (Jarausch and Geyer 2003). Individuals fashion coherent stories about their own lives by conversing with family members, looking at photo albums or writing formal curricula vitae. Groups like the German refugees from the East promote their common interests by organising themselves around accounts of their shared suffering so as to claim compensation. National governments seek to create political cohesion via school curricula, holiday commemorations, public museums and the like. Even some transnational entities such as the UN or NGOs like Greenpeace fashion historical narratives that justify their existence and promote their values. At best, such an approach can detect, in Jan-Werner Müller's words, only a '"thin" transnational European memory' at present.

Although 52 per cent of respondents profess a positive image of the EU in the Eurobarometer survey of July 2007 (No. 67), few individuals consider their memories as explicitly European. No doubt, the core values of European citizens, such as peace (52 per cent), respect for human life (43 per cent) and human rights (41 per cent), and the perceived attributes of the EU, such as human rights (38 per cent), democracy (38 per cent) and peace (36 per cent), owe much to the traumatic experiences of the twentieth century, but this connection is not articulated in a shared view of the past (Eurobarometer No. 66). Moreover, not a single one of Eurobarometer's 285 specialised reports addresses the views of European citizens concerning the past. Instead, fragmentary evidence from memoirs suggests that leading political figures such as Helmut Kohl do have explicit views of European history. In the former chancellor's case, a terrible memory of war and suffering made him think in European terms (Kohl 2004). But the overwhelming majority of ordinary Europeans can hardly be supposed to be framing their recollections in a European fashion.

Interest groups may lobby fiercely in Brussels, but their historical self-images tend to be intensely particularistic, leaving hardly any room for a European sensibility. In surveying associations seeking to promote their aims with the EU, Hartmut Kaelble (2007) has gone so far as to call them an emergent civil society on the European level. But most groups such as veterans' associations remain focused on national themes of sacrifice, since the rewards that they claim can be obtained only by welfare state legislation. Some minorities like the Catalans might look to the regional policy of the EU to bolster their independence, but their legitimising narratives remain utterly self-absorbed. A few civic initiatives such as the Karlspreis, bestowed annually by the city of Aachen, or foundation efforts such as Eustory, the youth history competition sponsored by the Körber Foundation, do seek to foster a European historical consciousness. But their impact so far has been rather slight.

Even more self-centred are the national governments, since they focus their efforts on promoting national cohesion rather than European cooperation. Except for a recent Franco-German textbook (Geiss and Le Quintrec 2006), school curricula remain solidly focused on the history of each respective nation. Public holidays also recall founding myths, such as the French Revolution, and celebrate military victories in national terms (see Clemens Maier in this volume). Monuments honour national heroes rather than significant Europeans. Museums of national history, such as the Norwegian resistance museum in Oslo, or of the military, such as the French War Museum, or of technology, such as the Deutsche Museum in Munich, spotlight the achievements of their own nationals, even if the subject (resistance, war, technological development) is by definition inter-or transnational. Although some self-representations, such as the 2006 exhibition on the Enlightenment in the Bibliotheque Nationale de France, make a valiant effort to embed their story in a European context, the latter merely tends to serve as a backdrop.

International organisations have even less explicit interest in Europe, even if many of them originated there and receive significant support from the Old Continent. While the League of Nations in Geneva merely replaced the defunct Concert of Europe, the location of the UN in New York signalled a wider scope. Similarly, the agendas of the International Monetary Fund, the World Trade Organization and the World Bank are global in intent. NGOs like Greenpeace or Médicins Sans Frontières have strong European roots but focus on universal concerns. Only as a refuge from the depredations of globalised capitalism during the melt-down of the financial system has Europe risen again in public estimation, because the nation state seems too small to defend its citizens effectively. But the intense pressure from political and economic migrants poses the question of how successful a 'fortress Europe' mentality can be in the long run, especially if it ignores its historical debt to influences from Africa and Asia. Beyond the reluctant acknowledgement of help by colonial troops during the world wars, such global issues have yet to make an impression upon the memory culture.

To make up this deficit, the European Union has itself begun efforts to create a shared memory culture by funding historical research and helping with the establishment of an integration museum in Brussels (Harding 2005). In the negotiations about the accession of new members, the European Parliament has tried to formulate something like an *acquis historique*, sketching rough outlines of a common understanding of the past.[2] Central to this endeavour has been the Holocaust standard, a frank admission of responsibility for perpetrating or collaborating with genocide. However, this imperative fails to address the difficult question of what to do with communist crimes such as the Soviet campaign of de-kulakisation (see Arfon Rees in this volume). Stressing the metaphysical singularity of the Holocaust militates against recognising the perhaps equally grave violation of civilisational norms by the Soviets. Moreover, some EU candidates are still largely in denial of their own misdeeds, such as the Turks in regard to the Armenian massacre. The intermittent discussions have yet to come to grips with other vexing questions, such as the mass population movements of German expellees and Polish resettlers after the Second World War.

Negative Lessons

The quest for transnational commonalities in European memories of the twentieth century has found it easier to derive negative lessons than to discover positive sources of pride. The phrasing of the preamble of the European Constitution has remained rather vague because some secularised countries want to appeal to the Enlightenment while more religiously oriented governments insist upon including positive references to Christianity. The impressive catalogue of human rights included in the document has therefore derived its significance more from a general realisation of past evils that needed to be avoided than from a specific delineation of common values that would bind the community together in the present (Joerges et al. 2007). This failure is regrettable, because it tends to lock thinking about Europe into a negative mode. Europe has become a kind of insurance policy against the repetition of prior problems rather than a positive goal, based upon a shared vision for the future. What are the chief cautionary tales that make up European memories?

Most basic has been the lesson of the Second World War: the necessity of avoiding war in Europe at all costs (see Stefan Berger in this volume). Even many victors were shocked by the 50 million people killed, untold cities destroyed and economies ruined. American visitors saw Europe in a Stone Age struggle for mere survival – as a continent that had lost its dominance over the rest of the world. Hence, the founders of integration, including Robert Schuman, Alcide de Gasperi and Konrad Adenauer, strove to prevent the repetition of such carnage, even at the cost of giving up some national sovereignty. Commemorations of the Second World War therefore sought to balance the validation of sacrifice among the winners with a loss of national meaning by the losers through a transnational message of the general destructiveness of war. Instead of repeating messages of intense nationalisation through a 'cult of the dead' as after the First World War, remembrances of the Second World War sought a measure of reconciliation by emphasising shared suffering. Yet the resulting pacifism provided little guidance for how to deal with the moral dilemmas of the Cold War, ethnic cleansing in the Balkans and the religious fanaticism of the Near East.

Another later and even more powerful message has been derived from a growing awareness of the genocide committed in the Holocaust (see Cecilie Felicia Stokholm Banke in this volume). In the catalogue of accusations of the Nuremberg trials, a new category – 'crimes against humanity' – was added, somewhat as an afterthought. But by the 1970s, literary evocations and filmic depictions of the suffering in the concentration camps had coalesced into a new concept, named after a burnt offering in Old Testament language, the 'Holocaust'. This American neologism, which was focused largely on the 'annihilation of Jews', quickly spread to Europe because of its powerful appeal as a kind of secularised 'civil religion' in which racism is outlawed and tolerance is commanded. While more Europeans had some contact with the process than they were willing to admit, in contrast to the war, this was a memory of sympathy – created largely by the media, education and politics – for the victims of Nazi crimes. Although the location of the genocide was Europe, the politicisation of the concept through the Stockholm conference turned into a universal standard, central to but transcending European memory.

More limited has been the impact of the condemnation of communist crimes after the fall of the Berlin Wall (see Péter Apor in this volume). In contrast to the lasting appeal of anti-fascism as vigilance against neo-Nazi tendencies, the anti-communist crusade lost much of its utility with the end of the Cold War. Moreover, its power had been regionally limited to the countries in the former Soviet bloc, which suffered directly from Stalinist repression. Western efforts, such as *The Black Book of Communism*, have had less resonance than Eastern initiatives to establish memorials to victims of communism. The lack of international cooperation among people harmed by communist repression also reduces its visibility in the media.

Due to the support of anti-communist commemoration by the right, leftist intellectuals have been reluctant to confront the crimes committed by a progressive ideology, based on values of the Enlightenment. Since much of the communist killing might be considered incidental rather than systematic, its memorialisation has a certain 'me too' quality, still oriented on the Holocaust standard.

Least remembered is the anti-imperialist lesson based on the hasty and contentious process of decolonisation after the Second World War. In contrast to the legacy of communism, the problematic colonial heritage is largely limited to Western Europe. Public memory in the former mother countries seems ambivalent, torn between an admission of guilt due to exploitation and lingering pride in the achievements of empire. In his contribution to this volume, Jan Jansen suggests that this is a problem of domestic politics, because descendants of imperial elites favour concealment and celebration of their civilising mission, while migrants from the colonies retain memories of suffering. Unlike the establishment of Holocaust memorials and anti-communist commemorations, memories of imperialism have been externalised to the former colonies where the suffering took place. This understandable displacement of guilt from the centre facilitates amnesia and offers right-wing politicians like Sarkozy opportunities to relativise responsibility over decolonisation. The intensely national coding of empire also means that this topic has hardly become an issue for Europe as a whole.

The dominant strands of transnational memories in Europe therefore seem to have an almost nightmarish quality. As products of large-scale suffering, from war to genocide, from repression to exploitation, they create hortatory narratives, pointing to dire consequences if certain dangerous tendencies are not stopped in time. Moreover, in the realm of public debate, the victims of militarism, fascism, communism and imperialism clamour for attention, vying for sympathy and compensation in turn. In East Germany, this has led to a competition over memory sites, since the Nazi prisons and camps were also used by the Soviets and the Stasi, creating two groups of survivors who have attached contradictory memories to the same memorial. This argumentation *ex negativo* strengthens Mark Mazower's picture (1998) of Europe as a dark continent, given to extraordinary violence, rather than emphasising the learning processes of overcoming hostility. This nightmare memory is based on experiences of suffering that are likely to diminish in time and are unlikely to serve as a lasting bond in the future.

Positive Alternatives

In order to avoid the pitfall of historical propaganda, the search for positive alternatives can pursue several promising options. However, repeating the creation of national narratives of the nineteenth century on a European level is a problematic course, since it will only result in duplicating nationalist mistakes on a larger scale. Inventing a common past by selecting merely those elements which lead to the current integration process will provide a highly biased and incomplete set of memories that fail to do justice to the complexity of pasts on the Old Continent. Harmonising disparate recollections into one generalised memory culture will disregard the long history of mutually inflicted suffering and overlook the rich diversity that characterises Europe in the first place. While the EU should support efforts to debate the elements of a shared memory, it must refrain from mandating a 'Brussels version' from above, because imposed memories tend not to produce viable roots. What methods might be more appropriate for reconciling plurality with unity in European memories?

A first step might be a concerted drive to stop the perpetuation of nationalist memories within the countries of the EU. Since public memory culture is a product of nation states, there is still an amazing amount of chauvinism in monuments, museums and commemorations that needs to be expurgated. At the same time, new tendencies of re-nationalisation ought to be resisted, especially when they lead to fresh mythologising about the past, as in Eastern Europe or former Yugoslavia (see Senadin Musabegović in this volume). To achieve this goal, the European public needs to support internal critics, such as the Polish KARTA Centre, who are working to provide a more self-critical view of the past that freely admits a nation's crimes against their own citizens and also against their neighbours. At the same time, the example of the bilateral school textbook commissions ought to be implemented further in order to eliminate the propagation of hateful stereotypes in textbooks. Similarly, in some intractable issues like the Beneš decrees, international commissions of historians might be able to mediate. Finally, symbolic acts of contrition are sometimes surprisingly effective in decreasing hostility.

A second move could be a transnational effort to recover the many connections that transcend boundaries and form a shared underpinning in Europe. Ancient churches, castles and cities of the pre-national period testify to the transmission of styles and ideas across regions. But even after the establishment of nation states, much trade and migration ignored national boundaries, with railroad networks or canals linking people and towns. While nationalisation of language did, indeed, serve to divide countries, other elements of visual and musical culture travelled freely, making it hard to locate painters or composers within a single national context. Even in the political realm, major ideologies spread from country to country, creating a European-wide horizon of liberalism or socialism; revolutionary outbursts inspired each other in 1789, 1848, 1918 and 1989; and solutions to urban problems were copied freely elsewhere. These few hints suffice to indicate that much of what connected Europeans in one place to another does not need to be invented but rather recovered. As I have argued elsewhere (Jarausch 2007), the material is there. It remains only for viewpoints and representations to change.

A third initiative would consist of an attempt to link national memories by rendering their multiple interdependencies visible. Breaking through the walls of separate suffering requires recognising the 'other' as equally afflicted. This is relatively easy for cross-cutting events, like the Great Depression, which might be nationally inflected but follow a similar pattern everywhere, leaving traces that resemble each other. It might be more difficult in bloody conflicts such as wars. However, it is a truism that it takes two to fight, that is, that another side is always present – even in nationalist accounts. Treating this other not just as a stereotypical enemy but as a collection of human beings would create an opening for sharing experiences – leading to the astonishing discovery that these might be similar to one's own. The remarkable transformation of former enemies into 'comrades' decades after vicious battles take place is an encouraging example of how memory can metamorphose with time by making the similarity of fighting more important than the former hostilities. The effort to link memories would need patient listening and open telling (see Stanisław Tyszka in this volume).

Finally, a pluralised approach to memories of Europeans ought to remain critical of any agenda aimed at creating a 'super-memory' for Europe. Hitler's effort to turn a losing war into a European crusade against communism indicates that the usually positive label of 'Europe' can also contain more sinister meanings. Similarly, most trade unions are not at all happy with the neo-liberal colouring of the EU's economic policy and the lack of a social dimension. National political leaders are time and again incensed by the effort of Brussels bureaucrats to expand their jurisdiction into areas not clearly demarcated as their purview. The failed referenda have shown that many European citizens are suspicious of the elite character of the integration project, which has paid insufficient attention to democratic participation. As Wolfgang Kaschuba suggests in this volume, a fundamentalist conception of Christian Europe pitted against Islam only provokes further hostility. Recent examples suggest that historians need to remain vigilant with regard to the goals that motivate various efforts to create a streamlined European memory.

Instead of having a Euro-memory mandated from above, Europeans need to reconcile their clashing recollections through a transnational discussion from below. Such an effort will require a European-wide debate about which strands to include in a common memory, thereby constituting a public sphere in which to discuss appropriate commemorations. This process of selecting, comparing and sharing memories is primarily a task for civil society – for concerned individuals and relevant interest groups – rather than national governments. It must begin with local efforts at dialogue which could then expand into larger networks, cutting across borders, much as in the decentralised approach suggested for defusing the Polish-German controversy over creating a museum about the expulsions. It should also involve young people as much as possible, because they find it easier to transcend historic enmities. More promising than tedious compromises by government commissions would be a grass-roots debate, which, in seeking unity, might preserve plurality. Successful examples of encounters in places such as Genshagen or Krzyżowa (Kreisau) show that this can actually be achieved.

Historians as Critics

In this emerging discussion, historians have a crucial role to play in developing a critical stance towards European memories. The deadly consequences of nationalist historiography have shown that scholars must above all avoid the 'Treitschke trap' of propagandising for a nation state – even on a larger European scale.[3] By deconstructing the relationship between the national project and the claim to professional objectivity, the postmodern critique has pointed out the constructed nature of master narratives. This realisation allows historians to analyse 'memory', not as a quasi-natural phenomenon, but as the product of conscious actions taken by a multitude of individuals, groups and governments who seek to shape public recollections in a certain way. In order not to become themselves naive promoters of Euro-memory, scholars ought to recognise their responsibility for commenting critically on the accuracy and intent of memory construction. Instead of remedying a claimed European 'myth deficit', they should demythologise current efforts to create a new integrationist memory (Schmale 1997).

One strategy not to be blinded by Euro-enthusiasm is to hold the European project to a moral standard derived from the troubled history of the Old Continent. How one should respond to the construction of a Euro-memory depends entirely upon the meaning with which the container 'Europe' is being filled. If the purpose is hegemonic or dictatorial, as under Napoleon or Hitler, then Europe must be resisted at all costs. But if the intent is liberating, as during the French Revolution or the collapse of communism, then it ought to be applauded. Did it not take incessant warfare, religious persecution and material exploitation to produce among critical minds a cluster of values such as human rights, social equality and racial tolerance, which now form the basis of civilised existence? These ideals inform a core of aspirations that can serve as a yardstick employed by historians to comment on the progress of the European project sympathetically and, at the same time, critically. However, it must be remembered that the goal is not Europe for its own sake but rather the realisation of a more humane life.

Ultimately, any effort to Europeanise memories must come to terms with the Faustian paradox that characterises European history. On the one hand, Europe has been an extraordinarily dynamic, innovative and expansive continent, producing untold wealth and holding dominion over vast swaths of the earth. On the other hand, Europe has also been incredibly destructive, devastating and deadly, spreading war and causing immense suffering for its own citizens as well as others. Honest memories therefore contain a wealth of contradictions, soaring to the highest cultural and artistic achievements and plunging to the depths of the grossest atrocities committed by humankind. The continent that produced antibiotics also invented the concentration camp. Both aspects are, as the medical experiments of the SS show, intimately intertwined. If they are to be truthful, European memories therefore have to reflect the destructive as well as the constructive elements of the past. As the guardians of the cultural memory of the past, historians are charged with keeping this duality in the public view. Perhaps through their critical efforts, they can contribute to making Europe's better potential prevail in the future.

Notes

1. Since most references in the text refer to contributions in this volume, notes have been kept to a minimum. For fuller citations, see Jarausch and Lindenberger (2007).
2. This neologism suggests a parallel to the *acquis communautaire* of European law, which the EU requires all new members to accept during negotiations for accession.
3. Heinrich von Treitschke was a famous liberal historian in the nineteenth century who agitated for the creation of a German national state while claiming to write objective scholarly history.

REFERENCES

Abécassis, F. and Meynier, G. (eds.) (2008), *Pour une histoire franco-algérienne: En finir avec les pressions officielles et les lobbies de mémoire* (Paris).

Adler, N. (1993), *Victims of Soviet Terror: The Story of the Memorial Movement*. (Westport).

Adorno, T. W. (1997), *Ob nach Auschwitz sich noch Leben Lasse: Ein Philosophisches Lesebuch* (Frankfurt am Main).

Agamben, G. (2000), *Il tempo che resta: Un comento alla Lettera ai Romani* (Torino).

Agnew, J. and McDermott, K. (1996), *The Comintern: A History of International Communism from Lenin to Stalin* (Basingstoke).

Aldrich, R. (2005), *Vestiges of the Colonial Empire in France* (Basingstoke).

Alexander, J. (2004), 'In the Social Construction of Moral Universals: The "Holocaust" from War Crime to Trauma Drama', in *Cultural Trauma and Collective Identity*, (ed.) J. Alexander, R. Eyerman, B. Giesen, N. Smelser and P. Sztompka (Berkeley and London), 196–263.

Amendt, G. (1999), 'Wer wie was, wieso weshalb warum: Psychogramm einer neuen Kriegsgeneration' *Freitag*, 7 May, http://www.freitag.de/1999/19/99190102.htm.

Amis, M. (2003), *Koba the Dread: Laughter and the Twenty Million* (London).

Andall, J. and Duncan, D. (eds.) (2005), *Italian Colonialism: Legacy and Memory* (Oxford).

Apor, P. and Trencsényi, B. (2007), 'Fine-Tuning the Polyphonic Past: Hungarian Historical Writing in the 1990s', in *Narratives Unbound: Historical Studies in Post-Communist Eastern Europe*, (ed.) S. Antohi, B. Trencsényi and P. Apor (Budapest and New York), 1–99.

Arendt, H. (1963), *Eichmann in Jerusalem: A Report on the Banality of Evil* (London).

Arnold, S. R. (1994), '"Das Beispiel der Heldenstadt wird ewig die Herzen der Völker erfül-len!" Gedanken zum sowjetischen Totenkult am Beispiel des Gedenkkomplexes in Vol-gograd', in *Der politische Totenkult: Kriegerdenkmäler in der Moderne*, (ed.) R. Koselleck, R. Jeismann and M. Jeismann (Munich), 351–74.

Ash, T. G. (2002), 'Trials, Purges and History Lessons: Treating a Difficult Past in Post-Com-munist Europe', in *Memory and Power in Post-War Europe: Studies in the Presence of the Past*, (ed.) J.-W. Müller (Cambridge), 265–82.

Ashplant, T. G., Dawson G. and Roper, M. (eds.) (2004), *Commemorating War: The Politics of Memory (Memory and Narrative)* (New Brunswick).

Assmann, A. (1991), 'Zur Metaphorik der Erinnerung', in *Mnemosyne: Formen und Funk-tionen der kulturellen Erinnerung*, (ed.) A. Assmann and D. Harth (Frankfurt am Main), 13–35.

_____ (1996), 'Texts, Traces, Trash: The Changing Media of Cultural Memory', *Representa-tions* 56: 123–43.

_____ (1999a), *Erinnerungsräume: Formen und Wandlungen des kulturellen Gedächtnisses* (Munich).

_____ (1999b), 'Ein deutsches Trauma? Die Kollektivschuldthese zwischen Erinnern und Vergessen', *Merkur: Deutsche Zeitschrift für Europäisches Denken* 53, no. 12: 1142–54.

_____ (2001), 'History and Memory', in *International Encyclopedia of the Social and Behavioral Sciences*, vol. 10, (ed.) N. J. Smelser and P. B. Baltes (Oxford), 6822–9.

_____ (2002), 'Gedächtnis als Leitbegriff der Kulturwissenschaften', in *Kulturwissenschaften: Forschung – Praxis – Positionen*, (ed.) L. Musner and G. Wunberg (Vienna), 27–45.

_____ (2006a), 'Memory, Individual and Collective', in *The Oxford Handbook of Contextual Political Analysis*, (ed.) R. E. Goodin and C. Tilly (Oxford), 210–24.

_____ (2006b), *Der lange Schatten der Vergangenheit: Erinnerungskultur und Geschichtspolitik* (Munich).

_____ (2006c), 'History, Memory, and the Genre of Testimony', *Poetics Today* 27, no. 2: 261–73.

_____ (2006d), 'On the (In)compatibility of Guilt and Suffering in German Memory', *German Life and Letters* 59, no. 2: 187–200.

_____ (2008), *Einführung in die Kulturwissenschaft: Grundbegriffe, Themen, Fragestellungen*. 2nd rev. ed. (Berlin).

Assmann, J. (1988), 'Kollektives Gedächtnis und kulturelle Identität', in *Kultur und Gedächtnis*, (ed.) J. Assmann and T. Hölscher (Frankfurt am Main), 9–19.

_____ (1995), 'Collective Memory and Cultural Identity', *New German Critique* 65: 125–33.

_____ ([1992] 2007), *Das kulturelle Gedächtnis: Schrift, Erinnerung und politische Identität in frühen Hochkulturen*, 6th ed. (Munich).

Auden, W. H. (1937), *Spain* (London).

August, T. G. (1985), *The Selling of the Empire: British and French Imperialist Propaganda, 1890–1940* (Westport).

Bacon, E. (2002), 'Church and State in Contemporary Russia: Conflicting Discourses', *Journal of Communist Studies and Transitional Politics* 18, no. 1: 97–126.

Bacon, E., Renz, B. and Cooper, J. (2006), *Scrutinising Russia: The Domestic Politics of Putin* (Manchester).

Bacon, E. and Wyman, M. (2002), *Contemporary Russia* (Basingstoke).

Bakhtin, M. M. (1981), *The Dialogic Imagination: Four Essays by M. M. Bakhtin*, (ed.) M. Holquist, (trans.) C. Emerson and M. Holquist (Austin).

_____ (1986), *Speech Genres and Other Late Essays*, (ed.) C. Emerson and M. Holquist, (trans.) V. M. McGee (Austin).

Bal, M. (1999), 'Introduction', in *Acts of Memory: Cultural Recall in the Present*, (ed.) M. Bal, J. Crewe and L. Spitzer (Hanover and London), vii–xvii.

Bancel, N. and Blanchard, P. (1999), 'De l'indigène à l'immigré: Images, messages et réalités', *Hommes et Migrations* 1207: 6–29.

Bancel, N., Blanchard, P. and Gervereau, L. (eds.) (1993), *Images et colonies: Iconographie et propagande coloniale sur l'Afrique française de 1880 à 1962.* (Paris).

Bandić, D. (1980), *Tabu u tradicionalnoj kulturi Srba* (Belgrade).

_____ (1997), *Carstvo zemaljsko i carstvo nebesko* (Belgrade).

Banke, C. F. S. (2004), 'Ny Antisemitisme i Europa?' DIIS-brief 39, Copenhagen.

Bann, S. (1990), 'Clio in Part: On Antiquarianism and the Historical Fragment', in *The Inventions of History: Essays on the Representation of the Past* (Manchester), 100–21.

Barkan, E. (2000), *The Guilt of Nations: Restitution and Negotiating Historical Injustices* (New York).

Barnett, C. (1986), *The Audit of War: The Illusion and Reality of Britain as a Great Nation* (London).

_____ (1995), *The Lost Victory: British Dreams, British Reality, 1945–1950* (London).

Barou, J. (ed.) (1993), *Mémoire et integration* (Paris).

Bartetzky, A., Dmitrieva, M. and Troebst, S. (eds.) (2005), *Neue Staaten – neue Bilder? Visuelle Kultur im Dienst staatlicher Selbstdarstellung in Zentral- und Osteuropa seit 1918* (Cologne).

Bartov, O. (2004), 'The Holocaust as "Leitmotif" of the Twentieth Century', *Zeitgeschichte* 31: 315–27.

Bauer, M. (2006), 'Schlimme Kommunisten: Sandra Kalniete spricht in Hamburg über das halbierte Gewissen', *Süddeutsche Zeitung*, 18/19 February, 14.

Bauer, Y. (2002), *Rethinking the Holocaust* (New Haven).

Bauman, Z. (1989), *Modernity and the Holocaust* (New York).

Baussant, M. (2002), *Pieds-noirs: Mémoires d'exils* (Paris).

Bax, M. (2000), 'Barbarization in a Bosnian Pilgrimage Center', in *Neighbors at War: Anthropological Perspectives on Yugoslav Ethnicity, Culture, and History*, (ed.) J. M. Halpern and D. A. Kideckel (University Park), 187–202.

Beck, U. (1998), *Was ist Globalisierung?* (Frankfurt am Main).

Beckett, F. (2004), *Stalin's British Victims* (Stroud).

Bell, D. (2006), 'Introduction: Memory, Trauma and World Politics', in *Memory, Trauma and World Politics: Reflections on the Relationship between Past and Present*, (ed.) D. Bell (Basingstoke), 1–29.

Ben-Ghiat, R. (2005), 'The Secret Histories of Roberto Benigni's *Life is Beautiful*', in *Jews in Italy under Fascist and Nazi Rule*, (ed.) J. D. Zimmerman (New York), 330–49.

Berg, P. A., Eikli, E. and Stordahl, T. E. (1995), *Fritt Norge* (Oslo).

Berger, S. (2003), *The Search for Normality: National Identity and Historical Consciousness in Germany since 1800* (Oxford).

_____ (2005), 'A Return to the National Paradigm? National History Writing in Germany, Italy, France and Britain from 1945 to the Present', *Journal of Modern History* 77, no. 3: 629–78.

Bernecker, W. L. (1989), 'Neutralität wider Willen: Spaniens verhinderter Kriegseintritt', in *Kriegsausbruch 1939*, (ed.) H. Altrichter and J. Becker (Munich), 153–77.

Bertrand, R. (2006), *Mémoires d'empire: La controverse autour du 'fait colonial'* (Bellecombe-en-Bauges).

Betz, F.-U. (2005), 'Das andere Mahnmal', *Zeit online* 19 May, http://www.zeit.de/2005/21/ITS_neu?page=all (accessed 3 May 2007).

Beyen, M. (2002), '"Elle est de plus en plus noire, la masse des flamingants": Comment s'est forgée l'image de l'occupation et de la répression en Flandre 1945–2000', in *Collaborations et répression: Un passé qui résiste*, (ed.) J. Gotovitch and C. Kesteloot (Brussels), 99–113.

Bhabha, H. K. (ed.) (1990), *Nation and Narration* (London).

Bidussa, D. (1994), *Il Mito del Bravo Italiano* (Milan).

Billig, M. (1995), *Banal Nationalism* (London).

Binder, B., Kaschuba, W. and Niedermüller, P. (eds.) (2001) *Inszenierung des Nationalen: Geschichte, Kultur und die Politik der Identitäten am Ende des 20. Jahrhunderts* (Cologne).

Blanchard, P., Bancel, N. and Lemaire, S. (eds.) (2005), *La fracture coloniale: La société française au prisme de l'héritage colonial* (Paris).

Błoński, J. ([1987] 1990), 'The Poor Poles Look at the Ghetto', in *My Brother's Keeper: Recent Polish Debate on the Holocaust*, (ed.) A. Polonsky (London), 34–52.

Bodnar, J. (1992), *Remaking America: Public Memory, Commemoration, and Patriotism in the Twentieth Century* (Princeton).

Bömelburg, H.-J. (2007), 'Zwischen imperialer Geschichte und Ostmitteleuropa als Geschichtsregion: Oskar Halecki und die polnische "jagiellonische Idee"', in *Vergangene Größe und Ohnmacht in Ostmitteleuropa: Repräsentationen imperialer Erfahrung in der Historiographie seit 1918*, (ed.) F. Hadler and M. Mesenhöller (Leipzig), 99–130.

Bon, S. (2005), *Testimoni della Shoah. La Memoria di Salvati: Una Storia del Nord Est* (Gorizia).

Bonwetsch, B. (2006), 'Erinnerungskultur und Traditionspflege im postsowjetischen Russland', in *'Transformationen' der Erinnerungskulturen in Europa nach 1989*, (ed.) B. Faulenbach and F.-J. Jelich (Essen), 221–6.

Booth, W. J. (2006), *Communities of Memory: On Witness, Identity, and Justice* (Ithaca).

Born, H. and Stemmer, K. (1996), *Damnatio memoriae: Das Berliner Nero-Porträt* (Mainz).

Bosworth, R. ([1993] 1994), *Explaining Auschwitz and Hiroshima: History Writing and the Second World War 1945–1990* (London and New York) (published first in London, and the following year in London and New York).

_____ (1998), *The Italian Dictatorship* (London).

Botz, G. (1983), 'Methoden- und Theorieprobleme der historischen Widerstandsforschung', in *Arbeiterbewegung – Faschismus – Nationalbewusstsein: Festschrift zum 20jährigen Bestand des Dokumentationsarchivs des österreichischen Widerstandes und zum 60. Geburtstag von Herbert Steiner*, (ed.) H. Konrad and W. Neugebauer (Vienna), 137–51.

Bourdieu, P. (1989), 'Social Space and Symbolic Power', *Sociological Theory* 7: 14–25.

Boym, S. (1994), *Common Places: Mythologies of Everyday Life in Russia* (Cambridge, MA).

Branche, R. (2005), *La guerre d'Algérie: Une histoire apaisée?* (Paris).

Bravo, A. (2005), 'The Rescued and the Rescuers in Private and Public Memories', in *Jews in Italy under Fascist and Nazi Rule*, (ed.) J. D. Zimmerman (New York), 311–20.

Breuss, S., Liebhart, K. and Pribersky, A. (1995), *Inszenierungen: Stichwörter zu Österreich* (Vienna).

Brix, E., Bruckmüller, E. and Steckl, H. (eds.) (2004–5), *Memoria Austriae*, 3 vols. (Vienna).

Brooks, R. L. (1999), *When Sorry Isn't Enough: The Controversy over Apologies and Reparations for Human Injustice* (New York).

Broué, P. (2003), *Communistes contre Staline: Massacre d'une génération* (Paris).

Brubaker, R. (2004), *Ethnicity without Groups* (Cambridge, MA).

Bruneteau, B. (2003), *'L'Europe nouvelle' de Hitler: Une illusion des intellectuels de la France de Vichy* (Monaco).

Brunnbauer, U. (ed.) (2004), *(Re)Writing History: Historiography in Southeast Europe after Socialism* (Münster).

Bryce, J. ([1888] 1995), *The American Commonwealth, Vol. 1*. Introduction by G. L. McDowell. Indianapolis.

Bryld, C. and Warring, A. (1998), *Besættelsestiden Som Kollektiv Erindring: Historie og Tradisjonsforvaltning af Krig og Besættelse 1945–1997* (Frederiksberg).

Bucur, M. (2002), 'Trauma, Nationalism and the Memory of World War II in Romania', *Rethinking History* 6, no. 1: 35–55.

Bucur, M. and Wingfield, N. M. (eds.) (2001), *Staging the Past: The Politics of Commemoration in Habsburg Central Europe, 1848 to the Present* (West Lafayette).

Bunting, M. (2004), *The Model Occupation: The Channel Islands under German Rule, 1940–1945* (London).

Burgwyn, H. J. (2005), *Empire on the Adriatic: Mussolini's Conquest of Yugoslavia 1941–1943* (New York).

Buruma, I. (2006), *Murder in Amsterdam: The Death of Theo van Gogh and the Limits of Tolerance* (New York).

Butterfield, H. (1931), *The Whig Interpretation of History* (London).

Čajkanović, V. (1973), *Mit i religija u Srba* (Belgrade).

Carpi, D. (1977), 'The Rescue of Jews in the Italian Zone of Occupied Croatia', in *Rescue Attempts during the Holocaust: Proceedings of the Second Yad Vashem International Historical Conference*, Jerusalem, 8-11 April, 465–525.

Castells, M. (1997), *The Information Age: Economy, Society and Culture* (Malden).

Caute, D. (1964), *Communism and the French Intellectuals* (London).

Chafer, T. and Sackur, A. (eds.) (2002), *Promoting the Colonial Idea: Propaganda and Visions of Empire in France* (Basingstoke).

Chalmers, D. J. (1996), *The Conscious Mind: In Search of a Fundamental Theory* (Oxford).

_____ (1999), 'Précis of the Conscious Mind', *Philosophy and Phenomenological Research* 59, no. 2: 435–38.

Childs, P. and Williams, P. (1997), *An Introduction to Post-colonial Theory* (Hemel Hempstead).

Chrétien, J.–P. (ed.) (2008), *L'Afrique de Sarkozy: Un déni d'histoire* (Karthala).

Cohen, W. B. (2002), 'The Algerian War, the French State and Official Memory', *Historical Reflections* 28: 219–39.

_____ (2003), 'The Algerian War and the Revision of France's Overseas Mission', *French Colonial History* 4: 227–39.

Cole, T. (1999), *Selling the Holocaust: From Auschwitz to Schindler. How History is Bought, Packaged, and Sold* (New York).

Collotti, E. (1997), 'Sulla Repressione Italiana nei Balcani', in *La memoria del Nazismo nell'Europa di Oggi*, (ed.) Leonardo Paggi (Firenze), 181–208.

_____ (2003), *Il Fascismo e gli Ebrei: Le Leggi Razziali in Italia* (Roma-Bari).

Collotti, E. and Klinkhammer, L. (1996), *Il Fascismo e l'Italia in Guerra: Una Conversazione fra Storia e Storiografia* (Roma).

Čolović, I. (2000), *Politika simbola* (Belgrade).

Conan, E. and Rousso, H. (1998), *Vichy: An Ever-Present Past*, (trans.) N. Bracher (Hanover).

Confino, A. (1997), 'Collective Memory and Cultural History: Problems of Method', *American Historical Review* 102, no. 5: 1386–403.

_____ (2005a), 'Introduction', in *Histories and Memories of Twentieth-Century Germany*, (ed.) A. Confino, special issue of *History and Memory* 17, no. 1/2: 296–322.

_____ (2005b), 'Remembering the Second World War, 1945–1965: Narratives of Victimhood and Genocide', *Cultural Analysis* 4: 46–75.

Connelly, M. (2004), *We Can Take It! Britain and the Memory of the Second World War* (Harlow).

Connerton, P. (1989), *How Societies Remember* (Cambridge and New York).

Conquest, R. (1986), *The Harvest of Sorrow: Soviet Collectivization and the Terror Famine* (London).

Corbea-Hoisie, A., Jaworski, R. and Sommer, M. (eds.) (2004), *Umbruch im östlichen Europa: Die nationale Wende und das kollektive Gedächtnis* (Innsbruck).

Coslovich, M. (ed.) (1997), *Racconti dal Lager* (Milan).

Coughlin, B. and Olick, J. K. (2003), 'The Politics of Regret: Analytical Frames', in *Politics and the Past: On Repairing Historical Injustices*, (ed.) J. C. Torpey (Lanham), 37–62.

Courtois, S. (1999a), 'Introduction: The Crimes of Communism', in *The Black Book of Communism: Crimes, Terror, Repression*, (ed.) S. Courtois et al. (Cambridge, MA, and London), 1–32.

_____ (1999b), 'Conclusion: Why?' in *The Black Book of Communism: Crimes, Terror, Repression*, (ed.) S. Courtois et al. (Cambridge, MA, and London), 727–58.

_____ (2003–4), 'Que reste-t-il du PCF?' *Communisme* 76–7: 252–7.

Courtois, S. and Panné, J.-L. (1999), 'The Shadow of the NKVD in Spain', in *The Black Book of Communism: Crimes, Terror, Repression*, (ed.) S. Courtois et al. (Cambridge, MA, and London), 333–52.

Crane, S. A. (1997), 'Writing the Individual Back into Collective Memory', *American Historical Review* 102, no. 5: 1372–85.

Cristea, G. and Radu-Bucurenci, S. (2008), 'Raising the Cross: Exorcising Romania's Communist Past in Museums, Memorials and Monuments', in *Past for the Eyes: Cinema and Museums in Representing Communism in Eastern Europe after 1989*, (ed.) O. Sarkisova and P. Apor (Budapest), 273–303.

Csáky, M. (2002), 'Gedächtnis, Erinnerung und die Konstruktion von Identität: Das Beispiel Zentraleuropas', in *Nation und Nationalismus in Europa: Kulturelle Konstruktionen von Identitäten. Festschrift für Urs Altermatt*, (ed.) C. Bosshart-Pfluger, J. Jung and F. Metzger (Vienna), 25–49.

Dabag, M. (2001), 'Erinnerung ohne Orte: Warum auch Deutschland den Genozid an den Armeniern Anerkennen Sollte', *Frankfurter Allgemeine Zeitung*, 9 February.

Dallin, A. (1988), 'The Uses and Abuses of Russian History', in *Soviet Society and Culture: Essays in Honor of Vera S. Dunham*, (ed.) R. L. Sheldon and T. L. Thompson (Boulder), 181–94.

Danilov, V. P. (ed.) (1999–2001), *Tragediya Sovetskoi Derevni*, vols. 1–3 (Moscow).

Darieva, T. and Kaschuba, W. (eds.) (2008), *Representations on the Margins of Europe: Politics and Identities in the Baltic and South Caucasian States* (Chicago).

Davies, N. (1996), *Europe: A History* (London).

Davies, R. W. (1989), *Soviet History in the Gorbachev Revolution* (Basingstoke).

_____ (1997), *Soviet History in the Yeltsin Era* (Basingstoke).

Davies, R. W. and Wheatcroft, S. G. (2004), *The Years of Hunger: Soviet Agriculture, 1931–1933* (Basingstoke).

_____ (2006), 'Stalin and the Soviet Famine of 1932–33: A Reply to Ellman', *Europe-Asia Studies* 58, no. 4: 65–33.

De Felice, R. (2001), *The Jews in Fascist Italy: A History* (New York).

de Haan, I. (1997), *Na de Ondergang: De Herinnering aan de Jodenvervolging in Nederland 1945–1995* (Amsterdam).

De Roche, S. (2006), 'Un tempio della memoria per Roma', *Ideazione*, 2 February.

Del Vecchio, G. and Pitrelli, S. (2007), 'Non Aprite l'Olocausto', *l'Espresso*, 7 June.

Derderian, R. L. (2002), 'Algeria as a *lieu de mémoire*: Ethnic Minority Memory and National Identity in Contemporary France', *Radical History Review* 83: 28–43.

Di Sante, C. (ed.) (2005), *Italiani senza Onore: I Crimini in Jugoslavia e i Processi Negati (1941–1951)* (Verona).

Diner, D. (ed.) (1988), *Zivilisationsbruch: Denken nach Auschwitz* (Frankfurt am Main).

_____ (2003), 'Restitution and Memory: The Holocaust in European Political Cultures', *New German Critique* 90: 36–45.

Dintenfass, M. (2000), 'Truth's Other: Ethics, the History of the Holocaust, and Historiographical Theory after the Linguistic Turn', *History and Theory* 39, no. 1: 1–20.

Douglas, L. (1998), 'The Shrunken Head of Buchenwald: Icons of Atrocity at Nuremberg', *Representations* 63: 39–64.

Draaisma, D. (2000), *Metaphors of Memory: A History of Ideas about the Mind* (Cambridge and New York).

Dreyfus, M., Groppo, B., Ingerflom, C., Lew, R., Pennetier, C., Pudal, B. and Wolikow, S. (eds.) (2000), *Le siècle des communismes* (Paris).

Du Camp, M. (1852), *Egypte, Nubie, Palestine et Syrie: Dessins photographiques recueillis pendant les années 1849, 1850 et 1851* (Paris).

Duchhardt, H. and Kunz, A. (eds.) (1997), *'Europäische Geschichte' als historiographisches Problem* (Mainz).

Dugin, A. N. (1999), *Neizvestnyi Gulag: Dokumenty i Fakty* (Moscow).

Duhovski, D. (2002), 'Kolaboracija i Otpor u Hrvatskoj 1941–1945', in *Religija, Društvo i Politika: Kontroverzna Tumačenja i Približavanja*, (ed.) T. Bremer (Bonn), 26–39.

Duroselle, J.-B. (1990), *L'Europe: Histoire de ses peuples* (Paris).

Eastlake, E. (1857), 'Photography', *London Quarterly Review* 101: 442–68.

Ebbinghaus, A. and Roth, K. H. (1992), 'Vorläufer des "Generalplans Ost": Eine Dokumentation über Theodor Schieders Polendenkschrift', *1999: Zeitschrift für Sozialgeschichte des 20. und 21. Jahrhunderts* 7, no. 1: 62–94.

Elenius, L. (1995), *Den Barnlösa Byn: Bland Ungklarlar och Änkor och Annat Folk i Vettasjärvi* (Östersund).

_____ (2001), *Både Finsk och Svensk: Modernisering, Nationalim och Språkförändring i Tornedalen 1850–1939* (Umeå).

_____ (2006a), *Nationalstat och minoritetspolitik* (Lund).

_____ (2006b), 'The Use of Ethnonyms in the Course of Minority Policy in the Fenno-Scandinavia', in *Minority Policies, Culture and Science* (Studies in Northern European Histories 1) (Luleå), 55–69.

_____ (2009a), 'Förändrade identifikationer på Nordkalotten', in *Fredens konsekvenser: Samhällsförändringar i norr efter 1809* (Studier i norra Europas historia 7/Studies in Northern European Histories 7), (ed.) L. Elenius et al. (Luleå), 25–36.

_____ (2009b), 'Kategoriernas makt på Nordkalotten', in *Är vi inte alla minoriteter i världen? Rättigheter för urfolk, nationella minoriteter och invandrare* (Studier i norra Europas historia 8/Studies in Northern European Histories 8), (ed.) L. Elenius (Stockholm), 80–97.

_____ (2009c), 'Norden som minoritetspolitiskt experiment', in *Är vi inte alla minoriteter i världen? Rättigheter för urfolk, nationella minoriteter och invandrare* (Studier i norra Europas historia 8/Studies in Northern European Histories 8), (ed.) L. Elenius (Stockholm), 265–281.

Eley, G. (2002), *Forging Democracy: The History of the Left in Europe, 1850–2000* (New York).

Elias, N. (1995), *Über den Prozeß der Zivilisation: Soziogenetische und psychogenetische Untersuchungen* (Frankfurt am Main).

Ellman, M. (2005), 'The Role of Leadership Perceptions and of Intent in the Soviet Famine of 1931–34', *Europe-Asia Studies* 57, no. 6: 823–41.

_____ (2007), 'Stalin and the Soviet Famine of 1932–33 Revisited', *Europe-Asia Studies* 59, no. 4: 663–93.

Elster, J. (1998), 'Coming to Terms with the Past: A Framework for the Study of Justice in the Transition to Democracy', *Archives Européennes de Sociologie* 39: 7–48.

Epstein, C. (2003), *The Last Revolutionaries: German Communists and Their Century* (Cambridge, MA, and London).

Erdősi, P. (2000), 'A Kulturális Örökség Meghatározásának Kísérletei Magyarországon', *Regio* 11: 26–44.

Eriksen, A. (1995), *Det Var Noe Annet Under Krigen: 2. Verdenskrig i Norsk Kollektivtradisjon* (Oslo).

_____ (1997), '… "Norge Er Atter Fritt!" Om den Norske Markeringen av 50-årsjubileet for Frigjøringen', *Tradisjon* 1: 3–12.

Evans, R. J. (1989), *In Hitler's Shadow: West German Historians and the Attempt to Escape from the Nazi Past* (London).

_____ (1997), *In Defence of History* (London).

_____ (2000), 'Blitzkrieg und Hakenkreuz', *Frankfurter Rundschau*, 16 September.

Fabre, G. (1999), *L'elenco. Censura Fascista e Autori Ebrei* (Torino).

_____ (2005a), *Mussolini Razzista. Dal Socialismo al Fascismo: La Formazione di un Antisemita* (Milan).

_____ (2005b), 'Il Museo Della Shoah che Verrà Costruito a Roma', *Panorama*, 21 September.

Farmer, S. (1999), *Martyred Village: Commemorating the 1944 Massacre at Oradour-sur-Glane* (Berkeley).

Faulenbach, B. (2006), 'Erinnerungskulturen in Mittel- und Osteuropa als wissenschaftliches und geschichtspolitisches Thema', in *'Transformationen' der Erinnerungskulturen in Europa nach 1989*, (ed.) B. Faulenbach and F.-J. Jelich (Essen), 11–21.

Felman, S. (1992), *Testimony: Crises of Witnessing in Literature, Psychoanalysis and History* (New York).

Ferry, J.-M. (2000), *La question de l'Etat européen* (Paris).

Finkelstein, N. G. (2000), *The Holocaust Industry* (London).

Finkielkraut, A. (1987), *La défaite de la pensée* (Paris).

_____ (1992), *Remembering in Vain: The Klaus Barbie Trial and Crimes against Humanity* (New York).

Finzi, R. (1997), *L'università Italiana e le Leggi Antiebraiche* (Rome).

Flacke, M. (2004a), 'Erinnerungen', in *Mythen der Nationen: 1945 – Arena der Erinnerungen, Begleitband zur Ausstellung*, (ed.) M. Flacke (Berlin), 7–12.

_____ (ed.) (2004b), *Mythen der Nationen: 1945 – Arena der Erinnerungen* (Berlin).

Flood, C. and Frey, H. (2000), 'History Writing: From the Annales to the Institut d'Histoire du Temps Présent', in *Currents in Contemporary French Intellectual Life*, (ed.) C. Flood and N. Hewlett (Basingstoke), 56–75.

FNACA (Fédération Nationale des Anciens Combattants en Algérie, Maroc et Tunisie) (1999), *Lieux et Liens du Souvenir, 1952–1962* (Paris).

Focardi, F. (1999), 'Alle Origini di una Grande Rimozione: La Questione dell'anti-Semitismo Fascista nell'Italia Dell'immediato Dopoguerra', *Horizonte* 4: 135–70.

_____ (2005), *La Guerra della Memoria: La Resistenza nel Dibattito Politico Italiano dal 1945 a Oggi* (Rome).

Focardi, F. and Klinkhammer, L. (2004), 'The Question of Italy's War Crimes: The Construction of a Self-Acquitting Myth (1943–1948)', *Journal of Modern Italian Studies* 9, no. 3: 330–48.

Foong Khong, Y. (1992), *Analogies at War: Korea, Munich, Dien Bien Phu and the Vietnam Decisions of 1965* (Princeton).

François, E. and Schulze, H. (2001), 'Einleitung', in *Deutsche Erinnerungsorte*, 3 vols. (ed.) E. François and H. Schulze (Munich), 1:9–24.

Frazon, Z. K. and Horváth, Z. (2002), 'A Megsértett Magyarország: A Terror Háza Mint Tárgybemutatás, Emlékmű és Politikai Rítus', *Regio* 13: 303–47.

Frei, N. (ed.), (2006), *Transnationale Vergangenheitspolitik: Der Umgang mit Deutschen Kriegsverbrechen in Europa nach dem Zweiten Weltkrieg* (Göttingen).

Friedländer, S. (1992), *Probing the Limits of Representation: Nazism and the 'Final Solution'* (Cambridge, MA).

――― (1993), *Memory, History, and the Extermination of the Jews of Europe* (Bloomington).

――― (2000), 'History, Memory and the Historian', *New German Critique* 80 (Spring/Summer): 3–15.

Friese, H. (ed.) (2002), *Identities: Time, Difference, and Boundaries* (Oxford and New York).

Fritzsche, P. (2002), 'Walter Kempowski's Collection', *Central European History* 35: 257–67.

Frye, N. (1957), *Anatomy of Criticism: Four Essays* (Princeton).

Fryer, P. (2007), 'Coping with Transition: Rural Indigenous Communities in the Russian North', in *Cross-Cultural Communication and Ethnic Identities* (Studies in Northern European Histories 5), (ed.) L. Elenius and C. Karlsson. (Luleå), 319–329.

――― (2009), 'Urfolks rättigheter och rättvisa på Kolahalvöns landsbygd', in *Är vi inte alla minoriteter i världen? Rättigheter för urfolk, nationella minoriteter och invandrare* (Studier i norra Europas historia 8), (ed.) L. Elenius (Stockholm), 186–202.

Fuglehaug, W. (1995), 'Veteraner paraderte på Karl Johan', *Aftenposten*, 8 May.

Furet, F. (1978), *Penser la Revolution française* (Paris).

――― (1988), 'La France unie …', in *La République du centre: La fin de l'exception française*, (ed.) J. Furet, J. Julliard and P. Rosanvallon (Paris), 13–66.

――― (1999), *The Passing of an Illusion: The Idea of Communism in the Twentieth Century*, (trans.) D. Furet (Chicago and London).

Furet, F., Julliard, J. and Rosanvallon, P. (eds.) (1988), La République du centre: La fin de l'exception française (Paris).

Gassama, M. (ed.) (2008), L'Afrique répond à Sarkozy: Contre le discours de Dakar (Paris).

Geiss, P. and Le Quintrec, G. (eds.) (2006), *Histoire/Geschichte: L'Europe et le monde depuis 1945/Europa und die Welt seit 1945* (Paris and Leipzig).

Geras, N. (1998), *The Contract of Mutual Indifference: Political Philosophy after the Holocaust* (London).

Gerner, K. (1999), 'A Moveable Place with a Moveable Past: Perspectives on Central Europe', *Australian Journal of Politics and History* 45, no. 1: 3–19.

Gerő, A. (2006), *Imagined History: Chapters from Nineteenth- and Twentieth-Century Hungarian Symbolic Politics* (Boulder and New York).

Geyer, M. (1994), 'Resistance as Ongoing Project: Visions of Order, Obligations to Strangers, and Struggles for Civil Society, 1933–1990', in *Resistance against the Third Reich 1933–1990*, (ed.) M. Geyer and J. W. Boyer (Chicago), 325–50.

Giesen, B. (ed.) (1991), *Nationale und Kulturelle Identität: Studien zur Entwicklung des Kollektiven Bewußtseins in der Neuzeit* (Frankfurt am Main).

――― (2004), *Triumph and Trauma* (Boulder).

Gigerl, M. (2006), 'Constructing Austrian Identity after 1945: The Austrian "State Book" Österreich (1948) and the "State Film" 1 April 2000 (1952)', Unpublished paper given at the conference 'Image and Identity in Contemporary Europe', Bangor University, 7–9 September 2006.

Gilcher-Holtey, I. (2001), *Die 68-er Bewegung* (Munich).

Gillis, J. R. (ed.) (1994), *Commemorations: The Politics of National Identity* (Princeton).

Gilroy, P. (2004), *After Empire: Melancholia or Convivial Culture?* (London).

Girard, R. (1989), *The Scapegoat* (Baltimore).

Girvin, B. and Roberts, G. (eds.) (1999), *Ireland and the Second World War: Politics, Society and Remembrance* (Dublin).

Glassberg, D. (1996), 'Public History and the Study of Memory', *Public Historian* 18, no. 2: 7–23.

Goebel, S. (2001), 'Intersecting Memories: War and Remembrance in Twentieth-Century Europe', *Historical Journal* 44, no. 3: 853–8.

_____ (2007), *The Great War and Medieval Memory: War, Remembrance and Medievalism in Britain and Germany, 1914–40* (Cambridge and New York).

Goldstone, R. J. (2001), 'From the Holocaust: Some Legal and Moral Implications', in *Is the Holocaust Unique?* (ed.) A. S. Rosenbaum (Oxford), 41–47.

Gorkin, J. (1978), *Les communistes contre la Révolution espagnole* (Paris).

Górny, M. (2007), 'From the Splendid Past into the Unknown Future: Historical Studies in Poland after 1989', in *Narratives Unbound: Historical Studies in Post-Communist Eastern Europe*, (ed.) S. Antohi, B. Trencsényi and P. Apor (Budapest), 101–72.

Graziosi, A. (1996), *The Great Soviet Peasant War: Bolsheviks and Peasants, 1917–1933* (Cambridge, MA).

Gretkowska, M. (2002), 'Scheda', *Wprost*, no. 1007, 17 March.

Griffiths, E. (2009), 'Stalin: The Second Coming', *Times Literary Supplement*, 20 January, 14.

Gross, J. (2005), 'France and Algeria: Performing the "Impossible Memory" of a Shared Past', in *Memory, Empire, and Postcolonialism: Legacies of French Colonialism*, (ed.) A. G. Hargreaves (Lanham), 216–34.

Gross, J. T. (2001), *Neighbors: The Destruction of the Jewish Community in Jedwabne, Poland* (Princeton).

Gruber, H. (1991), *Anti-Semitismus im Mediendiskurs: Die Affäre 'Waldheim' in der Tagespresse* (Frankfurt am Main).

Habermas, J. (1985), 'Die Krise des Wohlfahrtsstaates und die Erschöpfung Utopischer Energien', in *Die Neue Unübersichtlichkeit* (Frankfurt am Main), 141–63.

Halbwachs, M. ([1925] 1994), *Les cadres sociaux de la mémoire* (Paris).

_____ (1950), *La mémoire collective* (Paris).

_____ (1985), *Das Gedächtnis und Seine Sozialen Bedingungen* (Frankfurt am Main).

_____ (1992), *On Collective Memory* (Chicago and London).

Halecki, O. (1924), 'L'Histoire de L'Europe Orientale, sa Divisions en Epoches, son Milieu Géographique, et ses Problèmes Fondamentaux', in *La Pologne au Vᵉ Congrès International des Sciences Historiques à Bruxelles 1923* (Varsovie: Comité National Polonais du Ve Congrès d'Histoire), 73–94.

_____ (1950), *The Limits and Divisions of European History* (London and New York).

_____ (1952), *Borderlands of Western Civilization: A History of East Central Europe* (New York).

Hall, P. (2000), *Den Svenskaste Historien* (Stockholm).

Hanisch, E. (1994), *Der lange Schatten des Staates: Österreichische Gesellschaftsgeschichte im 20. Jahrhundert* (Vienna).

Hansen, M. B. (1996), '*Schindler's List* Is Not *Shoah*: The Second Commandment, Popular Modernism, and Public Memory', *Critical Inquiry* 22, no. 2: 292–312.

Haraway, D. (1995), 'Situiertes Wissen: Die Wissenschaftsfrage im Feminismus und das Privileg einer partialen Perspektive', in *Die Neuerfindung der Natur: Primaten, Cyborgs und Frauen*, (ed.) C. Hammer and I. Stieß (Frankfurt am Main and New York), 73–97.

Harding, G. (2005), 'Brussels Sprouts Museum for Europe', 24 August, http://www.spacewar.com/news/europe-05l.html.

Hargreaves, A. G. (ed.) (2005), *Memory, Empire, and Postcolonialism: Legacies of French Colonialism* (Lanham).

Harrison, N. (2003), *Postcolonial Criticism: History, Theory, and the Work of Fiction* (Cambridge).

Haslinger, P. (2005), 'Von der Erinnerung zur Identität und zurück: Zur aktuellen Debatte über die Vertreibungen in Ostmitteleuropa', in *Diktatur – Krieg – Vertreibung: Erinnerungskulturen in Tschechien, der Slowakei und Deutschland seit 1945*, (ed.) C. Cornelißen, R. Holec and J. Pešek (Essen), 473–88.

Hauge, J. C. (1988), 'Velkomsthilsen til Regjeringens Gjester', in *Manuskripter* (Oslo).

Hauptmann, G. (1974), *Sämtliche Werke: Nachgelassene Werke; Fragmente*, vol. 11 (Frankfurt am Main).

Hechter, M. (1999), *Internal Colonialism: The Celtic Fringe in British National Development* (New Brunswick and London).

Heer, H., Manoschek, W., Pollak, A. and Wodak, R. (eds.) (2003), *Wie Geschichte gemacht wird: Zur Konstruktion von Erinnerungen an Wehrmacht und Zweiten Weltkrieg* (Vienna).

Heer, H. and Naumann, K. (eds.) (1995), *Vernichtungskrieg: Verbrechen der Wehrmacht 1941– 1944* (Hamburg).

Hehlmann, W. (1965), *Wörterbuch der Psychologie*, 4th ed. (Stuttgart).

Hein, A. (1994), 'Denkmäler der sowjetischen Ära in Estland', in *Bildersturm in Osteuropa: Die Denkmäler der kommunistischen Ära im Umbruch*, (ed.) ICOMOS (Munich), 69–75.

Heller-Roazen, D. (1999), *Remnants of Auschwitz: The Witness and the Archive* (New York).

Henke, K.-D. and Woller, H. (eds.) (1991), *Politische Säuberung in Europa: Die Abrechnung mit Faschismus und Kollaboration nach dem Zweiten Weltkrieg* (Munich).

Henneberg, K. C. von (2004), 'Monuments, Public Space, and the Memory of Empire in Modern Italy', *History and Memory* 16: 37–85.

Heretz, L., Mace, J. and Procyk, O. (1986), *Famine in the Soviet Ukraine, 1932–1933: A Memorial Exhibition* (Cambridge, MA).

Hettne, B. (ed.) (1999), *Globalism and the New Regionalism* (London).

———— (2004), *Från Pax Romana till Pax Amerikana* (Stockholm).

Heumann, K. (2001), 'Hugo von Hofmannsthal: "Die Wege und die Begegnungen" sowie Reden und Aufsätze zwischen 1901 und 1907', Phil. diss. (Wuppertal).

Heyden, U. van der and Zeller, J. (eds.) (2002), *Kolonialmetropole Berlin: Eine Spurensuche* (Berlin).

Hilberg, R. (1961), *The Destruction of the European Jews* (London).

———— (1988), 'Development in the Historiography of the Holocaust', in *Comprehending the Holocaust: Historical and Literary Research*, (ed.) A. Cohen, J. Gelber and C. Wardi (Frankfurt am Main).

Hirsch, M. (1997), *Family Frames: Photography, Narrative, and Postmemory* (Cambridge, MA).

———— (2001), 'Surviving Images: Holocaust Photographs and the Work of Postmemory', in *Visual Culture and the Holocaust*, (ed.) B. Zelizer (New Brunswick), 215–46.

———— (2002), 'Nazi Photographs in Post-Holocaust Art: Gender as an Idiom of Memorialization', in *Crimes of War: Guilt and Denial in the Twentieth Century*, (ed.) O. Bartov, A. Grossmann and M. Nolan (New York), 19–40.

Hobsbawm, E. (1994), *The Age of Extremes: The Short Twentieth Century, 1914–1991* (London).

———— (1998), *On History* (London).

Hobsbawm, E. and Ranger, T. (eds.) ([1983] 1992), *The Invention of Tradition* (Cambridge).

Hockerts, H. G. (2005), 'Grenzen und Räume der Wiedergutmachung: Die Entschädigung für NS-Verfolgte in West- und Osteuropa', *Geschichte in Wissenschaft und Unterricht* 56, no. 5/6: 292–8.

Hockerts, H. G. and Kuller, C. (eds.) (2003), *Nach der Verfolgung: Wiedergutmachung nationalsozialistischen Unrechts in Deutschland?* (Göttingen).

Hollis, W. (1999), *Democratic Consolidation in Eastern Europe: The Influence of the Communist Legacy* (Boulder).

Holmes, O. W. (1980), 'The Stereoscope and the Stereograph', in *Photography, Essays and Images: Illustrated Readings in the History of Photography*, (ed.) B. Newhall (New York and Boston), 53–61.

Hölscher, L. (1989), 'Geschichte und Vergessen', *Historische Zeitschrift* 249: 1–17.

House, J. (2001), 'Antiracist Memories: The Case of 17 October 1961 in Historical Perspective', *Modern and Contemporary France* 9: 355–68.

House, J. and MacMaster, N. (2006), *Paris 1961: Algerians, State Terror and Postcolonial Memories* (Oxford).

Huener, J. (2003), *Auschwitz, Poland, and the Politics of Commemoration, 1945–1979* (Athens).

Huntington, S. (1996), *The Clash of Civilizations and the Remaking of World Order* (New York).

Huyssen, A. (1995), *Twilight Memories: Marking Time in a Culture of Amnesia* (New York and London).

Ichijo, A. and Spohn, W. (eds.) (2005), *Entangled Identities: Nations and Europe* (Aldershot).

ICOMOS (International Council on Monuments and Sites) (1994), *Bildersturm in Osteuropa: Die Denkmäler der kommunistischen Ära im Umbruch* (Munich).

Inglehart, R. (1990), *Culture Shift in Advanced Industrial Society* (Princeton).

Ireland, S. (2005), 'The Algerian War Revisited', in *Memory, Empire, and Postcolonialism: Legacies of French Colonialism*, (ed.) A. G. Hargreaves (Lanham), 203–15.

Israel, G. and Nastasi, P. (1998), *Scienza e Razza nell'Italia Fascista* (Bologna).

Ivaldi, G. (2006), 'Beyond France's 2005 Referendum on the European Constitutional Treaty: Second-Order Model, Anti-Establishment Attitudes and the End of the Alternative European Utopia', *West European Politics* 29, no. 1: 47–69.

Ivnitskii, N. A. (1995), *Golod 1932–1933 Godov* (Moscow).

_____ (1996), *Kollektivisatsiya i Raskulachivanie (Nachalo 30x Godov)* (Moscow).

Jackson, J. (1999), 'Historians and the Nation in Contemporary France', in *Writing National History: Western Europe since 1800*, (ed.) S. Berger, M. Donovan and K. Passmore (London), 239–51.

Jacobelli, J. (ed.) (1988), *Il Fascismo e gli Storici Oggi* (Roma-Bari).

Jahan, S. and Ruscio, A. (eds.) (2007), *Histoire de la colonisation: Réhabilitations, falsifications et instrumentalisations* (Paris).

Jahn, P. (2005), *Triumph und Trauma: Sowjetische und postsowjetische Erinnerungen an den Krieg 1941–1945* (Berlin).

Jarausch, K. H. (2007), 'Konfligierende Erinnerungen: Nationale Prägungen, Verständigungsversuche und europäische Geschichtsbilder', in *'Schmerzliche Erfahrungen' der Vergangenheit und der Prozess der Konstitutionalisierung Europas*, (ed.) C. Joerges, M. Mahlmann and U. K. Preuß (Wiesbaden), 15–25.

Jarausch, K. H. and Geyer, M. (2003), *Shattered Past: Reconstructing German Histories* (Princeton), 317–41.

Jarausch, K. H. and Lindenberger, T. (eds.) (2007), *Conflicted Memories: Europeanising Contemporary Histories* (New York).

Jaworski, R. (2003), 'Alte und neue Gedächtnisorte in Osteuropa nach dem Sturz des Kommunismus', in *Gedächtnisorte in Osteuropa: Vergangenheiten auf dem Prüfstand*, (ed.) R. Jaworski, J. Kusber and L. Steindorff (Frankfurt am Main), 11–25.

_____ (2004), 'Geschichtsdenken im Umbruch: Osteuropäische Vergangenheitsdiskurse im Vergleich', in *Umbruch im östlichen Europa: Die nationale Wende und das kollektive Gedächtnis*, (ed.) A. Corbea-Hoisie, R. Jaworski and M. Sommer (Innsbruck), 27–44.

Jeismann, M. (2000), 'Schuld – der Neue Gründungsmythos Europas? Die Internationale Holocaust-Konferenz von Stockholm (26.–28. Januar 2000) und eine Moral, die nach Hinten Losgeht', *Historische Anthropologie* 8: 454–58.

_____ (2001), *Auf Wiedersehen Gestern: Die Deutsche Vergangenheit und die Politik von Morgen* (Stuttgart).

_____ (2006), 'Zur Zukunft. Erinnerungsanspruch: Sandra Kalnietes Rede über Europa', *Frankfurter Allgemeine Zeitung*, 18 February, 40.

Jenkins, R. (2004), *Social Identity* (London and New York).

Joerges, C., Mahlmann, M. and Preuß, U. K. (eds.) (2007), *'Schmerzliche Erfahrungen' der Vergangenheit und der Prozess der Konstitutionalisierung Europas* (Wiesbaden).

Joerges, C. and Singh Ghaleigh, N. (eds.) (2003), *Darker Legacies of Law in Europe: The Shadow of National Socialism and Fascism over Europe and Its Legal Traditions* (Oxford).

Jönsson, C., Tägil, S. and Törnquist, G. (2000), *Organizing European Space* (London).

Judt, T. (1992), *Past Imperfect: French Intellectuals, 1944–1956* (Berkeley).

_____ (1993), 'Die Vergangenheit ist ein anderes Land: Politische Mythen im Nachkriegseuropa', *Transit* 6: 87–120.

_____ (2002), 'The Past Is Another Country: Myth and Memory in Post-War Europe', in *Memory and Power in Post-War Europe: Studies in the Presence of the Past*, (ed.) J.-W. Müller (Cambridge), 157–83.

_____ (2005), *Postwar: A History of Europe since 1945* (New York).

_____ (2006), *Geschichte Europas von 1945 bis zur Gegenwart* (Munich and Vienna).

Judt, T. and Lacorne, D. (eds.) (2004), *Language, Nation, and State: Identity Politics in a Multilingual Age* (New York).

Kaelble, H. (2007), 'A European Civil Society?' in *Conflicted Memories: Europeanising Contemporary Histories*, (ed.) K. H. Jarausch and T. Lindenberger (New York), 209–20.

Kalniete, S. (2004), 'Old Europe, New Europe', speech at the opening of the 2004 Leipzig Book Fair, 24 March, http://www.mdr.de/DL/1290734.pdf.

_____ (2005), '"Ich werde nie ein ganz freier Mensch sein": Sandra Kalniete über den GULag, das Elend ihrer Familie und die Gleichgültigkeit des Westens', *Frankfurter Allgemeinen Sonntagszeitung*, 13 November, 9.

_____ (2006a), 'Europa: Wiedervereinigung der Geschichte', speech at the annual meeting of EUSTORY, Hamburg, 16 February.

_____ (2006b), 'Verdrängter Gulag – Europas gespaltene Erinnerung', *Die Welt*, 16 February, http://www.welt.de/data/2006/02/16/846362.html.

Kämpfer, F. (1994), 'Vom Massengrab zum Heroenhügel: Akkulturationsfunktionen sowjetischer Kriegsdenkmäler', in *Der politische Totenkult: Kriegerdenkmäler in der Moderne*, (ed.) R. Koselleck, R. Jeismann and M. Jeismann (Munich), 328–49.

Kandel, E. R. and Schwartz, J. H. (2000), *Principles of Neural Science* (New York).

Kansteiner, W. (2002), 'Finding Meaning in Memory: A Methodological Critique of Memory Studies', *History and Theory* 41: 179–97.

_____ (2006), *In Pursuit of German Memory: History, Television, and Politics after Auschwitz* (Athens, OH).

Kaplan, R. (1993), *Balkan Ghosts: A Journey through History* (New York).

Karge, H. (2006), 'Dalla "memoria congelata" allo scontro del ricordo: I monumenti commemorativi della seconda guerra mondiale nella Jugoslavia di Tito', *Memoria e ricerca: Rivista di storia contemporanea* 21: 81–99.

_____ (2008), 'Im Reservat der Zeit: Kriegserinnerung und Schule im sozialistischen Jugoslawien', in *Kriegserinnerung und Kriegsverarbeitung in Südosteuropa: Zum kulturellen Umgang mit Kriegserfahrungen in Südosteuropa im 19. und 20. Jahrhundert*, (ed.) W. Höpken (Munich).

Karlsson, K.-G. (1993), 'History Teaching in Twentieth-Century Russia and the Soviet Union: Classicism and Its Alternatives', in *School and Society in Tsarist and Soviet Russia*, (ed.) B. Eklof (New York), 204–23.

_____ (1998), 'Nationalism, Ethno-National Conflicts and History in South Caucasus', in *Contrasts and Solutions in the Caucasus*, (ed.) O. Høiris and S. M. Yürükel (Aarhus), 128–39.

_____ (1999), *Historia Som Vapen: Historiebruk och Sovjetunionens Upplösning 1985–1995* (Stockholm).

_____ (2002a), 'Europe's Eastern Outpost? The Meanings of "Europe" in Baltic Discourses', in *The Meanings of Europe: Variety and Contention within and among Nations*, (ed.) M. af Malmborg and B. Stråth (Oxford and New York), 169–90.

_____ (2002b), 'History in Swedish Politics: The "Living History" Project', in *European History: Challenge for a Common Future*, (ed.) A. Pók, J. Rüsen and J. Scherrer (Hamburg), 145–62.

Karlsson, K.-G. and Zander, U. (eds.) (2003), *Echoes of the Holocaust: Historical Culture in Contemporary Europe* (Lund).

_____ (2004), *Holocaust Heritage: Inquiries into European Historical Cultures* (Malmö).

_____ (2006), *The Holocaust on Postwar Battlefields: Genocide as Historical Culture* (Malmö).

Kaschuba, W. (2007), 'Ethnische Parallelgesellschaften? Zur Kulturellen Konstruktion des Fremden in der Europäischen Migration', in *Zeitschrift für Volkskunde* 1: 65–85.

Keane, J. (1988), 'More Theses on the Philosophy of History', in *Meaning and Context: Quentin Skinner and His Critics*, (ed.) J. Tully (Cambridge), 204–17.

Kendall, W. (1969), *The Revolutionary Movement in Britain 1900–21* (London).

Kershaw, I. and Lewin, M. (eds.) (1997), *Stalinism and Nazism: Dictatorships in Comparison* (Cambridge).

Kertész, I. (2003), *Die Exilierte Sprache* (Frankfurt am Main).

Keval, S. (1999), *Die schwierige Erinnerung: Deutsche Widerstandskämpfer über die Verfolgung und Vernichtung der Juden* (Frankfurt am Main and New York).

Khlevniuk, O. V. (2004), *The History of the Gulag: From Collectivization to the Great Terror*, (foreword) R. Conquest (New Haven and London).

Klein, K. L. (2000), 'On the Emergence of Memory in Historical Discourse', *Representations Special Issue: Grounds for Remembering* 69 (Winter): 127–50.

Klein, N. M. (1997), *The History of Forgetting: Los Angeles and the Erasure of Memory* (London and New York).

Klinkhammer, L. (2003), 'Kriegserinnerung in Italien im Wechsel der Generationen', in *Erinnerungskulturen: Deutschland, Italien und Japan seit 1945*, (ed.) L. Klinkhammer, C. Cornelißen and W. Schwentker (Frankfurt am Main), 333–43.

_____ (2006a), *Stragi Naziste in Italia (1943–44)* (Rome).

_____ (2006b), 'Die "Achse" im Krieg: Protokoll einer Podiumsdiskussion zur Erinnerungskultur und Geschichtspolitik in Italien und Deutschland', *Quellen und Forschungen aus italienischen Archiven und Bibliotheken* 86: 656–95.

Kłoczowski, J. (2006), 'Oskar Halecki (1891–1973)', in *Nation and History: Polish Historians from the Enlightenment to the Second World War*, (ed.) P. Brock, J. D. Stanley and P. J. Wróbel (London), 429–42.

Kneževic, S. (1994), 'Die Denkmäler der sozialistischen Ära in Kroatien', in *Bildersturm in Osteuropa: Die Denkmäler der kommunistischen Ära im Umbruch*, (ed.) ICOMOS (Munich), 49–53.

Knigge, V. (2002), 'Von der Unselbstverständlichkeit des Guten: Gedächtnis – Bildung – Verantwortung', lecture on the fiftieth anniversary of the Max-Planck-Gymnasiums in Bielefeld, 6 July, http://www.mpg-bielefeld.de/schulinfos/knigge_rede.pdf.

Knigge, V. and Mählert, U. (2005), 'Der Kommunismus im Museum: Formen der Auseinandersetzung in Deutschland und Ostmitteleuropa', in *Das historische Museum: Labor, Schaubühne, Identitätsfabrik*, (ed.) G. Korff and M. Roth (Frankfurt am Main).

Kohl, H. (2004), *Erinnerungen 1930–1982* (Munich).

Kohser-Spohn, C. and Renken, F. (eds.) (2006), *Trauma Algerienkrieg: Zur Geschichte und Aufarbeitung eines tabuisierten Konflikts* (Frankfurt am Main).

Koljević, N. (1991), 'Istočnici srpske kulture', *Javnost*, 9 February.

Kolstö, P. (ed.) (2005), *Myths and Boundaries in South-Eastern Europe* (London).

Köppen, M. (1997), 'Von Effekten des Authentischen – *Schindlers Liste*: Film und Holocaust', in *Bilder des Holocaust. Literatur – Film – Bildende Kunst*, (ed.) M. Koppen and K. R. Scherpe (Cologne), 145–70.

Korff, G. and Roth, M. (eds.) (1990), *Das historische Museum: Labor, Schaubühnem Identitätsfabrik* (Frankfurt am Main).

Koselleck, R. (2002), *The Practice of Conceptual History: Timing History, Spacing Concepts*, (trans.) T. S. Presner (Stanford).

_____ (2003), 'Die bildliche Transformation der Gedächtnisstätten in der Neuzeit', in *La Mémoire: Actes du 35ème congrès annuel de l'AGES*, (ed.) J.-C. Margotton and M.-H. Pérennec (Lyon), 7–34.

Kostro, R. and Merta, T. (eds.) (2005), *Pamięć i odpowiedzialność* (Cracow and Wrocław).

Kovacs, E. and Seewann, G. (2006), 'Halbherzige Vergangenheitsbewältigung, konkurrenzfähige Erinnerungspolitik: Die Shoa in der ungarischen Erinnerungskultur', in *'Transformationen' der Erinnerungskulturen in Europa nach 1989*, (ed.) B. Faulenbach and F.-J. Jelich (Essen), 189–200.

Kovacs, J. M. (ed.) (1994), *Transition to Capitalism: The Communist Legacy in Eastern Europe* (New Brunswick).

Kreis, G. (1985), 'Die schweizerische Neutralität während des Zweiten Weltkrieges in der historischen Forschung', in *Les Etats neutres européens et la Seconde Guerre mondiale*, (ed.) L.-E. Roulet (Neurenburg), 29–53.

_____ (2000), *Die Rückkehr des J-Stempels: Zur Geschichte einer Schwierigen Vergangenheitsbewältigung* (Zurich).

_____ (2002a), 'Zurück in den Zweiten Weltkrieg: Zur schweizerischen Zeitgeschichte der 80er Jahre', *Schweizerische Zeitschrift für Geschichte* 52: 60–68.

_____ (2002b), 'Zur Bedeutung der 1990er Jahre für den Ausbau der schweizerischen Zeitgeschichte', *Schweizerische Zeitschrift für Geschichte* 52: 494–517.

Kristeva, J. (1982), *Powers of Horror: An Essay on Abjection* (New York).

Kroh, J. (2005), 'Holocaust Transnational: Zur Institutionalisierung des Holocaust-Gedenkens', *Blätter für Deutsche und Internationale Politik* 50: 741–50.

Kundera, M. (1983), 'Un Occident kidnappé ou la tragédie de l'Europe centrale', *Le Débat*, 27 November, 2–24.

Kurilo, O. (ed.) (2006), *Der Zweite Weltkrieg im Deutschen und Russischen Gedächtnis* (Berlin).

Kuroń, J. and Modzelewski, K. (2001), 'Cena Reprywatyzacji', *Gazeta Wyborcza* 27 January, 13.

Kurtović, M. (1990), 'Gađali su srpsku zastavu', *Javnost*, 22 December.

Kushner, T. (1994), *The Holocaust and the Liberal Imagination: A Social and Cultural History* (Oxford).

Kvenangen, P. G. (2002), 'Kväner och Rättigheter i Karesuando-området', *Samefolket*: 5.

Kverndokk, K. (2000), '"De Kjempet de Fallt de Gav Oss Alt" – om den Rituelle Bruken av Norske Krigsminnesmerker', Hovedoppgave (MA thesis), University of Oslo.

Kvist, W. (1999), 'Kväner. "En Glömd Minoritet Stiger Fram"', *Met-aviisi*: 4.

Lagrou, P. (1997), 'Victims of Genocide and National Memory: Belgium, France and the Netherlands 1945–65', *Past and Present* 154: 181–222.

_____ (2000), *The Legacy of Nazi Occupation: Patriot Memory and National Recovery in Western Europe, 1945–1965*. Studies in the Social and Cultural History of Modern Warfare (Cambridge).

Laignel-Lavastine, A. (2004), 'Fascism and Communism in Romania: The Comparative Stakes and Uses', in *Stalinism and Nazism: History and Memory Compared*, (ed.) H. Rousso (Lincoln and London), 157–93.

Langer, L. L. (1995), *Admitting the Holocaust* (New York).

Lantto, P. (2000), *Tiden Börjar På Nytt: En Analys av Samernas Etnopolitiska Mobilisering i Sverige 1900–1950* (avh.) (Umeå).

_____ (2003), *Att Göra Sin Stämma Hörd: Svenska Samernas Riksförbund, Samerörelsen och Svensk Samepolitik 1950–1962* (Umeå).

Lanzmann, C. (1994), 'Holocauste, la representation impossible', *Le Monde*, 3 March.

Lavabre, M.-C. (1994), *Le fil rouge: Sociologie de la mémoire communiste* (Paris).

Lazar, M. (2005), *Le communisme: Une passion française* (Paris).

Lazarevska, A. (1993), *Sarajevski pasijans* (Sarajevo).

Le Goff, J. (1988), *Histoire et mémoire* (Paris).

Leconte, D. (1980), *Les pieds-noirs: Histoire et portrait d'une communauté* (Paris).

Lefeuvre, D. (2006), *Pour en finir avec la repentance coloniale* (Paris).

Leggewie, C. (2007), 'Equally Criminal? Totalitarian Experience and European Memory', *Tr@nsit online*, http://iwm.at/index.php?option=com_content&task=view&id=580&Itemid=584.

Leinemann, J. (2006), 'Ein glückliches Volk: Deutschland, ein Sommermärchen – die Fußball-WM wird zur nationale Love Parade', *Der Spiegel*, reprinted in *Spiegel Jahreschronik 1*, 126–30, http://www.spiegel.de/jahreschronik/0,1518,452551,00.html.

Leitz, C. (2000), *Nazi Germany and Neutral Europe during the Second World War* (Manchester).

Leo, A. (1992), 'Antifaschismus und Kalter Krieg: Eine Geschichte von Einengung, Verdrängung und Erstarrung', in *Brandenburgische Gedenkstätten für die Verfolgten des NS-Regimes: Perspektiven, Kontroversen und Internationale Vergleiche*, Ministerium für Wissenschaft, Forschung und Kultur des Landes Brandenburg (Berlin), 74-80.

LeSueur, J. D. (2001), *Uncivil War, Intellectuals and Identity: Politics during the Decolonisation of Algeria* (Philadelphia).

Levi, P. ([1986] 1993), *Die Untergegangenen und die Geretteten* (Munich).

Levy, D. and Sznaider, N. (2001), *Erinnerung im Globalen Zeitalter: Der Holocaust* (Frankfurt am Main).

——— (2006), *The Holocaust and Memory in the Global Age* (Philadelphia).

Lévy, E. (2002), *Les maîtres censeurs: Pour en finir avec la pensée unique* (Paris).

Levy-Bruhl, L. (1965), *The 'Soul' of the Primitive* (London).

Liauzu, C. (2005), 'Les historiens saisis par les guerres de mémoires coloniales', *Revue d'histoire moderne et contemporaine* 54: 99–109.

Liauzu, C. and Manceron, G. (2006), *La colonisation, la loi et l'histoire* (Paris).

Liljefors, M. (2002), *Bilder av Förintelsen: Mening. Minne. Kompromettering* (Lund).

Lillteicher, J. (2006), 'West Germany and Compensation for National Socialist Expropriation: The Restitution of Jewish Property, 1947–1964', in *Coping with the Nazi Past: West German Debates on Nazism and Generational Conflict, 1955–1975*, (ed.) P. Gassert and A. E. Steinweis (Oxford), 79–95.

Linenthal, E. (1995), *Preserving Memory: The Struggle to Create America's Holocaust Museum* (New York).

Loker, Z. (1993), 'Documentation: The Testimony of Dr. Edo Neufeld. The Italians and the Jews of Croatia', *Holocaust and Genocide Studies* 7, no. 1: 67–76.

Loomba, A. (2006), *Kolonialism/Postkolonialism: En Introduktion Till Ett Forskningsfält* (Stockholm).

Lotman, Y. (1992), *Kultura i Vzryv* (Moscow).

Loupan, V. and Lorrain, P. (1994), *L'argent de Moscou: L'histoire la plus secrète du PCF* (Paris).

Loy, R. (1997), *La Parola Ebreo* (Torino).

Lübbe, H. (2001), *'Ich entschuldige mich': Das neue politische Bußritual* (Berlin).

Lüdtke, A. (1993), 'Coming to Terms with the Past: Illusions of Remembering, Ways of Forgetting Nazism in West Germany', *Journal of Modern History* 65: 542–72.

Lundmark, L. (1999), 'Kvänerna Är Ingen Urbefolkning', *Samefolket*: 10.

——— (2001), 'Risk För Etniskt Krig?' *Om: Ordfront Magasin* 7/8.

——— (2005), *Om Kväner, Birkarlar och ILO*. Unpublished manuscript, written on behalf of the Investigation about Hunting and Fishing Rights.

Luthar, O. and Luthar, B. (2006), 'Historische Darstellung oder/als Vergangenheitspolitik? Zur Entstehung einer radikalen Umdeutung der Kriegs- und Nachkriegsgeschichte Sloweniens', *Zeitgeschichte* 33, no. 3: 135–46.

Lyotard, J.-F. (1986), *Das postmoderne Wissen: Ein Bericht* (Vienna).

Macdonald, S. (ed.) (2000), *Approaches to European Historical Consciousness: Reflections and Provocations* (Hamburg).

MacKenzie, J. M. (ed.) (1986), *Imperialism and Popular Culture* (Manchester).

MacMaster, N. (1997), *Colonial Migrants and Racism: Algerians in France 1900–62* (New York).

_____ (2002), 'The Torture Controversy (1998–2002): Towards a "New History" of the Algerian War?', *Modern and Contemporary France* 10: 449–59.

Maffesoli, M. (1996), *The Time of the Tribes: The Decline of Individualism in Mass Society* (London).

Maier, C. S. (1993), 'A Surfeit of Memory? Reflections on History, Melancholy and Denial', *History and Memory* 5, no. 2: 136–52.

_____ (2002), 'Hot Memory … Cold Memory: On the Political Half-Life of Fascist and Communist Memory', *Tr@nsit online*, http://www.iwm.at/index.php?option=com_content&task=view&id=316&Itemid=481.

Main, I. (2008), 'How Communism is Displayed? Exhibitions and Museums of Communism in Poland', in *Past for the Eyes: Cinema and Museums in Representing Communism in Eastern Europe after 1989*, (ed.) O. Sarkisova and P. Apor (Budapest), 369–98.

Majerus, B. (n.d.), 'Besetzte Vergangenheiten: Erinnerungskulturen des Zweiten Weltkriegs in Luxemburg – eine historiographische Baustelle', unpublished paper.

Malia, M. (1999), 'Foreword: The Uses of Atrocity', in *The Black Book of Communism: Crimes, Terror, Repression*, (ed.) S. Courtois et al. (Cambridge, MA, and London), ix–xvi.

Malmborg, M. af and Stråth, B. (2002), 'Introduction: The National Meanings of Europe', in *The Meanings of Europe: Variety and Contention within and among Nations*, (ed.) M. af Malmborg and B. Stråth (Oxford and New York), 1–25.

Manceron, G. (2003), *Marianne et les colonies: Une introduction à l'histoire coloniale de la France* (Paris).

Manceron, G. and Remaoun, H. (1993), *D'une rive à l'autre: La guerre d'Algérie de la mémoire à l'Histoire* (Paris).

Mandler, P. (2002), *History and National Life* (London).

Mangos, S. (2007), *A Monumental Mockery: The Construction of the National Holocaust Memorial in Berlin* (Berlin).

Manoschek, W. (2002), 'Vernichtungskrieg. Verbrechen der Wehrmacht 1941 bis 1944: Innenansichten einer Ausstellung', *Zeitgeschichte* 29: 64–75.

Mantelli, B. (2000), 'Die Italiener auf dem Balkan 1941–1943', in *Europäische Sozialgeschichte: Festschrift für Wolfgang Schieder*, (ed.) C. Dipper, L. Klinkhammer and A. Nützenadel (Berlin), 57–74.

_____ (2004), 'Gli Italiani in Jugoslavia 1941–1943: Occupazione Militare, Politiche Persecutorie, Crimini di Guerra', *Storia e Memoria* 1: 23–37.

March, L. (2002), *The Communist Party in Post-Soviet Russia* (Manchester and New York).

Marchal, G. P. (2006), *Schweizer Gebrauchsgeschichte: Geschichtsbilder, Mythenbildung und Nationale Identität* (Basel).

Marchart, O. (2005), 'Das historisch-politische Gedächtnis: Für eine politische Theorie kollektiver Erinnerung', in *Transformationen gesellschaftlicher Erinnerung: Studien zur "Gedächtnisgeschichte" der Zweiten Republik*, (ed.) C. Gerbel et al. (Vienna), 21–49.

Margalit, A. (2002), *The Ethics of Memory* (Cambridge, MA).

Mark, J. (2008), 'Containing Fascism: History in Post-Communist Baltic Occupation and Genocide Museums', in *Past for the Eyes: Cinema and Museums in Representing Communism in Eastern Europe after 1989*, (ed.) O. Sarkisova and P. Apor (Budapest), 333–67.

Mauss, M. (1997). 'Gift, Gift', in *The Logic of the Gift: Toward an Ethic of Generosity*, (ed.) A. D. Schrift (London), 28–32.

Mazower, M. (1998), *Dark Continent: Europe's Twentieth Century* (London).

McDougall, J. (2007), 'Sarkozy and Africa: Big White Chief's Bad Memory', *openDemocracy*, 7 December, http://www.opendemocracy.net/article/democracy_power/africa/sarkozy_africa.

Medvedev, R. (2000), *Zagadka Putina* (Moscow).

Meier, C. (2007), 'Gedenkrede auf Reinhart Koselleck', in *Reinhart Koselleck 1923–2006: Reden zur Gedenkfeier am 24. Mai 2006. Bielefelder Universitätsgespräche und Vorträge 9* (Bielefeld).

Merridale, C. (1996), 'Death and Memory in Modern Russia', *History Workshop Journal* 42, no. 1: 1–18.
_____ (2005), *Ivan's War: The Red Army 1939–1945* (London).
Meyer, T. (2005), *Die Ironie Gottes: Religiotainment, Resakralisierung und die Liberale Demokratie* (Wiesbaden).
Michnik, A. (1999), 'Kłamstwo w Cieniu Shoah', *Gazeta Wyborcza*, 3 August, 1.
_____ (2001), 'Poles and the Jews: How Deep the Guilt?' *New York Times*, 17 March.
Milcakov, J. (2006), 'Poetik und Politik (Geschichte und Literatur zwischen "Sozrealismus" und "Realsozialismus")', in *Geschichte (ge-)brauchen. Literatur und Geschichtskultur im Staatssozialismus: Jugoslavien und Bulgarien*, (ed.) A. Richter and B. Beyer (Berlin), 19–32.
Miles, W. F. S. (2005), 'Third World Views of the Holocaust', *Journal of Genocide Research* 6, no. 3: 371–93.
Milosavljević, O. (2002), *U tradiciji nacionalizma* (Belgrade).
Milward, A. (2000), *The European Rescue of the Nation-State*, 2nd ed. (London).
Minsky, M. L. (1988), *The Society of Mind* (New York).
Mirzoeff, N. (1999), *An Introduction to Visual Culture* (London).
Mischi, J. (2006), 'La révolution au nom de la tradition: Mise en scène historique de l'implantation communiste dans l'Allier', in *Concurrence des passés: Usages politiques du passé dans la France contemporaine*, (ed.) M. Crivello et al. (Aix-en-Provence), 119–129.
Moeller, R. G. (1996), 'War Stories: The Search for a Usable Past in the Federal Republic of Germany', *American Historical Review* 101, no. 3: 1008–48.
_____ (2000), 'Geschichten aus der "Stacheldrahtuniversität": Kriegsgefangene im Opferdiskurs der Bundesrepublik', *Werkstatt Geschichte* 26: 23–46.
Moore, N. and Whelan, Y. (eds.) (2007), *Heritage, Memory and the Politics of Identity: New Perspectives on the Cultural Landscape* (Aldershot).
Morawiec, M. (2006), 'Oskar Halecki (1891–1973)', in *Europa-Historiker: Ein Biographisches Handbuch*, (ed.) H. Duchhardt et al. (Göttingen), 215–39.
Moretti, M. (2005), 'Chi Ha Paura del Museo della Shoà?' *Shalom*, 26 March.
Morgan, K. (2001), 'Parts of People and Communist Lives', in *Party People, Communist Lives: Explorations in Biography*, (ed.) J. McIlroy, K. Morgan and A. Campbell (London), 9–28.
Morin, E. (1987), *Penser l'Europe* (Paris).
Mosse, G. L. (1975), *The Nationalization of the Masses: Political Symbolism and Mass Movements in Germany from the Napoleonic Wars through the Third Reich* (New York).
Müller, J.-W. (2000), *Another Country: German Intellectuals, Unification and National Identity* (New Haven).
_____ (2002a), 'Introduction: The Power of Memory, the Memory of Power and the Power over Memory', in *Memory and Power in Post-War Europe*, (ed.) J.-W. Müller (Cambridge), 1–35.
_____ (ed.) (2002b), *Memory and Power in Post-War Europe: Studies in the Presence of the Past* (Cambridge).
_____ (2007a), *Constitutional Patriotism* (Princeton).
_____ (2007b), 'Europäische Erinnerungspolitik Revisited', *Tr@nsit online*, http://iwm.at/index.php?option=com_content&task=view&id=574&Itemid=590.
Musabegović, S. (2008), *Rat-konstitucija totalitarnog tijela* (Sarajevo).
Nabulsi, K. and Stråth, B. (2001), 'Europe: A View from Within and from the Outside', in *Ett Udvidgat EU*, (ed.) H.-Å. Persson (Lund), 61–75.
Nattermann, R. (Forthcoming), 'Humanitäres Prinzip oder politisches Kalkül? Luca Pietromarchi und die italienische Politik gegenüber den Juden im besetzten Kroatien', in *Die 'Achse' im Krieg: Politik, Ideologie und Kriegführung 1939–1945*, (ed.) L. Klinkhammer, A. Osti-Guerrazzi and T. Schlemmer.
Neil, L. (1999), *Architecture and Revolution: Contemporary Perspectives on Central and Eastern Europe* (London and New York).
Neiman, S. (2002), *Evil in Modern Thought: An Alternative History of Philosophy* (Princeton).

Newhall, B. (1986), *The History of Photography from 1839 to the Present* (New York).

Nidam-Orvieto, I. (2005), 'The Impact of Anti-Jewish Legislation on Everyday Life and the Response of Italian Jews, 1938–1943', in *Jews in Italy under Fascist and Nazi Rule*, (ed.) J. D. Zimmerman (New York), 158–81.

Niethammer, L. (1992), 'Orte des kollektiven Gedächtnisses', in *Brandenburgische Gedenkstätten für die Verfolgten des NS-Regimes: Perspektiven, Kontroversen und internationale Vergleiche*, Ministerium für Wissenschaft, Forschung und Kultur des Landes Brandenburg (Berlin), 95–104.

_____ (2000), *Kollektive Identität: Heimliche Quellen einer Unheimlichen Konjunktur* (Reinbek).

Nietzsche, F. (1980), *On the Advantage and Disadvantage of History for Life*, (trans.) P. Preuss (Indianapolis).

Niven, B. (2002), *Facing the Nazi Past: United Germany and the Legacy of the Third Reich* (London).

Nora, P. 1961. *Les français d'Algérie* (Paris).

_____ (ed.) (1984–92), *Les Lieux de mémoire* (Paris).

_____ (1989), 'Between Memory and History: Les Lieux de Mémoire', *Representations* 26, Special Issue: *Memory and Counter-Memory* (Spring): 7–24.

_____ (1990), *Zwischen Geschichte und Gedächtnis* (Berlin).

_____ (1996), 'General Introduction: Between Memory and History', in *Realms of Memory: The Construction of the French Past*, Vol. I: *Conflicts and Divisions*, (ed.) L. D. Kritzman (New York), 1–20.

_____ (2001), 'Mellan Minne och Historia', in *Nationens Röst – Texter om Nationalismens Teori och Praktik*, (ed.) S. Sörlin (Stockholm), 363–389.

Novick, P. (1999), *The Holocaust in American Life* (Boston and New York).

Nützendadel, A. and Schieder, W. (eds.) (2004), *Zeitgeschichte als Problem: Nationale Traditionen und Perspektiven der Forschung in Europa* (Göttingen), 7–24.

Ó Drisceoil, D. (2006), 'Neither Friend nor Foe? Irish Neutrality in the Second World War', *Contemporary European History* 15, no. 2: 245–53.

Olecki, K. (2004), 'Żydzi Wracają po Swoje', *Newsweek Polska* 14: 14–21.

Olick, J. K. (1999), 'Collective Memory: The Two Cultures', *Sociological Theory* 17: 333–48.

Olsen, E. H. (1995), 'Store Øjeblikke i Maj: 50-Året for befrielsen Blev Fejret Eftertrykkeligt Over Hele Landet', *FV-Frihedskampens Veteraner* 142: 7–13.

Onken, E.-C. (2007), 'The Baltic States and Moscow's 9 May Commemoration: Analysing Memory Politics in Europe', *Europe-Asia Studies* 59, no. 1: 23–46.

Orwell, G. (1966), 'Looking Back on the Spanish Civil War (1943)', in *Homage to Catalonia* (Harmondsworth), 225–47.

Oscherwitz, D. (2005), 'Decolonizing the Past: Re-visions of History and Memory and the Evolution of the (Post)colonial Heritage', in *Memory, Empire, and Postcolonialism: Legacies of French Colonialism*, (ed.) A. G. Hargreaves (Lanham), 189–202.

Osti Guerrazzi, A. (2005), *Caino a Roma: I Complici Romani della Shoah* (Rome).

Özdemir, C. (2001), 'Langer Gang am Bosporus: Was gegen eine Armenien-Resolution Spricht', *Frankfurter Allgemeine Zeitung*, 5 April.

Packard, J. M. (1992), *Neither Friend nor Foe: The European Neutrals in World War II* (London).

Paczkowski, A. (2004), 'Nazism and Communism in Polish Experience and Memory', in *Stalinism and Nazism: History and Memory Compared*, (ed.) H. Rousso (Lincoln), 242–61.

Pakier, M. (2007), 'Agnieszka Holland's *Europa, Europa* as a Critical Voice in the Polish Debate on the Second World War', in *Collective Traumas: Memories of War and Conflict in 20th Century Europe*, (ed.) C. Mithander, J. Sundholm and M. H. Troy (Brussels), 143–77.

Panteleiev, M. (1994–5), 'La terreur stalinienne au Komintern en 1937–1938: Les chiffres et les causes', *Communisme* 40–1: 37–53.

Passerini, L. (2003), 'Memories between Silence and Oblivion', in *Contested Pasts: The Politics of Memory*, (ed.) K. Hodgkin and S. Radstone (London and New York), 238–54.

_____ (ed.) (2005), *Memory and Totalitarianism* (New Brunswick and London).

Patriarca, S. (2001), 'Italian Neopatriotism: Debating National Identity in the 1990s', *Modern Italy* 6, no. 1: 21–34.

Paxson, M. (2005), *Solovyovo: The Story of Memory in a Russian Village* (Bloomington).

Pedersen, I. K. (1985), 'Lørdag er en Festdag', *Politiken*, 3 May.

Pedersen, S. (2006), *Lappekodisillen i Nord 1751–1859* (Tromsö).

Pendas, D. O. (2006), *The Frankfurt Auschwitz Trial, 1963–1975: Genocide, History and the Limits of the Law* (Cambridge).

Penrose, R. (1997), *The Large, the Small and the Human Mind* (Cambridge).

Perel, S. (1992), *Europa, Europa* (Warsaw).

_____ (1993), *Ich war Hitlerjunge Salomon* (Munich).

Peter, R. (1950), *Dresden: Eine Kamera klagt an.* (Dresden).

Petrie, J. (2000), 'The Secular Word HOLOCAUST: Scholarly Myths, History, and 20th Century Meanings', *Journal of Genocide Research* 2, no. 1: 31–63.

Phillips, K. R. (ed.) (2004), *Framing Public Memory* (Tuscaloosa).

Picciotto Fargion, L. (1991), *Il Libro della Memoria: Gli Ebrei Deportati dall'Italia 1943–1945* (Milan).

Pijpers, A. (2006), 'Now We Should All Acknowledge Our Holocaust Guilt', *Europe's World* (Autumn): 124–7.

Pingel, F. (2000), *The European Home: Representations of 20th Century Europe in History Textbooks* (Strasbourg).

Plato (1987), *Theaetetus*, (trans.) R. A. H. Waterfield (Harmondsworth).

Poliakov, L. and Sabille, J. (1956), *Gli Ebrei sotto l'Occupazione Italiana* (Milan).

Politkovskaya, A. (2004), *Putin's Russia: Life in a Failing Democracy*, (trans.) A. Tait (London).

_____ (2007), *A Russian Diary*, (trans.) A. Tait (New York).

Pollak, A. (2003), 'Vergangenheit und Reflexion: Konsens- und Streitlinien im Umgang mit der NS-Vergangenheit in Österreich', in *Zeitgeschichte als Streitgeschichte. Grosse Kontroversen seit 1945*, (ed.) M. Sabrow, R. Jessen and K. G. Kracht (Munich), 326–46.

Popović, J. (2003), 'Humanistička i bogočovečanska kultura i Svetosavska filosofija kulture', in *Srpska konzervativna misao*, (ed.) M. Đorđević (Belgrade), 49–56.

Popović, M. (1977), *Vidovdan i časni Krst: Ogled iz književne arheologije* (Belgrade).

Portelli, A. (1999), 'Le Fosse Ardeatine e la Memoria: Rapporto su un Lavoro in Corso', in *Le Memorie della Repubblica*, (ed.) L. Paggi (Firenze), 89–154.

_____ (2001), *L'Ordine È Già Stato Eseguito* (Rome).

_____ (2003), *The Order Has Been Carried Out: History, Memory, and Meaning of a Nazi Massacre in Rome* (New York).

Pradarelli, M. (2006), 'Legge Calpestata, la Shoah a Roma', *l'Espresso*, 25 October.

Presser, J. (1965), *Ondergang: De vervolging en verdelging van het Nederlandse jodendom 1940–1945* ('s Gravenhage).

Price, M. E. (2002), 'Memory, the Media and NATO: Information Intervention in Bosnia-Hercegovina', in *Memory and Power in Post-War Europe: Studies in the Presence of the Past*, (ed.) J.-W. Mueller (Cambridge), 137–54.

Probst, L. (2002), 'Europäisierung des Holocaust – eine neue Zivilreligion für Europa?' *Kommune: Forum für Politik, Ökonomie, Kultur* 20, no. 7: 42–5.

Prodi, R. (2004), 'A Union of Minorities', Seminar on Europe – Against Anti-Semitism, for a Union of Diversity, Brussels, 19 February.

Quack, S. (2007), 'Divided History – Common Memory? A Question of the Culture of Memory in the European Union', lecture at the European Union Studies Center, CUNY, New York, 28 February, http://web.gc.cuny.edu/Eusc/activities/paper/Quack07.htm.

Quemeneur, T. (2001), 'La mémoire mise à la question: Le débat sur les tortures dans la guerre d'Algérie, Juin 2000–Septembre 2001', *Regards sur l'actualité* 276: 29–41.

Raben, R. (2002), 'Koloniale Vergangenheit und Postkoloniale Moral in den Niederlanden', in *Verbrechen Erinnern: Die Auseinandersetzung mit Holocaust und Völkermord*, (ed.) V. Knigge and N. Frei (Munich), 90–110.

Radnóti, S. (2001), 'Az Üvegalmárium: Esettanulmány a Magyar Korona Helyéről', *Beszélő* 6: 36–68.

Radosh, R., Habeck, M. R. and Sevostianov, G. (eds.) (2001), *Spain Betrayed: The Soviet Union in the Spanish Civil War* (New Haven and London).

Radstone, S. (2000), 'Working with Memory: An Introduction', in *Memory and Methodology*, (ed.) S. Radstone (Oxford), 1–22.

Rawls, J. (1993), *Political Liberalism* (New York).

_____ (1999), *The Law of Peoples; with "The Idea of Public Reason Revisited"* (Cambridge, MA).

Raybaud, A. (1997), 'Deuil sans travail, travail sans deuil: La France a-t-elle une mémoire coloniale?' *Dédale* 5–6: 87–104.

Reed, J. (2001), 'Poland's President Seeks to Lay His Country's War Guilt to Rest: Sixty Years after a Massacre of Hundreds of Jews by Their Catholic Neighbours, an Official Apology Will Be Made', *Financial Times*, 7 July.

Rees, E. A. (1998), 'Stalin and Russian Nationalism', in *Russian Nationalism, Past and Present*, (ed.) G. Hosking and R. Service (Basingstoke), 77–106.

Renan, E. ([1882] 1994), 'Qu'est-ce qu'une nation?' in *Nationalism*, (ed.) J. Hutchinson and A. D. Smith (Oxford and New York), 17–18.

Renken, F. (2006), *Frankreich im Schatten des Algerienkrieges: Die Fünfte Republik und die Erinnerung an den Letzten Großen Kolonialkonflikt* (Göttingen).

Rév, I. (2005), *Retroactive Justice: Prehistory of Post Communism* (Stanford).

Rey, D. (2003), 'Erinnern und Vergessen im postdiktatorischen Spanien', in *Zeitgeschichte als Streitgeschichte: Grosse Kontroversen seit 1945*, (ed.) M. Sabrow, R. Jessen and K. G. Kracht (Munich), 347–69.

Ricoeur, P. (2004), *Memory, History, Forgetting* (Chicago and London).

Rioux, J.-P. (1993), 'Les français et la mémoire de l'Algérie', in *L'Algérie des français*, (ed.) C.-R. Ageron (Paris), 15–19.

Ristović, M. (2002), 'Kolaboracija u Srbiji u II Svetskom Ratu: Istoriografski i (ili) Politički Problem', in *Religija, Društvo i Politika: Kontroverzna Tumačenja i Približavanja*, (ed.) T. Bremer (Bonn), 10–25.

Rochlitz, I. (Forthcoming), *Accident of Fate: A Personal Account, 1938–1945*.

Rodell, M. (2005), 'Monuments and the Places of Memory', in *Memory Work: The Theory and Practice of Memory*, (ed.) A. Kitzmann, C. Mithander and J. Sundholm (Frankfurt am Main), 105–29.

Rodogno, D. (2003), *Il Nuovo Ordine Mediterraneo: Le Politiche di Occupazione dell'Italia Fascista in Europa (1940–1943)* (Torino).

Rosenburg, T. (1996), *The Haunted Land: Facing Europe's Ghosts after Communism* (New York).

Rosenfeld, G. D. (1999), 'The Controversy That Isn't: The Debate over Daniel J. Goldhagen's *Hitler's Willing Executioners* in Comparative Perspective', *Contemporary European History* 8: 249–73.

Rosenzweig, R. and Thelen, D. (1998), *The Presence of the Past: Popular Uses of History in American Life* (New York).

Rotfeld, A. (2007), 'Do Głowy mi nie Przyszło Żądać Odszkodowania', *Gazeta Wyborcza*, no. 52, 2 March, 2.

Rother, B. (2001), *Spanien und der Holocaust* (Tübingen).

Rousso, H. (2001), *Vichy: L'Evénement, la mémoire, l'histoire* (Paris).

_____ (2004a), 'Introduction', in *Stalinism and Nazism: History and Memory Compared*, (ed.) H. Rousso and R. J. Golsan, (trans.) L B. Golsan, T. C. Hilde and P. S. Rogers (Lincoln), 1–22.

_____ (ed.) (2004b), *Stalinism and Nazism: History and Memory Compared*, (ed.) R. J. Golsan, (trans.) L B. Golsan, T. C. Hilde and P. S. Rogers (Lincoln).

_____ (2007), *Le régime de Vichy* (Paris).

Rüsen, J. (1997), 'The Logic of Historizisation: Metahistorical Reflections on the Debate between Friedländer and Broszat', *History and Memory* 9, no. 1–2: 113–44.

_____ (2001), 'Holocaust Memory and Identity Building: Metahistorical Considerations in the Case of (West) Germany', in *Disturbing Remains: Memory, History, and Crisis in the Twentieth Century*, (ed.) M. Roth and C. Salas (Los Angeles), 252–70.

_____ (2004), 'Interpreting the Holocaust: Some Theoretical Issues', in *Holocaust Heritage: Inquiries into European Historical Cultures*, (ed.) K.-G. Karlsson and U. Zander (Malmö), 35–62.

Rystad, G. (1982), *Prisoners of the Past? The Munich Syndrome and Makers of American Foreign Policy in the Cold War Era* (Lund).

Ryymin, T. (2003), *'De Nordligste Finner', Fremstillingen av Kvenena i den Finske Litterære Offetligheten 1800–1939* (Tromsö).

_____ (2004), 'Histori, Fortidsforestilling og Kvensk Identitetsbygging', in *Fortidsforestillingar: Bruk og Misbruk an Nordnorsk Historie. Rapport fra det 27. Nordnorske Historieseminar, Hamarøy september 2002*, (ed.) Einar Niemi (Tromsö).

Sabrow, M. (2000), *Geschichte als Herrschaftsdiskurs: Der Umgang mit der Vergangenheit in der DDR* (Cologne).

Said, E. S. (1997), *Orientalism* (Stockholm).

Sakwa, R. (2004), *Putin: Russia's Choice* (London and New York).

Samuel, R. (1994), *Theatres of Memory*, Vol. 1: *Past and Present in Contemporary Culture* (London).

Sandberg, L. (1995), 'Himmelstrebende Frihetsmonument', *Aftenposten*, 8 May.

Sanders, P. (2005), *The British Channel Islands under German Occupation, 1940–1945* (Jersey).

Sarfatti, M. (1994), *Mussolini contro gli Ebrei: Cronaca dell'Elaborazione delle Leggi del 1938* (Torino).

_____ (2000), *Gli Ebrei nell'Italia Fascista: Vicende, Identità, Persecuzione* (Torino).

_____ (2006), *The Jews in Mussolini's Italy: From Equality to Persecution* (London).

Sassatelli, M. (2002), 'Imagined Europe: The Shaping of a European Cultural Identity through EU Cultural Policy' *European Journal of Social Theory* 5: 435–51.

Sauter, M. (2002), 'Memories in Conflict – Conflicting Memories: Reconciling Conflicting Cultural Memories', International Colloquium of Philosophy and the Social Sciences, Institute of Philosophy, Academy of Sciences of the Czech Republic, Prague, 10–14 May.

Schalk, D. L. (1999), 'Has France's Marrying Her Century Cured the Algerian Syndrome?' *Historical Reflections* 25: 149–64.

_____ (2002), 'Of Memories and Monuments: Paris and Algeria. Fréjus and Indochina', *Historical Reflections* 28: 241–53.

Schieder, T. (1978), 'The Role of Historical Consciousness in Political Action' *History and Theory* 17, no. 4: 1–18.

Schivelbusch, W. (2001), *The Culture of Defeat: On National Trauma, Mourning, and Recovery* (New York).

Schmale, W. (1997), *Scheitert Europa an seinem Mythendefizit?* (Bochum).

Schorske, C. (1981), *Fin-de-siècle Vienna: Politics and Culture* (New York).

Schudson, M. (1992), *Watergate in American Memory: How We Remember, Forget, and Reconstruct the Past* (New York).

Schwarz, B. (1982), '"The People" in History: The Communist Party Historians' Group, 1945–56', in *Making Histories: Studies in History-Writing and Politics*, (ed.) R. Johnson, G. McLennan, B. Schwarz and D. Sutton (Minneapolis), 44–95.

Shelah, M. (1991), *Un debito di gratitudine: Storia dei rapporti tra l'esercito italiano e gli ebrei in Dalmazia (1941–1943)* (Rome).

Shepard, T. (2006), *The Invention of Decolonization: The Algerian War and the Remaking of France* (London).

Shermer, M. and Grobman, A. (2000), *Denying History: Who Says the Holocaust Never Happened and Why Do They Say It?* (Berkeley).

Shore, C. (2000), *Building Europe: The Cultural Policies of European Integration* (London).

Simmel, G. (1983), 'Soziologie des Raumes', in *Schriften zur Soziologie* (Frankfurt am Main), 221–41.

Skjalg, F. (1995), 'Dronningen hedret kvinnene', *Aftenposten*, 8 May.

Skoutelsky, R. (2000), 'Militants et militaires: Les volontaires des Brigades internationales', in *Militantisme et militants*, (ed.) J. Gotovitch and A. Morelli (Brussels), 41–53.

Slater, J. (1994), *Teaching History in the New Europe* (London).

Smith, A. D. (1981), *The Ethnic Revival* (Cambridge).

_____ (1986), *The Ethnic Origins of Nations* (Oxford).

Snyder, T. (2002), 'Memory of Sovereignty and Sovereignty over Memory: Poland, Lithuania, and Ukraine, 1939–1999', in *Memory and Power in Post-War Europe: Studies in the Presence of the Past*, (ed.) J.-W. Müller (Cambridge), 39–58.

Soar, D. (2007), 'Bile, Blood, Bilge, Mulch', *London Review of Books*, 4 January.

Sohn, O. (2000), *Fra Folketinget Til Celle 290: Arne Munch-Petersens Skæbne* (Copenhagen).

Sontag, S. (2001), *On Photography* (New York).

Sørensen, N. A. (2005), 'Narrating the Second World War in Denmark since 1945', *Contemporary European History* 14, no. 3: 295–315.

Southgate, B. (2005), *What is History For?* (London and New York).

Spartaco, C. (2004), *I Campi del Duce: L'internamento Civile nell'Italia Fascista (1940–1943)* (Torino).

Speth, R. (1999), 'Europäische Geschichtsbilder heute', in *Umkämpfte Vergangenheit: Geschichtsbilder, Erinnerung und Vergangenheitspolitik im internationalen Vergleich*, (ed.) P. Bock and E. Wolfrum (Göttingen), 159–75.

Spiegelman, A. (1986), *Maus: A Survivor's Tale* (New York).

Steiner, G. (1961), *The Death of Tragedy* (New York).

Steinlauf, M. C. (1997), *Bondage to the Dead: Poland and the Memory of the Holocaust* (Syracuse).

Stephan, F. (2002), *Die Europavorstellungen im deutschen und im französischen Widerstand gegen den Nationalsozialismus 1933/40 bis 1945*, PhD diss., Universität Stuttgart, http://elib.uni-stuttgart.de/opus/volltexte/2003/1409/pdf/Band01.pdf.

Stone, D. (2004), 'Memory, Memorials and Museums', in *The Historiography of the Holocaust*, (ed.) D. Stone (Houndmills), 508–32.

Stora, B. (1991), *La gangrène et l'oubli: La mémoire de la guerre d'Algérie* (Paris).

_____ (1999), *Le transfert d'une mémoire: De 'l'Algérie française' au racisme anti-arabe* (Paris).

_____ (2005), 'Quand une mémoire (de guerre) peut en cacher une autre (coloniale)', in *La fracture coloniale: La société française au prisme de l'héritage colonial*, (ed.) P. Blanchard, N. Bancel and S. Lemaire (Paris), 57–65.

_____. (2007), *La guerre des mémoires: La France face à son passé colonial. Entretiens avec Thierry Leclère* (La Tour d'Aigues).

Strasser, P. (2005), 'Das kulturelle Erbe auf internationalem Parkett', in *Bricolage: Innsbrucker Zeitschrift für europäische Ethnologie* 3: 52–77.

Stråth, B. (2000a), 'Introduction: Myth, Memory and History in the Construction of Community', in *Myth and Memory in the Construction of Community: Historical Patterns in Europe and Beyond* (Multiple Europes No. 9), (ed.) B. Stråth (Brussels), 19–46.

_____ (ed.) (2000b), *Europe and the Other, Europe as the Other* (Brussels).

_____ (2002), 'A European Identity: To the Historical Limits of a Concept', *European Journal of Social Theory* 5: 387–401.

_____ (2005), 'Europa: Welche Werte und welche Geschichte?' in *Zeit-Geschichten: Miniaturen in Lutz Niethammers Manier*, (ed.) J. John, D. van Laak and J. von Puttkammer (Essen).

Stroop, J. (1943), *Es gibt keinen jüdischen Wohnbezirk in Warschau mehr!* (Warschau), http://www.holocaust-history.org/works/stroop-report/jpg/strp001.jpg.

Sturken, M. (1997), *Tangled Memories: The Vietnam War, the AIDS Epidemic, and the Politics of Remembering* (Berkeley and London).

_____ (1998), 'The Remembering of Forgetting: Recovered Memory and the Question of Experience', *Social Text* 57: 103–25.

Sundhaussen, H. (1994), 'Okkupation, Kollaboration und Widerstand in den Ländern Jugoslawiens 1941–1945', in *Europa unterm Hakenkreuz: Die Okkupationspolitik des deutschen Faschismus (1938–1945), Ergänzungsband 1: Okkupation und Kollaboration*, (ed.) W. Röhr (Berlin and Heidelberg), 349–65.

Szűcs, J. (1983), 'The Three Historical Regions of Europe: An Outline', *Acta Historica: Revue de l'Academie des Sciences de Hongrie* 29: 131–84.

Talbot, W. H. F. (1980), 'Some Account of the Art of Photogenic Drawing', in *Photography, Essays and Images: Illustrated Readings in the History of Photography*, (ed.) B. Newhall (New York and Boston), 23–31.

Talmon, J. (1952), *The Origins of Totalitarian Democracy* (London).

Taylor, J. (1994), 'Kodak and the "English" Market between the Wars', *Journal of Industrial Design* 7, no. 1: 29–42.

Thénault, S. (2005a), 'France-Algérie: Pour un traitement commun du passé de la guerre d'indépendance', *Vingtième Siècle* 85: 119–28.

_____. (2005b), *Histoire de la guerre d'indépendance algérienne* (Paris).

Thomas, J. (1996), *Time, Culture and Identity: An Interpretive Archaeology* (London and New York).

Thompson, A. (2005), *The Empire Strikes Back? The Impact of Imperialism on Britain from the Mid-Nineteenth Century* (Harlow).

Tierney, S. (2002), 'The Search for a New Normativity: Thomas Franck, Post-modern Neotribalism and the Law of Self-Determination', *European Journal of International Law* 13, no. 4: 941–60.

Tobiesen, N. (1995), 'Laserlys Blev Saboteret', *Politiken*, 6 May.

Todorov, T. (2003), *Hope and Memory*, (trans.) D. Bellos (London).

Todorova, M. (2006), 'The Mausoleum of Georgi Dimitrov as *Lieu de Mémoire*', *Journal of Modern History* 78: 377–411.

Tolz, V. (1998), 'Forging the Nation: National Identity and Nation Building in Post-Communist Russia', *Europe-Asia Studies* 50, no. 6: 993–1022.

Tomanić, M. (2001), *Srpska crkva u ratu* (Belgrade).

Torpey, J. C. (2001), '"Making Whole What Has Been Smashed": Reflections on Reparations', *Journal of Modern History* 73: 333–58.

Tossavainen, M. (2003), 'Calendar, Context and Commemoration: Establishing an Israeli Holocaust Remembrance Day', in *Echoes of the Holocaust: Historical Culture in Contemporary Europe*, (ed.) K.-G. Karlsson and U. Zander (Lund), 59–80.

Troebst, S. (2003), '"Intermarium" and "Wedding to the Sea": Politics of History and Mental Mapping in East Central Europe', *European Review of History/Revue Européenne d'Histoire* 10, no. 2: 293–321.

_____ (2005a), '"Was für ein Teppich?" Postkommunistische Erinnerungskulturen in Ost(mittel)europa', in *Der Kommunismus im Museum: Formen der Auseinandersetzung in Deutschland und Ostmitteleuropa*, (ed.) V. Knigge and U. Mählert (Cologne), 31–54.

_____ (2005b), *Postkommunistische Erinnerungskulturen im Östlichen Europa: Bestandsaufnahme, Kategorisierung, Periodisierung/Postkomunistyczne Kultury Pamięci w Europie Wschodniej: Stan, Kategoryzacja, Periodyzacja* (Wrocław).

_____ (2005c), 'Jalta versus Stalingrad, GULag versus Holocaust: Konfligierende Erinnerungskulturen im grösseren Europa', *Berliner Journal für Soziologie* 15, no. 3: 381–400.

_____ (2005d), 'Holodomor oder Holocaust?' *Frankfurter Allgemeine Zeitung*, 4 July, 8.

_____ (2006a), 'Von Nikita Chruščëv zu Sandra Kalniete: Der *lieu de mémoire* "1956" und Europas aktuelle Erinnerungskonflikte', *Comparativ* 16, no. 1. 150–70.

_____ (ed.) (2006b), *Vertreibungsdiskurs und Europäische Erinnerungskultur* (Osnabrück).

_____ (2007a), 'Vom *Spatial Turn* zum *Regional Turn*? Geschichtsregionale Konzeptionen in den Kulturwissenschaften', in *Dimensionen der Kultur- und Gesellschaftsgeschichte: Festschrift für Hannes Siegrist zum 60. Geburtstag,* (ed.) M. Middell (Leipzig), 143–59.

_____ (2007b), 'Das Europäische Netzwerk Erinnerung und Solidarität: Eine zentraleuropäische Initiative zur Institutionalisierung des Vertreibungsgedenkens 2002–2006', *Zeitgeschichte* 34, no. 1: 43–57.

Tumarkin, N. (1994), *The Living and the Dead: The Rise and Fall of the Cult of World War II in Russia* (New York).

Uhl, H. (2003), 'Zeitgeschichtsforschung und "österreichisches Gedächtnis"', in *Zeitgeschichte(n) in Österreich: HistorikerInnen aus vier Generationen, Anlässlich '30 Jahre Zeitgeschichte', Zeitgeschichte* 30, no. 6: 341–56.

_____ (2004), 'Vom Opfermythos zur Mitverantwortungsthese: Transformationen des "Österreichischen Gedächtnisses"', in *Mythen der Nationen: 1945 – Arena der Erinnerungen,* (ed.) M. Flake (Berlin), 481–508.

_____ (2006), 'From Victim Myth to Co-Responsibility Thesis: Nazi Rule, World War II, and the Holocaust in Austrian Memory', in *The Politics of Memory in Postwar Europe,* (ed.) R. N. Lebow, W. Kansteiner and C. Fogu (Durham), 40–72.

_____ (2008), 'From Discourse to Representation: "Austrian Memory" in Public Space', in *Narrating the Nation: The Representation of National Narratives in Different Genres,* (ed.) S. Berger, L. Eriksonas and A. Mycock (New York), 207–21.

URO (United Restitution Organization) (ed.) (1962), *Judenverfolgung in Italien, den italienisch besetzten Gebieten und in Nordafrika* (Frankfurt am Main).

Utzon, S. (1985), 'Æg og Tomater Mod Schlüter', *Politiken,* 5 May.

van der Leeuw-Roord, J. (2001), 'Euroclio, a Cause for or Consequence of European Historical Consciousness', in *History for Today and Tomorrow: What Does Europe Mean for School History?* (ed.) J. van der Leeuw-Roord (Hamburg), 249–68.

van Vree, F. (2005), 'The Stones of Treblinka', in *Neue Staaten – neue Bilder? Visuelle Kultur im Dienst staatlicher Selbstdarstellung in Zentral- und Osteuropa seit 1918,* (ed.) A. Bartetzky, M. Dmitrieva and S. Troebst (Cologne), 199–208.

Varner, E. R. (2004), *Mutilation and Transformation:* Damnatio memoriae *and Roman Imperial Portraiture* (Leiden).

Verdery, K. (1991), *National Ideology under Socialism: Identity and Cultural Politics in Ceaușescu's Romania* (Berkeley).

Veser, R. (2005), 'Feindliche Einladung', *Frankfurter Allgemeine Zeitung,* 1 March, 1.

Vigna, X., Vigreux, J. and Wolikow, S. (2006), *Le pain, la paix, la liberté: Expériences et territoires du Front populaire* (Paris).

Vigreux, J. and S. Wolikow (2003), 'Introduction', in *Cultures communistes au xxᵉ siècle: Entre guerre et modernité,* (ed.) J. Vigreux and S. Wolikow (Paris), 7–13.

Virgili, F. (2003), *Shorn Women: Gender and Punishment in Liberation France* (Oxford).

Voigt, K. (1989–93), *Zuflucht auf Widerruf: Exil in Italien 1933–1945,* 2 vols. (Stuttgart).

Von Lucius, R. (2005a), 'Zwei Geschichtsdeutungen: Die Baltischen Länder Wollen die EU für ihre Sicht des "9. Mai" Gewinnen', *Frankfurter Allgemeine Zeitung,* 16 February, 10.

_____ (2005b), 'Kriegsende brachte weiteres Morden', *Frankfurter Allgemeine Zeitung,* 3 March, 9.

von Plessen, M. (ed.) (2003), *Idee Europa: Entwürfe zum 'Ewigen Frieden'* (Frankfurt am Main).

Wägenbaur, T. (ed.) (1998), *The Poetics of Memory,* Stauffenburg Colloquium 45 (Tübingen).

Wallerström, T. (2006), *Vilka var Först? En Nordskandinavisk Konflikt Som Historisk-Arkeologiskt Dilemma* (Stockholm).

Wandycz, P. S. (1992), 'East European History and Its Meaning: The Halecki-Bidlo-Handelsman Debate', in *Király Béla Emlékkőnyv. Háború És Társadalom. War and Society. Guerre et société. Krieg und Gesellschaft,* (ed.) P. Jónás et al. (Budapest), 308–21.

Warring, A. (1987), '40 År Efter: Historiebevidsthedens og Historieformidlingens Samfunds-mæssige Betydning Belyst Gennem en Analyse af Iscenesættelsen af 40 Årsjubilæet for Danmarks Befrielse og Dets Manifestation i Massekulturen', PhD diss., Roskilde University.

Watson, R. S. (1994a), 'Making Secret Histories: Memory and Mourning in Post-Mao China', in *Memory, History, and Opposition under State Socialism*, (ed.) R. S. Watson (Santa Fe), 65–85.

_____ (ed.) (1994b), *Memory, History, and Opposition under State Socialism* (Santa Fe).

Weber, H. (1969), *Die Wandlung des deutschen Kommunismus: Die Stalinisierung der KPD in der Weimarer Republik* (Frankfurt am Main).

Weckel, U. (2003), 'The Mitläufer in Two German Postwar Films: Representation and Critical Reception', *History and Memory* 15, no. 2: 64–93.

Weight, R. (2000), *Patriots: National Identity in Britain 1940–2000* (London).

Weinrich, H. (1997), *Lethe: Kunst und Kritik des Vergessens* (Munich).

Wells, L. (ed.) (2000), *Photography: A Critical Introduction* (London).

Wenk, S. and Eschebach, I. (2002), 'Soziales Gedächtnis und Geschlechterdifferenz: Eine Einführung', in *Gedächtnis und Geschlecht: Deutungsmuster in Darstellungen des national-sozialistischen Genozids*, (ed.) I. Eschebach, S. Jacobeit and S. Wenk (Frankfurt am Main), 13–38.

Werth, N. (1999), 'A State against Its People: Violence, Repression, and Terror in the Soviet Union', in *The Black Book of Communism: Crimes, Terror, Repression*, (ed.) S. Courtois et al. (Cambridge, MA, and London), 33–268.

Wertsch, J. V. (1998), *Mind as Action* (New York).

_____ (2002), *Voices of Collective Remembering* (Cambridge).

West, N. M. (2000), *Kodak and the Lens of Nostalgia: Cultural Frames, Framing Culture* (Charlottesville).

White, A. (1995), 'The Memorial Society in the Provinces', *Europe-Asia Studies* 47, no. 8: 1343–66.

White, H. (1973), *Metahistory: The Historical Imagination in Nineteenth-Century Europe* (Baltimore).

Whitling, F. (2009), 'Memory, History and the Classical Tradition', in *European Review of History: Revue européenne d'histoire* 16, no. 2: 235–53.

Wiesel, E. (1991), *The Accident* (New York).

Winter, J. (2000), 'The Generation of Memory: Reflections on the "Memory Boom"', *Contemporary Historical Studies: Bulletin of the German Historical Institute* 27: 80–2.

_____ (2006), *Remembering War: The Great War between History and Memory in the Twentieth Century* (New Haven and London).

Winter, J. and Sivan, E. (1999), *War and Remembrance in the Twentieth Century* (Cambridge and New York).

Wintle, M. (2006), 'Visual Representations of Europe in the Nineteenth Century: The Age of Nationalism and Imperialism', in *A Companion to Nineteenth-Century Europe 1789–1914*, (ed.) S. Berger (Oxford and Malden, MA), 11–28.

Wittgenstein, L. (2001), *Tractatus Logico-Philosophicus* (London and New York).

Wodak, R., de Cillia, R., Reisigl, M., Liebhart, K., Hofstatter, K. and Kargl, M. (1998), *Zur diskursiven Konstruktion von nationaler Identität* (Frankfurt am Main).

Wood, N. (1999), *Vectors of Memory: Legacies of Trauma in Postwar Europe* (Oxford).

Woolf, S. (2003), 'Europe and its Historians', *Contemporary European History* 12, no. 3: 323–37.

Wyman, D. (ed.) (1996), *The World Reacts to the Holocaust* (Baltimore and London).

Yakovlev, A. (2004), *A Century of Violence in Soviet Russia* (London).

Young, J. E. (1993), *The Texture of Memory: Holocaust Memorials and Meaning* (New Haven).

Young, R. (2001), *Postcolonialism: An Historical Introduction* (Oxford).

Zander, U. (2003), '*Holocaust* at the Limits: Historical Culture and the Nazi Genocide in the Television Era', in *Echoes of the Holocaust: Historical Culture in Contemporary Europe*, (ed.) K.-G. Karlsson and U. Zander (Lund), 255–92.

Zaremba, M. (2004), 'Zorganizowane Zapominanie o Holocauście w Dekadzie Gierka: Trwanie i Zmiana', *Kwartalnik Historii Żydów* 2: 216–24.

Zemskov, V. N. (2005), *Spetstposelentsy v SSSR 1930–1960* (Moscow).

Zernack, K. (1977), *Osteuropa: Eine Einführung in seine Geschichte* (Munich).

Zolla, E. (1998), *Che cos'è la tradizione* (Milan).

Zuccotti, S. (1987), *The Italians and the Holocaust: Persecution, Rescue, Survival* (New York).

Archives

Norges Hjemmefrontmuseum, Oslo (NHM)
195 Dda 0011 Høytider; 195 Dda 0014, 32.5 50 årsjubileet

Statsministerens kontor, København (Copenhagen)
04-28/1962-70; 04-28/1962-70: 1; 057-6 I Udvalget for 40-året; 051-19, 1992 I; 051-4, 1995

Statsministerens kontor, Oslo
Komiteen til forberedelse av 50Års jubileet for frigjøringen (Frigjøringskomiteen) 1992. 'Delinstillingen til regjeringen. Om reising av et frihetsmonument og et forsvarsmonument avgitt 5. november 1992'.

Stortingets arkiv, Oslo
Stortinget 1965. 'Programmet ved minnemøtet i Stortingssalen 8.mai 1965', Minnemøtet i stortingssalen den 8. mai 1965 – 20-årsdagen for frigjøringen i 1945.

Komitéen til forberedelse av 25-års jubileet for frigjøringen, Stortingets Arkiv, Minnemøtet i Stortinget den 8. mai 1970.

Saksnr. 94/811, Frigjøringsjubileet 1995.

INDEX

www.ingramcontent.com/pod-product-compliance
Lightning Source LLC
Chambersburg PA
CBHW060023030426

42334CB00019B/2147